Selling British Columbia

Michael Dawson

Selling British Columbia:
Tourism and Consumer Culture,
1890-1970

UBCPress · Vancouver · Toronto

15 14 13 12 11 10 09 08 07 06 05 04   5 4 3 2 1

Printed in Canada on acid-free paper

Library and Archives Canada Cataloguing in Publication

Dawson, Michael, 1971-
   Selling British Columbia : tourism and consumer culture, 1890-1970 /
Michael Dawson.

   Includes bibliographical references and index.
   ISBN 0-7748-1054-8 (bound): ISBN 0-7748-1055-6 (pbk.)

   1. Tourism – British Columbia – History. 2. Tourism – British Columbia –
Marketing – History. 3. Consumption (Economics) – Canada – History. I. Title.

G155.C3D29 2004   338.4'791711044   C2004-902934-7

Canadä
UBC Press gratefully acknowledges the financial support for our publishing program of the Government of Canada through the Book Publishing Industry Development Program (BPIDP), and of the Canada Council for the Arts, and the British Columbia Arts Council.

This book has been published with the help of a grant from the Canadian Federation for the Humanities and Social Sciences, through the Aid to Scholarly Publications Programme, using funds provided by the Social Sciences and Humanities Research Council of Canada, and with the help of the K.D. Srivastava Fund.

UBC Press
The University of British Columbia
2029 West Mall
Vancouver, BC V6T 1Z2
604-822-5959 / Fax: 604-822-6083
www.ubcpress.ca

"I know just the place that will suit you" said I. "It's more English than England ... To speak about money-making is considered rotten bad form ... The Victorians ... never lie awake nights fretting about the filthy lucre."

> — E.A. Powell, "Autobirds of Passage: The Island Highway," *Sunset* magazine (1914)

God Save the Queen ... 'cause Tourists are moneeeeeeey.

> — The Sex Pistols, c. 1977

Contents

Illustrations

Tables

Acknowledgments

Objectively, the low point of this whole process occurred on an otherwise pleasant day in June 1998. While I was returning to Vancouver from a research trip to Oregon and Washington states, my devoted '88 Chevy Sprint was totalled just south of Bellingham when it was involved in a multiple rear-ender initiated (ironically enough given the topic of this book) by an inattentive cross-border shopper from North Vancouver. Persons less paranoid than me would likely dismiss a Canadian tourist in the United States barrelling his automobile into the back of a car filled with research notes on the development of tourism and consumerism in North America as pure coincidence. I know better. This event – coupled with a National Archives employee's attempt to charge me an international postage rate on a shipment of photocopies from Ottawa to Vancouver a year earlier – alerted me early on to the possibility that this project would not be completed quickly or easily.

Finishing a project such as this entails persevering through what seems like an endless series of Pyhrric epiphanies. Many people have helped me to negotiate the arduous route to completing this book. I came to Queen's to do my MA in 1993 in part because a very wise professor at UBC told me that I could "do a lot worse than work with Ian McKay." I told Ian this the first day I met him. He laughed. I considered that a good sign. It was. I stayed at Queen's for my PhD for two reasons. One was Ian. The other was Karen Dubinsky. Karen has provided me with innumerable insights, sage advice, and constant encouragement over the past decade. Many thanks as well to James Carson, John Holmes, and, especially, Keith Walden for their insights and ideas.

My thanks to Alisa Apostle for allowing me to read her completed PhD dissertation. Thanks are also due to Todd McCallum and Jim Kenny, who commented on early versions of some of the chapters, and to Yvonne Place, who now rightly occupies an almost mythic place among history graduate students at Queen's for her ability to negotiate the administrative maze that is the School of Graduate Studies. My thanks also to Alan MacEachern, Linda Sproule-Jones, and Scrap and Carol Hawtin for on-the-road accommodation arrangements. The exceptional service from the staff at the City of Vancouver Archives (especially Donna MacKinnon) as well as archival depositories at the Nanaimo Community Archives, the University of Washington, the Washington State Archives, the University of Oregon, the British Columbia Archives (especially David Lemieux), and the University of Victoria was most appreciated. Also appreciated is the financial assistance that came by way of Ontario Graduate Scholarships, Donald S. Rickerd Fellowships, a Joseph Engler Dissertation Fellowship, the School of Graduate Studies at Queen's, as well as professional development funds at the University of Northern British Columbia.

I completed the final draft of the book while working as a sessional instructor in the History Program at the University of Northern British Columbia from the fall of 2000 until the summer of 2003. Sessional work is no easy task, but it was made immeasurably more enjoyable by the faculty and administrative staff at UNBC. A hearty thank-you to everyone up in Prince George, especially Gordon Martel, Jon Swainger, and, of course, Pat Norris. Thanks also to my students, who (on most occasions anyway) made a daunting teaching load a great deal of fun.

My thanks also to Jean Wilson and the rest of the crew at UBC Press, as well as the anonymous reviewers. Parts of this book first appeared as "From 'Business as Usual' to 'Salesmanship in Reverse': Tourism Promotion in British Columbia during the Second World War," *Canadian Historical Review* 83, 2 (2002): 230-54, and as "Taking the 'D' out of 'Depression': The Promise of Tourism in British Columbia, 1935-1939," *BC Studies* 132 (2001-2): 31-56. I thank both journals for allowing me to include that material in the pages that follow.

A number of friends and colleagues have provided valuable support over the past few years. In particular, Ross Cameron, Russ Johnston, Helen Harrison, and Todd McCallum provided ideas and encouragement, while both Helen and Todd graciously vacated our shared office at Queen's for long periods of time in order to let me "organize" my material on their desks. A hearty salute as well to the "Madison" crew! I would also like to acknowledge my parents, who have offered nothing less than unflinching support and encouragement for my academic endeavours. And, finally, my thanks to Catherine Gidney for her love, support, and encouragement. This book is for her. (Of course, I expect to get one in return.)

Michael Dawson
Vancouver, BC

Acronyms

ACRA   Auto Courts and Resorts Association of British Columbia
BCGTB   British Columbia Government Travel Bureau
BITD   Bureau of Industrial and Tourist Development
CGTB   Canadian Government Travel Bureau
CTB   Canadian Travel Bureau
EPA   Evergreen Playground Association
GVPB   Greater Vancouver Publicity Bureau
GVTA   Greater Vancouver Tourist Association
GVVCB   Greater Vancouver Visitors and Convention Bureau
PNTA   Pacific Northwest Tourist Association
TAV   Tourist Association of Victoria
TTDA   Tourist Trade Development Association of Victoria and
         Vancouver Island
VDTA   Victoria Development and Tourist Association
VIDA   Victoria and Island Development Association
VIPB   Victoria and Island Publicity Bureau
VTA   Vancouver Tourist Association

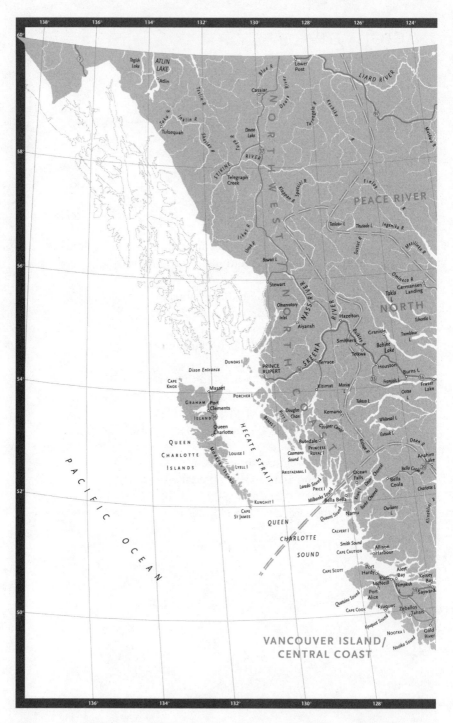

Map 1 Map of British Columbia, showing regions and highway systems, 1997

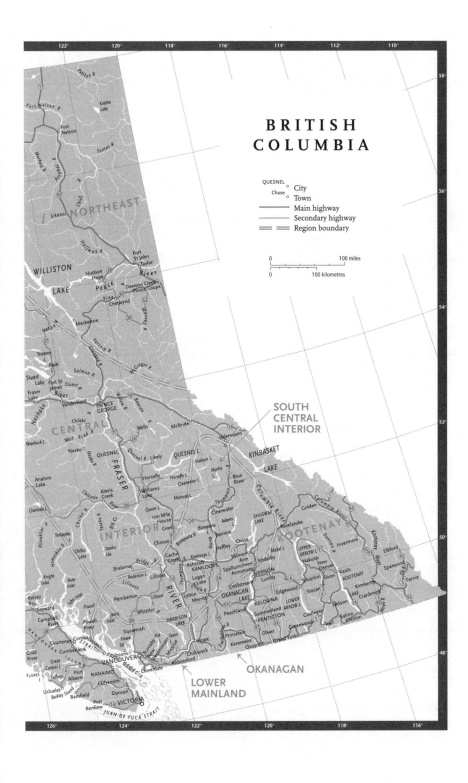

Selling British Columbia

Introduction:
Tourism and Consumer Culture

Amusing, and perhaps apocryphal, anecdotes circulated throughout British Columbia during the summer of 1986. Vancouver was hosting a World's Fair, Expo '86, which meant that it was also hosting a great many American tourists. Television interviews with Expo information bureau staff produced a litany of humorous responses to a query seemingly on everyone's mind: What is the strangest question American tourists have asked you so far? Typical examples, eagerly offered up by amused Expo staffers, included American tourists' queries as to where they might be able to exchange their Alberta currency for British Columbia's legal tender, whether or not souvenir Canadian flags were available in any other colours besides the seemingly ubiquitous and prosaic red and white, and what time the Canadian pavilion, bedecked with decorative sails, departed for Vancouver Island. These needling anecdotes undoubtedly reflected the anti-American strain within Canadian nationalism – a strain that enjoyed renewed strength as a result of growing concerns about the federal government's announced plans to pursue a Free Trade Agreement with the United States.[1]

Yet the mocking of visitors to what was then Vancouver's most popular tourist attraction also reflected a widespread, and generally unfavourable, image of tourists. Our attitudes toward tourists reveal our often hypocritical evaluation of the consumer culture in which we live. We have all come in contact with tourists – either on the street or behind service counters. And most of us have been tourists ourselves. Yet tourism is popularly understood as inducing a precipitous decline in human behaviour – one very much in keeping with the most damning criticisms of consumers as unthinking and simple-minded.[2] Tourists are frequently parodied and held up as the epitome of ignorance. Rarely, however, do we detect such failings in ourselves. As Patricia Jasen perceptively reminds us, we prefer to think of ourselves as "travellers" rather than "tourists." Tourists, we tell ourselves, are content to accept inauthentic experiences; we, however, insist on authenticity.[3]

Yet if tourists are consistent objects of ridicule, the tourism industry itself is recognized as a powerful and important economic player. The World Tourism Organization (WTO) boasts that the travel and tourism industry currently accounts for roughly 10 percent of the world's gross domestic product. Tourism, the WTO explains, is "the world's largest export earner." In 2000 the WTO reports, "foreign currency receipts from international tourism reached US$476 billion ... outstripping exports of petroleum products, motor vehicles, telecommunications equipment, textiles or any other product or service."[4] Tourism is also a major player in the Canadian economy. In 2001 Canada ranked ninth internationally in terms of its popularity as a tourist destination (19.7 million international visits) and eighth as a tourism earner (US$10.8 billion).[5] Statistics Canada's latest report estimates that tourism is responsible for nearly 600,000 jobs in Canada.[6]

These are heady numbers. Both Statistics Canada and the World Tourism Organization are generally credited for offering realistic assessments of tourism's economic impact. Statistics Canada, for example, reminds observers that of those 600,000 Canadian tourism jobs a great many of them offer only part-time employment.[7] Historically, however, organizations gathering tourism statistics have lacked either the sophisticated analysis required to produce accurate statistics or the motivation to overcome their own boosterish approach to information gathering. For example, in her recent study of the Canadian Travel Bureau (CTB), a federal government organization created in 1934 to encourage the development of Canada's tourism industry, Alisa Apostle notes an important distinction between the CTB's reporting procedures and those of the Dominion Bureau of Statistics (DBS). In its annual report for 1938, the CTB claimed that the nation's tourism industry contributed over $270 million to the Canadian economy. In its annual report for the same year, however, the DBS arrived at a much lower figure. The difference? The DBS elected to factor in not only the estimated amount of money spent by tourists in Canada (as the CTB had done) but also the amount of money Canadians had spent abroad. In short, the DBS statistics reflected Canada's net rather than gross revenue from tourism. The larger estimate of expenditures was politically useful for the CTB not only for justifying its existence within the federal bureaucracy but also in its campaigns to convince Canadians of tourism's economic importance.[8] Moreover, in the early 1940s, the DBS revised its information-gathering techniques and developed a more accurate understanding of both the duration of American visits and the amount of money these visitors were spending in Canada. These results also challenged the legitimacy of earlier inflated figures.[9] To a certain extent, then, historians must acknowledge the "flexibility" of such statistical data and refrain from jumping to hasty conclusions about what these statistics really tell us.

Still, despite these concerns, one can be reasonably confident in noting that, like tourism elsewhere in the Western world, tourism in British Columbia grew steadily throughout the twentieth century. International tourist arrivals at the twenty most popular tourist destinations in the world increased dramatically during the postwar era, from 25 million in 1950 to 457 million in 1990 (see Table 0.1). Similarly, Table 0.2 illustrates the steady increase in annual US visitors to British Columbia during the middle of the twentieth century from under 300,000 in 1926 to over three

Table 0.1

International tourist arrivals, 1950-90

Year	Arrivals
1950	25 million
1960	69 million
1970	166 million
1980	288 million
1990	457 million

Source: World Tourism Organization. Table adapted from Charles R. Goeldner, J.R. Brent Ritchie, and Robert W. McIntosh, *Tourism: Principles, Practices, Philosophies*, 8th ed. (New York: John Wiley and Sons, 2000), 9.

Table 0.2

Estimated total number of US automobile passengers entering British Columbia from the United States, 1926-71

Year	Passengers
1926	272,303
1931	339,016
1936	260,454
1941	451,038
1946	535,785
1951	1,016,000
1956	1,300,000
1961	1,763,000
1966	2,307,617
1971	3,071,600

Note: Figures for 1941 and 1946 are based on the number of vehicles crossing the border and multiplied by three (the average number of passengers whom tourist authorities estimated travelled in each car).
Sources: Greater Vancouver Tourist Association Annual Reports, 1926-36; British Columbia Government Travel Bureau Annual Reports, 1941-71.

million in 1971. In the decades after 1971, this number continued to increase. In 1998 4.7 million American tourists visited British Columbia.[10]

The increase in tourist accommodation similarly suggests the growth of tourism in British Columbia. On the eve of the Second World War, British Columbia boasted just 300 auto camps within its borders.[11] By 1954 this number had more than quadrupled to 1,300.[12] In their examination of accommodation on Vancouver Island, Ross Nelson and Geoffrey Wall demonstrate that this dramatic growth continued throughout the postwar era. Between 1945 and 1965, in fact, the number of accommodation establishments on Vancouver Island increased threefold.[13] By 1988 British Columbia boasted 650 hotels, roughly 750 motels, and a variety of smaller forms of accommodation that offered a combined 74,000 rooms for visitors.[14]

The growth of tourism in British Columbia during the twentieth century depended upon several factors, including increased spending power and available leisure time of potential visitors and dramatic improvements in the province's transportation infrastructure. The 1930s and 1940s witnessed a substantial increase in paid vacations for workers in North America, and this increase combined with the sustained period of postwar prosperity to make vacations an increasingly central component of modern life for many North American families.[15] In 1900, for instance, expenditures on recreation accounted for 3 percent of American consumption; by 1990 that figure had doubled to 6 percent.[16]

During the second half of the twentieth century, the ability of visitors to travel throughout British Columbia was improved dramatically by an extensive road-building program. In the late 1930s, one participant in a "See B.C. First" promotional caravan from Vancouver to the Kootenays decried the province's rudimentary road system as "a system of building roads for political reasons, beginning everywhere and ending nowhere," which "discourage[d] all but the seasoned traveller."[17] The lack of navigable roads in British Columbia was due primarily to the difficulties involved in imposing an efficient road network on the province's mountainous geography.[18] Moreover, during the early part of the twentieth century, British Columbia followed a pattern familiar in other Canadian provinces when it directed its road-building energies to ensure that the best roads connected the province with the United States.[19] As Map 2 illustrates, visitors' access to the interior of the province in 1930 was greatly restricted. A sustained highway-building program spearheaded by the W.A.C. Bennett Social Credit governments in the 1950s and 1960s opened up vast areas of the province that had hitherto been considered impenetrable by most travellers and, of course, increased tourists' access by automobile to the scenery of the province's northern and interior regions. By the 1990s, paved highways allowed easy access to these areas (see Map 1).

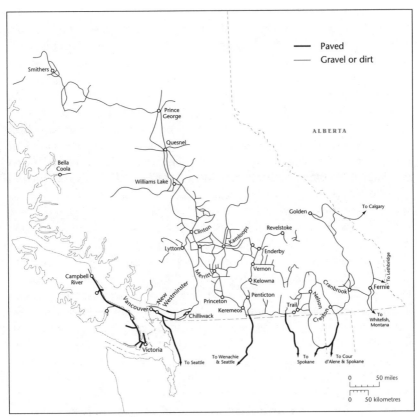

Map 2 Principal roads of British Columbia, 1930

Most early histories of tourism in North America focused primarily upon the changing circumstances that allowed the industry to grow.[20] Those observing the growth of tourism in British Columbia and elsewhere frequently noted the importance of key developments such as increased leisure time, greater disposable income, and technological advances in transportation. These were important observations, for they clearly revealed the changing, and growing, realm of leisure in the lives of North Americans. But these observations overshadowed other equally important lessons that the history of tourism can provide. In particular, such observations overlooked a dramatic transformation in tourism during the twentieth century: its incorporation into a burgeoning culture of consumption. More recent histories of tourism have begun to explore important links between tourism, nation building, and consumption, and it is, in fact, the connection between tourism and consumerism that is the central focus of this book.[21]

As Richard Wightman Fox and Jackson Lears pointed out two decades ago, the emergence of a consumer society is marked not simply by an "abundance of televisions and automobiles" but also by a cultural transformation that witnesses the replacement of "a value system based on work, sacrifice, and saving" with a "consumer ethic."[22] But just what is that consumer ethic, and is it possible to settle upon a workable definition of "consumer culture?" There are, it seems, both procedural and substantive approaches to such a definition. On the procedural side, sociologist Don Slater offers the following six characteristics as key components of our consumer culture. First, it is a culture in which "core social practices and cultural values, ideas, aspirations and identities are defined and oriented in relation to consumption rather than to other social dimensions such as work or citizenship, religious cosmology or military role." The dominant values of this culture are (from a pessimistic point of view) materialistic, hedonistic, and narcissistic and (from an optimistic standpoint) based on individual sovereignty and freedom of choice. Second, a consumer culture "is mediated by market relations." Individuals no longer "make the goods through which we reproduce everyday life." Instead, we choose "between a range of alternative commodities produced by institutions which are not interested in need or cultural values but in profit and economic values." Third, the market relations that dominate this consumer culture are "anonymous and in principle universal." The scope and scale of commodity distribution is such that very little face-to-face contact between producer and consumer ever occurs. As a result, "the consumer is not a known 'customer' but an anonymous subject who can only be imagined and constructed as an *object* – the target of a marketing drive, the profile produced by a market survey, a mass market or market segment." Closely related to the phenomenon of consumer anonymity is the understanding that, in spite of the real economic restrictions placed on an individual's ability to purchase a given commodity, "the consumption of commodities is treated *in principle* as the activity of the entire population." Fourth, consumer culture equates freedom with an individual's ability to choose how to spend one's money. Hence the popular rhetoric of "consumer sovereignty" – the idea that it is the individual consumer who holds the real power in society. Fifth, in a consumer culture, "the constant desire for more and constant production of more desires ... is widely taken to be not only normal for its denizens but essential for socio-economic order and progress." And sixth, in a consumer culture, individuals constantly negotiate their status and their identity through the acquisition of consumer goods – and, as a result, status and identity are more fleeting and changing in modern life than they were in premodern societies.[23] Clearly one would wish to assign varying degrees of significance to these characteristics depending upon the time and place one is examining. And certainly other observers have chosen a more substantive approach of delineating the features of a consumer society. Celia Lury, for example, has chosen a much more tangible series of characteristics, including "the political organization by and of consumers," "the increasing visibility of different forms of shopping," an increasing availability of consumer credit, and "the increasing visibility of so-called consumer illnesses" such as compulsive shopping.[24]

Overall, consumerism can best be understood as a lifestyle associated with the frequent consumption of mass-produced goods and services. A consumer society or culture, then, is one in which the purchasing, accumulating, and consuming of goods and services is a chief priority for many individuals. Consuming these goods and services is certainly given greater value in a consumer society than, say, leisure time. Proponents of consumerism point to its ability to provide reasonably secure access to a variety of desirable products and services. They also champion the liberating possibilities associated with the availability of these goods and services. Critics of consumerism, on the other hand, decry the waste and extravagance that result from what they term a "disposable" culture and suggest that the availability of such a wide range of products leads to passivity among the public, not just in the shopping mall, but in the polling booth as well.[25]

Only in the past decade or so have historians directed their efforts to writing about the making of our "consumer culture" and the arrival of a "consumer society" in Canada. For the most part, these studies demonstrate that consumerism began to take hold in Canada at the end of the nineteenth century and was visibly altering the cultural landscape by the 1920s. Several studies have examined this first wave of consumerism, noting both its emancipating and its destabilizing effects. The pleasures and opportunities of shopping at Toronto's Industrial Exhibition, for example, were for many rural Canadians balanced by the possibility of falling victim to confidence men as well as a profound sense of concern over what impact this new atomistic existence might have on them and their communities. The impact of commercialized forms of leisure on women and the working class, we have learned, was similarly dramatic. For women, commercial amusements and department stores provided a degree of liberation – although for single women in Toronto during this era such opportunities came hand in hand with rigorous scrutiny by moral reformers concerned that such activities would have adverse effects upon their morality.[26] The deleterious effects of "mass culture" on the working class have similarly been explored, as have workers' tendencies to adopt the tenets of consumerism for their own purposes either to maintain older notions of "respectability" or to finance necessary purchases.[27]

The other period that has received increasing attention is the era of

economic expansion that followed the Second World War. In his examination of the baby boom generation, for instance, Doug Owram has
demonstrated the extent to which the consumer culture of the 1950s and
early 1960s served to reinforce a sense of generational unity among Canadian teenagers that not only lured them away from institutional religion
and adult-monitored activities such as scouting but also helped to inculcate in them the sense of entitlement that inspired the radical protests
of the late 1960s.[28] In her analysis of consumers' motivations concerning
the purchasing of furniture and household appliances in the postwar era,
Joy Parr has revealed the extent to which many Canadian families "made
do" with older technologies while exhibiting a decidedly rational form
of decision making when it came to purchasing new items. This important study clearly illustrates the limitations inherent in simplistic models of consumer behaviour. Yet Parr's impressive and nuanced discussion
is focused solely on consumer durables used in the home. We still await
a similar analysis of consumers' motivations concerning goods and services that might be termed "luxuries" rather than "necessities" by their
owners (e.g., toys, entertainment, and travel).[29]

Less analyzed in Canada is the development of the culture of consumption during the intervening period between the economic boom of
the 1920s and the end of the Second World War. For the most part, the
years from 1930 to 1945 are portrayed primarily as a period in which
consumers went without. At most, these years of economic depression
and war are portrayed as a period of "conspicuous underconsumption"
that contributed to a pent-up urge to purchase consumer goods and experiences after 1945. One aim of this book is to underscore the continuities
and connections between the interwar years and the postwar era in order
to chart a more thorough and balanced understanding of the roots of the
fully fledged consumer culture that emerged in Canada after the Second
World War. If, as Bryan Palmer has suggested, the 1920s served as the first
act of the "Theatre of Mass Culture" before a curtain descended and signalled a fifteen-year intermission that would end with postwar prosperity, this book endeavours to pull back the curtain and investigate what
was taking place on stage during the intermission.[30] Rather than seeing
the period between 1930 and 1945 as a hiatus in the development of our
consumer culture, this book makes room at the front of the stage for the
developments of the Great Depression and the Second World War in order
to draw out the significance of this era in the development of tourism
promotion and consumerism in general.

Recent historical work on the United States and Europe points to
the 1930-45 period as an important turning point in the emergence of
consumerism. In her examination of the American New Deal, for example, historian Lizabeth Cohen highlights the centrality of the Great

Depression in the emergence of "a mass consumer economy and society" in the United States. While historians examining the expansion of consumerism "inevitably focus on eras of economic prosperity, such as the 1920s and the 1950s," she explains, such an approach "misses the crucial role that state policy-making played in creating a postwar world where mass consumption not only shaped the economy, but also altered the political realm, becoming a new vehicle for delivering the traditional American promises of democracy and egalitarianism." The Great Depression, Cohen argues, was "a crucial period of modern American state building" that "established the groundwork for the centrality of consumption and consumers in the postwar era."[31] Similarly, in his survey of the rise of consumerism in the United States, Gary Cross devotes a refreshingly unorthodox amount of energy to examining both the Great Depression and the Second World War. His findings are illuminating. While millions of Americans cut back expenditures in light of the economic downturn of the 1930s, an equally common response was "a refusal to retrench" as many Americans proved "unwilling to abandon the 'luxuries' of the 1920s." Moreover, he reminds us, "manufacturers did not simply wait for the recovery." They employed new sales techniques and creative advertising campaigns throughout the 1930s and embarked upon a concerted effort during the Second World War to prepare Americans "for an era of private consumption after the war."[32] In an earlier study of European and North American attitudes toward leisure time and money, Cross similarly took issue with existing interpretations "biased by the victory of consumerism after 1945" and therefore of limited use in examining "the historical origins of mass-consumer society." Instead, he pointed to the 1930s as the key period in which workers, traumatized by the social stigma attached to idleness, were now willing to abandon their claims to shorter workdays and increased leisure time in favour of increased pay and the promise of increased access to consumer goods.[33] Interestingly, Cross noted that the holiday served as an important arena in which the desires for leisure time and money could be reconciled as vacations came to be seen increasingly as opportunities to participate in "the magic of uninhibited spending."[34]

While historians have been relatively slow to embrace the possibilities of the history of consumerism, the academic study of tourism has flourished in the past few decades, especially among sociologists. Firmly rooted in a sociological approach, many scholars examined tourism in an attempt to decipher our motivations and experiences under the conditions of modernity. These studies focus primarily on the human desire for unique and fulfilling experiences. In his path-breaking 1976 study of tourism, for example, Dean MacCannell offered tourist travel as the epitome of the modern experience by drawing a parallel between sightseeing and the desire to transcend the fragmented and discontinuous experience of

postindustrial society.[35] More recently John Urry offered a more historically informed examination of this phenomenon that documents the extent
to which tourists' experiences are constructed by tourism professionals eager
to produce new and more alluring attractions.[36] While this emphasis on
the tourists' pursuit of experiences is on one level very revealing, it is also
very restricting. Colin Campbell's claim that tourism "does not involve
the purchase of products, but of experiences," illustrates the limitation of
this approach.[37] Given the emphasis that the tourist industry itself places
on the importance of tourist expenditures on goods and services ranging
from meals and transportation costs to souvenirs, it is clear that tourism
is as much about purchasing goods and services as it is about obtaining
"authentic" experiences. A 1979 questionnaire circulated to package tour
participants in Vancouver, for example, found that the "largest proportion
of respondents used their free time for dining and shopping."[38]

To reconcile the sociological emphasis on experience with the tourism
industry's emphasis on expenditures, it is useful to turn to the work of
the late cultural critic Raymond Williams on advertising. For Williams,
advertising was a "magic system." The purpose of advertising, he argued,
was to instill even the most mundane of products with a sense of desir-
ability by associating them with a particularly rewarding experience.[39]
Since the onset of the Great Depression, tourism in British Columbia and
elsewhere has been expected to perform that function. Tourism promotion
has become a method of making local goods and services desirable to
outsiders by endowing them with an aura of unique experience. The purpose of this book, then, is to examine and explain the transformation
of tourism promotion from a specialized form of civic boosterism to an
economic strategy geared to the provision of mass-produced goods and
services that are fully enmeshed with a culture of consumption.

Chapter 1 examines early tourism promotion efforts in Vancouver and
Victoria. It begins by examining the motivations of tourists visiting British
Columbia during the late nineteenth century and the early twentieth century and then explores the manner in which civic tourism organizations
were created in order to capitalize upon tourists' conflicting responses to
the experience of modernity. It also examines the promotional material
produced to lure tourists to British Columbia when tourism had yet to
be incorporated fully into North America's emerging consumer culture.

Chapter 2 examines the activities of tourism promoters in the 1920s
and early 1930s. It illustrates the extent to which promotional organizations in Victoria and Vancouver joined with similar organizations in the
American Pacific Northwest in an attempt to woo tourists to the region.
Most importantly it demonstrates the ways in which British Columbia's
tourism promoters sought to incorporate the latest lessons of modern advertising into their arsenal of promotional techniques. These new approaches

combined with the economic dislocation of the Great Depression to reorient their conception of tourism promotion away from its original incarnation as a method of luring settlement and investment and toward a new rationale: maximizing tourist expenditures.

Chapter 3 focuses on the efforts of tourism promoters to obtain government recognition of their efforts. Focusing on the establishment of the provincial government travel bureau in 1937-38, this chapter demonstrates the extent to which the new consumerist conception of tourism was embraced as a free-enterprise solution to the Great Depression. The demand for the provincial government to take tourism seriously was imbued with both a rhetoric of entitlement and a sense of idealism – a combination that reflected not just the desperation of the times but also the extent to which tourism represented an alluring vision of the future that promised economic and cultural renewal while leaving the economic system intact. This chapter also reminds us that Canada's emerging consumer culture was contested by those least likely to benefit from the established political and economic order.

Chapter 4 examines the consolidation of the tourism industry in British Columbia during the Second World War and challenges earlier assumptions about tourism in North America that have suggested that tourist travel all but ceased during the war itself. Now able to enlist the support of the state in their cause, tourism promoters in British Columbia embarked upon a determined effort to employ the powers of the state both to increase the scale and scope of their advertising campaigns and to regulate the activities of private tourist resort operators. Their endeavours were designed to maximize tourist travel to the province both during and after the war.

Chapter 5 documents the manner in which tourism promoters in British Columbia responded to the challenges of an increasingly competitive marketplace during the 1950s and 1960s. It analyzes newspaper and magazine campaigns as well as promotional films and the creation of local tourist attractions in order to demonstrate how both government and civic organizations selectively drew upon the colonial history of British Columbia in order to differentiate the province from other popular tourist destinations during the postwar period.

Finally, Chapter 6 examines the extent to which tourism promotion in the postwar era had become an institutionalized government policy to alleviate regional economic underdevelopment during an era of dramatic province building. It also documents the extent to which the government and local tourism organizations attempted to sell tourism as a public good to residents of British Columbia. Having gained the support of the state, tourism's advocates now turned their attention to civil society and undertook a sustained campaign to inculcate the values of hospitality in the general public by utilizing conduits such as the public school system and the province's university.

A few words about the scope of this book. I do not pretend here to offer a comprehensive history of tourism in British Columbia. I focus, instead, on examining the incorporation of tourist travel into an emerging culture of consumption. To maintain this tight focus, many important aspects of the history of twentieth-century tourism – such as its environmental impact, the role of tourist trade entrepreneurs, and the increasing power of large corporations, as well as the experience of tourist workers and host indigenous populations – remain, for the most part, beyond the book's scope.[40] Moreover, as with all historical study, historians of tourism in British Columbia must acknowledge the limitations of their sources. The internal records of the provincial government's tourist bureau, I was informed early on, no longer exist; the records of the leading publicity bureau in Victoria are sparse. Fortunately, a significant collection of tourism records remains intact for the Vancouver Tourist Association, but only for the post-1926 period.

Throughout the 1990s, Canadian historians debated (sometimes productively, sometimes not) the merits and demerits of both political and social history. Staunch supporters of the latter approach may well find themselves disappointed with the seeming dearth of information about tourists' experiences in this book. As an academic historian educated during debates about "national" history, I found myself drawn to cultural history in part because it seemed to be the most effective method of reconciling political and social history. As Fox and Lears rightly remind us in reference to the American context, "it is impossible to understand the cultures of ordinary Americans without appreciating the ways those cultures are influenced and delimited by the ideas, plans, and needs of the powerful." Indeed, they have gone so far as to suggest that "the study of dominant elites – white, male, educated, affluent – is a critically important part of social history."[41] Fox and Lears thus emphasize the importance of focusing on the *producers* as well as the consumers of mass culture. And it is the producers of mass culture who form the core subject of this book.

Recent Canadian examinations of mass culture have tended to prioritize a consumer- or audience-led approach. For example, in her study of nineteenth-century Canadian exhibitions, E.A. Heaman emphasizes the extent to which exhibition audiences played a central role not only in determining the success of the fairs but also in developing alternative readings to the dominant narratives that the fairs' creators had in mind when they originally designed their displays. Drawing upon the work of Michel de Certeau, Heaman explains that the audience itself played an active role in determining how they experienced the fair: "One might read resistance in the acts of fair-goers who told to admire a prize cow, instead laughed at its obesity and subverted the intended meaning. Or they might flock to the races instead of the lecture hall. The sum total of these actions altered the shape of the exhibition, installing the popular reading as the determining one."[42] Similarly, in her examination of *Chatelaine* magazine in the 1950s and 1960s, Valerie J. Korinek ably demonstrates that readers of the magazine were not passive consumers who always accepted the "preferred meaning" of an editorial, article, or short story uncritically. Instead, *Chatelaine*'s audience offered a variety of "alternative" and "oppositional" readings of the magazine's contents.[43]

Such studies serve two important purposes. First, they reinforce the liminal nature of communication – a phenomenon first explored in the Canadian historical context by Keith Walden in his examination of grocery store window displays in turn-of-the-century Toronto.[44] Second, they reinforce the important observation that, again in the words of Fox and Lears, "it will not do to view" consumer culture "as an elite conspiracy in which advertisers defraud the 'people' by drowning them in a sea of glittering goods. The people are not that passive; they have been active consumers, preferring some commodities to others. They have also been more than consumers; they have pursued other goals in their leisure besides consumption."[45] And, of course, there have been instances of popular (albeit not terribly effective) resistance to this burgeoning culture of consumption.[46]

These are important and, in the aforementioned cases, well argued and innovative observations that offer us a more realistic sense of how cultural texts are communicated. Where we have to be wary, however, is in ascribing too much power to those who were the targets, rather than the initiators, of the cultural discourses. To suggest, as Heaman does, that "historical agency ... lay with the audience rather than the organizers of exhibitions" runs the risk of eliminating the role of cultural producers from the equation entirely.[47] Moreover, as the literature stands right now, we know very little about the actions and ideologies of the producers of mass culture in Canada.[48] And to gain a full understanding of how and when our consumer culture emerged, we need to understand the apparatus that was put in place to foster consumer demand. Thus, if previous studies have tended to tip the historical balance in favour of the consumers of mass culture, this book is offered as a counterweight that focuses on the production of mass culture rather than its reception. It is a study, to paraphrase Thomas Frank's summary of his own work, of "cultural production rather than reception, of power rather than resistance."[49] It is a book motivated by the concern that, in endeavouring to avoid the pitfalls of the critical theory associated with Horkheimer and Adorno, we risk writing a history of consumerism that underestimates the degree to which the producers of consumer culture have had the upper hand.

1

Boosterism and Early Tourism Promotion in British Columbia, 1890-1930

It is the common remark of visitors from the United States that Victorians have mastered the art of combining business with pleasure.

— British Columbia Board of Trade, *Victoria, British Columbia: Past and Present*, c. 1900

Order and Opportunity

In a 1921 article for the "Women's Section" of *Saturday Night* magazine, Irene Todd recounted her journey along the Pacific Coast from Prince Rupert to Vancouver.[1] The attractions and events that Todd chose to highlight for the magazine's readers were in some ways predictable. Near Prince Rupert, for example, Todd drew her readers' attention to the "softly breathing sea" and the "shaggy islands over which a few stars kept watch." Farther south she enthusiastically paid tribute to the way in which a sunrise "broke over the snowy summits of the mountains of British Columbia tinging them with crimson and gold." Nor could she forget "the beauty of those early morning hours as we glided over the pearly waters down that winding passage between two quivering walls of vivid green formed by the steep spruce clad banks."[2] British Columbia's natural beauties were clearly a significant part of her travel experience.

More surprising, perhaps, was Todd's emphasis on more utilitarian attractions. As prominent as the anecdotes about natural attractions in her article were descriptions of industrial and technological achievements. The Grand Trunk Pacific steamer that transported Todd and the other passengers was, in her recollection, "shining and trim, glistening with light from stem to stern, her engines throbbing in eagerness to be off on her 800 mile journey through the fiords and inlets of the North Pacific coast." Prince Rupert Harbour itself was also worthy of sustained comment: "The longshoremen hurried to and fro, stowing away great loads of freight ... There was the whine of block and tackle, the clanking of chains, the splash of water against the wharves, and the chug-chug of the gasoline engines of the halibut fishing boats, and the Indian Salmon fishing boats, that lay out in the path of the moon." A stop to take on passengers at Swanson Bay was also worthy of a detailed retelling. Swanson Bay, after all, boasted "one of the largest industries on the Pacific

Coast" – Whalen Pulp and Paper Mills – and employed 700 people. On this trip, then, industry also sparked Todd's interest.[3]

Most interesting here is the manner in which Todd intertwined observations about nature and industry. For her, the steamer, no less than the snow-capped mountains, was, in her account, deserving of attention, and her focus seems to have been as much on the industrial possibilities of her travel destination as on its natural setting. In her article, both aspects of modernity are given voice: an angst-ridden search for escape into nature, and a celebration of and fascination with the twin driving forces of the modern world, technology and capitalism.[4] The ease with which Todd reconciled the splendour of the natural world and the wonders of technology is reminiscent of what Leo Marx has identified as "the rhetoric of the technological sublime."[5] As David Louter has recently demonstrated, some early-twentieth-century tourists to the American west saw no difficulty in reconciling the most modern of machines, the automobile, with the region's natural wonders. For such travellers, the automobile offered convenient access to national parks and mountains, with minimal impact upon the environment when compared with the effects of railways. Seen "in this light," Louter explains, "parks were a kind of national commons for nature and machines."[6]

Todd, then, was not alone. In fact, her motivations for travelling and recording her experiences were shared by many other travellers in British Columbia between 1890 and 1930. Some were local residents and journalists anxious to publicize the province; many more were visitors from afar keen to detail their experiences for the magazine-buying public. By examining what these writers chose to highlight and how they responded to the natural and human-made attractions that they visited, it is possible to get a sense of why people toured British Columbia in the early part of the twentieth century. Such accounts are particularly important because during this era there was, for the most part, no accurate way of measuring tourist demand or even the number of tourists visiting the province. Tourism promoters anxious to expand the tourist trade would likely have consulted, as we are about to do, the pages of major periodicals such as *Saturday Night, Maclean's,* and *Sunset* to glean an understanding of why tourists travelled and what could be done to encourage more of them to visit the province.[7]

This chapter focuses on both tourists and tourism promoters in order to illustrate an important but overlooked aspect of the history of tourism. While contemporary tourism promotion efforts are measured primarily by the amount of money that visitors are convinced to spend at a given destination, early tourism promotion in British Columbia had a different rationale – one closely related to boosterism. Many travellers sought to evade the debilitating effects of modern life by retreating to the province's wilderness. But, like Todd, they were also intrigued by the economic opportunities and the wonders of industrial production that they saw in British Columbia. Analyzing the activities of tourists and tourism promoters during this era gives us a window onto the nature of tourism before it was incorporated into a burgeoning culture of consumption.

To date, research on tourism and tourism promotion in Canada during the late nineteenth and early twentieth centuries has emphasized the extent to which tourism promoters recognized tourists' desire to escape the modern world in favour of wilderness adventures.[8] In Atlantic Canada, the region most studied by tourism scholars, the tourist trade was seen as an alternative to the fishery and a means of diversifying local economies. Local clubs and government regulators endeavoured to set aside a significant portion of the region's fish and game for visiting American tourists, who were willing to pay handsomely for the privilege of gaining access to the region's wildlife resources. These promotional efforts focused on the benefits of obtaining a direct but temporary infusion of cash from visiting American hunters and fishers.[9] Nascent tourism promotion bodies in British Columbia, however, saw tourism as a strategy for luring settlers and agricultural and industrial development to the province. They shared this approach with booster organizations throughout western Canada that advertised their towns and cities as wilderness preserves in the hope that deep-pocketed eastern investors would be convinced to settle in the west.[10] This recognition of tourism as a catalyst for industrial development was not unique to Canada. During the interwar years, South Africa employed tourism promotion as a method of luring American capitalists to its shores.[11] Similarly, in the years leading up to its independence in 1962, government officials in Jamaica attempted to secure much-needed American investment by tailoring the colony's tercentenary celebrations to suit the sensibilities of American tourists.[12] The political climate of both South Africa in the 1920s and Jamaica in the 1950s focused explicitly on nation building and the exporting of natural resources. It also reflected a sense of optimism about future resource development. The similarities to British Columbia at the turn of the century are striking. In a recent survey of late-nineteenth-century British Columbia politics, R.A.J. McDonald has urged historians to recognize the extent to which the province's politicians embraced the possibilities of modernity.[13] Moreover, as Jean Barman notes, the turn of the century marked a period of growing self-confidence as provincial leaders eagerly anticipated a resource extraction boom.[14] Such anticipation reflected a sense of optimism about the province's economic future. It was very likely this optimism that encouraged British Columbians to see tourism as a catalyst, rather than an alternative, to industrial and agricultural development. To this end, organizations in Victoria and Vancouver sought to capitalize upon tourists' ambiguous reactions to the modern world. Indeed, while much of the historical literature examining public reaction to the onset of modernity in North America focuses primarily on the search for *order* in this period of dramatic change brought about by industrial capitalism,[15] the evidence from British Columbia suggests that North Americans were equally as determined in their search for something else: *opportunity*.

Evading Modernity

Many tourists travelled to escape the hectic pace of modern life – at least temporarily. In a 1908 article appearing in *Saturday Night* magazine, for example, P.A. O'Farrell of New York City saw in British Columbia's Arrow Lake country the opportunity to temporarily trade the hustle and bustle of the "Big Apple" for the relaxing sight of orchards, gardens, and lawns. In contemplating the building of a chalet near the mountains, O'Farrell hoped to "escape from that species of tiger hunt that prevails in Wall Street."[16] Poet and travel writer Ernest McGaffey was more ambiguous in his evaluation of the modern world. In a 1913 article for *Sunset* magazine, McGaffey hailed Vancouver Island as a place where "a Modern Metropolis Touches the Margin of a Pristine Wilderness." Victoria, he trumpeted, was a place where "Scenery and Commerce Meet." The island's properties, McGaffey explained, made it an ideal destination for world-weary citizens of North America – albeit one in which they could maintain contact with the world of commerce.[17] Both O'Farrell and McGaffey celebrated British Columbia's restorative powers, and their observations were echoed many times over by other travellers.

Recording her 1915 trip to the Kootenays for *Maclean's* magazine, for example, Mrs. Arthur Spragge, the author of an earlier book describing her 1887 trip from Ontario to the Pacific Coast via the Canadian Pacific Railway, praised the region's dry air and sporting opportunities but paid particular tribute to Sinclair Hot Springs, which possessed radium for fighting disease.[18] This concern for the health-giving properties of vacation destinations was widely shared.[19] "If the open road fever seizes you," E.A. Vandeventer encouraged readers of *Sunset* magazine in 1925, "do not resist it, for nothing links health building with pleasure more surely than does change of scenery and climate in the fresh air."[20] In a 1928 report on ski-jumping in Revelstoke for *Maclean's*, J.E. March noted the growing popularity of skiing as an antidote to the drudgery of an increasingly bureaucratized world. In earlier times, March noted, the actual skiing had been left "to the stark enthusiasts; now everybody does it." "Important and portly men who seriously and solemnly manage every kind of business," March reported, "now spend a week or two each winter attempting feats which almost appal[l] their children."[21]

The same year *Saturday Night* offered a lengthy list of the health advantages that could be secured by visiting British Columbia. Its coastal mountain range, for example, offered a bevy of winter sports, including skiing, tobogganing, and snowshoeing. In reminding its readers of the important role of play in daily life, the magazine pointed to the many opportunities that existed in the province for big-game hunting, sailing, fishing, and golfing. Less active readers could make use of Vancouver's many beaches. Vancouver was, after all, "one of the healthiest cities on the North American Continent. Its climate, the geographical situation, its modernity all help to make it so, but there is added to those factors the magnificent sea bathing which every citizen and visitor alike enjoy." The properties of the Pacific Ocean, according to the author, not only improved one's health but also encouraged one to relax and have fun: "The waters of the mid-North Pacific Ocean have a refreshing buoyancy, an invigorating tang which assist[s] the thousands of visitors to enjoy the many beaches." Victoria also boasted many beaches. In fact, the two cities in combination supplied such a generous choice of beaches for visitors that, in the eyes of *Saturday Night,* the visitor to British Columbia could not fail "to enjoy the sparkling waters with their health-giving and re-freshing properties."[22]

According to some observers, a vacation's health-giving properties also played a key role in maintaining an *orderly* and productive society.[23] In a 1904 article for *Sunset* magazine, for example, George Eldredge under-scored the importance of vacations, not just for the vacationer, but also for society in general. In his view, vacations contributed to self-improvement and efficiency – two key attributes for the modern person. According to Eldredge, a man was either a productive citizen striving for self-improvement or a "shirk" who held back society by "taking out of the common fund all he can and paying back less than he can." The deliberately lazy were "vagrants – no matter whether he [sic] be clothed in rags or in broad-cloth – a foe to mankind" – and as such deserved, and received, little sympathy or support from the state. Eldredge had little time for this group. His attention was directed instead to another, less recognized type of "shirk." Many men remained unproductive, he explained, not through laziness but through ignorance. "There is one false idea which prevails among this unfortunate class of men which is very largely responsible for the smallness of result in their lives," Eldredge explained, "the idea that a man can work 365 days in a year and accomplish good results." Rest and relaxation were necessary ingredients in production. Quite aside from religious considerations, he suggested, productive citizens required "one day of rest in every seven" and should "spend that day in the way best calculated to refresh his whole nature." "The man who is ambitious to do the most and best work will," Eldredge argued, "if he be wise, take a month out of his summer each year and invest it in pure air and sunshine." Like a well-harvested field, the productive citizen then should "let himself lie fallow for four weeks; and then go back to his business with zest and earnestness, to accomplish more in the next eleven months than he could possibly have done in all the twelve otherwise."[24]

A quarter of a century later, in 1929, *Sunset*'s advice for readers remained largely unchanged. To alleviate the high number of suicides and mental health problems among businesspeople, household science expert Gladys Denny Shultz urged the magazine's readers to divert themselves from "this strange devotion to coins and bits of paper." Businesspeople, Shultz advised, should concentrate more on the challenge of competing in business than on the monetary aspects of their occupation. Moreover, Shultz echoed Eldredge's call for more emphasis on rest and enjoyment away from the workplace. In her discussion of a dedicated yet unproductive female worker, she explained that the woman worked "like a slave, getting through mountains of detail, staying overtime, working herself into a state of nervous irritability, working gray hair into her head and worried lines into her forehead. Working so hard, all the time, in fact, that she loses her perspective entirely and has nothing fresh to contribute to anything." Rest, relaxation, and play provided the necessary antidote to this condition, she argued, by improving one's mental health and workplace productivity.[25]

It would be overly simplistic, of course, to assume that visits to British Columbia were undertaken purely in pursuit of a calculated period of rest. Focusing again on travellers' experiences as they were recorded in magazines provides insight into how these visitors themselves represented their experiences and their relationships to the natural and technological wonders that they were viewing. Travellers to British Columbia shared a pursuit common to many other travellers of the era: a desire for sublime experience.[26]

A 1913 trip to Capilano Canyon just north of Vancouver, for example, allowed Toronto journalist Mary Adelaide Snider to immerse herself in nature and escape from the pressing concerns of daily life. Peering in awe at the gigantic skunk cabbage and dandelions, Snider reported, "you feel like Alice in Wonderland, you are so small by comparison with familiar things." When she crossed the bridge into the centre of the canyon, her removal from modern life was complete: "Forgotten are your perplexities – forgotten everything – there is *nobody* in the universe." A venture across a gorge on a narrow plank produced just the sensation she sought: "You do not care. You are uplifted above fear by the wonder of the woods."[27]

Kitty Hardcastle's 1913 trip to the Rockies produced similar results. "Amidst the impressive grandeur of that mountain scenery how finite mere humans seemed!" she mused. Hardcastle experienced the "ecstacy of inhaling the pure mountain air" and embraced the opportunity "to sense the solitude and listen to the mountain sounds all indescribably sweet."[28] Ernest McGaffey also found it difficult to find the words to describe the scenery on Vancouver Island. He was awed by the island's "rivers and canyons savage in their grandeur and beauty, and forests gray with the rime of ages."[29]

For many travellers, the natural surroundings provided a religious allure. E.A. Powell found the scenery along the Island Highway so impressive "that we felt a trifle awed and spoke in whispers when we spoke at all, as though we were in the nave of a great cathedral."[30] When the journalist and future wheat financier Norman Lambert visited the Rockies in 1915, words failed him in his attempt to record the scene: "Description is futile," he wrote, "because the experience is not one of the eye and the senses: it is spiritual."[31] Face to face with the mountains and gigantic trees of Bella Coola, Guy Rhoades was awed into silence. He described himself as "helpless" and at first unable to convey the beauty of the area. Having recovered enough to write down his thoughts, he announced that "here one can feel the presence of the spirits of the upper world, and one begins to realise how logical the religious beliefs of the Indians really are."[32] Nature, however, was not the only antidote to the enervating side effects of modernity. Former "boom" towns could offer reassurance as well. In 1922 Charles Lugrin Shaw found serenity in the most peaceful of places: the Barkerville graveyard. For Shaw, the graveyard "seemed to fit in as one of the obvious features, because here was the place where people lived in the past, where the slightest suggestion of the modern seemed like an intrusion."[33]

Clearly, then, one overwhelming motivating factor for tourists in British Columbia before 1930 was the desire to escape from the hustle and bustle of the modern world. Many early travellers to British Columbia shared a desire to escape from the repetitiveness and dreariness of daily life. This yearning for causal potency and authentic experience has been noted by other scholars focusing on other contexts and activities ranging from the private correspondence and published writings of English Canadian imperialists living in Montreal to art aficionados in Toronto eager to celebrate Tom Thomson's manly virtues.[34] Similarly, in the American context, Anne Farrar Hyde has argued that, between 1885 and 1915, "many people began to question assumptions about the gifts of modernity and technology."[35] The travellers' accounts of British Columbia detailed here emphasize, in many ways, the breadth of this antimodern yearning in Canada between 1890 and 1930.

Embracing Modernity

Yet there are elements in these travellers' tales that jar with their antimodern rhetoric. To be sure, these writers advocated vacations to promote physical recovery and offered their readers detailed retellings of their spiritual communions with the province's sublime mountain scenery. However, their feelings of awe toward the sublimity of nature also engendered a desire to conquer the very topography that produced these feelings. For example, when fish and game enthusiast Edward Sandys visited the Great Asulkan Glacier near Rogers Pass in 1890, he recorded not only his tribute to the sublime health-restoring scenery but that of his American travelling partner as well. In doing so, he also alluded to an "indescribable sense of awe" in peering up at the glacier. When Sandys suggested climbing the glacier itself, his "little" American companion bowed out. Sandys proceeded to climb partway up the side of the glacier and then slid down "toboggan style." There coexisted within Sandys and many other travellers both an admiration for nature and a desire to conquer the landscape to which they had retreated.[36] W.E. Raney's 1899 trip along the Old Cariboo Road was also punctuated by a dangerous encounter with nature, and Raney too employed the theme of American inferiority in recounting his tale. Informed that two Americans from New York had proclaimed themselves scared of the dangerous road from Lillooet to Golden Cache, Raney felt obliged to tackle the route and boasted of his accomplishment.[37] The sense of superiority and causal potency that came with conquering one's fear was not solely the domain of male travellers. On her 1913 trip to the Rockies, Kitty Hardcastle savoured the opportunity to demonstrate her bravery. When several other female travellers panicked the night before a scheduled trip to see the Takakkaw Falls, Hardcastle and her companion relished the opportunity to reassure them of their safety.[38]

Waterfalls and glaciers were not the only natural wonders that intimidated and provoked travellers in British Columbia; less remarkable sections of the landscape evoked similar feelings. In his retelling of the Vancouver Automobile Club's 1922 trip through Southern British Columbia, Percy Gomery offered readers a rugged tale of individual achievement: "Travelling by motor-boat, row-boat, dugout canoe, wagon, pack-horse and for two score miles struggling unaided through deserted and overgrown trails," he explained, his party triumphed over the province's mountainous geography.[39]

Travel writer E.A. Powell was convinced that conquest over nature could come in more portable and tasty forms. In response to his colleague's complaint that they had done little hunting or fishing during their journey up the Pacific Coast from Mexico, Powell challenged his travelling companion (and *Sunset*'s readers) to just wait "until we get over to Vancouver island. You won't need to unstrap your fishing rods or your gun either. A man I know told me that up in the unfrequented interior of the island you can spear salmon with a pitchfork and kill all the pheasants you want with a club."[40]

Another method of conquering nature was through the collection of knowledge. In a manner reminiscent of eighteenth-century European travel writers who diligently recorded the characteristics of their colonial possessions, visitors to British Columbia detailed the province's natural properties for their readers.[41] Bird enthusiast Hamilton M. Laing, for instance, dedicated his entire 1920 tour between Hope and Princeton to a detailed examination and recording of the wide variety of flowers found in the region.[42] Interest in science was not restricted, of course, to botany. A reporter visiting the Cariboo Road for *Saturday Night* found equally fascinating the ways in which science was employed to find gold and other minerals.[43] Mary Adelaide Snider's 1913 trip to Capilano Canyon was incomplete, her guide insisted, without a detailed explanation and exploration of the nearby timber flume.[44]

Often an interest in conquering or controlling nature combined with a fascination with scientific achievements to produce, in many travellers' accounts, a list of entrepreneurial opportunities in agriculture and industry for their readers to contemplate. During his journey along the Cariboo Trail, for example, E.A. Powell took time to explain to his readers the immense impact that the Grand Trunk Pacific was bound to have on the province. When completed, he explained, it "will open up to civilization and exploitation the rich mines and vast forests of northern British Columbia and the limitless prairies of the Peace river country."[45] Mrs. Arthur Spragge's 1915 journey to Golden allowed her the opportunity to document the region's improving irrigation system and declare that small fortunes were to be made growing fruits and vegetables.[46] Norman Lambert drew his readers' attention to the various canneries and copper deposits near Hazelton.[47] Frequently a tribute to the province's climate was combined with an example of a success story to emphasize the economic opportunities present. P.A. O'Farrell found the climate and soil of the Arrow Lake country to be "all that are desirable for men or women who love open air life and bracing mountain air, and an occasional hunt for cariboo and elk." "One rancher told me," he continued, "that he realized 800 dollars off one acre of fruit."[48]

These visitors to British Columbia were not simply rebelling against the enervating effects of modern life; they were, in fact, fascinated by the possibilities of modern technology, and they certainly were not averse to contemplating ways to capitalize and profit from the natural world to which they were temporarily retreating. As such, these travellers took a utilitarian approach to tourism – one that had been popular throughout the eighteenth century. As Ian Ousby explains, eighteenth-century travellers were motivated not by nostalgia but by a desire to investigate and experience the scientific advancements of the modern world. Motivated as they were by this spirit of enquiry, such travellers placed a great deal of importance on firsthand, empirical knowledge.[49] Early travellers to British Columbia thus combined their desire to temporarily evade the debilitating effects of modern life with a keen interest in locating and embracing industrial and agricultural opportunities.[50]

During the first two decades of the twentieth century, civic leaders in Victoria and Vancouver worked diligently to attract as many visitors as possible. They did so with the hope that even a brief visit to the province would convince these travellers to invest and settle in British Columbia. As the articles appearing in magazines such as *Maclean's, Saturday Night,* and *Sunset* suggest, many nineteenth-century visitors to British Columbia were drawn to a great extent to the province's hinterland. Communication requirements along with more tangible advantages such as roads ensured that British Columbia's two largest centres, Victoria and Vancouver, led the way in tourism promotion and that these two cities reaped most of the benefits that such promotional efforts produced.

Victoria, Vancouver, and the Establishment of Civic Tourist Associations

While British Columbia's entry into Confederation in 1871 alleviated several financial problems plaguing the former Crown colony, it left Canada's newest province in a precarious position. The Confederation agreement relieved the province of its mounting debt, but it did not immediately solve British Columbia's most pressing requirement: economic development. During the last three decades of the nineteenth century, governing coalitions in the province's Legislative Assembly focused their efforts on securing population and investment capital for the province. The chief means of obtaining these ingredients for economic development was a permanent transportation link with eastern North America – a link finally provided by the eventual completion of the Canadian Pacific Railway (CPR) in 1885.

Between the founding of Vancouver in 1886 as the CPR's western terminus and the outbreak of the Great War, R.A.J. McDonald has argued, British Columbia "was transformed economically from an outward-looking maritime society connected by the Pacific Ocean to California, Great Britain, and various points on the Pacific Rim, into an inward-looking continental community." The catalysts for this reorientation were the railways. Completion of the Central Pacific Railway at San Francisco in 1869 was supplemented, between 1883 and 1893, by the completion of three other transcontinental railways farther north in the Pacific Northwest.[51] Completion of transcontinental railway lines to the US Pacific Northwest in the early 1880s meant that it was now practical for local boosters "to lure tourists along with home seekers and investors" to Idaho, Washington, and Oregon.[52] Similarly, the completion of the CPR provided civic leaders in

Victoria and the new city of Vancouver with a much more efficient means of luring potential settlers to their settlements.

The CPR, like other North American railways, had identified tourism as an important source of supplementary income to help alleviate the company's mounting debt. Throughout the late nineteenth century, railway companies in the western United States built hotels along their lines to capitalize upon the American public's growing interest in transcontinental travel.[53] The Southern Pacific Railroad's Hotel Del Monte in Monterey (opened in 1880), the Denver and Rio Grande Railroad's Antlers Hotel in Colorado Springs (opened in 1881), and the Northern Pacific's Canyon Hotel (built in 1913), which overlooked the Grand Canyon, all offered well-to-do tourists stately and comfortable accommodation for their travel adventures. Between 1896 and 1920, in fact, the Santa Fe Railroad built no fewer than seventeen large hotels.[54] Similarly, the CPR commenced construction on three restaurant stops in British Columbia in 1886 (Mount Stephen House at Field, Glacier House near Rogers Pass, and Fraser Canyon House at North Bend), each of which contained six or seven bedrooms. Construction on a much larger hotel in Vancouver began in July 1886, and the Hotel Vancouver opened its doors to visitors in May 1887. A few months later work was completed on the Banff Springs Hotel in Alberta.[55] By the first decade of the twentieth century, these hotels would combine with others, such as the Chateau Frontenac in Quebec (completed in 1893) and the Algonquin Hotel in St. Andrew's, New Brunswick (brought under CPR management in 1905), to give the company a network of hotels across the country.

The CPR had another effect, of course, on the provincial economy. Bolstered by its position as the CPR's western terminus, Vancouver supplanted the provincial capital of Victoria as the province's leading port, and throughout the 1890s Victoria's economy was outpaced by Vancouver's. In 1890, Victoria's exports were six times greater than Vancouver's. By 1903, these positions were dramatically reversed, and Vancouver's exports exceeded Victoria's by a ratio of three to one.[56] It was in this context that the province's capital city embraced the possibilities of civic boosterism.

In the competition to lure industrial development and settlers at the turn of the century, cities throughout North America conducted publicity campaigns championing their local amenities and promising tax concessions and monetary grants to companies willing to set up shop within their boundaries. Between 1907 and 1915, for example, the town of Maisonneuve, Quebec, undertook a systematic newspaper advertising campaign supplemented with several promotional pamphlets in an attempt to lure industry to what local officials claimed was "Le Pittsburg du Canada."[57] Coexisting with this desire to promote urban growth, however, was a concern about the dangers of urbanization. Disease, crime, prostitution, and "rampant materialism" were all seen as evil by-products of city life. In response, urban reformers launched "collectivist" campaigns to clean up urban centres in an attempt "to impose order on the chaos of city life." By 1900 the beautification of the city, through the creation of parks and wide boulevards, had emerged as a popular solution to the problems and perils of city life.[58]

While civic leaders in eastern urban centres embarked upon urban reform campaigns, many civic leaders in the nascent communities of the west engaged in beautification programs in order to attract investment and settlement. Between 1890 and 1910, civic leaders in Seattle were motivated to construct "an attractive system of parks and boulevards" and to advertise these amenities "not ... so much from a spirit of reform as from a desire for commercial growth, civic pride, and a spirit of rivalry with other Northwest cities."[59] Similar motivations among civic leaders on the Canadian Prairies during the late nineteenth and early twentieth centuries resulted in a sustained period of boosterism in which community leaders embarked upon vigorous campaigns to improve local infrastructure and lure investment in an attempt to foster economic growth.[60] Frequently such campaigns emphasized the city's favourable living conditions. Civic leaders in Saskatoon, for example, attempted to offer prospective residents an inviting and reassuring image of the city by promoting its local parks, hotels, and bridges. Such symbols, David Neufeld explains, offered potential newcomers a vision of Saskatoon that emphasized opportunities for financial gain in an attractive but secure setting.[61]

British Columbia's capital city was not immune to this spirit of boosterism. Among the earliest attempts to publicize Victoria was the 1891 booklet *Victoria Illustrated,* published by the *Colonist* newspaper. This booklet was dedicated to selling the city's industrial, agricultural, and settlement opportunities to outsiders. Focusing chiefly on the city's "natural advantages," *Victoria Illustrated* reflected the booster spirit of the time. Along with writing lengthy profiles of economic opportunities ranging from mining and fishing to agriculture and wholesale trade, its authors did their best to underscore the advantageous living conditions that the city offered. They highlighted both the "salubrity" of the city's climate and its "pastoral" yet "majestic" setting in an attempt to lure investors to Victoria. Detailed monthly rainfall and temperature charts were included as statistical proof of the city's climatic health-giving advantages.[62]

Early city boosters elsewhere along the Pacific Coast produced similar promotional material. A January 1893 issue of *Facts Seattle* produced by the Seattle Chamber of Commerce highlighted for potential settlers evidence of the city's population growth, noted its superior climate, and listed among its amenities a plethora of schools, churches, and banks. The potential investor was informed that the "principal resources within a radius of 120 miles of Seattle, and tributary thereto, are the immense growth of superior timber, vast deposits of iron and coal ... precious metals, stone and lime," while opportunities also existed in "agriculture, fishing, manufacturing and shipping." The pamphlet also highlighted the city's two transcontinental railway connections to the eastern United States.[63]

Facts Seattle was part of a sustained campaign undertaken by civic leaders in Seattle between 1890 and 1910 in which organizations such as the Seattle Chamber of Commerce distributed promotional literature aimed at luring settlers and investors to the city.[64] The most successful promotional campaign of the era, however, belonged to the city of Los Angeles. Between the 1860s and the 1930s, Los Angeles was transformed from a small town with dirt streets to the fourth largest urban centre in the United States and to a city that led that nation "in agriculture, motion pictures, and aircraft production." The chief catalyst of this growth was the city's Chamber of Commerce, which concentrated its efforts on luring investors and settlers from the American midwest to the city in order to take advantage of its warm and dry climate.[65] Anxious to withstand the economic challenge posed by its rapidly developing mainland neighbour and intrigued by the ongoing success of Los Angeles, Victoria's business community turned to tourism promotion at the turn of the century. In doing so, as we shall see, local initiatives, rather than the Montreal-based CPR, played the leading role in promoting the city as a tourist destination.

The Tourist Association of Victoria

Tourism has had neither a timeless nor an intrinsic association with British Columbia's provincial capital. While visitors included the city on their cruise itineraries along the Pacific Coast as early as the 1870s, the number of visitors remained low until the city undertook a sustained campaign to promote tourism at the turn of the century.[66] Victoria's first steps toward tourism promotion were, in fact, tentative. This is not surprising since the city retained its central role in the province's commercial development into the 1890s.[67] In the fall of 1890, however, with Vancouver's economy quickly developing, the city's Board of Trade turned its attention for the first time in a concentrated manner to the question of publicizing Victoria. In October of that year, the board created an Advertising Committee to explore the possibility of publicizing the city's investment opportunities as well as its "equable climate and fine scenery."[68] By April 1891, having impressed upon the provincial government the importance of publishing a pamphlet to benefit the province, the board undertook its first direct step in the direction of promotional activity by offering its services in gathering statistics for a book soon to be published under the auspices of the *Colonist* newspaper – very likely *Victoria Illustrated*.[69]

In the late 1890s, the Board of Trade loaned the use of its name to efforts aimed at advertising the city as a Klondike outfitting centre, and the board was becoming more involved in supplying and publishing information designed to attract travellers to the city.[70] By October 1899, the board had concluded that a concerted effort should be made to advertise the city and that "annual subscriptions" should be solicited in order to publicize "the trading advantages of Victoria and its attractions to tourists."[71] With this decision, the board immersed itself in the Pacific Northwest's fledgling network of tourism promoters. One member was sent to a convention in Kamloops aimed at organizing a Provincial Good Roads Association. Three more were invited to embark upon a publicity excursion organized by the Seattle Chamber of Commerce.[72]

In 1900 and 1901 the board helped to design a booklet to advertise the city entitled *Victoria, British Columbia: Past and Present.*[73] This publication offered a portrait of Victoria as a city that provided visitors with the chance to immerse themselves in local natural attractions and to observe firsthand the city's industrial development possibilities. Under the heading "Panoramic and Picturesque," for example, it called readers' attention both to the attractive smaller islands nearby and to "ships being towed to the lumber mills ... [and] steamers speeding to all points of the coast and to the Orient and Australia."[74] And, in late December 1901, as a sign that the board was now convinced more than ever of the importance of tourists to the city's welfare, it began proceedings to approach the Canadian Pacific Railway with the idea of having the company construct a tourist hotel in Victoria.[75] While the push for a tourist hotel was a clear sign that tourism was gaining more attention from the board, it would not accomplish this task alone. The key player in the negotiations with the CPR was the city's newly formed Tourist Association.

Organized tourism promotion in Victoria was the product of a cooperative effort among the city's business and community leaders, but one figure played a leading role: the indefatigable Herbert Cuthbert. Cuthbert was born in Wakefield, England, in 1865 and had taken up a career in Victoria at the turn of the century as both a real estate agent and the part owner of an auction house.[76] The energetic Cuthbert arrived in Victoria in October 1891 and, quickly struck by the possibilities of the city's new market building, became the market's largest tenant by obtaining consignments of various types of produce and beef cattle. When this undertaking was halted by a smallpox epidemic, Cuthbert persevered to organize a new market and became a director of the local Agricultural Association. He also took a leading role in city improvements by spearheading a campaign to have the city build a stone embankment to replace the old wooden bridge across Government Street.[77] Cuthbert's desire to develop the city's market and improve local pedestrian walkways reflected the wider agenda of the contemporary urban reform movement.[78]

Cuthbert outlined his support for tourism promotion in a July 1900 letter published in the Victoria *Daily Colonist*. Victoria's image as a "pleasure and health resort," he explained, must be spread throughout North America and Britain. But he was equally anxious to ensure that the flattering depictions of the city in guidebooks could be backed up by developments in the city itself. Civic improvements, including permanent roadways, pleasure grounds, and a revitalized inner harbour, Cuthbert argued, were necessary to maximize the city's allure as a tourist destination. To justify his recipe for success, Cuthbert drew a comparison between Victoria's potential as a seaside resort and previous success stories in Britain.[79] "I know of several cities in England that could not compare with Victoria, and that fifty years ago had not over 1,000 inhabitants which have now from 20,000 to 75,000 people," he explained, primarily because of their civic leaders' far-sighted decision to provide "attractions and entertainment for the visitors." The result, he argued, was prosperity. Both Blackpool and Southport, Cuthbert maintained, owed their "popularity and their largely increased population to the establishment of winter gardens and such places of entertainment." Visitors lured to Victoria by such entertainments might stay "for a day ... a week, a month or more, and many of them would become permanent residents." The resulting word-of-mouth publicity would also ensure that "Victoria's importance as a commercial and mining centre would be advertised more by these visitors coming amongst us than by anything else." As a local entrepreneur, Cuthbert also recognized the immediate benefits of such visits: "Our hotels would be filled," he noted, before drawing upon his experience as co-owner of a local auction house to predict that "the auctioneers would have a larger and more profitable business."[80]

Less than a year later, Cuthbert again publicly admonished his fellow Victorians to take the possibilities of tourism promotion seriously, this time in an interview with a *Daily Colonist* reporter. On this occasion, he was armed with evidence detailing the development of a tourist destination closer to home: Seattle. In Seattle, Cuthbert explained, the value of business and residential properties was increasing dramatically. The impetus behind this development was the willingness of Seattle businesspeople to combine efforts and transcend individual self-interest. This willingness had allowed the city to prosper despite the fact that Seattle's cost of living was higher, and its quality of life was lower, than Victoria's. Victoria businesspeople could remedy this situation, Cuthbert claimed, only by following the lead of their southern counterparts. Victoria would attract a large number of residents only if its "citizens would lay themselves out to attract visitors and home seekers" by "providing amusements and entertainment for residents and visitors."[81]

As Cuthbert championed tourism's possibilities in print, the local business community took tentative steps toward the creation of a tourist association. A preliminary meeting in November 1901 suggested a good deal of interest in such an organization on the part of Victoria's business leaders and prompted the *Daily Colonist* to suggest that "the organization in Victoria of an efficient Tourists' Association [is] a certainty." The tourist movement, the newspaper explained to its readers, was "one that ought to appeal to every business man, for the expenditure by tourists is large." Saint John, New Brunswick, it reported, had obtained $2.5 million from tourist revenue in 1900. Confident that Victoria possessed both "the attractions that will bring tourists" and "the territory to draw from," the *Daily Colonist* restlessly awaited the day when information about the city reached potential tourists and a "golden harvest" resulted. Subscriptions totalling $5,000, the newspaper suggested, would get a tourist association up and running.[82]

With the necessary funding secured, the Tourist Association of Victoria (TAV) was formed in February 1902. In giving its final report, the association's Provisional Committee, headed by Mayor Charles Hayward, echoed the rhetoric of boosterism that Alan Artibise has identified with community leaders on the Prairies and proclaimed that its great success in canvassing funds for the new organization was evidence that the association had "secured the sympathy of all classes of the community."[83] Besides Mayor Hayward, the Provisional Committee was comprised of prominent business and civic leaders, including hotel proprietors Stephen Jones and G.A. Hartnagle, industrialists D.R. Ker and A.B. Fraser Sr., clothing store proprietor and Alderman W.G. Cameron, and journalists Frank I. Clarke and Charles H. Lugrin.[84] While these men came from a variety of political and religious backgrounds,[85] and indeed pursued quite different occupations, they all shared two key characteristics. They were heavily involved in voluntary community activities, and their financial security depended upon the overall prosperity of the city itself. These men shared a sense of civic duty and were imbued with a dedication to philanthropy common among businesspeople of the time.[86]

Aims and Activities of the TAV

While the *Daily Colonist* tempted local businesses with visions of a "golden harvest" of free-spending visitors, the leaders of the TAV remained focused on promoting tourism in order to attract settlement and investment.[87] Cuthbert had little time for observers who suggested that Victoria would not benefit from industrial development. In fact, he maintained that the tourist association should be dedicated to luring new factories to the city and that commercial interests must not be neglected in the city's efforts to become both a tourist resort and a leading centre of economic development in the Pacific Northwest. Cuthbert also emphasized the important role that the association played in encouraging agricultural development. Concerted campaigns to lure prospective farmers to southern Vancouver Island, he explained, were necessary not only to build up these rural communities but also to stimulate industrial activity in Victoria itself.[88] Such aims were reminiscent of the goals associated with nineteenth-century international exhibitions, which offered countries such as Canada an opportunity to showcase natural resources with the hope of securing new "immigrants, capital, and markets."[89]

Cuthbert's position was publicly endorsed by other prominent men. Charles H. Lugrin stressed the connection between tourists and the region's fisheries. Drawing upon his earlier experience as a lawyer and journalist in the Maritimes, Lugrin pointed to the example of New Brunswick, where the provincial government had taken a leading role in encouraging visitors to make use of that province's fishing opportunities.[90] As a less flattering example, Lugrin pointed to the State of Maine: "the most barren, worthless portions" of that state "had been made valuable through advertising their attractions as hunting and fishing resorts." Lugrin urged the association to focus first on potential US customers west of the Mississippi before turning gradually to include the eastern coast of the United States and Canada. He also stressed the lucrative British market, in which "there were many people of wealth who counted distance as an obstacle easily overcome when there was something worth seeing and good sport at the other end."[91]

A Mr. Mackenzie was among the eager supporters of the association and drew his inspiration from a recent report in the Seattle *Post-Intelligencer* – a report that he suggested "was in itself ... a sufficient reason for the formation of a tourist association in Victoria." The report documented the large numbers of tourists visiting California who would be returning to the east by way of the northwest (many by way of Portland). What irked the Seattle newspaper was the city's lack of promotional literature in California that might woo these travellers farther north.[92] Mackenzie considered this a valuable lesson for Victoria. So did the *Daily Colonist*. Under the heading "Advertise Victoria," the newspaper published an interview with M.P. Benton, general agent for the Burlington Railroad in Seattle, detailing the vast number of potential visitors to the city who had travelled from the east to vacation in California and were contemplating a northern route home. If Seattle "can attract any number of tourists from Southern California," the *Daily Colonist* reasoned, "surely if Victoria's thousand and one beauty spots were adequately advertised in the southern land, any who came as far north as Seattle would be morally sure to pay Victoria a visit."[93] Such reasoning would lead, in the near future, to a great deal of cooperation between tourism promoters in Seattle, Victoria, and Vancouver.

With agreement upon the aims of the association, TAV members embarked upon a number of different activities, all of which were designed to develop the city's economy. Their efforts included a sustained local drive to beautify the city and modernize its infrastructure, a vigorous campaign to improve transportation routes to Victoria and expand the city's available accommodation, a concerted effort to advertise the city's attractions through promotional trips and the distribution of tourist literature, and, of course, a constant campaign to raise funds to support these various initiatives.

By July 1902, the *Daily Colonist* reported, great strides had been taken in improving the city's appearance. Many transportation companies, it noted, were "becoming alive" to the city's attractions "and have commenced to profit by the increase of travel." The involvement of the town's citizenry could be seen "in the permanent character of the public works" now under way. The city's main streets "are being paved with wooden blocks," it reported. The beautification campaign was substantial: "Concrete sidewalks are being laid. Some acres of the harbor are in the course of reclamation. The handsome stone embankment is almost completed and the low lands behind are being filled in."[94] The association concentrated its early efforts on upgrading the city's attractions. The Standing Committee on Hotels and Sea Bathing quickly embarked upon a plan to establish a sea-bathing resort by the summer of 1903. Transportation itself, it was hoped, would also become an attraction. The association introduced the Tally Ho Coach, a horse-drawn carriage that would enliven the city's streets while providing visitors with a guided tour of selected attractions six months of the year.[95] Three years later, in 1906, the TAV continued to devote a good deal of energy to improving the city's boulevards and bathing facilities.[96]

The drawing power of civic improvements remained dependent upon Victoria's ability to overcome one of its chief limitations: its distance from major population centres. One way in which the Tourist Association sought to overcome its geographical isolation from the rest of North America was by appealing to the CPR. In August 1903, Cuthbert appealed to the CPR's passenger agent in Vancouver for assistance in fostering travel through the mountains from Alberta, and by December 1903 the association had succeeded in convincing the CPR to reduce its winter rates from Manitoba and the Northwest Territories to allow the Prairie population "the opportunity of taking a vacation in the enjoyment of our mild climate."[97] Cuthbert also supplied the CPR's Vancouver office with promotional literature bound for British nationals residing in Japan and China.[98] Accommodation, however, remained a chief concern – one that required a combined effort on the part of the newly formed Tourist Association and the Board of Trade.

The Board of Trade had approached the CPR in December 1901 about the possibility of a tourist hotel, but the company was at first lukewarm to the board's suggestion. Sir Thomas Shaughnessy initially refused the request because of his railway's many other commitments and because of the existence of a good-quality hotel, the Driard, in the city already. Continued pressure on the part of the board and the Tourist Association throughout 1902, however, softened the CPR's position.[99] By May 1903, Shaughnessy had agreed to recommend to his company that a tourist hotel be built on the city's inner harbour. The hotel would cost not less than $300,000 and was dependent upon the citizens of the city transferring to the CPR the necessary land free of cost, furnishing free water, and exempting the company from taxation for fifteen years.[100]

Establishment of the Empress Hotel, Cuthbert would later recall, provided the city with more than just additional accommodation. It also convinced the CPR to develop the E&N Railway and to make Victoria the home port for its Pacific fleet.[101] The TAV's efforts to beautify the city, improve its transportation links with the surrounding area, and expand its accommodation were clearly designed to enhance the experience of tourists once they had decided to visit Victoria. But city beautification and improved transportation links would prove beneficial only if outsiders could be convinced to take advantage of these developments. The association's major undertaking, then, was a campaign to convince travellers to visit the city in the first place.

The TAV was determined to alert businesspeople in eastern North America to the economic opportunities in Victoria, and it frequently sent Herbert Cuthbert to deliver the message in person. A 1903 tour of large population centres in the east afforded Cuthbert the opportunity to inform easterners of the city's possibilities. In Toronto Cuthbert employed lectures to bring Victoria's temperate climate to the attention of the Canadian Club, the Canadian Manufacturers' Association (CMA), the Toronto Board of Trade, and the Business Men's League.[102] The TAV's conception of tourism's function as a means to further Victoria's industrial development was underscored when CMA members arrived in town later that year. Cuthbert wrote to both Mayor Alexander G. McCandless and Premier Richard McBride explaining that, "of all [the] visitors we have had in the city during the last two years," the members of the CMA "are the most important." It was crucial, Cuthbert explained, that the CMA members be encouraged to see British Columbia "both as a market for Canadian goods and as an outlet for the investment of Canadian capital."[103]

Cuthbert's duties also included frequent trips throughout the Pacific Northwest to distribute promotional literature. In June 1904, Cuthbert toured Washington and Idaho in an effort to promote fruit-growing opportunities near Victoria. On such trips, he distributed circulars and copies of the association's promotional pamphlets. His intended audience was clear: potential investors and settlers. In North Yakima, for instance, he enthusiastically reported that the "people here are all very well-to-do, and we are getting a good deal of business from here."[104]

His travels also allowed Cuthbert to investigate the success of other tourism centres. A 1904 trip to southern California provided him with the opportunity to lecture his fellow Victorians on developments in that state. He was particularly impressed by Pasadena and encouraged Victorians to replicate Pasadena's successes locally "by boulevarding" Victoria's streets, "throwing down its fences, and laying broad cement sidewalks, bordered with velvety emerald greensward." Such tours also allowed Cuthbert to emphasize the economic impact of tourist travel, and he did so on this occasion by reporting that Santa Barbara was bringing in five million dollars per year from tourists.[105] Primarily, however, such tours were designed to disseminate promotional material about Victoria.

Early tourist booklets focused directly on commercial development. For example, the TAV's 1905 publication *An Outpost of Empire* championed Victoria as "The Tourist and Commercial City of the Canadian Far West" and printed endorsements from a British editors' delegation paying homage to both the city's beauty and the province's agricultural and industrial opportunities.[106] The centrality of commercial concerns is apparent as well in promotional literature distributed on behalf of individual hotels. The Hotel Dallas's guide to Victoria began by boasting of the hotel's close proximity to the city's "commercial centre." Both the city's steady increase in population and the continual expansion of the city limits figure prominently in the hotel's description of Victoria. Here too the city's favourable climate was highlighted, as were a variety of burgeoning industries, including iron and boiler works, sawmills, chemical works, and shipbuilding. In fact, according to the Dallas, "every industry is well represented by many flourishing firms of old standing and respectability." Recreational pursuits, including hunting, fishing, boating, and cycling, were also highlighted. The booklet offered not simply a list of things to see and do but also a list of commercial opportunities to pursue and a variety of reasons to relocate one's family and business in Victoria.[107]

Not surprisingly promotional literature also addressed readers' concerns about modernity. A 1902 Tourist Association of Victoria publication explained that Victoria boasted "every pastime to give the health-seeker and tourist more buoyant strength to equip him for this 'strenuous' modern life." The pamphlet enthused that the "wealth of picturesque islands" in the Gulf of Georgia "out-rivals the more widely known Thousand Isles," and it reported that "the combination of bold and picturesque country with old-fashioned English homes, their beautiful gardens and air of comfort and contentment makes Victoria a delightful residential city." The city also boasted "a veritable feast of pastimes," including boating, driving, mountain climbing, bathing, hunting, and fishing. The city's climate, moreover, was "devoid of extremes of heat or cold," and "sunstrokes and prostrations from the heat are afflictions only known to Victorians through newspaper reports from other parts of the world." Thus, Victoria was the ideal destination for "those who desire to escape from the enervating heat of the middle and eastern states." Victoria, readers were informed, "has not the hustling business methods of Chicago, nor the nerve-destroying habits of New York." Instead, "conservative business methods, health, happiness and contentment are the features identified with Victoria."[108]

A 1903 TAV publication acknowledged Victoria's place as "the leading Tourist and health resort of the Pacific North West" but also highlighted the city's "varied commercial and industrial enterprises." These included farming, lumber mills, copper and gold mining, salmon canneries, and shipbuilding.[109] The 1907 edition of the TAV's *An Outpost of Empire* described Victoria as "a hive of industry" that "offers many excellent business and manufacturing opportunities." These included agriculture, poultry and dairy farming, and fishing. Victoria's position as a "manufacturing centre" ensured that it could draw upon Vancouver Island's "immense iron and coal deposits." Eschewing the more reserved approach of earlier tourist literature, this publication included a list of opportunities for entrepreneurs on its back page.[110]

Tourist literature was careful, of course, to avoid painting a portrait of Victoria as an underdeveloped community desperate for investment. A 1915 pamphlet, for example, attempted to strike the right balance by listing new industries that Victoria required, which included woollen mills and a steel industry, alongside a discussion of the city's existing and prosperous industries.[111] To entice visitors to entertain the thought of settling in Victoria, promotional literature also highlighted the city's social life, its low level of taxation, and its abundant supply of high-quality hospitals and schools.[112] These pamphlets also encouraged settlement by directing potential settlers to information resources. The 1905 edition of the TAV's *Outpost of Empire* informed readers that the provincial government, "through its Horticultural department, will assist intending settlers with practical information upon all matters pertaining to fruit culture."[113]

This promotional literature also emphasized that the city attracted the right sort of visitors and settlers. A 1903 TAV publication, for example, outlined a direct causal link between local agricultural successes and the ethnic makeup of the population. Farming near Duncan and Cowichan, it explained, was pursued on "some most excellent farms and ranches, in the hands of a very desirable class of English settlers."[114] Another booklet describing Victoria's rapid economic expansion ascribed these results to both its climate and the makeup of its population. The fact that Victoria was one of the wealthiest cities in Canada was "greatly owing to the fact that on account of the salubrity of its climate and other attractions it offers to people of wealth and refinement a delightful place of residence. It is a peculiarly British town and the citizens are proud of the fact." The racial makeup of the city also offered optimism for the future. Vancouver Island's "immense and practically inexhaustible natural resources" were now free to be capitalized upon by this population. Moreover, the sheer volume of resources remaining was due, in part, to the previous economic inactivity of the region's Aboriginal population: "Where, but a few years ago, the native races held undisputed sway and waged their tribal wars," the pamphlet explained, "the strong arm of the settlers has hewn a home and the long neglected land returns an hundred fold."[115]

The 1907 pamphlet *Impressions of Victoria* also highlighted the city's English characteristics. Trumpeting the city as "A Bit of England on the Shores of the Pacific," it promised readers plants, shrubs, and flowers peculiar to England as well as popular sports from the "Old Land." Along with championing the city's healthy climate and housing opportunities, *Impressions of Victoria* attempted to make a tangible link between the city's Englishness and England's own industrial achievements. "The Island of Vancouver is larger than the kingdom of Ireland and almost as large as England," it explained, adding that its "almost limitless undeveloped riches in iron, coal, copper, timber and fisheries" meant that it had "all the potential wealth that made England 'the workshop of the world.'"[116]

Similar messages graced the TAV's promotional posters. Posters distributed to the Southern Pacific Railway Company lauded Victoria as "A Bit of England on the Shores of the Pacific."[117] A coloured poster produced in March 1906 championed the city's temperate climate and described Victoria as "The Finest Residential City in America." The poster's central images, the James Bay embankment, the post office block, the Empress Hotel, and the provincial legislature buildings, were surrounded by halftone images of "sheep, orchard, farming and industrial scenes in and near to Victoria, the idea being to portray the commercial and shipping industries, together with the special opportunities the environs offer to settlers desirous of engaging in orcharding, mixed farming and dairying."[118]

The same year a Victoria *Daily Times* editorial underscored and endorsed the motivation behind these promotional campaigns. In praising the TAV's efforts, the editorial maintained that the key measure of the association's success is "not to be found in the presence of transient wayfarers who have come to spend a portion of their holidays here, but in the sales of property made to well-to-do farmers and business men who, having acquired competencies, are in quest of the most congenial possible places of residence in which to take the rest they have earned by years of devotion to duty."[119] TAV activities were centrally focused on developing the city's industrial and agricultural infrastructure by encouraging outsiders to invest and settle in and around Victoria.

Civic beautification and promotional campaigns required money, and the campaigns to raise funds to support these endeavours revealed that TAV members considered these projects and promotional campaigns to be in the interests of all Victorians. During the TAV's first years of operation, its operating expenses ranged between $8,000 and $10,000 a year. Grants from the City of Victoria usually accounted for between 60 and 80 percent of the association's revenue.[120] To raise additional funds, the association solicited firms throughout the city, attempting to convince them of the importance of tourism promotion, and often stressed the ways in which these businesses benefited from the association's efforts. Cuthbert informed the Permanent Home Building Society of Victoria, for instance, that a crucial part of the association's work was "to increase the number of permanent residents here," work that must certainly "have a considerable influence on the business of your company."[121] Even individual citizens, Cuthbert hoped, could be swayed to contribute to the association through self-interest. Writing to Joan Dunsmuir, widow of coal magnate Robert Dunsmuir, Cuthbert described the TAV's efforts as "devoted to the advertising of the city generally as a place of residence and as a resort for tourists." He emphasized the benefits that local businesses had derived from such efforts but made special mention of the tendency of the association's work "to increase the price of real estate throughout the city."[122] Similarly, he told James Thompson of the Hudson's Bay Company in Victoria that the TAV's successful campaign to have the CPR build the Empress Hotel had ensured that "in some portions of the city real estate has increased in value over 100 per cent." The CPR's upcoming publicity campaigns would undoubtedly increase the city's population, Cuthbert explained, and further increase the value of the HBC's land holdings.[123]

The association also solicited funds from the city itself. Writing to the mayor in 1903 to seek a substantial improvement to the city's grant of $2,000, Cuthbert did his best to champion the association's cause. "Above everything else," Cuthbert reminded the mayor, "this tourist movement in the City was made possible by the contributions of the City Council and the business men." It had already "resulted in the awakening of the C.P.R. to the advantages of the City from a tourist standpoint." To add a competitive edge to his argument, Cuthbert informed the mayor that even after adding in the voluntary subscriptions from individuals and businesses the Tourist Association of Victoria found itself with "$2,000 per year less" than its rivals in Vancouver. A contribution to tourism, Cuthbert reminded the mayor, also had a direct bearing on his government through increased taxes. "Two years ago Victoria, as a resort and residential city was almost unknown in the ticket offices of the large Railway Co's or to those in search of such a resort," Cuthbert explained. "To-day it is the best advertised individual city on the continent. This is how your money is used, and the city is not expending in this way as much as in former years."[124]

Keen to expand their city's population base and to ward off the mounting economic challenge posed by Vancouver, Victoria's community leaders turned to tourism promotion. In doing so, they not only focused on beautifying their city and improving its transportation links to the larger population centres in North America, but they also embarked upon publicity campaigns that featured promotional booklets and speaking tours. To underwrite these initiatives, they drew upon civic grants as well as individual subscriptions. Not surprisingly, and much to the chagrin of Victoria's civic boosters, similar tactics were soon employed by Victoria's chief rival, Vancouver.

The Vancouver Tourist Association

> The Tourist Association of the city of Vancouver has more than twice the revenue enjoyed by our association. Flippant persons might retort that it needs it, as it has less than half the attractions of this city from a tourist's point of view.
>
> — Editorial, Victoria *Daily Colonist*, 28 January 1903[125]

Only months after the founding of the Tourist Association of Victoria, Vancouver's business community created one of its own. In late June 1902, local businesspeople circulated a petition calling upon the city's mayor, Thomas F. Neelands, to hold a meeting on the subject. According to the Vancouver *Daily Province*, "nearly all the prominent professional and business men of the city" signed the petition.[126] Attendance at the meeting itself, held on 26 June, was sparse, but among those present support for a tourist association was unanimous, and it was agreed that such an association was necessary "to advertise the city as a pleasure resort, and in every way possible to bring Vancouver to the attention of outsiders."[127]

By early July 1902, the Vancouver Tourists' Association (VTA) was up and running. Fred Buscombe, a prominent china and glass merchant and a future mayor of Vancouver, served as its first president. As with the TAV in Victoria, the VTA's executive committee was comprised of local business leaders. The VTA's executive committee for 1909, for example, included significant representation from the real estate, insurance, and legal professions as well as two representatives from the CPR (see Table 1.1). Of the three leading VTA figures during the association's early years of operations, two men, F.J. Proctor and J.R. Seymour, were in the real estate business and were likely to benefit directly from VTA activities luring settlers and investment into the city. The other leading figure was J.J. Banfield, a notary public and insurance agent.

To raise money for the new association, subscription lists were posted in business centres, banks, and larger stores throughout the city, and by 11 July over $5,000 in subscriptions had been secured.[128] VTA members quickly formed committees focusing on reception, entertainment, and literature.[129] By mid-July, the association had established its headquarters in the Fairfield building on Granville Street, and within a week numerous visitors were dropping in to the headquarters in search of tourist information. The newly organized "Tally-Ho" trips around Stanley Park were also proving popular.[130]

The VTA also played a leading role in the city's beautification movement. According to R.A.J. McDonald, the leaders of Vancouver's City Beautiful movement were motivated by a number of different concerns, including a desire to impose social order on the city's population, public-spirited philanthropy, and boosterism. The VTA took the lead in advancing the "commercial thrust for beautification."[131] For example, at its first meeting, the association's secretary, H.W. Findlay, was instructed to draft communication to the City Council emphasizing "the immediate necessity of certain improvements at English Bay," namely benches, seats, and "proper sanitary arrangements."[132]

Table 1.1

Vancouver Tourist Association executive committee, 1909

Member	Occupation
John J. Banfield	Notary public and insurance agent
Robert Cassidy	Barrister and solicitor
Charles B. Foster	Assistant general passenger agent, CPR
William Godfrey	Manager, Bank of British North America
W.H. Hargrave	Unknown
Richard Marpole	General executive assistant, CPR
John P. McConnell	Publisher, Ford-McConnell Ltd.
Frederick J. Proctor	Real estate and insurance
Charles David Rand	Real estate and stock broker
Joseph R. Seymour	Real estate and insurance
Rochford H. Sperling	General manager, BC Electric Railway and Vancouver Gas
George E. Trorey	Managing director, Henry Birks and Sons Jewellers
John Williams	Unknown

Sources: Henderson's City of Vancouver and North Vancouver Directory, 1909; Vancouver *Daily Province* 21 January 1909: 10.

As in Victoria, tourism promoters in Vancouver hoped to benefit from a close relationship with the CPR, and the association planned to approach the company quickly in the hope of securing "special transportation rates, and the arrangement of special summer excursions from points in the interior to Vancouver."[133] But what most interested Vancouverites were material advantages that the CPR could bring their way. When the company offered the city land for the purpose of building a golf course, the *Daily Province* enthusiastically supported the proposed facility. Such an endeavour would "aid this city in coming to the front as a golf centre," the newspaper explained, while relaying the position of CPR general superintendent, and VTA member, Richard Marpole, who "cited the fact that at all the winter resorts to the south of this city golf links are to be found, and they are looked upon as one of the strong points in drawing that class of people which this city is now so anxious to secure."[134] Marpole, like early tourism promoters in Victoria, saw tourism promotion as a strategy that would attract rich visitors, not simply for their spending power but also for their investment potential.

Vancouverites did not expect the CPR to supply all of their city's attractions. The VTA embarked upon its own campaign to make the city more attractive to potential visitors, and the local business community was not short on ideas to improve Vancouver's fortunes. In championing the inauguration of train service to the fishing centre of Steveston, the *Daily Province* suggested that tourists would be among those drawn to this "quick and efficient medium of transportation." Closely related to this endeavour was the possibility of a market site being constructed in the city, "whereat the produce of the Delta country may be disposed of by the farmers."[135] Local fishers and farmers, Vancouverites had accepted, would benefit greatly from an increase in visitors. The association's first secretary, H.W. Findlay, the advertising manager for the *Daily Province,* also wasted little time in bringing attractions to the city. Findlay wrote letters to interests across the province soliciting collections and items from mineral and agricultural industries so that they might be exhibited for visitors at the association's headquarters. Findlay was sent, along with various fruits, vegetables, and grains, a sampling of "Indian and other curios" – an indication, perhaps, that Native culture could eventually be appropriated as a natural resource and tourist attraction.[136]

Vancouver's tourism promoters were aware, of course, of the activities of their Victoria counterparts. William Godfrey, manager of a local branch of the Bank of British North America, and a VTA member, had returned from a trip to the provincial capital in 1902 overwhelmed by the success of that city's tourist association. "Every citizen seems to be directly interested," he explained, "for it appeals to him as something that is bringing immediate results." Godfrey was also impressed with the "detailed management" of the TAV office and championed the city's advertising efforts.[137] That the two cities were in direct competition with one another was not lost on the *Daily Province*. The same year the newspaper printed a statement by a local resident explaining how, in at least one instance, Victoria had trumped Vancouver's efforts to attract wealthy visitors. "Two of the wealthiest men of Penang, China arrived in Vancouver by the last *Empress*," he explained. "They both had an unlimited amount of money and were willing to spend it." Both were "charmed" by Vancouver but "had heard so much of the attractions of Victoria," as advertised by the TAV, "that they were impatient to spend the rest of their stay ... in that city." The moral of the story, of course, was that Vancouver lacked Victoria's profile. "The only literature showing Vancouver's points of interest that the travelers could obtain," the *Daily Province* reported, "was what was supplied by the C.P.R. Co. on the steamers crossing the Pacific."[138]

To overcome this publicity deficit, the VTA embarked upon a sustained promotional campaign. During 1907, for example, the association distributed 60,000 illustrated books, 70,000 folders and guides, 2,000 government bulletins, and hundreds of maps not only to the CPR and other railways but also to the Office of the High Commissioner in London as well as to leading hotels, libraries, and information bureaus throughout the world. In addition, a VTA representative travelled to Winnipeg and other population centres on the Prairies to deliver lectures accompanied by stereoscopic slides. The results of similar past endeavours, VTA president F.J. Proctor announced, were clearly paying dividends. In the past year, VTA headquarters had responded to approximately 2,000 letters of inquiry about the city, while roughly 5,000 visitors had dropped in on the headquarters itself – a visit that allowed them to view the VTA's display of fruits and minerals from throughout British Columbia.[139] Two years later the association spearheaded a vigorous publicity campaign to coincide with the Alaska-Yukon-Pacific Exposition in Seattle (see Figure 1.1).[140]

Overall, the VTA inherited the mantle of the city's leading public relations body from the Vancouver Board of Trade and took a more aggressive position in advertising the city to outsiders in order to promote its commercial and industrial development. The association's leading members were drawn primarily from the real estate sector, but, as Fred Buscombe's tenure as president suggests, merchants also held prominent positions. Like their counterparts in Victoria, tourism promoters in Vancouver endeavoured to convince potential investors to visit their city with the hope that such a visit would convince them to return as permanent contributors to sustained economic development. And like tourism promoters in Victoria, VTA members recognized the important role that the CPR and railway travel played in the tourist business.

Figure 1.1 Vancouver Tourist Association poster, 1909. One of a thousand VTA posters printed to champion Vancouver as an attractive city for investors at the Alaska-Yukon-Pacific Exposition in Seattle in 1909.
Source: Philip T. Timms, photo, courtesy of City of Vancouver Archives, CVA 677-565.

Conclusion

Like visitors in search of Nova Scotia folklore, admirers of Tom Thomson paintings, and readers of the romantic stories of Mounted Police heroism, travellers to British Columbia between 1890 and 1930 welcomed the opportunity to escape from the pressures and concerns of modern life.[141] As Marguerite S. Shaffer explains in her examination of early-twentieth-century tourists' motivations for visiting the American west, such "white, upper- and middle-class citizens" who were "threatened not only by increased immigration, labor unrest, and racial diversity, but also by a sense of powerlessness and 'weightlessness' manifested in modern urban-industrial living," embraced tourism in order to "regain some sense of security and self-control."[142] But while such tourists journeyed to British Columbia to escape from the enervating effects of modernity, they were also determined to embrace the economic opportunities that modern life made possible. The province's vast forests, for example, were not simply awe-inspiring natural cathedrals; they were also raw materials awaiting industrial production. Similarly, British Columbia's coastline and interior regions offered tourists not only the sublime spectacle of mountain scenery but also industrial opportunities ranging from canneries to copper mining. Tourists visiting British Columbia embraced the promise of modernity as much as they attempted to evade its unsettling side effects.

Anxious to develop the province, and aware of visitors' motivations, civic organizations in Victoria and Vancouver turned to tourism promotion in an attempt to attract potential investors. Early efforts at tourism promotion were thus very local in nature and relied to a great extent on the cooperation of large railway companies such as the CPR. The involvement of both local businesspeople and city governments was representative of the intensely competitive boosterism that has been associated with the establishment of communities on the Prairies. In the 1910s and 1920s, however, new tourism organizations would emerge to consolidate a more cooperative approach to tourism promotion. The most important of these organizations, the Pacific Northwest Tourist Association, would be led by Victoria tourism promoter Herbert Cuthbert.

2

From the Investment to the Expenditure Imperative: Regional Cooperation and the Lessons of Modern Advertising, 1916-35

The interwar years ushered in a new era of tourist travel in North America as railway transportation and hotel accommodation yielded pride of place to the automobile and the auto camp. In 1910, just 500,000 Americans owned cars. By 1920 over eight million cars were registered in the United States. Even before automobile travel became widespread during the 1920s, middle-class tourists were abandoning the regimentation of railway travel and hotel accommodation for the freedom and flexibility of auto travel.[1] The 1920s confirmed the arrival of this new era of tourist travel. Between 1921 and 1929, automobile traffic passing between British Columbia and Washington state at the Blaine border crossing increased fivefold, while the number of train passengers passing through the same port of entry in 1929 had dropped to a fifth of the total number recorded in 1919.[2]

The dramatic expansion – some would say democratization – of tourist travel in North America during the 1920s has been noted and examined by a wide variety of scholars.[3] Relatively unexamined, however, is the changing nature of tourism promotion that accompanied this transition. The late 1920s and early 1930s witnessed a transformation not just in the scope of tourist travel in North America but also in the rationale behind tourism promotion itself. As the travelling public grew in number, the investment imperative that had dominated the promotional campaigns of civic tourist associations gave way to a new emphasis on tourist expenditures. One was focused now not on the tourist as a potential investor in BC *production* but on his or her economic impact as a *consumer*. This chapter examines the activities of tourism promoters in Victoria and Vancouver during this era in which a more cooperative interurban approach to advertising coincided with tourism promoters' adoption of modern advertising techniques.

Regional Cooperation and the Investment Imperative
In their determination to elicit greater community support and to succeed in the increasingly competitive business of attracting tourists, promoters

in both Victoria and Vancouver frequently reinvented and renamed their tourist associations. In April 1906, for instance, Tourist Association of Victoria members chose to rename the association the Victoria Development and Tourist Association (VDTA) in recognition of the association's determination to foster economic development and to acknowledge its merger with another local booster organization, the 100,000 Club, which was determined to see the city's population reach 100,000 people by 1910.[4] Less than three years later, in December 1908, VDTA directors agreed to transform their organization into a branch of a new island-wide coalition that would allow island communities to form a "systematic system of advancing the interests of the Island."[5] Originally termed the Vancouver Island Development League, this organization was later renamed the Vancouver Island Development Association (VIDA). In January 1909, Vancouver Tourist Association directors agreed to change their association's name to the Vancouver Information and Tourist Association in part to emphasize the fact that the organization performed the function of an information bureau and did not restrict its activities solely to civic beautification.[6] Such manoeuvres reflected tourism promoters' desire to consolidate local support for their initiatives, and, as is clear in the case of the VIDA, they constituted a recognition that local interests should at times yield to regional ones.

Anxious to compete directly with California for tourists, but unable to accomplish this task with the limited funding they could muster from private subscriptions and civic grants, tourism promoters in Victoria and Vancouver increasingly opted to pool their resources with other communities throughout the Pacific Northwest. In an attempt to overcome local rivalries between publicity bureaus throughout the region, for example, representatives from civic tourist associations in British Columbia, Washington, and Oregon gathered in Tacoma, Washington, in October 1916 to plot strategy and organize a new umbrella organization for promoting tourism in the Pacific Northwest. Originally termed the North Pacific Coast Tourist Association, the organization was barely a month old before it was renamed the Pacific Northwest Tourist Association (PNTA) in deference to noncoastal communities in the region.[7] To organize the association, fifty-four delegates from Washington, Oregon, and British Columbia met on 11 October at Tacoma's Commercial Club. British Columbia's delegates included representatives of the Vancouver and Victoria Boards of Trade, civic politicians, as well as several representatives of the cities' manufacturing and industrial interests. The Victoria Chamber of Commerce was represented at the October 1916 meeting by coal-mining agent Joshua Kingham, whose colleagues greeted his glowing report on the international meeting with enthusiasm.[8] No representatives from the province outside Vancouver and Victoria were present – a deficiency that likely contributed to the association's untimely termination in 1923.[9] The PNTA was funded by government grants from the Oregon, Washington, and BC legislatures. Washington and Oregon contributed an appropriation of $25,000 annually, while British Columbia was expected to contribute half that amount.[10]

Regional cooperation was not an entirely new approach in 1916. In 1904, Victoria's Herbert Cuthbert told the Nelson *News* that the Tourist Association of Victoria (TAV) always encouraged eastern visitors to visit the Kootenays either on the way to Victoria or on their way back home – though Cuthbert quickly turned this particular interview into an opportunity to sell Kootenay residents themselves on the benefits of visiting Victoria.[11] Seemingly more genuine were his connections with American publicity organizations. In early 1906, for example, Cuthbert attended a meeting of the "See America" League in Tacoma and was the only official Canadian delegate to the "See America First" congress in Salt Lake City. This association was dedicated to encouraging travel in North America rather than Europe.[12] In February 1906, the Vancouver Tourist Association and the TAV cooperated in promoting travel to Victoria and Vancouver while participating at a fair in Portland, Oregon.[13] Later that year Cuthbert joined leading businesspeople from Washington on a three-week publicity tour of major centres in California.[14] But the formation of the PNTA signalled an advance in cooperative publicity initiatives, in terms of both the number of communities involved and the scale and scope of their promotional campaigns.

Victoria itself was well represented on the PNTA executive. Alderman A.E. Todd was named president, while Herbert Cuthbert was elected to the powerful post of executive secretary. Three vice presidents were elected, one each from Oregon, Washington, and British Columbia.[15] From his position as executive secretary, Cuthbert would emerge as perhaps the most powerful figure in Pacific Northwest tourism promotion. His decision to leave Victoria for Seattle and his new position with the PNTA stemmed, in part, from a dispute over civic funding for the TAV and, more specifically, his salary. The hesitancy on the part of Victoria City Council and the larger business community to contribute generously to TAV activities reflected the extent to which many in the community believed that the costs of tourism promotion should be borne by those few businesspeople, such as hotel owners, who seemed to benefit most directly from tourism.[16] As PNTA executive secretary, however, Cuthbert railed against such short-sighted appraisals of tourism's economic benefits.

Cuthbert's new position allotted him an unprecedented opportunity to promote tourism. For Cuthbert and the PNTA, tourism was not an industry unto itself; it was a means to agricultural and industrial development. Tourists, for Cuthbert, were a particular type of people. A tourist, he explained, was a "self made man." He was someone with money, "and nine times out of ten he has his eyes open for new opportunities and investments – he is a keen businessman and can see these opportunities without their being advertised; he can find them for himself once you have got him here." What was important was to get these potential investors to visit Victoria in the first place. "First let us get the population, get the tourist here and let him see what we have got," Cuthbert argued. "Industries will follow as night follows day."[17] The same was true of agricultural development, he maintained. "Tourist travel is the modern colonizer," he explained. "You do not see any campaigns for settlers to take up homesteads on free government lands as there used to be," he reasoned. Instead, the Pacific Northwest had embarked upon a new phase of development. "The new people who are coming to us now are those who are able to purchase improved or partially improved properties and have some money to get along with until their properties are in the producing stage, if they are not already self sustaining, and these people come to us," Cuthbert emphasized, "chiefly as tourists, either by rail, by automobile or by sea." To support his analysis, Cuthbert pointed to statistics illustrating that "60 per cent of the Southern California population originally went there as visitors."[18] As secretary of the PNTA, Cuthbert now broadened his rhetoric to include all of British Columbia, Washington, and Oregon.

PNTA campaigns reflected Cuthbert's continued confidence in tourism's ability to lure industrial and agricultural development to the region, and the association's promotional undertakings were substantial. In 1922, Cuthbert boasted that the organization had issued six tons of booklets. This massive campaign included the distribution of 85,000 maps, 50,000 pamphlets, 25,000 general booklets, as well as five additional runs of 10,000 booklets focusing on automobiling, fishing, golfing, mountaineering, and yachting. These booklets were supplemented by Cuthbert's coordinating meetings with chambers of commerce and commercial clubs in California, his addresses to twenty-three conventions in the Pacific Northwest, as well as newspaper and magazine advertisements.[19]

In one pamphlet entitled *The Pacific Northwest: The World's Greatest Out of Doors*, British Columbia was termed "The Switzerland of America." The booklet contained pictures of Capilano Canyon, picturesque islands, and the bathing beach at English Bay. The pamphlet's text, however, contained not romantic words offering moving commentary on the sights but raw economic data for the potential investor. "British Columbia is 700 miles long by 400 miles wide, with an area of 395,000 square miles," the text began. "It is equal to 24 Switzerlands." The pamphlet then detailed production statistics for the province's fisheries, mining, lumber, agriculture, and stock-raising industries. Once the potential investor's appetite had been whetted with these statistics, the province's recreational opportunities were efficiently documented. Fishing, hunting, golfing, yachting, sea bathing, and automobiling were all possibilities amid the province's pastoral scenery.[20]

The PNTA's newspaper and magazine advertisements carried similar messages. PNTA ads generally portrayed families enjoying outdoor activities. Men could be seen golfing, fishing, and hunting, while women swam or joined the men hiking. Family camping trips were also depicted. The text accompanying these scenes, however, reflected the investment imperative that guided PNTA activities. In one ad featuring men, women, and children partaking in outdoor activities under the heading "The Lure of the Great Pacific Northwest," readers were provided with a list of the region's attractions. Trout streams, golf courses, sea beaches, national parks, and forest reserves combined with the region's climate to offer visitors "bright, cool days with sound, restful sleep every night." But such attractions were not meant to provide a complete break from the modern world. This was certainly a "land of enchantment ... of family happiness and contentment," but it was also a land of "opportunity" (see Figure 2.1).

Another advertisement featuring a giant apple urged visitors to "Come to the Land Where the Apples Grow." British Columbia, Oregon, and Washington, the ad maintained, offered visitors the opportunity to "enjoy the temperate climate where the evergreens grow, where Nature has been most lavish in her gifts, not only of wonderful scenery, but of great latent wealth." Here again the rhetoric of economic opportunity emerged side by side with the promise of rest and relaxation. Moreover, the ad continued, "if you are contemplating a change of residence because you desire a different climate, or are in ill health, or from any other cause, you will find the Pacific Northwest the one land on earth in which life is worth living" (see Figure 2.2).

In its attempt to attract investors and settlers from farther east, the PNTA directed some advertisements toward people visiting California. The PNTA invited visitors to return home via the Pacific Northwest and explained that "the knowledge acquired of the whole Coast, the people you will meet, the business opportunities which may be taken advantage of, together with the wonderful scenery and facilities for every kind of recreation will more than justify you in adopting this northern route" (see Figure 2.3). A similar advertisement employing the heading "Climate, Scenery, Sport and Comfort" not only described the region's natural attractions in romantic terms but also employed business calculations. Thus, the Pacific Northwest's "magnificent forests" contained "twelve hundred billion feet of merchantable timber." And, along with its lakes and "rugged sea coast," readers were called upon to visit the region's "fertile valleys with undulating meadows, orchards either in blossom or laden with their golden fruit, or the waving grain fields" (see Figure 2.4).

PNTA advertising campaigns offered potential visitors the promise of spectacular scenery and a wide variety of outdoor activities. But these campaigns also directed the reader's attention to investment opportunities throughout the Pacific Northwest. The association's promotional activities thus reflected the determination of British Columbia's tourism promoters to attract what they deemed to be the necessary ingredients for economic development: population, capital, and entrepreneurial know-how.

By 1923 the PNTA faced a battle for its survival. The association depended upon annual appropriations from the BC, Washington, and

Figure 2.1   Pacific Northwest Tourist Association advertisement.

Source: UOA, Drake Papers, Box 1, File 1, c. 1922. Courtesy of the Division of Special Collections and University Archives, University of Oregon Library System.

Figure 2.2 Pacific Northwest Tourist Association advertisement.

Source: UOA, Drake Papers, Box 1, File 1, c. 1922. Courtesy of the Division of Special Collections and University Archives, University of Oregon Library System.

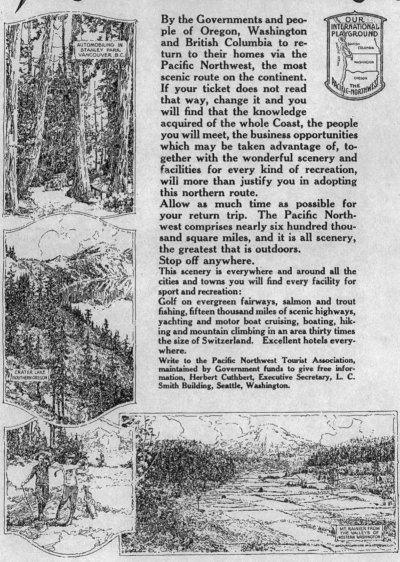

Visitors to California are Invited

By the Governments and people of Oregon, Washington and British Columbia to return to their homes via the Pacific Northwest, the most scenic route on the continent. If your ticket does not read that way, change it and you will find that the knowledge acquired of the whole Coast, the people you will meet, the business opportunities which may be taken advantage of, together with the wonderful scenery and facilities for every kind of recreation, will more than justify you in adopting this northern route.

Allow as much time as possible for your return trip. The Pacific Northwest comprises nearly six hundred thousand square miles, and it is all scenery, the greatest that is outdoors.

Stop off anywhere.

This scenery is everywhere and around all the cities and towns you will find every facility for sport and recreation:

Golf on evergreen fairways, salmon and trout fishing, fifteen thousand miles of scenic highways, yachting and motor boat cruising, boating, hiking and mountain climbing in an area thirty times the size of Switzerland. Excellent hotels everywhere.

Write to the Pacific Northwest Tourist Association, maintained by Government funds to give free information, Herbert Cuthbert, Executive Secretary, L. C. Smith Building, Seattle, Washington.

Figure 2.3   Pacific Northwest Tourist Association advertisement.

Source: UOA, Drake Papers, Box 1, File 1, c. 1922. Courtesy of the Division of Special Collections and University Archives, University of Oregon Library System.

Figure 2.4 Pacific Northwest Tourist Association advertisement.

Source: UOA, Drake Papers, Box 1, File 1, c. 1922. Courtesy of the Division of Special Collections and University Archives, University of Oregon Library System.

Oregon governments, and when the 1923 Washington and Oregon appropriations were cancelled the association's tenure as the leading tourism promotion body in the region was over. British Columbia's finance minister, John Hart, followed the lead of his American counterparts.[21] Aware of the organization's impending demise, but stubbornly hoping it might continue, the PNTA's directors recounted their accomplishments over the previous six years. While the San Francisco *Chronicle* had earlier praised the PNTA for its role in increasing tourist spending in the Pacific Northwest from $7 million a year under what it termed the "old competitive plan" to $35 million a year, the PNTA executive focused on a broader realm of achievements.[22] The PNTA, the executive suggested, was chiefly responsible "for having the Pacific Northwest become a recognized summer resort region, and in being appreciated as the summer playground of America." "The tide of summer tourist travel," they argued, had been turned to the region "at a time when there was little, if any organized travel to this section." Tourist agencies and railway companies had been convinced to design new itineraries that included the Pacific Northwest and "to prolong the stay of visitors who were passing through" the region. Before the PNTA arrived on the scene, they estimated, 70,000 tourists had visited the region annually. By 1923, that figure had reached 700,000. Before the association began its activities, there were no auto camps to speak of; now there were 250. Hundreds of tourists had elected to settle in the region. After just six years of operation, the directors triumphantly announced, "the Pacific Northwest has become a trademark ... in resorts," and "every city, town and village has benefitted from this travel."[23]

Like the San Francisco *Chronicle,* Herbert Cuthbert was certainly aware of the monetary infusion that visitors to the Pacific Northwest were providing to cities such as Victoria and Vancouver, and in his public pronouncements he explained that tourist expenditures benefited not just hotel owners but also farmers, local businesspeople, and governments.[24] Indeed, by 1920, Cuthbert was anticipating the rhetoric of the next generation of tourism promoters. "Every mountain top, every fishing stream, every lake, every highway through our primeval forest, every sea beach, has a monetary value that can be sold, and yet they are never delivered," he explained. "We receive money for no other natural resource in the same way."[25] But for Cuthbert, the money that tourists left behind on their visits was of secondary concern. Foremost in his mind throughout his tenure in Victoria and then with the PNTA in Seattle was the desire to employ tourism as a strategy to encourage investment and settlement. His aim was to populate the Pacific Northwest with "the right kind of people, who have money, and who are not brought here to take the places of people who are already employed." It was only in passing, he explained, that tourists left behind "immense sums of ready cash with us."[26] With the demise of the PNTA, Cuthbert moved to Portland to become manager of the Portland Visitors Bureau. He died in Portland in 1931. His death was marked by the Victoria *Daily Colonist*, which lauded him for his contributions to Victoria's tourist trade.[27] As the rest of this chapter demonstrates, his passing marked the end of an era in which tourism promotion was understood by its chief supporters as a strategy for soliciting settlers and investors and signified the arrival of a new "consumerist" era in which tourist expenditures became the tourist trade's primary rationale.

Victoria, Vancouver, and the Lessons of Modern Advertising

By the 1920s, an advertising industry anxious to promote the consumption of everything from automobiles to zinnias had taken shape in North America. The amount of money spent on advertising in the United States is estimated to have climbed from $682 million in 1914 to just under $3 billion in 1929 as large corporate advertising firms now concentrated in New York City battled one another for the chance to sell goods and services to North Americans.[28] Indeed, by 1917 97 percent of all national advertising in the United States was placed through advertising agencies.[29] As Russell Johnston has demonstrated in his analysis of the emergence of professional advertising in Canada, such modern advertising was based on a scientific and systematic approach that drew upon applied psychology and market research to design and place advertising copy in mass-circulation magazines and newspapers.[30] Throughout the 1920s and 1930s, North American advertising agencies and their customers embraced a variety of innovations ranging from radio advertising to an increased emphasis on visual imagery in advertising copy. In their determination to promote tourist travel to British Columbia, tourism promoters in Victoria and Vancouver increasingly embraced the possibilities of these innovations and came to echo Madison Avenue's claims that consistent advertising could usher in an era of unending economic growth.

With Herbert Cuthbert's departure to the PNTA, a new force emerged in Victoria tourism circles. His name was George Warren. Warren was born in San Francisco in 1887. A former clerk and stenographer for Western Union, he also worked for the Bank of California before visiting Victoria in 1912 and deciding to stay there. (Warren was thus representative of the type of tourist that Cuthbert had worked to lure to the city.) As a young man in San Francisco, Warren developed two attributes that would serve him well in his future endeavours: enterprise and community spirit. At the age of fourteen, Warren learned that the nearby town of Point Richmond would be provided with postal delivery service on the condition that the citizens provide their own mailboxes. The enterprising Warren wasted little time in ordering over 400 mailboxes from Buffalo and sold them for a dollar a piece. Seven years later he spearheaded a campaign to acquire "a much-needed main sewer for a San Francisco suburb by raising a public subscription to pay interest on bonds and [by] acting as a liaison man between the city and the banks."[31]

After moving to Victoria, Warren quickly built up what the *Daily Colonist* would later term "the largest sickness, accident and casualty insurance business on the Island." Buoyed by his success in the insurance business in his new hometown, Warren joined the VIDA in 1918 and served as chairman of the association's Finance Committee. In the early 1920s, he assumed important leadership positions in the city's two key business organizations. In 1921 he became the managing secretary of the Chamber of Commerce, a post that he would hold until 1954, when he resigned for health reasons. In January 1922, Warren relinquished managerial control over several insurance companies to become the commissioner of the VIDA, which was now renamed the Victoria and Island Publicity Bureau (VIPB), a position that he would retain until 1960. He secured this position, in part, because his earlier business interests had allowed him a significant degree of contact with up-island communities – an important attribute at a time when Victoria's tourism promoters were embracing the possibilities of regional cooperation. Throughout his career in the provincial capital, he belonged to a wide variety of community organizations, including the Victoria and Island Athletic Association, the Victoria Rotary Club, the Tyee Club, the Gizeh Temple for all BC, and the Victoria Jitney Association.[32]

Under Warren's leadership, the VIPB worked successfully to expand auto-camp accommodation and improve ferry service to Vancouver Island from Washington. In fact, Warren played a leading role in securing both a good-quality road from Victoria to Sidney and in establishing the Mill Bay ferry, which transported vehicles across Vancouver Island's Saanich Inlet.[33] In 1921 Warren spearheaded a campaign to inaugurate ferry service between the mainland and Vancouver Island. Until then, the only method of transporting automobiles to the island involved removing windshields and deflating tires in order to ship the vehicles by steamer. In 1921 the ferry service, which operated between Sidney and Anacortes, Washington, consisted of two boats, "a former kelp-harvesting barge and a temperamental paddlewheel steamer," which between them brought roughly 400 vehicles to the island. By 1960, when Warren stepped down as commissioner, ferries were bringing 234,000 cars to the island annually.[34]

The VIPB also expanded its promotional activities, in part, by employing a new slogan, "Follow the Birds to Victoria." The slogan itself was created in 1918 for a pamphlet coauthored by Warren entitled *The Call of Victoria*. To maximize the effect of its promotional literature, the VIPB erected signs and billboards throughout the Pacific Northwest ostensibly indicating the route that one should take to follow the birds to the provincial capital.

These signs went unchallenged in Oregon and Washington; however, when a VIPB sign reading "Follow the Birds to Victoria – More Sunshine, Less Rain" was erected in Vancouver in 1922, Vancouver's tourism promoters, angered by this public reminder that their city endured more annual precipitation than did Victoria, voiced their displeasure.[35] Not even this brazen publicity stunt, however, could prevent sustained cooperation between tourism promoters in Victoria and Vancouver throughout the 1920s and 1930s.

While Warren would remain the dominant figure in Victoria tourism promotion circles, the promotional work of the Vancouver Information and Tourist Association, renamed the Greater Vancouver Publicity Bureau (GVPB) in 1922, was performed more by committee than by a single individual. As Table 2.1 indicates, the GVPB drew its leaders primarily from the city's burgeoning service sector. Between 1925 and 1936, the day-to-day operations of the GVPB were under the direction of its commissioner, Charles H. Webster, a former member of the advertising department of the Vancouver *World* and a man quick to praise the virtues of modern advertising.[36] The GVPB itself expanded dramatically during the 1920s. Between 1923 and 1926, its membership more than doubled to 1,309 members.[37] In addition to its members' private subscriptions, the GVPB relied upon municipal grants. In 1926, for example, it received $20,000 from the City of Vancouver. Smaller sums of $1,000 and $500 were received from the municipality of Point Grey and the New Westminster Board of Trade respectively.[38]

By the mid-1920s, the majority of VIPB and GVPB publicity campaigns were carried out cooperatively. In addition to their own publicity endeavours, the VIPB was involved in five cooperative campaigns while the GVPB contributed to three cooperative campaigns to supplement its own efforts. The earliest of these joint advertising initiatives involved cooperation not just between Victoria and Vancouver but also with cities in Washington.

Table 2.1

Greater Vancouver Publicity Bureau presidents, 1928-39

President	Year	Occupation
Brenton S. Brown	1928, 1929	Insurance agent
O.B. Allan	1931	Jeweller and optician
J.C. McPherson	1932	Real estate agent
Harold Darling	1933	Insurance agent
Ernest H. Adams	1934, 1935	Vice president, BC Electric Railway
Dr. G.H. Worthington	1936-38	Medical doctor
Elmer Johnston	1939	President, Johnston National Storage

Sources: *Who's Who in British Columbia*, 1931, 1941, 1944-46; *Henderson's Greater Vancouver Directory*, 1923.

In 1923 the GVPB joined with the VIPB and tourism promotion bodies in Seattle, Tacoma, and Bellingham as charter members of a group rather awkwardly termed the Puget Sounders and British Columbians Associated. Their promotional campaigns focused chiefly on bringing investment to the Pacific Northwest. Membership fees for the new association totalled $33,000 and were set proportionally according to the population of each member city. The GVPB invested $8,800 in the advertising scheme, while the VIPB contributed $2,200. Both organizations drew their contributions from their own advertising budgets, which, in turn, were comprised of civic grants and private subscriptions. The US cities of Seattle, Tacoma, and Bellingham contributed $15,400, $4,400, and $2,200 respectively.[39] Puget Sounders' campaigns relied upon large daily newspapers as well as "prominent motor and outing magazines" to reach roughly six million readers.[40] As Figures 2.5 and 2.6 suggest, the organization's advertisements, focused as they were on attracting investment and settlement, retained a good deal in common with PNTA campaigns.

In 1926 the GVPB and the VIPB joined forces again to lure winter tourist traffic to the Pacific Coast through what was termed the "Prairie Winter Campaign." The GVPB contributed $6,000, and the VIPB contributed $2,000, to conduct a campaign that featured 109 ads in major daily newspapers and farm journals in Manitoba, Saskatchewan, and Alberta – publications boasting a total circulation of 525,000 or, as the GVPB triumphantly reported in its 1926 annual report, "practically every English-speaking home" in the region.[41] The same year the GVPB and the VIPB joined forces to convince the provincial government to grant them an appropriation of $25,000 to advertise the province in eastern Canada. Advertising copy in this campaign focused on "the general advantages of all sections of the Province dealing with the natural resources, industries and general subjects" as well as tourist activities, including hunting, fishing, golfing, and motoring. These advertisements appeared primarily in major metropolitan newspapers such as the Toronto *Globe,* the Toronto *Mail,* the Montreal *Star,* and the Montreal *Gazette.* Advertisements were also placed in the *Ontario Teachers'* magazine. Each advertisement, the GVPB estimated, reached 1,390,768 readers. By 1929, when provincial funding for the eastern publicity campaign was cut to $15,000, the two associations still succeeded in placing 264 ads in thirty-nine daily papers with an estimated weekly circulation of 3,093,300 readers.[42]

In addition to these three joint advertising endeavours with the GVPB, the VIPB contributed to at least two other cooperative publicity campaigns. One was run by a group of Washington hotel owners known as the Southwestern Washington Hotel Men's Association. In 1926, this campaign succeeded in placing ten billboards in California and distributing 100,000 posters in its attempt to lure Californians to the Pacific Northwest.[43] The

THE EVERGREEN PLAYGROUND

Modern Cities
in Marvelous Scenic Settings!

NATURE has built a wondrous "sky-line" for the metropolitan cities of the Evergreen Playground. She has lavished her loveliness in their surroundings.

There's Tacoma, for instance! The greatest scenic attraction of the West, Rainier National Park, is less than three hours distant. Ice caves, vast snow fields, 28 glaciers! Or Seattle! Two hours takes you into the heart of the Cascades, Snoqualmie Pass, Green River Gorge, Hoods Canal, lakes like Crescent and Quinault.

And Bellingham—gateway to Mt. Baker National Forest, destined to be one of the foremost spots of tourist interest in the West. Famous Chuckanut Drive only a few moments away with its constellation of San Juan Islands below.

Or Vancouver! Here again scenic attractions are at your door, the wonderful Marine Drive, Stanley Park with its marvelous natural beauty, Capilano Canyon! Victoria, too! The grandeur of the Malahat Drive, the magnificent peaks of Strathcona National Park! The famous Butchart Gardens.

The Evergreen Playground is a vacation paradise. Every summer sport is at its best in this cool green summerland. There's fishing in lake, stream and salt water; mountain climbing, skiing, tobogganing, sailing, canoeing, fresh and salt water bathing, golf on evergreen courses—an endless number of summer joys in ideal summer weather.

Write for booklet, "The Evergreen Playground." It tells in picture and story the wonders of this great Vacation Land. It will help you plan your trip more easily. Address 213, Chamber of Commerce Bldg., Seattle.

Puget Sounders & British Columbians · Associated
A Non-Profit Organization representing the citizens of
TACOMA · SEATTLE · BELLINGHAM · VICTORIA · VANCOUVER
NO RED TAPE AT THE INTERNATIONAL BORDER

Figure 2.5 Puget Sounders and British Columbians Associated advertisement, 1926. This ad by the Puget Sounders championed both the region's "modern cities" and its scenery in an attempt to lure visitors to the Pacific Northwest. *Source: Sunset* 56, 5 (1926): 99.

Figure 2.6 Puget Sounders and British Columbians Associated advertisement, 1927. This ad by the Puget Sounders championed both the region's temperate climate and its recreational possibilities.

Source: Sunset 58, 6 (1927): 61.

other initiative was more limited in scope: a 1924 cooperative agreement with the Seattle Chamber of Commerce establishing a joint information bureau at Yellowstone National Park.[44]

The GVPB's publicity department also distributed pamphlets as well as photographs and stories for newspapers and magazines to transportation companies, automobile clubs, and information bureaus. In addition, the GVPB's editorial department also contributed to the publicity campaign by sending out well over forty newspaper stories. These "editorials," according to the board of directors, "were special stories dealing with either automobile trips, yachting trips, fishing, big game hunting, hiking, and some stories dealing with climate, living conditions, and ... industrial development." This department was also responsible for distributing a "clip sheet" of human-interest stories to newspapers "written strictly according to newspaper style" and bearing eye-catching headlines. The "clip sheet" thus allowed news editors at newspapers across the continent to draw upon the GVPB's collection of suggestive articles on Vancouver to fill in gaps in their daily publications. The GVPB was confident that news editors were "gradually learning to depend on this sheet as a source of information." A survey of eastern Canadian newspapers suggested that "approximately forty per cent. of the papers use the stories, and that nearly sixty per cent. of the stories used are featured." The editorial department also assisted motion picture companies in the production of three films about British Columbia, including one on the province's industrial life and another focused on "parks and scenic drives." And, finally, the editorial department provided slides for exhibits at exhibitions such as the Toronto Fair, where visitors were shown "two dozen slides showing parks, residential, commercial and industrial scenes."[45]

Similarly, during the 1920s, the VIPB continued the campaign to convince entrepreneurs to visit British Columbia. The promoters were confident in the assumption that, once these visitors saw the economic opportunities available in manufacturing, mining, or farming, they would settle in the province and bring with them their investment capital and know-how. Like Herbert Cuthbert before him, George Warren pointed to Los Angeles as an example of a settlement that had "nothing but climate, miles from the seashore," but that had secured prosperity through publicity.[46] Agricultural and industrial opportunities, for example, were highlighted in the 1922 edition of the VIPB pamphlet *"Follow the Birds" to Victoria B.C.* The 1928 version of this pamphlet trumpeted the fact that "Victoria Welcomes New Industries" while noting that Victoria City Council was willing to offer industrial sites, taxation inducements, and cheap water in an effort to lure new industries.[47]

The "Follow the Birds" campaign was part of George Warren's determined effort to develop a "personality" for Victoria. "Communities must have personality and must have advertising if they are to forge ahead," he maintained. The key to this strategy was his important insight that "a community can be trade marked like a product."[48] Trademarks began to be widely employed by manufacturers in the 1870s as companies made a concerted attempt to differentiate their products from those of their competitors. But as Pamela Walker Laird explains, trademarks also served as "memory hooks for advertising appeals, acting as symbols with which promoters link[ed] their advertising messages to their products in the minds of consumers and middlemen." Trademarks were employed in an effort to "replace the traditional push of sales forces and middlemen with the modern pull of specific demand from consumers." A successful trademark, advertising agents and manufacturers recognized, could "help make demand relatively inelastic and minimize the impact of the business cycle by generating a constant level of specific demand."[49] Warren's eagerness to create a trademark for Victoria was but one of many instances in which tourism promoters adopted the techniques of modern advertising.

The fact that Warren sought to trademark Victoria by using a pictorial image was indicative of another development in modern advertising – an increasing emphasis on visual display. By the early 1930s, in fact, art had triumphed over written copy in national advertising campaigns in the United States. According to Roland Marchand, "the success of the tabloids, the movies, and the rotogravure sections pointed to the public's desire to absorb new ideas and information in visual form." Increased competition for consumers' attention combined with the belief that pictorial images aroused less psychological resistance than did written statements to ensure that advertising copy came to be seen as a necessary but secondary component of advertisements.[50] The VIPB was not alone among tourism organizations in capitalizing upon this insight. Tourism promoters in Vancouver embraced this technique as well. By 1928 the GVPB had embarked upon a new strategy in the production of its pamphlets. That year the GVPB's Editorial and Publicity Committee reported that its latest scenic booklet "deviates from the old time custom of story and illustrations and follows the more modern, and probably exceptional, plan of complete illustrations by full-page cuts, the letterpress being confined to fifty-word captions, written in a style interesting and at the same time descriptive of the scenic attractions of our great Province."[51]

Another key development in modern advertising was the use of radio broadcasts. The number of American families owning a radio increased dramatically from 20 percent in 1926 to 30 percent just two years later.[52] After 1925, Jackson Lears argues, "national advertising invaded the airwaves with stunning speed" as advertisers embraced radio advertising as an opportunity to introduce products to consumers in "a 'natural,' uncommercial atmosphere."[53] They were also eager to capitalize upon the promise of intimacy that radio offered. Radio advertising, as they understood it, enhanced the listener's sense that the advertiser's message was aimed solely at him or her.[54]

Not surprisingly, North American tourism promoters were quick to embrace the possibilities of this new medium.[55] By February 1924, George Warren had secured the use of the Centennial Church's radio to broadcast the VIPB's message. His radio addresses were aimed at potential visitors in both the United States and Canada and emphasized Vancouver Island's temperate climate along with its industrial and agricultural opportunities.[56] In 1928, tourism promoters in Vancouver made their first foray into radio publicity. From January until April, the GVPB embarked upon publicity work under the auspices of the *Vancouver Lumberjacks Radio Night Club* broadcast each Wednesday night from 10:30 until 11:30. "In addition to a scintillating programme of variety, dialogue, music, instrumental and vocal, built around the theme of a logging camp with the many characters attached to such an institution," GVPB commissioner Charles Webster embraced this opportunity to meditate "on the tourist, industrial and general attractions of this City and district" and to extend "an invitation to write for literature." During his ten- to fifteen-minute talks, Webster "interwove ... many interesting and fascinating legends of early day history, and what might be termed pre-historical Indian lore attached to this Province." The program elicited requests for information on the city from across the Prairies and throughout the United States.[57]

During 1928, the GVPB experienced its most "active" and "successful" season to date. That year its president, Brenton S. Brown, reported on an important development in the organization's activities. The bureau's activities were "broadening from year to year," he explained, "and the field of advertising activities has doubled and trebled during the past three years." Besides increasing in quantity, the organization's activities had undergone a qualitative change. "The work has been departmentalized," Brown wrote, "and carried on under the direction of committees."[58] The Advertising Committee, Brown reported, "would probably be considered the major committee," and as such it was responsible for the largest percentage of GVPB expenditures. In the first eleven months of 1928, the Advertising Committee had spent just under $40,000 on 651 newspaper and magazine advertisements reaching an estimated weekly circulation of sixteen million readers.[59] By 1928 the board of directors was keen to expand the campaign in Washington to cover eleven months of the year, while the eastern Canada campaign had been extended from May until August and now included the Maritime provinces.[60] The departmentalization of the GVPB mirrored a trend occurring among advertising agencies in the first decade of the twentieth century.[61] The move toward internal specialization and departmentalization was further evidence that organizations such as the GVPB were adopting a systematic approach to publicity that had been originated by advertising agencies.

Directors of both the GVPB and the VIPB acknowledged the extent to which their promotional campaigns had adopted modern advertising techniques, and they were quick to attribute the increasing number of tourists arriving in Vancouver and Victoria in the late 1920s to the miracle of modern advertising. Before 1926 GVPB directors had believed that the city's tourist business was necessarily confined to two brief seasons: July and August in the summer and January and February in the winter. GVPB members were now convinced that a determined foray into the world of advertising had produced what the association's directors had sought: a lengthening of these two separate seasons. As a result of the new emphasis on advertising the GVPB proclaimed, the number of passengers arriving by automobile increased by 15 percent in 1926 over the previous year. Areas that had been the target of advertising campaigns paid particular dividends. The increase in automobiles from California was 50 percent, while automobile traffic from elsewhere in Canada increased by 35 percent.[62] Similarly, VIPB directors estimated that the number of tourists visiting Victoria had increased from 250,000 in 1923 to 335,000 in 1926 and boasted that the promotional efforts that they believed had produced this increase had created a financial windfall for the city in the form of tourist expenditures.[63]

While earlier evaluations of tourism's economic contributions had emphasized visitors' investment potential, by the mid-1920s tourism promoters were beginning to employ a new method for calculating a tourist's economic value. Using the dominion government's estimate that each tourist spent ten dollars per day while visiting Canada and stayed on average for three days, the GVPB estimated the total tourist expenditure in British Columbia for 1926 to be $32,676,260.[64] GVPB officials, however, were unwilling to fully embrace the dominion government's methods for measuring tourist expenditures. Their own observations convinced them that "a greater number of the tourists on vacation spent at least a month in British Columbia."[65] Similarly the VIPB concluded that the 370,000 tourists visiting Victoria in 1928 spent roughly $3.5 million in the city during their stay.[66]

The sustained increase in tourism during the late 1920s allowed those involved in tourism promotion, such as GVPB commissioner Webster, to champion tourism's economic power more forcefully. In November 1928, for example, Webster announced that "the tourist industry of Canada now ranks amongst the Dominion's chief business interests." Citing a report from the federal Department of Railways and Canals, Webster explained that in 1927 over $276 million was spent by foreign tourists in Canada. Such a contribution to the Canadian economy placed tourism behind wheat exports but ahead of building permits, pulp and paper, and mineral production. Webster also drew on a recent editorial appearing in the *Monetary Times* championing the value of tourism to the Canadian economy "as an element in international trade." Tourism, the *Monetary Times* explained to its readers, was an "invisible export."[67]

Similarly the VIPB rejoiced in announcing annual increases in tourists to its members and the public at large. Such reports also emphasized that the bureau had been very active in the past year responding to inquiries from potential settlers. But whereas earlier public pronouncements on tourism had focused primarily on the tourist trade's ability to lure such settlers to Vancouver Island, pronouncements during the late 1920s focused increasingly upon the immediate infusions of cash that tourists injected into the local economy. In 1927, for example, the VIPB reported that the number of tourists visiting Victoria had increased markedly from 250,000 in 1923 to 335,000 in 1926. The fact that approximately 1.24 million people had visited the city in the past four years, the bureau reasoned, meant that these visitors had contributed roughly $12.4 million to the local economy. Moreover, this sizable sum of money had been obtained with a minimal outlay by the city itself – the VIPB had spent just $100,000 over the past four years on publicity. The fact that the VIPB's efforts to distribute informative articles about the island's lumber trade had led to "a large number of big deals hav[ing] been consummated" was welcome news – but it was no longer the stuff of headlines.[68] Headlines in the *Daily Times* and the *Daily Colonist* increasingly trumpeted tourism's cash-producing achievements. In February 1929, for example, headlines in the *Daily Colonist* told readers that the 370,000 people who had visited Victoria in 1928 had spent over $3.5 million.[69]

According to GVPB commissioner Webster, tourism was an economic windfall. "Money placed in circulation in the Province of British Columbia by tourists is new money that has become available to the people of our Province," he explained, "and it undoubtedly increases our general prosperity."[70] In the heady 1920s, Webster remained confident in tourism and the economy in general. He was pleased with his organization's activities and positive in his understanding of the role of tourism in the civic, provincial, and national economies. For a quarter of a century, the GVPB and other tourism promotion bodies in British Columbia had seen tourism primarily as a means to an end – a method for luring industrial and agricultural investment to the province. In the late 1920s, however, a growing awareness of the important impact of tourist expenditures was setting the stage for a new vision for tourism – one that saw tourism as an important economic endeavour in its own right. It was a transition from a tourism geared to enhancing industrial production to one embedded in a new culture and political economy of consumption. The onset of the Great

Depression would highlight both the difficulties in attracting further investment and the newly appreciated significance of tourist expenditures for the provincial economy.

100 for 1:
Advertising for Tourist Expenditures in the Great Depression

For tourism promoters, like many other people, the Great Depression arrived as a great surprise. In November 1929, for example, GVPB president Brenton S. Brown announced that he was delivering the most "progressive" report in the history of the association. Each and every department, he explained, had demonstrated "increased results."[71] The association's Membership Committee echoed Brown's optimism, suggesting that its recent slowdown in subscriptions would "entirely disappear after the new year." Vancouver, after all, was "showing ... continued progress and development on a solid basis."[72] The economic dislocation of the 1930s would eventually challenge this complacency – and encourage a new approach to tourism. But before turning to this development, it is important to note two important continuities in tourism promotion: a sustained faith in the power of advertising, and a continuing pattern of regional cooperation.

During the Depression, advertising agencies and national magazines in the United States preached the virtues of advertising despite the economic slowdown. In fact, they argued that "advertising appropriations should actually *increase* in times of economic depression" because sustained advertising campaigns would foster an economic recovery by increasing consumer demand.[73] Tourism promoters in Victoria and Vancouver shared this commitment to advertising. By 1931, for example, GVPB president O.B. Allan was reporting a "falling off in tourist traffic throughout the United States and Canada," but the resulting reduction in revenue did not produce a concomitant reduction in GVPB advertising. Indeed, Allan reported that "the apparent falling off in business is by no means a reason to curtail advertising." Sustained advertising and improved transportation and communication infrastructure, Allan and others reasoned, were the key factors of a healthy tourist trade. With little ability to improve the latter, particularly during the Depression, the GVPB worked diligently to augment the former. "We have been advertising consistently in the states to the south," Allan reported, "and are gratified to know that there has been a yearly increase in traffic from these sources. To cut down on our advertising there during the next year or two would mean the loss of the benefits accruing from years of steadily building up a 'Vancouver consciousness' in those states."[74]

Tourism promoters in British Columbia remained optimistic that a return to the heady days of the late 1920s was not far off. Faced with the economic dislocation of the early 1930s, for example, GVPB commissioner

Charles Webster outlined for GVPB members a decidedly rosy view of the past decade and concluded his brief history of the rise of tourism with encouraging words about the future. The rise of mass tourism, he explained, had been inaugurated during the years immediately following the Great War. "Fortunes, resulting from high prices of post-war years, came into existence," he reported, "causing an increased consumption of higher-priced commodities." One result of this pattern was a rise in transoceanic travel and world travel more generally. Moreover, "continued prosperity up to 1929 placed people on a travel-conscious plane that had never before been achieved. The financial situation of 1930, fore-runner of the so-called 'depression' of 1931, brought a new situation." A sudden decrease in travel was the result, although "automobile travel held up fairly well during that period." Yet Webster remained certain that the Depression had "not changed the desire for travel that has become inculcated in the hearts of the people and the trend to former conditions is noticeable this year. People are travelling again." What had decreased were tourist expenditures. The "general tendency to reduce salaries and other overhead, has shown decidedly in a reduced purchasing power," Webster explained, "thus decreasing the expenditures of travellers."[75]

Advertising executives had long championed their industry's ability to minimize and even eliminate business cycles by encouraging consumption, and in the 1920s and 1930s they continued to champion their industry as the most efficient method of counteracting overproduction. Like advertising executives who defended advertising's role as the enemy of disease and poverty in the 1920s, tourism promoters such as Webster remained surprisingly self-assured in the face of the Depression.[76] Confident in tourism's recovery, Webster envisioned both a higher calling and new responsibilities for the GVPB and other publicity organizations. Tourism, he suggested, offered what other economic pursuits could not: a way out of the Depression. "Vancouver and British Columbia are subject to the same World conditions that effect [sic] the trade and development of all other countries," Webster explained. Unfortunately British Columbians could do nothing to boost world markets and increase the demand for staples such as lumber, fish, and agricultural products. Tourism, he suggested, was different: "The tourist industry is the only one we have whose development lies in the hands of our people." Vancouver, and the province more generally, he suggested, were in a position to benefit from the sustained advertising effort of previous years.[77]

According to Webster, tourism had already done much to ease the strain of the Depression. He suggested that business conditions would have been far worse without the "loose" money brought in by tourists. Tourism expenditures were especially valuable, he reasoned, because they were spent directly with merchants, retailers, and service providers such as hotels and restaurants. This money then "gravitate[d] from these starting points to all sections of the community and the benefit from this new wealth is felt by all throughout the Province, because it increases the purchasing power of the people and also creates employment."[78]

This focus on tourist expenditures was not entirely new. Indeed, earlier tourism promoters such as Herbert Cuthbert had noted this aspect of tourism's economic contribution. What was new, however, was the degree of emphasis now placed on tourists' purchasing power, which had long been regarded as a welcome but secondary by-product of tourism promotion's primary objective: attracting investors and securing settlers. This new emphasis on tourism, as an important economic activity in its own right, was also illustrated in GVPB membership drives. The continuing economic dislocation of the Depression had convinced the GVPB's Executive Committee that a more determined approach to fund-raising would be necessary in the coming years – one that included returning to an earlier policy of soliciting subscriptions from service clubs. Potential subscribers were contacted by mail. The package that they received included a newly created booklet entitled *100 for 1,* which outlined the emerging philosophy of the GVPB. The booklet championed the role of advertising and "pointed out the direct effect of advertising in building up this great cash industry." To supplement this campaign, advertisements were placed in local newspapers "showing in graphic style the relationship of the tourist industry to the prosperity of the City."[79]

According to the GVPB's booklet, every dollar that Vancouver invested in advertising resulted in 100 new dollars in tourist expenditure. This increased emphasis on advertising was deemed necessary because of increased competition from vacation resorts around the world. Moreover, many countries and regions were setting aside ever larger amounts of money to invest in tourism advertising programs of their own. The tourist industry, the GVPB pamphlet argued, was responsible for roughly 13.5 percent of the province's total income for 1930. It was, in fact, the province's fourth largest industry – behind lumber, agriculture, and mining but ahead of fishing. Furthermore, the tourist industry had shown greater growth in the past decade than any of the other main industries, and the GVPB argued that "there is no reason why it should not show the same rate of increase during the next ten years." The key to ensuring such growth was advertising, and the appeal to businesspeople was direct: "More Advertising Means More Tourist Money Means More Business for All of Us." What was required, the GVPB pamphlet explained, was more financial support from the business community to guarantee these results.[80]

Advertising, then, continued to occupy a central place in GVPB activities. In 1931 the GVPB contributed approximately $27,000 toward regional campaigns. The association conducted campaigns focusing on Washington, the Canadian Prairies, and the Puget Sounders campaign directed at California. The eastern Canada campaign, however, was suspended. In March 1931, the Puget Sounders teamed with tourism bodies in Oregon and California to advertise nationally in the United States for the first time: a four-page advertisement in the *Saturday Evening Post*.[81] By the autumn of 1931, the GVPB had also seen fit to suspend its advertising campaign for the Prairies, relying instead on just the Washington campaign and the Puget Sounders national campaign in the United States.[82]

By November 1933, faced with declining automobile travel to the city and the lack of national conventions to buttress the tourist numbers, the GVPB had settled upon a new advertising strategy. Henceforth the bureau would concentrate its advertising expenditure in "particular districts" even though a concerted effort would be made to maintain continuity in as many districts as possible. Like preceding presidents, GVPB president Harold Darling underscored tourism's unique ability to increase British Columbians' "purchasing power" because of its freedom from "tariff walls and conditions in the trade-markets in the world."[83] The bureau itself, Commissioner Webster reported, was "becoming more and more recognized from day to day as a civic service institution."[84] In fact, in light of the Depression, GVPB members' sense of responsibility and duty toward the community was growing. For the GVPB's Membership Committee, the time had clearly come for tourism promoters to take a leading role in civic affairs. "Never before in the history of the Bureau," the committee announced, "has its importance to the prosperity of the community, through the scientific and consistent development of the tourist trade been brought so forcibly to the attention of our people."[85] By December 1934, a renewed sense of optimism emerged at the GVPB. Growing interest in tourism combined with "the recovery in business which is taking place" to bring a smile to the face of GVPB president E.H. Adams.[86] Drawing upon "the consensus of opinion that we have at last passed the 'travel depression' years," Webster reported, "renewed and increased activity" in the form of cooperative advertising was sure to follow.[87]

A consistent advertising program had been a key element in the GVPB efforts to weather the adverse effects of the Depression, and tourism promoters on Vancouver Island similarly championed the power of continuous advertising. In February 1931, despite facing a decline in revenues, the VIPB expanded its advertising program. In November 1931, an editorial in the Victoria *Daily Times* emphasized the importance of continuous advertising. The editorial supported Victoria mayor Herbert Anscomb's suggestion that the VIPB continue to increase its publicity efforts and issued a dire warning to businesses throughout the city. Only those establishments that continued to advertise their goods and services would be in a position to prosper once the Depression ended. Businesses that suspended advertising now, it suggested, would face dire consequences later on.[88] The VIPB's annual report, released in February 1932, suggested that the city's tourist trade was weathering the Depression better than other commercial pursuits in Victoria. Continuous advertising, bureau directors maintained, was necessary to increase both the number of tourists visiting the island and the amount of money that they spent.[89]

In February 1933, the Victoria *Daily Colonist* stressed the temporary nature of the present decline of the local tourist trade. Tourism, it argued, made a tremendous contribution to the nation's welfare, particularly in terms of "new money left in the country." While the Depression meant that tourists were holidaying less and confining their travels closer to home, this was only a "passing phase." When the economy recovered, tourism would again "rise to the heights of past years and no doubt continue to expand." The key for Victoria and other tourism-dependent communities was to "continue to concentrate its efforts on attracting attention in bad years as well as in good." The *Daily Colonist* praised the Victoria and Island Publicity Bureau for its efforts, particularly in attracting conventions to Victoria. These conventions, it suggested, resulted in "the expenditure of considerable sums of money, in addition to what is distributed in circulation by the regular stream of tourists."[90]

As the Depression worsened after 1932, the pressure to decrease the VIPB's activities increased. Like the GVPB, the VIPB responded to these pressures by cutting back on its expenses while continuing to promote Vancouver Island as a tourist destination as best it could. By February 1933, the VIPB reduced both salaries and operating expenses and moved to more affordable headquarters. It discontinued its Prairie and eastern Canada advertising campaigns and opted to halt the erection and improvement of billboards in favour of spending its publicity money on initiatives that utilized Seattle radio stations.[91]

The year 1935 marked the beginning of sustained improvement in the tourist business. In November, GVPB president E.H. Adams announced that the GVPB was now in a financial position to significantly increase its promotional activities. This enhanced ability to pursue potential tourists came at a time when more and more communities were entering the already stiff competition for tourists.[92] The Puget Sounders (now renamed the Evergreen Playground Association to mark the inclusion of members from Portland) remained, according to Adams, the GVPB's "leading and most effective medium." Increased financial support from GVPB subscribers as well as from Vancouver City Council allowed the GVPB to renew advertising campaigns in the Prairies and eastern Canada while doubling the size of the program in Washington and Oregon.[93]

With the number of potential tourists increasing, road conditions emerged as an increasingly important issue in 1935. GVPB commissioner

Charles Webster paid tribute to the provincial government's efforts to improve road access to the province's Kootenay region. The provincial government's road-surfacing program, Webster predicted, would increase the tendency of BC residents to travel to the region along BC roads rather than "making the journey over the highways of the State of Washington, which it must be admitted has been practically compulsory during recent years."[94] The GVPB continued to receive an increasing number of requests for travel information as well as for "data on practically all of British Columbia's basic industries."[95] The standing committees of the GVPB all produced reports documenting the "growing return to the tourist travel records of a few years ago."[96] The return of a significant number of annual conventions also signalled a return to "'normal' times" for the GVPB.[97] In 1936 GVPB president G.H. Worthington announced that the association's advertising appropriations had been increased across the board, and the number of tourists visiting the city continued to rise.[98]

The GVPB was convinced that its determination to continue advertising even during the worst years of the Depression was apparently now paying dividends. But the scale of advertising does not tell the entire story. Equally as important is the changing content of the advertising. As the GVPB and the VIPB increasingly came to see tourism promotion as an important economic pursuit in its own right, rather than a means to industrial and agricultural expansion, the content of the advertisements changed accordingly. The didactic tone of earlier copy was replaced by content that emphasized expenditure rather than investment opportunities. To maximize expenditure required increasing both the number of tourists and the duration of their visits. The best way to do this, many observers argued, was to offer Americans something exotic and foreign. In British Columbia, that meant capitalizing on both the province's imperial grandeur and the mystique surrounding its Aboriginal population.

Ethnicity as Spectacle: The Expenditure Imperative in Print
During the 1920s, the VIPB designed and distributed a series of questionnaires not only to provide the city's tourism promoters with valuable information concerning the number of people visiting the city but also to obtain insights into why tourists were choosing Victoria as a tourist destination. Here again was an example of BC tourism promoters adopting the techniques of modern advertising – this time by initiating rudimentary market research studies.[99] By 1928 these questionnaires had convinced George Warren and other local tourism promoters that the city's English atmosphere was an important drawing card. In response, the VIPB publicly urged the city's residents to promote the city's Englishness, even going so far as to request that oil companies on Vancouver Island join in by displaying Elizabethan architecture and Union Jacks at gas stations and

by ordering their employees to refer to gasoline as "petrol."[100] This particular initiative was unsuccessful, but the onset of the Depression further convinced British Columbia's tourism promoters of the importance of capitalizing on what made the province unique in the eyes of its visitors.

In a letter to Premier S.F. Tolmie in September 1930, for example, H.B. Thomson, chairman of the British Columbia Liquor Control Board, lamented the province's failure to capitalize on what he termed its "greatest selling point" – its Britishness. "We are ear-marked as British," Thomson claimed, "and visitors, particularly from the United States, expect to see something different." Unfortunately, he explained, this was rarely the case: "A man leaving Tia Juana [sic], Mexico, and motoring through to Vancouver, passes the usual series of gas stations, as hideous in their colourings as they are grotesque in their design. From observation he cannot tell when he crosses the Border." According to Thomson, British Columbia's small hotels and restaurants were too committed to an American design. These establishments, he argued, should emulate Victoria and introduce, "wherever possible, a black and white Tudor and Elizabethan style of architecture and design."[101]

Thomson was not alone in his views. In April 1932, he called Premier Tolmie's attention to an opinion piece written by former Victoria mayor Herbert Anscomb that had appeared in the March issue of *Island Motorist* magazine. Anscomb, then president of the VIPB, offered readers his opinion on the best ways to keep visitors returning to the island. Besides supplying fresh foods and maintaining an overall attractive appearance, Anscomb encouraged hotels and restaurants to enter into a more challenging cooperative venture: they must "Make British Columbia Different." American tourists, Anscomb warned, arrived in the province anxious to see something that provided a contrast with hometown sights and sounds. To provide American tourists with what they wanted, Anscomb and others suggested dramatically increasing the profile of the province's British component. "Let them see the Union Jack flying," Anscomb suggested. "English inns" would both "enhance the pleasure of their trip" and provide American tourists with "something to talk about." "Bowling greens, tennis lawns, quoit and archery grounds" would all increase the marketability of local restaurants and hotels, as would two rather prosaic symbols of English imperialism, "flowers and shrubbery." Two other English pastimes, fishing and shooting, were supported by Victoria's Chamber of Commerce, which had established a Fish and Game Conservation Committee to ensure a sustainable supply of fauna for visiting sportsmen.[102]

When the VIPB issued its 1932 questionnaire, the results created something of a stir in newspapers across the country. Suggestions by US tourists that Victoria was becoming increasingly "Americanized" produced an alarmed response from the Ottawa *Evening Journal*, which decried Canada's architecture, city planning, and countryside as increasingly carbon copies of those found in the United States. To buttress its case, the *Evening Journal* drew upon results from the bureau's survey, which implored Victoria not to "go modern." The *Evening Journal*'s view, however, was not shared by the Winnipeg *Tribune*, which suggested instead that Canadians cultivate rather than prune their continentalist roots. Canada, it reminded its audience, "is a part of America, and its people are, in the main, sprung from the same racial stocks as those of the United States." "If we have some American faults," it reasoned, "it does not follow that we have copied them from the Yankees." Moreover, a concerted plan to differentiate Canada from the United States signified both an uncouth desperation and a lack of foresight: "If the United States tourist desires something quaint and foreign adjacent to the borders of his own country, let Mexico supply it. Canada has other fish to fry, and it will be a dark day indeed when we forget that we are North Americans or 'go native' in order to entertain the light-minded." The Victoria *Daily Times* assured both major dailies and its own readership that the entire debate was much ado about nothing. Victoria's penchant for attracting tourists was neither at risk nor apparently in need of much attention. Victoria's attractions were, it explained, entirely natural. American visitors simply "take us as they find us," it suggested.[103]

In 1937 E.H. Adams, now president of the Evergreen Playground Association, entered the debate by urging tourism promoters to concentrate not only on attracting American tourists to Canada but also on "maintaining tourist interest" once they had arrived. To this end, he reminded his audience that to American tourists "Canada is a foreign land in which they may have expected to find something that is romantic or different to anything they have seen at home." In particular, he argued, these tourists sought attractions that were "a part of the British Empire, something that is traditionally British." Adams's tangible suggestion was a proliferation of scarlet-clad Mounted Policemen stationed in front of federal buildings across the country. The mountie, Adams reasoned, fulfilled several key requirements as a tourist attraction (see Figure 2.7). He was symbolic of Britain and therefore a foreign attraction. He was easily involved in ceremonies that could be converted into tourist attractions. And, since "people are travelling in greater numbers with moving picture cameras these days," his colourful attire and glamorous and romantic reputation would induce them to record his image and then "go home and show their friends and help indirectly to advertise Canada." "People are apt to get tired looking at buildings and scenery and as evening time comes on they want to rest," Adams advised. Ceremonies, pageants, music, and military displays should all play a role in maintaining visitor interest and ideally prolong visits to Canada. "Too often," Adams lamented, "we Americanize our attractions under the mistaken idea that the tourist from across the line will feel more at home." This was not what tourists wanted, he explained. Instead, they wanted to feel as if they were in a foreign country. Adams paid homage to the cities of Quebec and Victoria, both of which had maintained their "quaint atmosphere[s]" and historic backgrounds. "We should be what we are – Canadian and not a mixture of all the nationalities who come to us," he announced.[104] Another group that tourism promoters were increasingly inclined to emphasize in their promotional campaigns did not fit easily into either of Adams's two categories. Along with the province's British heritage, BC tourism promoters sought to capitalize upon the lore surrounding the province's Aboriginal population.

Earlier promotional literature, focused as it was on industrial and agricultural production, devoted very little copy space to the province's Aboriginal peoples. Tourist pamphlets frequently highlighted only the opportunity to visit museum collections of rare Native relics and curios.[105] The continuing resonance of scientific racism into the twentieth century meant that Native peoples continued to be viewed as unproductive and backward – hardly people who would leave a first impression that tourism promoters wanted potential settlers and investors to carry with them.[106] As E.A. Heaman has demonstrated, international exhibitors were also wary of employing Aboriginal artifacts and performers to promote Canada for fear of frightening potential settlers and investors. Indeed, Canadian exhibitors did what they could to promote the image of Canada as a safe, invigorating, and welcoming destination ideal for industrious Anglo-Saxon immigrants.[107]

Similar negative attitudes prevailed toward Aboriginal people among promoters of Yellowstone National Park. As Paul Schullery explains, "park administrators before 1900 did not see Indians the way later generations of tourism professionals would, as potentially an added 'attraction' to bring visitors to an area." In fact, "throughout the 1880s, complaints were published in the national press of Indians hunting or travelling in the park."[108] Such complaints arose from tousists who, to use Patricia Nelson Limerick's revealing phrase, "were people of means, people who wanted comfort and service, people for whom the era of conquest was a little too recent and raw."[109]

While advertisements for consumer products employed images of Aboriginal people to sell goods, their roles were tightly constrained. Ads in the United States focused on the savagery of Indians in order to construct an "other" against which the virtues of a modern consumer product could be contrasted. In 1900, for example, Ivory Soap launched an advertising series that ostensibly demonstrated the uplifting impact of its soap on the old unhygienic ways of Natives.[110] As Jeffrey Steele notes, such ads assured audiences that these Indians either belonged to a bygone time or were geographically isolated from the middle-class homes of the buying public.[111] The CPR's enthusiasm for Aboriginal imagery in its promotional campaigns might also be explained by the fact that tourists travelling its tracks generally secured only fleeting contact with Aboriginal people. As the British traveller Edward Roper noted on his trip through the Canadian west in 1890, the local population did not share travellers' enthusiasm for the exoticism of the Aboriginal population: "The Canadians seemed

Figure 2.7 Imperial authority as tourist attraction. E.H. Adams was not alone in advocating the use of the imperial grandeur of Mounties and bobbies to lure American tourists northward. Both the Evergreen Playground Association and the Greater Vancouver Publicity Bureau incorporated law and order images into their promotional campaigns.

Source: CVA, GVVCB papers, Series B, File 21, *Greater Vancouver Publicity Bureau Annual Report 1937* (reproduced with the permission of Tourism Vancouver); *Sunset* 76, 5 (1936): 13.

to regard them as a race of animals which were neither benefit nor harm to anyone, mentioning that they were surely dying out, and that when they were all gone it would be a good thing."[112] Such an image was the antithesis of the modern and progressive aura that tourism promoters in Victoria and Vancouver traditionally had sought to secure for their cities.[113]

With the growing emphasis on tourist expenditures, however, the mystical aura surrounding the province's Aboriginal population was apparently deemed more acceptable and, therefore, more useful. In 1935, for example, when W.T. Straith, chairman of a local beautification committee, took a leading role in updating and expanding Victoria's attractions by proposing a "sightseeing drive" to better capitalize upon Victoria's historical involvement in the fur trade, he lamented that "not enough attention has been paid in the past to the Hudson Bay tradition nor the Indian lore of Victoria." He hoped that a sightseeing drive might be developed "which would include these two factors as well as a view of the old Military and Naval Barracks and fortifications, the drydocks," and the "village of Esquimalt." Particular attention could be paid, he explained, to the Indian Reserve along Admirals Road. Here, Straith enthused, were "old unpainted houses with moss covered roofs" that were "typical of the Indians of the Coast." Visitors could partake of the "three common houses with the mud floors and holes in the roof for chimneys, and all the features of the large Indian common Houses." As authentic as this scene might seem to some, Straith was not willing to leave it in its natural state. "The Indian Reserve could be improved," he explained, "by having totem poles removed from other sites and war canoes could be arranged so as to be attractive to sightseers." There was even a place for the Aboriginal population itself in Straith's plan – albeit a restricted and secondary one: "The Indians themselves would no doubt visit this place in the summer and sell their Indian baskets, totem poles and other trinkets."[114]

Throughout the 1930s, the province's two largest cities continued to rely upon cooperative advertising campaigns. One of the most successful belonged to the Evergreen Playground Association (EPA). In 1936 the combined circulation of advertisements produced by the EPA was, according to VIPB commissioner George Warren, over 1.5 million readers. Some of the ads featured Victoria alone, while others featured it alongside other tourist destinations in the Pacific Northwest. The advertisements included coupons with which potential travellers could request information. The VIPB would then respond with "personal letters and descriptive folders" to those inquiring.[115] As Figures 2.8 through 2.10 indicate, EPA advertisements reinforced many of the key lessons and themes that the province's tourism promoters had been championing on their home turf.

The new emphasis on British and Aboriginal imagery in tourism promotion campaigns was part of a broad trend in advertising during the

Holiday this year in the Evergreen Playground

Fraser Canyon, from historic Cariboo Trail.

—and now for a COOL Summer Vacation! ...

... where you can spend the best holiday you have ever dreamed about. The Evergreen Playground of Washington and British Columbia is becoming the mecca of Pacific Coast holiday makers—largely because there's so much to see and do and each of the five cities is within comfortable distance of all points in the Playground.

It's an easy trip to make. At most, this great vacation land is only a one-to-three-days' journey from California cities. It offers you such a complete change of climate, of scenery, of sports and pastimes that even a few days here will invigorate you. (You can easily make the Circle Tour of all cities in two weeks.)

It's a sort of pot-pourri of every kind of vacation delight you have ever imagined! Evergreen forests, snow-capped mountains, fishing streams, waterfalls, acres of brilliant flower-gardens, velvety lawns, verdant valleys ... snow sports, riding, hunting, bathing, golf ... a trip to a "foreign" country, unusual shops and strange merchandise. You can breakfast in Tacoma and lunch on Mt. Rainier's snowy slopes! You can start your day at Bellingham and in two or three hours be at the top of Mt. Baker! You can sleep in Vancouver and before nightfall visit several gold mines in the now famous Bridge River district. You can lunch in Victoria and be in the Olympic Forest by tea time! Within half a day from Seattle, you can reach almost any point in the whole Evergreen Playground.

You will get more value and more variety out of your holiday budget if you come to the Evergreen Playground. Mail the coupon below for picture book—where to go and what to see while here.

FIVE PLAYGROUND CITIES

TACOMA. Rainier National Park and Mountain, glaciers, snow-sports.

SEATTLE. Hub of Evergreen Playground, on Puget Sound, gateway to Alaska and the Orient.

BELLINGHAM. Mt. Baker National Forest, and historic San Juan Islands.

VANCOUVER, Canada's western metropolis, world port, scenic hinterland, Cariboo Country and the Rockies.

VICTORIA. Capital of B. C., a miniature of Old England, Parliament Buildings, lovely gardens, great Island sportland.

While up here explore the Olympic Peninsula, 1,001,000 acres of virgin forests, snow-capped mountains, a rugged wonderland for sportsmen.

ᵀʰᵉ EVERGREEN PLAYGROUND

PUGET SOUNDERS & BRITISH COLUMBIANS ASSOCIATED

Puget Sounders & British Columbians Associated,
434 Chamber of Commerce Bldg., Seattle, Wash.
Please send me your FREE illustrated booklet.

Name ....

Address ....

Figure 2.8 Puget Sounders and British Columbians Associated advertisement, 1934. As competition for tourists increased, promoters in the Pacific Northwest emphasized the variety of attractions in the region. This ad offered a "pot-pourri" of delights that included "unusual shops and strange merchandise" from a "'foreign' country" – a telling message during the decade in which tourism promoters shifted their focus from attracting industry to maximizing tourist expenditures.

Source: Sunset 72, 6 (1934): 43.

Figure 2.9 "The family-next-door" visits the Evergreen Playground. Offering a "British Holiday" in a "Foreign Atmosphere," this 1936 EPA ad also emphasized the region's low summer fares and cost of living. Mention is also made of the Bonneville and Grand Coulee dams. By 1936, however, tourism was increasingly understood as a method of obtaining currency rather than investment.

Source: BCARS, Premiers' papers, Box 137, File 10, George I. Warren to Premier, 11 May 1936.

Figure 2.10 Evergreen Playground Association advertisement, 1936. Both English and Aboriginal content were employed in this EPA ad aimed at the California market.

Source: BCARS, Premiers' papers, Box 137, File 10, George I. Warren to Premier, 11 May 1936.

1930s. Ad workers employed the simplistic image of a variety of "folk" peoples in their advertisements in order to associate modern goods and services with the reassuring image of a preindustrial organic society – one that spoke of a more secure era far removed from the modern world.[116] The increasing acceptance of Aboriginal imagery in such advertisements undoubtedly owed something to the ascendance of cultural pluralism in scientific and scholarly studies of Aboriginal peoples during the 1920s.[117] In advertisements promoting tourism in British Columbia, however, images of Aboriginal culture likely owed their presence just as much to the expenditure imperative that increasingly shaped tourism promotion efforts.

Conclusion

In many historical accounts of leisure and tourism, the 1930s represent an era of economic restraint and sacrifice (a decade of "conspicuous underconsumption," one might say) that ushered in an era of conspicuous consumption in the postwar years.[118] Recent North American scholarship, however, has begun to chip away at the assumption that the 1930s were primarily an era of abstinence that contributed to a postwar tourist boom. In her study of vacations in the northeastern United States, for example, Cindy Aron reveals that vacations "remained a prevalent and popular American institution throughout the 1930s." In fact, while vacationing declined briefly in the early part of the decade, it expanded rapidly after 1935 when paid vacations were extended to a majority of industrial workers in the United States.[119] Peter Blodgett points to the US Park Service's advertising campaigns as playing a key role in increasing the number of visitors to the national parks in the early 1930s.[120] In Canada, recent studies of Niagara Falls, Ontario, and the province of Prince Edward Island both suggest that tourism outperformed other industries during the Depression.[121] While the Great Depression meant poverty and homelessness for many North Americans, those with disposable income continued to enjoy the pleasures of recreation and travel.[122]

In addition to acknowledging the fact that tourist travel did not grind to a halt during the Depression, it is important to recognize that the late 1920s and early 1930s witnessed a dramatic transformation in the rationale behind tourism promotion. Whereas earlier publicity campaigns had focused a good deal of energy on advertising the industrial opportunities of the province, by 1938 the GVPB was actively boosting its own industry: tourism. Its Publications and Editorial Committee now vaguely considered tourism a "stimulant to every industry" in the province and expended a good deal of energy publicizing the importance of the tourist industry itself.[123] As the following chapter reveals, the advent of large-scale government intervention in the tourist industry would confirm a transformation in the nature of tourism promotion – from a variant of boosterism to a crusade in pursuit of a direct cash infusion on the part of consumers. This transformation would witness two important shifts: the international and regional campaigns typified by the PNTA would cede pride of place to provincial and federal tourism bureaucrats, and BC tourism promoters would increasingly focus their efforts on the expanding middle class of the western United States at the expense of their earlier target audience, industrialists and agriculturalists from Britain and eastern North America.

3

Entitlement, Idealism, and the Establishment of the British Columbia Government Travel Bureau, 1935-39

During the first three decades of the twentieth century, local organizations in Victoria and Vancouver took the lead in fashioning an international tourism promotion network. Their first large-scale initiative, the Pacific Northwest Tourist Association, had benefited from a substantial but short-lived grant from the provincial government. Conversely, a second major endeavour, the Puget Sounders (later the Evergreen Playground Association), received no such assistance from the BC government. The provincial government's overall attitude to tourism promotion was ambiguous at best.

The workings of the government's own Bureau of Information tell a similar story. The bureau was created when the Bureau of Statistics and the Bureau of Immigration were combined in 1900. Established during a period of large-scale immigration into the province, the bureau was charged with compiling economic and demographic statistics, indexing the province's newspapers, and promoting immigration. Authority over the bureau, originally housed within the Department of the Provincial Secretary, was transferred to the minister of finance in 1907. Despite the publication and widespread distribution of bulletins on subjects as varied as industrial opportunities and fishing and hunting possibilities, the bureau's promotional undertakings were essentially conservative and passive; for the most part, the bureau contented itself with responding to inquiries from potential settlers and directed a disproportionate amount of publicity material to British rather than American or continental European centres. The scope of the bureau's activities also paled in comparison to the much larger immigration campaigns conducted by the CPR and the federal government.[1]

A series of disputes between the bureau's Secretary, H.W. Hart, and John Oliver's Liberal government in the early 1920s combined with funding cuts to terminate the bureau's operations in 1924. Almost immediately, however, the Bureau of Information was reborn with a larger budget and a broader mandate: to promote tourism and immigration. Between 1923 and 1930, the bureau's annual budget increased from just under $9,000 to over $62,000. Like the advertising campaigns of the Greater Vancouver Publicity Bureau (GVPB) and the Victoria and Island Publicity Bureau (VIPB), the Bureau of Information's promotional material also underwent an important transformation that recognized the changing nature of tourist travel: the statistic-laden bulletin series was abandoned in favour of a series of illustrated booklets aimed at motorists.[2] While the provincial government did not entirely abstain from tourism promotion during the first three decades of the twentieth century, its involvement was clearly sporadic. In light of the Depression, inducing the government to recognize tourism as an important economic activity worthy of direct and sustained government involvement became the primary concern of the province's local tourism organizations.

The existing literature on business activities and motivations during the Depression is sparse. Alvin Finkel, in what remains the most in-depth study of Canadian business during the Depression, has convincingly demonstrated that businesspeople successfully argued for state intervention in the economy in the hope of saving capitalism from itself and a growing socialist threat.[3] Michael Bliss, supporting a very different understanding of the causes of the Depression, also emphasizes the willingness of businesses to encourage government intervention in the form of price controls and increased government spending.[4] Coexisting with this call for government intervention, however, was another increasingly popular business strategy: cooperation. According to Bliss, collectivism among businesses was "endorsed in one form or another by almost all boards of trade, chambers of commerce, and trade associations in the country."[5] Indeed, the Canadian Pulp and Paper Association, supermarket chains, and the Canadian securities industry, among others, all sought government regulation in the hope of limiting harmful competition and halting declining prices. Their demands were supported by both the Canadian Manufacturers' Association and the Retail Merchants Association.[6]

Yet cooperation and the demand for government intervention in the economy do not tell the whole story. In particular, these strategies do not tell us much about the motivations behind tourism promotion or the ideological outlook of British Columbia's tourism promoters. Unlike either the heads of large corporations or small shopkeepers, tourism promoters did not necessarily stand to benefit directly from their endeavours. The promoters under examination here were not hotel owners, campground operators, or tour guides who profited directly from tourist expenditures. They were primarily civic-minded politicians and business leaders imbued with a more organic conception of their place in society.

This organic or "new liberal" conception of the relationship between the state and its citizens was also voiced in the demands made by ordinary citizens on their governments during the Depression. As Lara Campbell has demonstrated in her study of Ontario families and Great War veterans, ordinary citizens employed a rights-based discourse in arguing for a reciprocal relationship between themselves and the government in which the state was expected to assist them in finding employment or provide greater access to relief payments. This sense of entitlement, which expressed a desire for government action but did not call for a fundamental reshaping of the economic system, permeated their letters to premiers George Henry and Mitch Hepburn.[7] Tourism promoters in British Columbia harboured a similar sense of entitlement, imbued on occasion with a profound sense of regional alienation.

While tourism promoters sought government assistance in developing the tourist trade, their demands were limited to increased monetary grants and the formation of a government tourist bureau rather than widespread state intervention in the economy. Tourism itself, they proposed, rather than substantially increased government spending or new social programs, would provide a lasting solution to the economic, social, and cultural problems of the 1930s. British Columbia's tourism promoters advocated, in many ways, a free-enterprise solution to the Depression. In adopting this stance, they were echoing the sentiments of New Dealers in the United States, who had come to see consumer buying power as the key element in ending the Depression. As Lizabeth Cohen explains, "empowering the consumer seemed to many New Dealers a way of enhancing the public's stake in society and the economy while still preserving the free enterprise system." "With the Keynesian revolution," Cohen points out, "consumers became responsible for high productivity and full employment whereas a decade earlier that role had belonged to producers."[8] A similar "optimistic" version of Keynesianism in Canada, Robert M. Campbell argues, resulted in a response to the Depression on the part of the federal government that left the "basic allocation and distribution of resources" in the hands of the free market.[9] Tourism promoters in British Columbia championed tourist expenditures as a substitute for Canada's lagging domestic consumer demand and in doing so offered tourism promotion as an early tangible vision of a free-enterprise solution to the Great Depression.

"On to Nanaimo" and a "New Deal" for Vancouver Island: David Leeming and the Tourist Trade Development Association of Victoria and Vancouver Island

The GVPB had entered the 1930s in a strong position and weathered the early years of the Depression remarkably well. With Vancouver's reasonably diversified economy, the pressure to maximize tourist expenditures was growing but not intense. The city of Victoria was not so fortunate. Faced with a worldwide depression and intense competition from Vancouver, Victoria's civic officials and business leaders turned to tourism as an answer to their plight. In doing so, they embraced a new understanding of tourism's purpose and possibilities. In many ways, it was Victoria's plight and the response of its tourism promoters that most clearly highlight the transformation of tourism promotion in the 1930s.

During the late 1920s, the Victoria Chamber of Commerce maintained its preferred position as the city's economic watchdog. On issues regarding tourism, for example, it restricted itself for the most part to offering public endorsements of organizations such as the VIPB and limiting what it viewed as unnecessary government regulations that hindered the tourist business.[10] More pressing, of course, was the dramatic impact of the economic depression. Chamber discussions of the Depression generally focused on the need for increased business efficiency along with government restraint in the face of increasing demands for a loosening of the public purse. In November 1931, for instance, C.P.W. Schwengers, a past president of the chamber, returned from a fact-finding mission in New York and eastern Canada to remind his colleagues that "rigid economy was essential if prosperity was to be regained."[11] In March 1932, chamber president R.W. Mayhew reported on an unofficial chamber delegation that had teamed with a similar group from Vancouver to impress upon the provincial government the importance of "endeavor[ing] to balance the Provincial budget without increased taxation."[12]

Yet Chamber of Commerce discussions were not monopolized entirely by talk of provincial budgets. In its search for more direct and local answers to the Depression, tourism took on a greater importance than ever before. While chamber manager George Warren (still commissioner of the Victoria and Island Publicity Bureau) continued his contact work in the United States, Victoria's newly elected mayor, David Leeming, toured Washington, Oregon, and California in 1932 in order to address both the chamber and the VIPB on the subject.[13] As the economic situation worsened, Leeming stepped forward with a forceful suggestion: the time had arrived, he proposed, for tourism to take its place as the city's leading economic concern.

Leeming was born in suburban Manchester, England, in 1876. He arrived in Victoria with his family in 1893, and during his first five years in the city Leeming worked for a local real estate firm before starting up a family customs brokerage with his brothers. This operation grew into a shipping business, and Leeming Brothers Limited eventually operated five freighters along the coast. In 1909 the family firm abandoned both the shipping and the customs businesses in favour of real estate. During the 1920s, Leeming served as a director of the VIPB, and, for the four years leading up to his election as mayor in 1932, he served as the bureau's president. He served as mayor of Victoria until 1936 and remained very active on the city's Real Estate Board until he passed away in January 1939.[14]

As president of the VIPB, Leeming emphasized the unlimited possibilities of the tourist trade. But where earlier tourism boosters emphasized the connection between visitors and industrial and agricultural development, Leeming saw tourism's contributions differently. In an August 1929 speech to the local Gyro Club, Leeming drew his audience's attention to the amount of money that the tourist trade produced. He emphasized the importance of good-quality roads on the island and affordable ferry transportation to and from the mainland. Residents of Vancouver Island, he maintained, could "easily increase" their revenue from tourism by overcoming civic rivalries. Islanders, he explained, needed to "get together and co-operate in making [their] natural beauties more widely known." They could further increase their income by establishing more accommodations, more amusements, and a greater variety of entertainment facilities.[15] For Leeming, tourism promotion was primarily about maximizing tourist expenditures.

Over the next few years, Leeming formulated his plan, and in November 1934 he shared his ideas and concerns with his fellow Chamber of Commerce members. After reviewing "the economic losses suffered by the City in the last forty years," Leeming argued that "the only hope of the City was to extend its tourist trade." While reiterating the need for "sound common sense business principles" and acknowledging the city's ballooning relief rolls, Leeming pointed to tourism as the only viable answer to the Depression. Tourism, he explained, was the "one live endeavor that the City has been successful in during the past few years." The only way out of the Depression for the city of Victoria, he argued, was closer cooperation between the Chamber of Commerce, the VIPB, and a new association created under his guidance, the Tourist Trade Development Association of Victoria and Vancouver Island (TTDA). At their wits' end, the chamber's board of directors concurred: for the city of Victoria, tourism "seemed the last hope."[16]

Leeming reiterated his arguments a few weeks later when he informed the Rotary Club that tourism was the "only industry that cannot be taken away" from Victoria. To buttress his argument, he reminded his audience of past developments. The city's sealing industry had been destroyed through an adverse treaty agreement with the United States. The British naval base had been closed in 1905. And the CPR decision to establish its western terminus at Vancouver had cost Victoria its shipping businesses. What remained was the tourist trade – a pursuit that could not be taken away from the city. What was required, he maintained, was a concerted effort to build up this trade.[17]

Leeming's understanding of tourism's possibilities was very different from Herbert Cuthbert's. While Cuthbert had seen tourism as a means to further industrial growth, Leeming was convinced that Victoria's industrial era was over. Instead, he suggested, a tourist industry would emerge in place of traditional industries that had been lured away to Vancouver. "Tourists bring in a literal rain of gold," he explained to a Rotary Club audience in November 1934. "No tourist moves without paying spot cash for everything he receives." The need for this cash infusion was particularly pressing given the city's present financial predicament. Victoria's spiralling relief costs had left the city near bankruptcy, and appeals to the provincial government to alleviate the city's problems had been unsuccessful. With the city's social service costs increasing by 240 percent between 1930 and 1934, Victoria's only hope, Leeming maintained, was a well-formulated plan to increase the city's income from tourism.[18]

A sustained campaign publicizing Victoria to potential tourists, Leeming maintained, would result in unlimited wealth for businesses located on the southern part of Vancouver Island. "Publicity that is spasmodic is not worth much," he insisted, echoing earlier statements by tourism promoters in Victoria and Vancouver. What was required was a concerted effort. "When a public holiday comes along," he explained to a gathering of the Credit Granters' Association in November 1934, "you must forget it is your holiday and you must sell that holiday to visitors." Leeming reminded his audience that twelve million people lived along the Pacific Coast and characterized them as "the highest powered buyers and money spenders you will find everywhere in the world." To lure them to Victoria, he emphasized, required "the entire support of the citizens."[19]

The core of Leeming's plan was the TTDA. To launch this association, Leeming enlisted the help of T.H. Eslick, a "publicity expert" with international experience. He also established several working committees chaired by prominent city businesspeople. For example, R.H.B. Ker, president of the Brackman-Ker Milling company and president of the VIPB from 1925 and 1927, chaired the Finance Committee, while Harold Husband, the manager of Vancouver Island Coach Lines and the current VIPB president, chaired the Entertainment Committee. By the time the TTDA was up and running, twelve committees had been formed with 220 members.[20]

With the preliminary work out of the way, the first full-year TTDA campaign was launched in January 1935. An overflow crowd gathered in a local banquet hall and responded enthusiastically to the assembled speakers, who "emphasized the growth of holiday travel into one of the largest businesses of the nation, and stressed the importance of business-like handling of that trade." Here again Leeming spoke of the need for cooperation and the importance of unifying "the whole of Vancouver Island." Earlier civic battles and ill feelings between Victoria and communities on the northern part of the island had hindered the island's success in obtaining valuable road improvements. Leeming was determined to prevent his tourist trade initiative from falling victim to the same fate.[21]

Among the most vocal supporters of the new association was Victoria MLA and former Victoria mayor, Herbert Anscomb. He emphasized the overwhelming support that Leeming's plan had received from business-people throughout Vancouver Island. He also shared Leeming's optimism concerning the possibilities of the tourist trade: "It means a new lease of life for our hotels, rooming-houses, cafes, etc. All our merchants will benefit. Our transportation companies will benefit. In fact, practically all lines of business in the community get direct benefit from the tourist, and the longer the tourist stays with you the greater the benefits derived." Anscomb's endorsement of the TTDA was absolute; it was a solution whose time had come: "It seems that for the last year or two the people of every country have been waiting for somebody to lead them out of their troubles, and the citizens of Victoria are no exception ... Our Mayor is leading a movement which, if supported in the right way, will bring prosperity to this city."[22]

Two months later, in March 1935, an overflow crowd at the city's Royal Victoria Theatre gathered for what the *Daily Colonist* termed a "tourist mass meeting." So well attended was the meeting, the newspaper reported, that "several thousand persons were unable to gain admittance."[23] "The development of the tourist business means work and wages," Leeming told the audience. He estimated that a sustained effort at tourism promotion would produce $10 million a year for island communities.[24] At this meeting, representatives from throughout Vancouver Island were in attendance. According to Comox MLA L.A. Hanna, Vancouver Island had overcome its earlier divisions and "the Island, as a whole, was definitely behind the Tourist Trade Development Association." On that night, TTDA secretary Eslick was the main speaker, and he reiterated tourism's potential economic contribution while reinforcing the points that traditional industries had not served the island well and that tourism offered islanders an opportunity to help themselves out of their current situation. During his address, Eslick outlined the TTDA's five-year plan, which would depend upon "co-ordinated and co-operative community energy." The TTDA, he explained, would complement the work of the VIPB. While the VIPB continued to publicize Vancouver Island through advertising campaigns, the TTDA would focus on improving the island's entertainment facilities. For the year 1935, for example, the TTDA would focus its efforts on improving road signs, working toward the creation of a personal guide service, and coordinating entertainment programs throughout the island to avoid the prospect of local initiatives conflicting with one another. A similar meeting was to be held in Nanaimo in April.[25]

Leeming's TTDA aimed at improving both the city's financial position and the "actual financial betterment of every individual in the commu- nity." To promote these aims, Leeming and his followers embraced *coop- eration* as their watchword.[26] The TTDA was to provide an "Island-wide, non-political, non-sectarian, non-profit organisation" to lead Victoria out of the Depression. Leeming, as president, headed the organization's exec- utive council. While the Victoria section boasted a membership of roughly 250 "influential citizens," including representatives from more than eighty local organizations, branches of the association were also formed in twenty- two cities throughout the island and usually headed by a local mayor or reeve.

Drawing on the cooperative effort of communities throughout the island, TTDA members sought to "capitalise Vancouver Island's unique advan- tages as a pleasure resort and to create a permanent profitable Tourist Industry." (The very prominence of the phrase "Tourist Industry" was a telling indication of the new outlook.) To bring these plans to fruition, the association embarked upon a "carefully prepared five year, step-by-step plan to encourage and develop the Island's tourist trade possibilities." It would do so by encouraging "better transportation, suitable entertainment," and "wider publicity." The association was to become self-supporting through fund-raising efforts. Its efforts, moreover, were to remain firmly embedded in a self-help ethos and aimed to "foster a spirit of helpful comradeship between all Island communities, linking them up in one big co-operative effort." The association would complement, rather than com- pete with, the already established VIPB. The VIPB would continue to focus on publicizing the island and luring the visitor to its shores, while the TTDA would focus on "the internal work necessary to interest him, pro- long his visit, and induce him to return."[27]

The entire raison d'être of the new association suggested a new atti- tude toward the island's economic prospects and the possibilities of tour- ism. The "present commercial and financial conditions of Vancouver Island generally make the creation of new wealth from an undeveloped industry immediately and urgently necessary," a TTDA tract explained. The island's present "geographical, social and industrial conditions have retarded com- mercial development," and "thriving industries have been taken away," while "new enterprises to fill their place have not been found." Tourism had long been a means to such ends – a strategy for enticing industries to the island. In the context of the Depression, a new strategy was needed.

According to this circulated synopsis of the TTDA's mandate, its mem- bers were confident that tourism would bring them "an annual Island income greater than any to be derived from [their other] commercial pos- sibilities." Tourism, the TTDA suggested, was a welcome panacea for all that ailed the island. It would, TTDA members hoped, "create a permanent industry, for which our Island is peculiarly fitted, and which cannot be taken away from us." It would also help islanders to "secure new and better roads, to improve, extend and beautify our cities, to conserve and protect our natural assets, to provide modern recreational facilities, to enrich the cultural opportunities of our Island public, and to extend our municipal services."

Tourism's possibilities were seemingly endless. Tourism would not only "eventually reduce Island taxation below its present incidence" but also "increase business in all the wholesale and retail trades, and professions, create a new demand in the building and allied trades, benefit the farmer and all producers of raw materials, raise the value of real estate, increase permanent employment, make better wages possible, and build up our residential population."[28] While such pronouncements resembled an optimism epitomized by earlier promoters such as Herbert Cuthbert, there were important differences here as well. Tourism emerged here not as a strategy to draw industrial development to the island but as an alternative to such industries. Faced with decreasing success in attracting new industries and wary of Vancouver's penchant for poaching industries that did develop, Leeming and his supporters sought a more permanent basis for sustained economic development that would be sought on their own terms. "We believe the time has come for the people of Vancouver Island to help themselves out of the depression," the TTDA explained. Convinced that "the tourist dollar is the surest, safest and quickest way out, and that by real teamwork we can achieve a newer, greater and more permanent prosperity," the TTDA adhered closely to the tenets of liberalism and called upon the island's citizenry to join together in a communal effort to better the island's welfare. In doing so, it explained, individuals would also be serving their own self-interests.[29]

The campaign to garner support for the new association included, fittingly, an automobile tour. In February 1935, supporters of the TTDA travelled along the Island Highway to explain the association's aims to potential supporters in up-island communities. Press reports suggest that their message was heartily supported and that the association was endorsed by all of the communities visited. Support was forthcoming primarily because the smaller island communities saw this as the most acceptable plan for economic development. It was "a plan for the co-ordinated effort of the smaller communities in co-operation with Victoria to achieve benefits FOR THE ISLAND AS A WHOLE."

What resistance TTDA organizers confronted was based not on opposition to the plan itself but on the unease felt by the smaller island communities in dealings with the provincial capital. Doubts were expressed by some "that Victoria would initiate anything for the general good of the whole Island," while others reminded TTDA organizers that they did not wish to relive earlier experiences in which Victoria had "sought to dominate the Island, and had adopted a 'high-hat' attitude." Such concerns were assuaged by TTDA organizers, who assured potential supporters that "VICTORIA WAS EARNEST IN ITS EFFORTS TODAY to study and assist in the broader policy of Island development."[30]

TTDA organizers explained the workings of the organization to potential member communities. Each community would be responsible for raising its own funds for the entertainment of tourists. There would be, however, a coordinated effort to ensure that entertainment events did not overlap and compete directly with one another. Island communities would also co-operate to speak in a united voice in favour of tourist trade infrastructure such as highway improvements.[31] By April 1935, Mayor Leeming could proudly proclaim that the TTDA had "succeeded in arousing the enthusiasm of every community on the Island for Island-wide co-operation on Tourist Development." With twenty-two TTDA branches either formed or under way, the mayor announced, the stage was set for an "All-Island Rally" at Nanaimo at the end of April.[32] The "On to Nanaimo" rally, as it was labelled, garnered significant support and coverage from the media.

This new route to prosperity received particularly warm support from B.A. McKelvie, the managing editor of the Victoria *Daily Colonist*, who had briefly served as director of the provincial Bureau of Information from 1929 to 1930. McKelvie took up the TTDA's cause in his newspaper, and his support for a "New Deal" came entwined with a pronounced sense of regional alienation.[33] Amid the now heightened calls for a "new and more generous interpretation of the relations between the Province and the Dominion" – a veiled reference to British Columbia's demand for better terms in Confederation – McKelvie explained that there was also a necessity for a "readjustment of treatment between the Province of British Columbia and Vancouver Island." Annexation of the island in 1866 to the Crown Colony of British Columbia, McKelvie explained, was the cause of many of the island's present problems. Prior to annexation, he argued, "the Island was the most popular colony and was the commercial and industrial centre of the North Pacific." Union with British Columbia, he railed, had been "disastrous." "The Island's interests were sacrificed to those of the Mainland," he explained, "and with the passing years this system of preference has been developed to an alarming extent." McKelvie went on to detail the ways in which the mainland had won out in terms of revenue and expenditure, highway construction, and public works. As a keen supporter of the tourist trade, McKelvie noted the particular importance of highway development in the island's future. After all, "the future of Vancouver Island," he explained, "is largely associated with the tourist industry." Vancouver Island required "a better measure of consideration in the future than in the past," or "progress will be slower than before."[34]

McKelvie suggested that at stake was "an opportunity existing today for A REAL CONSOLIDATION OF ISLAND THOUGHT AND ACTION that is of the utmost importance, not only to Victoria, but to every part of the Island." "Such an opportunity," he suggested, "has not yet been offered since Colonial days." Victoria, he implored, must recognize that its own welfare was directly linked to that of other Island communities. In exhorting potential supporters to gather for the mass meeting in Nanaimo, McKelvie sounded a clarion call for a new era of tourist promotion: "SUCH A GATHERING WOULD CRYSTALLIZE ENTHUSIASM, LAY SOLIDLY THE FOUNDATIONS FOR A 'NEW DEAL' FOR VANCOUVER ISLAND, AND ESTABLISH A NEW ERA OF INTRA-ISLAND CO-OPERATION."[35]

David Leeming's death in 1939 appears to have cut short the life of the TTDA. The rhetoric surrounding its formation, however, is revealing. No longer considered simply a strategy employed to lure settlers and investment, by the mid-1930s tourism was clearly gaining acceptance as a viable economic industry in its own right. Soon an increasing number of civic leaders and businesspeople would lend their voices to the chorus calling for cooperation and sustained government involvement in tourism. Moreover, toward the end of the decade, these men would ascribe to tourism the ability to save the province and Western society from not only its economic predicament but its cultural malaise as well.

The Promise of Tourism and the Call
for Government Intervention

Statistical evidence of tourism's contribution to the Canadian economy became increasingly prominent during the Depression. Since 1928 the Dominion Bureau of Statistics (DBS) had undertaken a concerted effort to document the scope of Canada's tourist trade by tracking the number of automobiles entering Canada from the United States. As Alisa Apostle explains, this endeavour marked "the first attempts at state rationalisation of the industry" and was part of a broader international campaign to record and quantify tourism's economic importance.[36] Not surprisingly, tourism promoters in British Columbia seized upon the planning and publicity possibilities that this new information provided. In its *100 for 1* pamphlet, for example, the GVPB quoted DBS reports at length to demonstrate both the diversity of tourist expenditures and their importance for Canada's international balance of payments. According to dominion statistician R.H. Coats, "retail business, gas and oil stations, garages, hotels, restaurants, amusement places, sporting goods and clothing shops," along with other businesses, all benefited from tourism. DBS statistics also indicated that the tourist trade enjoyed a favourable international balance of payments during 1930 of over $165 million, second only to wheat.[37]

The provincial government was not blind to the prospects of tourism.

In November 1931, in fact, Premier S.F. Tolmie positively salivated at the thought of a road connecting Washington with Alaska. "If there is one line of activity which promises results with the least possible outlay to British Columbia," he surmised, "it is the tourist traffic." Tolmie looked forward with great anticipation to the day when the American press would report one morning that such a road had been completed.[38] Just who would pay for such a road, of course, was an entirely different matter.

As Tolmie contemplated such developments, support for tourism initiatives increased throughout the business community. An April 1932 public pronouncement by the Canadian Bank of Commerce championed the cause of the tourist industry. "Tourism is of ancient origin," it reminded Canadians, "but it has recently developed such great growth and financial importance as to command the active encouragement of the governments of at least fifty countries." The bank pronounced tourism Canada's most important contributor on the credit side of its balance of payments and warned of an impending reduction of ocean travel rates to Europe – a development that could threaten Canada's tourist industry "at a time when she is in the greatest need of it." The answer to this impending dilemma was government intervention. While "government economy" was a necessary and righteous concern amid the Depression, the bank strongly encouraged the dominion and provincial governments to take a "more progressive stand" in order to maintain Canada's share of the international tourist trade.[39]

In the media, as well, support was growing for the tourist industry. In May 1932, the Point Grey *News* endorsed a call for hotel operators to take greater notice of the tourist industry. The *News* suggested that, while it was easy to see the impact of other industries, such as lumber, mining, and fishing, it was difficult to distinguish tourists from other pedestrians as they walked along city streets. The key to obtaining the province's share of this boundless industry, it agreed, was advertising. British Columbians must sell their scenery in the same way that they had been selling other commodities.[40]

In September 1933, the Victoria *Daily Times* lamented the fact that too many British Columbians viewed the tourist business as "something of a fad and not worthy of serious consideration." Tourism, it argued, was Canada's "largest dividend payer" and, in fact, could be increased significantly if the various tourism promotion bodies across the country were more closely coordinated. The *Daily Times* encouraged the dominion government to take the lead in two ways. First, it wanted the dominion government to organize a general tourism promotion campaign to advertise Canada in the United States – "where seventy-five per cent of our guests come from each year." Second, it suggested the federal government find ways to induce the many communities, provinces, and organizations to cooperate and to coordinate their promotional efforts.[41]

The hopes and frustrations of British Columbia's more peripheral communities were also voiced in the media. In April 1932, the Ashcroft *Journal* drew upon and endorsed the Bank of Commerce's commercial letter and encouraged governments to become more involved in the tourist trade.[42] The following month the Prince Rupert *News* found fault with industry figures that stressed the wide distribution of the tourist dollar. These figures, it argued, were tied inextricably to the circulation of automobile traffic throughout the province – traffic that could not reach Prince Rupert, it lamented, because of the provincial government's unwillingness to sponsor a highway connecting this coastal community with the province's interior.[43]

The early 1930s thus saw a dramatic interest in increasing the role of governments in developing the tourist trade.[44] The spring of 1934 witnessed the inauguration of the Senate's Special Committee on Tourist Traffic – a committee that would give birth to the Canadian Travel Bureau (CTB).[45] Before the creation of the CTB, the federal government's involvement in tourism was, like its provincial counterpart in British Columbia, sporadic and uncoordinated. Before 1935, in fact, responsibility for the Canadian state's tourism initiatives had been divided between two government departments. Since 1911 the federal government's Parks Branch, housed in the Department of the Interior, had been charged with the responsibility of luring tourists to Canada's national parks. In 1926 a publicity branch was created in the Department of Trade and Commerce with the aim of luring investment into Canada.[46] The drive for the CTB was initiated by Senator W.H. Dennis of Halifax, who served as chairman of the Senate committee. In his final report, Dennis outlined the committee's recommendations. The tourist trade, he explained, was a matter of national concern. Alarmed by the dramatic drop in tourist expenditures in Canada (from over $300 million in 1929 to less than $118 million in 1933), the committee recommended the creation of a federal government travel bureau to coordinate the country's promotional campaigns.[47]

The CTB was established under the direction of R.J. Manion, minister of railways and canals, and was headed by Leo Dolan, a former newspaper reporter and journalist from New Brunswick, who had served as the director of the New Brunswick Bureau of Information and Publicity since 1931. Once Dolan was appointed CTB director on 24 July 1934, the organization wasted little time taking up an active role in tourism promotion: it began functioning in the first week of August and launched its first advertising campaign a month later. The CTB's mandate was "to co-ordinate and co-operate with existing tourist and travel organizations." Its advertising campaigns were thus general in scope, leaving to the individual provinces "the particular work of making better known the peculiar attractions in the respective provinces."[48] Dolan also maintained that the CTB's task was

one of attracting tourists to Canada. It was left to provincial and municipal organizations to provide accommodation and hospitality.[49] The creation
of the CTB, Alisa Apostle explains, marked not only the "establishment of
a centralised federal travel bureau at Ottawa" but also "the beginning of
discursive relationships among Canada as a nation, the federal government and tourism."[50]

The CTB's understanding of its contribution to the organic community of Canada echoed the optimism of media pronouncements in British
Columbia. According to Dolan, the "new dollar of wealth" brought in by
American tourists was widely distributed: "His dollar not only benefits
the merchant and the industrialist but also the agriculturalist." In fact,
Dolan supported the conclusion of one Ontario newspaper editor, who
claimed that selling a twenty cent ham sandwich to a visitor brought
more money into the Canadian economy than an entire pound of bacon
shipped to Britain.[51]

British Columbia, of course, was not without influence in the federal
government's tourist trade efforts. In November 1934, British Columbia's
tourism promoters flexed enough muscle to convince Dolan to visit western Canada. GVPB commissioner Charles Webster invited Dolan to attend
the GVPB's annual meeting – a meeting that would consist of almost
1,000 people and include representatives from Vancouver Island. Webster
and George Warren were, Dolan explained to his minister, R.J. Manion,
"perhaps the most enthusiastic in urging me to tour the west," and the
two had had, until the recent conference, "a feeling that we were not giving British Columbia much recognition in our plans." Dolan ascribed these
concerns to "merely one of those sectional suspicions which arise from
time to time, throughout Canada," and cheerfully reported to the minister that Webster and Warren had left a recent conference "perhaps the
two most enthusiastic delegates." To "capitalize [on] that enthusiasm and
to keep them strongly behind our plans," Dolan suggested, a trip out west
was advisable.[52]

One of British Columbia's most vociferous supporters of government
intervention in the tourist trade was R.J. Cromie, an ardent Liberal who
welcomed the opportunity to speak his mind publicly, even at the expense
of incumbent Liberals in Victoria and Ottawa.[53] Cromie took time out
from his duties as owner and publisher of the Vancouver *Sun* to telegram
Dolan in December 1935 with his suggestion that the CTB chief convince
the premiers to urge the dominion government to spend at least $1 mil-
lion and preferably $2 million on tourism that year. Cromie pointed to
California as a state with half of Canada's population that was spending
$3 million to attract tourists, and he concluded his message to Dolan with
an appeal to eastern Canadian businesspeople: "Eastern Canadians No
Longer Have [the] Railroading Romancing and Financing of a Growing

West to Make Money out of So [the] Only Alternative Is Tourists."[54] Dolan responded enthusiastically to Cromie's suggestion, forwarding it both to premiers attending a nearby conference and to his new minister, C.D. Howe. Cromie, Dolan informed Howe, "has been one of the most aggressive supporters of the tourist industry, and the Canadian Travel Bureau, in the entire country."[55]

Many influential citizens and groups in British Columbia were thus lending their voices to the increasingly loud calls for government intervention in the tourist trade. Unresolved, however, was the question of how to finance this more coordinated and more forceful approach to tourism promotion in British Columbia. For even after Duff Pattullo's Liberals replaced Tolmie's Conservatives in 1933, advances toward the provincial government continued to meet with little tangible success. Pattullo was elected on a reform platform that promised to pull British Columbia out of the Depression through a public works program, one that required the financial support of the federal government. Indeed, much of the premier's energies were devoted to his battles with Ottawa and his attempts to renegotiate British Columbia's place in Confederation.[56] As Cromie's efforts in his capacity as publisher of the Vancouver *Sun* reveal, even personal appeals could not spark an enthusiasm for tourism in the breast of Premier Pattullo.

In February 1935, Cromie wrote directly to Pattullo to make his case. He advocated a tourist drive similar to one taking place in Quebec. Such an effort, he suggested, was a "sure way to bring several millions of new money into the Province this Summer."[57] Cromie's personal letter to the premier was reinforced by a heavy-handed editorial in the Vancouver *Sun*. Stung by Cromie's public criticism of the government on this issue, Pattullo agreed that encouraging tourism was an admirable goal but cautioned that a large expenditure of money would not guarantee immediate results. The poor condition of the province's roads, he maintained, greatly limited the effectiveness of such an effort. Besides, he reminded Cromie, the province's financial situation made such a suggestion impossible. Pattullo's lukewarm response to Cromie's suggestion was also coloured by his focus on dominion-provincial relations, and Pattullo took this opportunity to chastise Cromie for placing the province's welfare at risk by publicly "sniping away at small stuff at a time when you should be rendering every possible assistance and sympathy." Cromie's tourism plan was, for Pattullo, little more than a distraction. "It would have been easy to go off on a tangent and accomplish nothing except a little notoriety," he argued. "It is much more difficult to have to sit tight under conditions which preclude making public all that takes place."[58]

Restless for action on his proposal, Cromie berated the premier for his "B.N.A. obsession," suggesting that Pattullo's approach was too "vague" and "distant" to produce results. Better, Cromie argued, to direct one's energy to something tangible, such as tourism. Road conditions were a problem, Cromie conceded, but they were less of a problem in the Lower Mainland and on Vancouver Island than throughout the rest of the province. Like a military general caught behind enemy lines, he suggested, the premier should focus upon saving the largest battalions rather than losing the entire army. "Government Ministers and employees are like General Headquarters Staff in war; they are back behind," he argued. "Businessmen," however, "are out in the front lines, and the business stores and hotels and garages throughout this province must have some more revenue." The tourist business, he glibly informed the premier, was "a setup." He suggested investing at least $100,000 in tourism promotion "because it is the one sure thing that we can get a return on this year." A tourism campaign would "carry itself," Cromie argued, if only the premier would "give it the push and get the people throughout the Province rallying behind you on it." A large-scale tourism campaign, Cromie argued, was "urgent and immediate and profitable, both in money and in public psychology."[59] Pattullo wouldn't bite. Focused as he was on dominion-provincial relations and what he saw as the "biggest fight since Confederation," he refused to turn his attention to "lesser issues" such as tourism. What was needed, he maintained, was a significant "realignment" of dominion-provincial powers; "anything else is just playing with the issue."[60]

This pointed exchange between the premier and the publisher of the *Sun* was but a private dress rehearsal for a very public fight that Pattullo would find himself embroiled in just a few weeks later. On 6 March 1935, a delegation of twenty business leaders from Vancouver and Victoria, including Cromie himself, descended on the provincial legislature to demand that the Liberal government include a $50,000 grant for tourism promotion in the upcoming budget. Their arguments were familiar ones. David Leeming, a key spokesperson for the Victoria contingent, emphasized the important role that tourist expenditures played in the provincial economy and reported that, having reached a high of $29 million in 1929, tourist expenditures in the province had dropped to $14 million in 1934. Vancouver Board of Trade president T.S. Dixon drew the government's attention to the increased competition that the province faced from tourism promoters in the United States. Such competition, he explained, had increased markedly in the past decade. In 1934, he reported, 21,000 automobiles from California entered Washington's Rainier Park, but only 4,000 entered British Columbia. Dixon was adamant that a sustained advertising drive by the provincial government would convince these tourists to travel farther north – and in doing so fill the government's coffers. The tourists who did enter the province, Dixon reminded the government, were responsible for roughly 13 percent of the revenue that it earned through gasoline taxes. Moreover, the delegation pointed to the promotional activities already undertaken by other governments. The province of Quebec, the delegation explained, had spent $200,000 on tourist advertising in 1934, while the BC government had seen fit to offer just $2,000 in grants to civic publicity bureaus in Victoria and Vancouver. Liberal MLA S.S. McKeen endorsed the delegation's proposals and reminded the government that businesses in Victoria and Vancouver were responsible for 75 percent of the province's tax revenue. The delegation, T.S. Dixon argued, simply wanted a say in how these tax dollars were being spent.[61]

Pattullo rejected the proposal. The delegation's message, however, was publicly endorsed by at least five Liberal members of the legislature.[62] Indeed, many legislators expressed their concern about returning to their constituencies in light of the defeat of this popular proposal. Tourism promotion, they explained, was a pursuit that many people connected with road development – an extremely popular and volatile issue throughout the province.[63] Pattullo initially explained that, while the entire legislature was sympathetic to the delegation's plan, the Bureau of Information's publicity grant had already been doubled from $15,000 to $30,000 in the budget. Two days later he took a harder line, explaining that the budget had already been finalized and that British Columbians from outlying areas were unlikely to look kindly upon a government that acceded to a last-minute funding request from the business leaders of the province's two largest cities.[64]

Reaction in the media to Pattullo's position was swift and pointed. A Vancouver *News Herald* editorial blasted the premier for turning down the proposal and berated his government for decreasing past advertising expenditures. "Criminal folly is not too strong a term to use," the *News Herald* explained, "in designating the past policy of government which has led to the gradual curtailment of grants for tourist advertising purposes." A $50,000 grant, the editorial maintained, was a small expenditure that would have produced both a substantial financial return in the form of tourist expenditures and a decrease in unemployment.[65] Cromie's Vancouver *Sun* similarly attacked the premier and charged that Pattullo was missing an opportunity to allow British Columbians to help themselves out of the Depression with a strategy that did not require help from Ottawa.[66]

On 12 March 1935, an entire page of the *Sun* was dedicated to the reprinting of letters supporting the newspaper's editorial stance endorsing the delegation's proposal. These letters emphasized the extent to which British Columbia's more isolated communities connected the issue of road building with tourism advertising as letter after letter spelled out their frustration with the uneven development of tourism in the province. The Vernon Board of Trade, for example, endorsed the delegation's proposal but lamented that tourism advertising would be meaningless unless tourists could gain easy access to the Okanagan: "To spend large sums of money on advertising our undeniable attractions with our roads in their present deplorable condition is analogous to a tradesman advertising his wares and then pulling down the blinds." The Kelowna Board of Trade offered a similar observation, while letters supporting the delegation's initiative were sent by boards of trade and local newspapers in Delta, Powell River, Penticton, Revelstoke, Nelson, Cowichan, Mission City, and Nanaimo. The *Sun* also delighted in reprinting letters from twelve MLAs, each of whom went on record acknowledging the economic importance of tourism.[67]

A week after the delegation first presented its proposal, the Vancouver *Sun* reported that MLAs were being inundated with requests from retail merchants to save the proposal and "had also been hearing by letters, and in vigorous terms, from hotel men, garage and service station proprietors, even beauty parlor operators, demanding reconsideration of what all consider a moderate request."[68] Behind the scenes, Liberal caucus members continued a vain attempt to get the government to reconsider the proposal.[69] As the summer tourist season came to a close in August, the *Sun* bitterly chastised the premier for his intransigence. The business community in Vancouver and throughout the province, an editorial lamented, had missed out on a golden opportunity: "Our own Premier Pattullo must feel proud to have turned down a nice, fat slice of this tourist business by refusing to join businessmen with fifty or even one hundred thousand dollars for tourist advertising and thereby give a boost to this profitable industry."[70]

Throughout 1935 support continued to build for government to play a larger role in the tourist industry. In mid-March Dr. W.A. Carrothers, chairman of British Columbia's Economic Council, an advisory body appointed by Pattullo in 1934 to gather information on the province's economy and offer policy recommendations, added his name to the growing list of public figures who were recognizing tourism as an important economic pursuit.[71] "Every tourist meal is an export," he explained, "and every article or service we can sell to our visitors will help to overcome the unbalanced condition of British Columbia's trade." For Carrothers, tourism promotion was part of a broad strategy to help the economy that included the building up of small industries and a determined effort to purchase products manufactured in British Columbia.[72]

In July 1935, VIPB commissioner George Warren drew British Columbians' attention to the promotional efforts undertaken by governments in other jurisdictions. Switzerland, New Zealand, Mexico, and Japan had all recently embarked upon aggressive advertising campaigns. Closer to home, Quebec was now spending almost $250,000 promoting tourism, while Ontario, New Brunswick, and Nova Scotia had all established provincial tourist bureaus. In view of this increased competition, he argued,

British Columbia required a government department devoted to increasing the province's share of tourist traffic. Despite the best efforts of the VIPB and the government's Bureau of Information, he maintained, more government money was required to compete both with international tourist destinations and with other provinces in Canada.[73]

Throughout 1936 the continued economic dislocation of the Depression drove home the need, in several BC communities, for increased investment. Often the perceived prerequisite for such investment was publicity. In March 1936, for example, G.E. Curtis, secretary of the New Westminster Board of Trade, wrote to Finance Minister John Hart to point out the "urgent need of up-to-date publicity enterprise on the part of New Westminster and the Fraser Valley." Tourist enquiries were increasing, he noted, and the opportunity to advertise the region's commercial opportunities must be capitalized upon. Publicity expenses, Curtis explained, would "return real dividends by bringing in new land owners, home owners and new industry to our City and the Fraser Valley areas." In doing so, he reminded Hart, these "dividends" would benefit the province as a whole.[74]

While communities such as New Westminster advocated a traditional use of tourism publicity, others embarked upon a new direction – one more closely aligned with David Leeming's plans for Victoria. While Curtis sought exposure for New Westminster's industrial opportunities, M.C. Ironside, secretary of the Nanaimo Board of Trade, saw a very different purpose for tourism publicity. In January 1936, Ironside wrote to Premier Pattullo in favour of a Convention of Provincial Governments designed to create a policy to preserve resources serving as tourist attractions. Alive to the possibilities of tourism for his own city, Ironside petitioned Pattullo for direct government intervention to protect a number of rivers, lakes, and streams from pollution and to enhance the conservation of fish and game. Ironside also advocated "the saving of belts of timber along our highways," presumably to foster a more enjoyable vacation experience for visitors to the province.[75] Absent from Ironside's appeal was any direct connection between tourism and industrial development.

By March 1936, the provincial government had been won over, and Finance Minister John Hart announced that the government was now prepared to devote more attention than in past years to tourism advertising. To facilitate a more extensive advertising campaign, the government announced that it would be doubling the Bureau of Information's publicity expenditures from $30,000 to $60,000. The bureau's commissioner, Major J. Gordon Smith, was reportedly hard at work designing a publicity program for the coming year.[76] In November 1937, the provincial government introduced legislation creating a Bureau of Industrial and Tourist Development (BITD). The BITD absorbed the old Bureau of Information and would be housed in the newly created Department of Trade and Industry.

Its mandate was to stimulate tourist traffic and to secure information and offer advice concerning the establishment of new industries in the province.[77]

In February 1938, Deputy Minister of Trade and Industry E.G. Rowebottom announced the formation of a seven-person provincial Tourist Council to be composed of four government members and three nongovernment members – one each from Vancouver, Victoria, and the interior. The government was now willing to spend $50,000 on tourist advertising during the coming year, and Rowebottom's announcement echoed the rhetoric of the civic leaders and businesspeople who had been lobbying his government so determinedly. Tourism, he explained, "is one of our fundamental industries and the government has determined to promote it with all its energy. I look on the tourist business as an export business – an invisible export. The tourists come here and spend their money and take nothing away except delightful memories and a determination to return." Rowebottom also endorsed recent pronouncements concerning the scope of the tourist industry, saying that a conservative estimate placed tourist expenditures in British Columbia at $30 million in 1937. Anxious to increase that amount, the government now recognized the importance of coordinating the activities of tourism promotion organizations.[78]

In November 1938, legislation was introduced expanding the Tourist Council from seven to thirteen members in an effort to obtain wider representation from communities throughout the province. This amendment also changed the name of the Bureau of Industrial and Tourist Development to the British Columbia Government Travel Bureau (BCGTB), giving the tourist trade an even more prominent place within the government bureaucracy. The new bureau's budget for tourist literature and advertising was increased to $105,000, more than double the $50,000 that its predecessor had been provided with the year before.[79]

On 10 January 1939, the expanded British Columbia Tourist Council officially came into being. E.G. Rowebottom, the deputy minister of trade and industry, was appointed as the body's permanent chairperson. The organization's twelve councillors included E.H. Adams of the GVPB and George Warren of the VIPB, an indication that tourism promoters in Vancouver and Victoria would be afforded the opportunity to influence government tourism policy. They were joined by J. Gordon Smith, the commissioner of the BCGTB; several powerful government bureaucrats, including J.V. Fisher, the assistant deputy minister of finance; and representatives from a number of smaller communities, including Nelson, Kamloops, and Prince Rupert.[80]

Pattullo was not wholly opposed to government intervention in the tourist trade; however, as the events of 1935 and 1936 reveal, it is clear that his government did not take the lead in this initiative.[81] Instead, a broad consensus was formed among interests likely to reap immediate gains from an increase in tourist traffic – the business leaders and local politicians of Victoria and Vancouver, and those who anticipated an economic windfall in the future, such as the business spokespersons from outside the Lower Mainland. In their demands, they voiced a sense of entitlement to direct government expenditures as well as an optimistic idealism about the possibilities of the tourist trade. Tourism promotion was now accepted as a recognized duty of the state, but the push for tourism to be taken seriously as an industry came primarily from business leaders and civic politicians, not from the provincial government. Given its genesis, it is not surprising that the new government travel bureau focused its duties on two key initiatives that had been championed by local tourism promoters in Vancouver and Victoria for the better part of a decade: advertising and coordination.

Advertising and Coordination: The Aims of the BCGTB

By 1936, then, the provincial government had been swayed by the increasing resonance of voices throughout the province advocating an expanded role for the government in tourism promotion, and in July of that year J. Gordon Smith, director of the Provincial Bureau of Information and Publicity, outlined his suggestions for the form that such government intervention should take.[82] Smith, an experienced newspaper reporter and civil servant, focused his suggestions primarily upon the government's coordinating activities, but his tenure as director of the BCGTB also marked a more direct foray for the government into tourism promotion and publicity.

Smith was born in Edinburgh, Scotland, in 1874. He moved to Montreal while still a child, and after briefly attending McGill University he joined the Montreal *Herald,* where he worked first in the art department before joining the editorial staff. After two years in the newspaper business (in Montreal and New York City), Smith moved to Victoria. There he was eventually successful in landing a position first with the *Daily Times* and then with the *Daily Colonist.* After serving as a correspondent first for the London *Daily Mail* and then for the London *Morning Post* during the Russo-Japanese War, Smith returned to Victoria and became the *Daily Colonist's* magazine editor. In 1912 he abandoned the newspaper business in favour of a new pursuit: tourism promotion.[83] His determination to develop the province's tourist trade led him to join the provincial civil service. Smith was motivated to do so by his belief that, "as the tourist industry was valuable and benefited everyone directly or indirectly, it should be considered the duty of the Government to promote it" – just as it was the government's duty to promote other basic industries "for the common welfare." After a five-year break in which Smith served in the Great War, he returned to the government's Bureau of Information, where he served throughout the 1920s, eventually becoming the bureau's director in 1930.[84] It was during the 1930s, however, that Smith would get an opportunity to play a leading role in the development of the tourist industry.

Advertising was to become a central component of BCGTB duties, and as early as 1931 Smith made his faith in advertising known. "Advertising is a necessity," he explained. "When it is considered that one motor manufacturing firm appropriates $6,000,000 a year for advertising," and "a chewing gum manufacturer spends $3,500,000," he reasoned, "the value in results must well be proportionate to the expenditure." He also pointed to a recent publication that demonstrated a "decline in business and profits of those firms which decided to retrench advertising expenditures in the period from 1921 to 1926."[85]

From within the provincial civil service, Smith championed the role of advertising, for he saw a direct cause-and-effect relationship between advertising and increased tourism revenues. In a 1938 address to Victoria's Real Estate Board, for example, Smith offered a revised version of Herbert Cuthbert's favourite topic, the California success story. In 1921, Smith explained, a small number of Los Angeles businesspeople had put together an advertising fund totalling $46,000 with the hope of extending the state's tourist season beyond the summer months. Within a few short years, the fund had increased to over $500,000. The results were dramatic. By 1937 tourism was California's second largest industry (behind petroleum), and tourists had spent roughly $280 million there.[86] Like Cuthbert before him, Smith was determined to model his efforts on the successful accomplishments of the city of Los Angeles. But while earlier endeavours to repeat the California success story had focused primarily on tourism's role in attracting settlers and investment, Smith focused his efforts on emulating Los Angeles's ability to maximize tourist expenditures.

Cognizant of the success enjoyed by California, New Mexico, and Quebec in marketing their ethnic heritage, Smith suggested that British Columbia's "historic background and native characteristics ... be utilized more." Under the suggestive heading "Artificial Stimulation," Smith urged that local promoters be encouraged to stimulate travel through local anniversaries and other celebrations. Aware of the increasing importance of shopping to the tourist experience, tourist expenditures could also be increased through a concerted attempt by manufacturers, importers, and retailers "to display and specially price lines which U.S. tourists can purchase to better advantage than at home." Smith also drew the government's attention to the success of excursion tours in New Zealand and suggested that transportation companies should be encouraged to conduct similar all-expense tours in British Columbia. Centralization could also play an important role in these more direct promotional suggestions, and Smith proposed augmenting the lure of the province's "sporting and recreational attractions" by creating a central agency dedicated to connecting travellers with "bona fide guides and outfitters."[87] Similar themes emerged in the earliest BCGTB advertisements (see Figure 3.1). In preparing these expanded advertising campaigns, the bureau enlisted the help of two advertising firms, Stewart-McIntosh Ltd. of Vancouver, and Clarke Advertising Service of Victoria.[88]

An increased advertising budget, however, was not enough. Smith was equally determined that promotional efforts be coordinated and complement each other. Acknowledging the difficulty presented in measuring tourist behaviour and the scope of the tourist industry, Smith emphasized the need to bring about a greater coordination of activities among the various local tourist organizations.[89] British Columbia's tourism promoters, he explained, needed to eliminate both duplication of effort and competition between tourist bureaus in order to carry out the important work that needed to be done to maximize tourist expenditures in the province.

Figure 3.1   Fishing, scenery, and the "thrilling enchantment" of the province's Native totem poles – all were featured prominently in the BCGTB's 1939 advertising campaign.

Sources (left to right): Sunset 82, 4 (1939): 10; *Sunset* 82, 6 (1939): 12; *Sunset* 82, 5 (1939): 8. Courtesy of University of Washington Libraries, Special Collections Division, UW 23580z, UW 23581z, and UW 23582z.

This important work included determined efforts to preserve the local character of popular tourist destinations, to improve access to popular attractions, to develop local handicrafts, and to encourage tourists to purchase products in local stores.[90]

Smith's plan would first see the coordination of all of the province's local tourist bureaus under the supervision of a provincial minister and delineated through a Tourist Act. The minister would be aided in this and other endeavours by an unpaid advisory body (the Tourist Council). Whereas local tourist bureaus would retain a focus on their community's immediate interests, the provincial government's actions would be based upon the principle that all British Columbians should share in the benefits of tourism, and thus the government's activities would be defined and carried out broadly, on a province-wide basis. The provincial travel bureau would aid in the centralization of tourism promotion activities by acting as a "clearing house" to collect and relay enquiries to districts throughout the province. The bureau would also be responsible for an official BC tourism promotion campaign and would produce "an advertising, publicity, and promotional plan" approved by the minister and supported by a specific vote in the legislature. Another key responsibility of this provincial tourist bureau would be ensuring cooperation with both Canadian and US government travel bureaus as well as the transportation, hotel, and automobile organizations. These, then, were to be the broad characteristics of the proposed provincial body. Coordination and centralization were clearly dominant concerns for Smith and other BC tourism promoters.[91]

Smith's approach was influenced by government activities in two very different regions of North America. Not surprisingly his attention was focused directly on the experience of US states in the Pacific Northwest. The "general trend," Smith explained, was to give state bureaus the responsibility of "State advertising and publicity plans, leaving civic and regional efforts exclusively to local enterprise." To date, he reported, twelve US states had established government travel bureaus, mostly in the past two years.[92] In designing British Columbia's state-sponsored tourist bureau, however, Smith did not restrict himself solely to the experience of governments in the Pacific Northwest. Impressed by the activities of the Quebec government, he suggested the establishment of a Tourist Traffic Act aimed largely at improving organization and adding cohesion to existing tourism promotion efforts. The Quebec government, like its BC counterpart, faced the daunting task of governing a large and diverse area, and a chief advantage of the "Quebec Plan" was its efficient organization of different parts of the province into regional tourist bureaus that could focus more directly on their communities' needs.[93]

If the trend of state governments in the Pacific Northwest had opened the BC government's eyes to the need for a state-sponsored tourism bureau, the Quebec government offered the promise of coherence, efficiency, and centralization that Smith desired. Moreover, the "nucleus" for such an organization already existed in British Columbia. The government's own Bureau of Information (now renamed the Bureau of Information and General Publicity) housed bureaucrats "equipped with experience and technical ability" to efficiently gather and relay the necessary information. In addition, Vancouver and Victoria both boasted established tourist bureaus, while various other cities throughout the province had Chambers of Commerce and other organizations that would provide valuable infrastructure. The creation of a Tourist Act would not only provide a way to divide the province into a number of official districts but could also provide the authority to "induce local interests to initiate District Tourist Bureaus" – thus providing a workable network that was easily monitored. Like its federal counterpart, the CTB, British Columbia's new government travel bureau was expected to provide a coordinating framework within which local tourist bureaus would operate.

The newly formed BCGTB enjoyed reasonably cordial relations with the CTB. The two bureaus cooperated in a number of areas, especially in the coordination of advertising campaigns. Advertising schedules were exchanged to avoid duplication of effort and advice exchanged concerning advertising in the United States.[94] The CTB's most extensive campaign was focused on the United States (from which Canada regularly drew over 90 percent of its tourist revenue). This interest in the United States was shared by tourism promoters in British Columbia. But the two approaches were not entirely similar. While BC tourism promoters focused their efforts almost entirely on the Pacific Coast, the CTB advertising campaign had a very different focus. The CTB's advertising appropriations targeted just 2.6 percent of its funds for advertising in the Pacific Northwest and 9.5 percent in the "southwest" zone, which included California. A full 84.9 percent of its appropriation was targeted at the US northeast (a group likely to visit Canada but much less likely to traverse the continent to visit British Columbia).[95] In its submission to the 1934 Senate committee, the BCGTB's precursor, the Provincial Bureau of Information and Publicity, had raised this issue in an effort to limit the coordinating powers of the proposed federal bureau, noting that "the chief markets of the Maritimes and of British Columbia are some thousands of miles apart."[96]

Not surprisingly, some tensions did emerge between the two bureaus. These tensions were focused mainly on the methods and content of advertising. In November 1936, Paul B. Thompson, an advertising representative for *Sunset* magazine, demanded that the CTB pay more attention to Canada's westernmost province. Thompson informed the CTB that the Vancouver advertising firm of Stewart-McIntosh was of the opinion that "there should be more advertising space used in *Sunset* by the Canadian Travel Bureau since *Sunset's* circulation of over two hundred thousand is practically all on the Pacific Coast."[97]

Nor were CTB activities without fault in the eyes of British Columbia's tourism promoters. An April 1938 CTB advertisement, for example, caught the eye of George Warren when it appeared in both *Fortune* and *Sunset* magazines. Frustrated over the previous two years by CTB advertisements that suggested that the country stretched only "from the Atlantic to the Rockies," Warren wrote to CTB chief Leo Dolan chastising the federal bureau for the present advertisement promoting the nation's national parks. The ad announced that, "From the snow-capped Rockies to the shores of Nova Scotia, great National Parks dot Canada" (see Figure 3.2). In response, Warren offered the CTB copywriters a geography lesson. Both Glacier National Park and Mount Revelstoke National Park were west of the Rockies, he reminded them. The danger in such advertising, Warren lamented, was particularly virulent with a regional magazine such as *Sunset* that had a large circulation in California. "A Californian who is not conversant with the geography of this part of the Coast," he explained, "would conclude that there was nothing to see, nothing worth while west of the Rockies."[98] An annoyed W. Lloyd Craig, director of the province's Bureau of Industrial and Tourist Development, joined Warren in chastising Dolan for the content of the recently circulated CTB magazine ads for the national parks.[99] Dolan's response suggested that he was unconvinced by the BC tourism promoters' reasoning but willing to address their concerns for the sake of continued cooperation. The "Rockies," Dolan maintained, meant all of British Columbia for "the vast majority of people."[100]

Increased BCGTB advertising in the future could alleviate such concerns, but during its early years concerns that British Columbia was being ill served by the CTB remained. In November 1938, for example, J. Gordon Smith made a point of writing to Dolan directly to express his concerns about the conduits for CTB advertising. Smith sought more attention in the CTB's newspaper schedule for newspapers in the western United States – the lifeblood of the BC tourist trade.[101] Smith also encouraged the CTB to decentralize its promotional activities. British Columbia, Smith suggested, was hampered by the CTB's very "general" approach to advertising and suggested that the "zoning of at least part of the work" of the CTB "would be advantageous." While the CTB advertised Canada very generally, Smith sought recognition of the country's "five distinct zones" in the form of direct appropriations from the CTB to the provincial bureaus. Decentralizing the national tourist campaign, he suggested, would produce better results.[102]

Dismissed as "small stuff" by Premier Pattullo in February 1935, by 1938

Soar to New Vacation Heights

IN

CANADA'S *Great*

NATIONAL PARKS

FROM the snow-capped Rockies to the shores of Nova Scotia great National Parks dot Canada. Each offers its own special appeal — teeming waters to fish, sporty golf courses, smart resorts, swimming, riding, camping, hiking, all to your taste in settings absolutely inspirational. National Parks vacations can be fitted to any budget and there's no red tape at the border. Full information and illustrated booklets from your nearest Canadian railway or steamship office, or write:

CANADIAN TRAVEL BUREAU
OTTAWA · CANADA

Figure 3.2 The offending advertisement. BC tourism promoters chastised their federal counterparts for excluding British Columbia from this ad promoting Canada's national parks.

Source: Fortune 17, 4 (1938): 42. Reproduced with the permission of the Canadian Tourism Commission.

the tourist trade boasted its own government bureau firmly ensconced within the provincial bureaucracy. The advent of the BCGTB provided the BC tourist trade with not only a more powerful voice in national advertising campaigns but also a degree of government recognition previously unknown in the province. The BCGTB's own promotional initiatives would expand greatly in the coming years, thus augmenting the efforts of the Greater Vancouver Publicity Bureau, the Victoria and Island Publicity Bureau, and cooperative organizations such as the Evergreen Playground Association.

Panacea and Protest: Progress, Peace, and Democracy

While businesspeople and politicians were intrigued by the economic possibilities of tourism promotion, the promise of tourism in British Columbia during the late 1930s also had a cultural dimension. Several supporters of tourism promotion in British Columbia championed tourism's potential to revive human progress, restore international peace, and defend democracy. As the many public pronouncements at public meetings and newspapers suggest, support for the development of the tourist industry in British Columbia was not limited to those involved in the tourist trade itself. It was also capturing the imagination of those not directly connected to the industry and, in the case of Gerry McGeer, those who had already gained a reputation for radical and idealistic solutions to the Depression.

Nowhere was the idealism of tourism promotion given more force or colour in British Columbia in the late 1930s than in the speeches of the former Vancouver mayor. By the mid-1930s, McGeer had both gained a reputation as an ardent defender of British Columbia's interests within Confederation and, with the onset of the Depression, embarked upon a sustained campaign for monetary reform. His interest in promoting the virtues of the tourist industry, which left economic recovery very much in the hands of consumers, reflected a far less dramatic rethinking of the state's role in the economy than that proposed in his earlier speeches and published works.[103]

McGeer, like many others, sought increased government recognition for tourism, and he outlined what he considered to be the main purposes behind the tourist trade in a January 1937 memorandum to his successor as mayor, George Miller. While earlier explanations of tourism's importance often emphasized the close relationship between tourist travel, settlement, and industrial and agricultural development, McGeer's rationale was very different: he focused chiefly on tourist expenditures.[104] Yet government support for tourism promotion would not simply alleviate the current economic dislocation, McGeer argued; it would also help to put Canada back on the road to progress. Tourism, McGeer suggested, possessed "moral as well as economic virtues." To buttress his argument, he drew upon the observation of the early-nineteenth-century Whig historian T.B. Macaulay. For McGeer, Lord Macaulay had foreseen what governments were only too slow to discover: that improvements in transportation produced both material and intellectual benefits. Such improvements, as Macaulay had announced in the second volume of his *History of England*, held the possibility of removing "national and provincial antipathies and ... join[ing] together all branches of the great human family." When Gerry McGeer surveyed the Canadian landscape in 1937, he saw a good degree of evidence to support Macaulay's supposition. "Our greatest cultural joy is found in travel," he announced, "and there is every indication that during the next 100 years travel will become the common privilege of every citizen in the land."[105]

According to the former mayor, a sustained effort by governments to develop the tourist trade would allow Canadians to continue on their appointed path to progress and harmony. It was a path, according to McGeer, that had been initiated in 1534 by Canada's first tourist: Jacques Cartier. And the country's history had since unfolded "as the brilliant record of romantic and venturesome tourists."[106] Along with the economic benefits that tourism promotion offered came the promise of a return to a linear route to progress and moral development from which Canadians had been diverted in recent years.

In the minds of tourism's champions, there were, in fact, two key elements of Western civilization that required protection in order to ensure the progress that McGeer envisioned: peace and democracy. Tourism, they suggested, would play a fundamental role in protecting both elements from looming ideological threats. If the Depression arrived as something of a surprise to Canadians, the Second World War did not. It is clear from the writings and musings of the country's tourism promoters that, from the mid-1930s onward, the possibility of war was a pressing concern.

As the decade progressed, tourism promoters became increasingly occupied with the possibility of war. In fact, the martial language of war pervaded some enthusiastic endorsements of the tourist trade itself, particularly those of Toronto publisher Wilber Philpott. Each year, Philpott wrote in a 1938 editorial for his *Liberty* magazine, the invading army of tourists returned to the United States "with an increasing share of Canada's thinking and good will transplanted in its native soil." Given the rising international tensions of the late 1930s, Philpott explained, tourism had an important peacekeeping role to play. "Wars spring from hatred, and hatred springs from misunderstanding," he argued. Misunderstanding, in turn, was caused by thinking of other nations "in the abstract." The abstraction of ideologies, Philpott proposed, could be circumvented by tourism: "The peace of this continent has been attained, and will be

sustained, because the tourist invasion forbids thinking in the abstract."
When "John Smith, Chicago, thinks of Bill Jones, Calgary, as friend and
neighbor," Philpott concluded, "the term 'foreigner' is as ill-timed as illog-
ical." Tourists for Philpott were Canada's "biggest export customer[s]," but
they also served a more philanthropic function. Tourists were ambassadors
who were helping to cement "the logical alliance of the Anglo-American
democracies which girdle the globe."[107]

Closely related to the issue of peaceful international relations was a
defence of democracy. On this topic, Leo Dolan, perhaps the most influential Canadian tourism promoter in the eyes of those supporting British
Columbia's tourist trade, offered the most eloquent championing of tourism's contributions to democratic government. While McGeer had reached
back to the nineteenth-century writings of Macaulay for inspiration, Dolan,
in an address to British hotelmen in New York City, cast his line back
even further in time. He paid tribute to the "inspiration of the light of
freedom" that flowed from the Magna Carta as well as the heritage of the
Declaration of the Rights of Man and Citizen and the American Declaration of Independence. A successful effort to increase tourism, he suggested, would help to spread the virtues of Western thought and protect
the world from lesser philosophies that, he explained, were "largely responsible for international discord and discontent." The close and friendly
relations between Canada and the United States were, of course, an example to the world, and it was thus the responsibility of the citizens of North
America to keep the idea of peace alive – through tourism. "There is no
agency that has won more for the promotion and development of this
amity among peoples of the world than the travel industry," Dolan suggested. "Today we hear of this or that axis being formed," he announced,
and he suggested that the existing "travel axis" between Britain, the United
States, France, and Canada be expanded to include other nations.

To conclude this particular address, Dolan joined Philpott in turning to
metaphors of war. Dolan described previous American visitors to Canada
as a friendly invading army that brought "friendliness instead of desola-
tion, leaving a trail of wealth rather than a trail of destruction." Not content with Philpott's metaphor of the invading army, Dolan saw tourism
as the basis for an alliance. Casting aside the fourth member of his vaunted
"travel axis," he then advocated the forging of "a new weapon for the
promotion of peace among the Anglo-Saxon democracies." Tourism would
be the catalyst to bring about "an even closer alliance" between the people of Britain, the United States, and Canada.[108]

Once a strategy for luring agriculturalists and industrialists to the Pacific
Northwest, by the late 1930s tourism was being recognized as a potent
moral force expected by some to promote a cultural recovery in the province, the nation, and perhaps the entire Western world. A similar optimism

infused tourism promoters' evaluation of the tourism industry's economic performance. The main struggle for tourism promoters throughout the decade, of course, had been for government recognition and involvement. As the decade came to a close, they could look triumphantly upon the British Columbia Government Travel Bureau and, in particular, upon its early foray into the world of tourism advertising. In 1937, the GVPB reported, Canada enjoyed a "record tourist year," and tourist expenditures exceeded 1929 levels for the first time.[109] British Columbia, GVPB secretary-manager R.A. Hutchison reported, "has more than kept pace in producing this new all-Canadian Record." In the past three years, he explained, "a steady gain of nearly 30% annually in tourist business has been maintained."[110] In 1938 Vancouver again enjoyed an increase in tourist traffic, despite a tourist season "replete with widely circulated reports of forest fires and riots, uncertain business conditions, wars and rumours of wars throughout the world."[111] An economic recession did, however, prevent tourist expenditures from reaching predicted record levels.[112] GVPB president G.H. Worthington looked forward to 1939, which would bring the royal visit of the king and queen as well as the opening of the new Hotel Vancouver and the Lions Gate Bridge – all of which were expected to have a positive impact upon tourist levels.[113]

British Columbia's tourism promoters, it must be said, appeared to be more comfortable (and perhaps more interested) in alleviating international problems and in pursuing more idealist goals such as democracy and peace than they were in addressing the social inequalities in their local communities. But if their attention often wandered from the immediate needs of local residents, it was at times refocused for them by some of British Columbia's more vociferous underprivileged residents. The extent to which tourism became embedded in the discussions and debates focusing on solutions to the Depression is indicated by the fact that some of the unemployed themselves saw tourism as a target worthy of their disdain.

Along with the direct economic impact that the Depression had on potential tourists, the economic dislocation of the 1930s had an indirect impact upon tourism promotion. In June 1938, following the sit-down strikes at Vancouver's art gallery and post office, for example, the plight of the unemployed in the Lower Mainland became an immediate concern for tourism promoters on Vancouver Island.[114] When several hundred unemployed protesters marched on Victoria, tourism promoters quickly became staunch supporters of government relief for the unemployed. Yet their calls for relief camps made reference not to the demonstrable needs of the unemployed but to the importance of removing unemployed protesters from the sight of American tourists.

Among the concerns forwarded to Premier Pattullo by the Victoria and Island Publicity Bureau was that expressed by William Clark, the manager of the Dominion Hotel in Victoria. Clark called attention not to the plight of the unemployed but to the plight of the travelling public. The presence of unemployed protesters in Victoria, Clark maintained, was "decidedly detrimental to the traveling public." A few days earlier, he reported, vehicles boarding the ferry to Vancouver Island "were hissed and booed." Such activity, Clark bemoaned, would nullify "the good work of the Publicity Bureau."[115]

The situation farther up the island was apparently worse. According to the manager of the Sunset Inn at Qualicum Beach, not a single guest had arrived at the inn during the previous week, whereas at the same time the previous year the inn had been "doing quite a good business." The intimidating sight of the unemployed protesters had turned potential guests away, and, the manager reported, "we amongst others have had to lay off employees and thus contribute to unemployment."[116] The answer, Clark explained, was for the provincial government to feed the unemployed in relief camps until relief work projects were under way.[117]

E.W. Hudson, manager of the Hotel Georgia in Vancouver, voiced considerable sympathy for his fellow hoteliers on the island. The "unemployed sitdown situation" in Vancouver had garnered a great deal of attention south of the border, and he urged the Victoria and Island Publicity Bureau to call upon the provincial government to resolve the situation. Hudson related the experience of "a prominent building contractor from Los Angeles" vacationing in Vancouver with his wife; they had intended to visit Victoria but, in light of "the unemployed situation," were now "afraid to go over" to the island and had returned south to Seattle instead. The couple had heard rumours that the ferries to Victoria were filled with the unemployed. Hudson admitted that this was only one case that probably cost the city of Victoria in the neighbourhood of fifty dollars in tourist expenditures but argued that, "if this is multiplied several hundreds of times, as doubtless it will be if this situation is not cleared up, you can readily see how much tourist revenue you and we are going to lose."[118] These concerns suggest that, despite all of the rhetoric that championed the widely distributed benefits of tourist expenditures, some British Columbians were unwilling to accept the suggestion that tourism operated in everyone's interest. Indeed, some unemployed workers in British Columbia targeted tourists in order to voice their frustrations with what they considered to be the government's misplaced priorities.

While these unemployed protesters vented their frustrations by antagonizing tourists en route to Vancouver Island, others found a less direct, more literary, medium for their anger. When a writer for the radical Victoria *Jobless Journal* sought to highlight the gap between his colleagues' daily experience and that of Premier Pattullo, the language of tourism pervaded the poem:

O, if I had a plane like Pattullo
O'r these high mountain ranges I'd fly,
And I'd fly to the City of Ottawa
Where they say all our grievances lie.
But now we're in British Columbia
And this is our domiciled home.
We've all had our fill of those train rides,
We no longer desire to roam.
So we *followed the birds to Victoria*
To try to prevail upon Duff
That it's work with a wage that we're after
So cut out this transient stuff.[119]

This writer remained unconvinced that tourism offered a promising solution to the unemployment crisis.

The Communist-organized Single Unemployed Protective Association had developed its own conceptions of proper humanitarian obligations and, of course, of the necessary plans for economic recovery. Demanding a "Genuine Works Programme" to end unemployment, for example, an editorial in the *Job-Seekers Journal* asked readers for their "moral support" to work toward a "guarantee that all Canadian youth will enjoy a future worthy of a country which has such noble traditions of Democracy and which is rich in all that should make life a thing of enduring happiness and prosperity."[120] The inaugural issue of the *Post Office Sitdowner's Gazette* also championed the strikers' activities as being "in accordance with peace and democracy."[121]

These unemployed British Columbians expressed a singular dislike of the rising popularity of tourism as an answer to the Depression and offered sarcastic versions of promotional material mimicking local tourist organizations. A mock tourist pamphlet produced by the Single Unemployed Committee, for example, wryly championed some of Vancouver's less traditional tourist attractions. "We have slums," the pamphlet announced, "which have been appraised by Slum Clearance experts, who testify that they lead even London, England, for dilapidation." Visitors should also be sure to track down a "most outstanding feature attraction ... the scenes at the Post Office and Art Gallery, where the youth and workers of this glorious civilization waste away." The pamphlet also targeted the infamous quality of the province's roads. "SEE VANCOUVER FIRST?" it offered, "Then swap your car for a Bull-Dozer and blast your way to our Natural beauties of the interior."[122]

The objections of the province's unemployed activists, not surprisingly, seem to have had little impact upon the activities and ideas of BC tourism promoters. The province's tourism promoters, along with many influential civic leaders, embraced tourism as a free-enterprise route out of the Depression. From our present vantage point, it is easy to dismiss the pronouncements of British Columbia's Depression-era tourism promoters as either hopelessly utopian schemes or shrewdly manipulative attempts to bring uneasy governments onside. Indeed, present-day readers may well be reminded of Thomas Friedman's recent formulation of "The Golden Arches Theory of Conflict Prevention," in which he suggested that nations with McDonald's restaurants (and which had embraced the free market) were less likely to wage war with one another.[123] But in trivializing these pronouncements, we risk overlooking an important point – the extent to which tourism (and now consumerism) was embraced as a pattern for future economic and cultural growth. Nor were British Columbia's tourism promoters alone in championing the cultural side effects of increased travel opportunities. In the United States, reluctant politicians were encouraged to have the government play a larger role in tourism promotion in part because travel and recreation would help the country to overcome internal dissension.[124] That the Nazis were similarly utilizing tourism as a means of strengthening national ties through their "Strength through Joy" initiative certainly calls into question any innate connection between tourist travel and peace.[125] But all of these examples, regardless of their ideological and military aims, speak to the optimistic manner in which tourism was embraced by civic leaders and governments during the 1930s.

In British Columbia, this optimism was tempered to a certain extent by the realization that much work remained to be done. British Columbia's overall travel picture for 1938 was described by GVPB secretary-manager R.A. Hutchison. British Columbia enjoyed a favourable balance of payments in tourism with the United States of over $4 million. Despite this favourable balance, however, the number of British Columbians travelling to the United States was higher per unit of population. According to Hutchison, this pattern resulted from a number of factors: the lack of highways into the interior of the province, the lack of loop highways required for round-trip sightseeing, a lack of tourist accommodations and resorts, and a lack of appreciation on the part of British Columbians for the scenic and recreational attractions of their own province.[126] The newly formed BCGTB would be expected to take the lead in ameliorating these problems. Born amid the economic dislocation of the 1930s, the BCGTB would emerge as a powerful coordinating body during the 1940s and would play a central role in consolidating the tourist trade as an industry in its own right.

Conclusion

First you must catch your American before you can sell him
anything, and that is the idea of a road to Alaska ... The Americans

are the richest people in the world. We are not jealous of that, but
if there is any legal way in which we can take some of their wealth
so long as I am premier we are going to try. We can not play golf
and drink afternoon tea, and expect these people to send us their
money by registered mail.

— Premier S.F. Tolmie, 21 June 1930[127]

As we have seen, Premier Tolmie was only partially correct in his evaluation of which activities were necessary to lure American tourists north
of the border. Americans were indeed unlikely to send their money by
registered mail; playing golf and drinking tea, however, had become increasingly prominent images in tourism promotion campaigns by the end
of the decade. Toward the end of the 1930s, individual and cooperative
campaigns by the GVPB and VIPB were supplemented by an advertising
campaign carried out by the newly formed BCGTB.

The creation of the BCGTB, with its mandate to advertise the province
and coordinate tourism promotion initiatives, was primarily the result of
public demand that reflected both a sense of entitlement and a sense of
idealism – albeit demand led by the business communities of Victoria and
Vancouver. Business leaders in those two cities gave voice to a sense of
entitlement when they urged the government to divert "their" tax dollars
to a large-scale tourism promotion campaign. A sense of regional grievance
imbued the rhetoric of David Leeming's TTDA. Of course, entitlement
could be voiced by governments as well: just as there was no shortage of
dominion-provincial tension during the Depression as the two levels of government implored one another to take responsibility for the plight of their
citizens, similar tensions emerged between the newly formed BCGTB and
its federal precursor, the CTB. And finally the more idealistic pronouncements of tourism's economic potential were matched by equally hopeful
suggestions concerning its cultural influence. Unemployed protesters challenged these pronouncements – reminding us that not all British Columbians embraced the possibilities of tourism (and consumerism) in the 1930s.
Nevertheless, this combination of entitlement and idealism had proven
successful in encouraging the provincial government to embrace tourism
as a free-enterprise solution to the Great Depression.

A 1940 BCGTB tourist brochure celebrating the opening of the Big
Bend Highway between Revelstoke and Golden allowed Premier Pattullo
to echo earlier tributes regarding the contribution of tourism and travel
to the betterment of society. Harkening back to the "earliest days of the
Fur Brigades," Pattullo paid tribute to this new section of the Trans-
Canada Highway. In completing this section, Pattullo announced, those
involved had removed "another stubborn barrier to uninterrupted travel"

and had made "another notable contribution to the cause of progress and human intercourse."[128] In the midst of the war that had broken out the year before, British Columbia's tourism promoters would pay surprisingly little adherence to this line of thought. Visions of progress and cultural exchange were pushed to the sidelines as a concern with the immediate condition of the tourist trade itself came increasingly to the fore.

4

The Second World War and the Consolidation of the British Columbia Tourist Industry, 1939-50

"Isms" are under a cloud these days, but one "ism" continues to be popular: namely, tourism.

— *Tourism: A British Columbia Industry* (BCGTB film, 1940)

Jules Hone welcomed the arrival of the Second World War with open arms. As a travel agent isolated in Montreal, where the war seemed distant and exciting, Hone hoped to capitalize upon British Columbia's more precarious position on the Pacific Coast. Unable to continue sending customers to tour Europe, Hone first approached British Columbia's premier Duff Pattullo in August 1941 with the idea of diverting his regular tourist traffic to Canada's West Coast.[1] When Japan attacked Pearl Harbor in December, however, his plans seemed to be threatened. Undaunted, Hone wrote to Pattullo's successor, John Hart, to suggest that, far from interfering with his plan, the Japanese threat to Canada's Pacific Coast actually bolstered his scheme: "Far from curtailing, or giving up Tourist propaganda, a more determined effort should be made. Blackouts and the more than remote possibility of Japanese attacks should not deter people visiting Vancouver, Victoria and other British Columbia centres. On the contrary, those remote threats should prove additional attractions, if presented as out-of-the-programme *thrills* without extra charge." In explaining how the war itself could be marketed as a tourist attraction, Hone was quick to justify the ethics of his proposal by outlining the contributions that tourism made to the war effort.

Hone suggested that his proposal merited serious consideration because of its potential contribution to national unity. In addition to providing Canadians with a "rest from war nerves and pressure fatigue," he hoped to convince both English and French speakers in eastern Canada to see the west "as a fundamental condition of enlightened citizenship, social eminence, successful enterprise, [and] nation-wide patriotism."[2] Hone thus rationalized his pursuit of profit in the midst of the war effort not only by noting its economic benefits but also by underscoring tourism's stabilizing effects upon civilian morale, individual health, and national unity.

Some observers, however, were uneasy with the role of tourism promotion during the war. Writing to the Vancouver *News Herald* in August

1943, a G. Florence complained that government tourism advertising was not simply a waste of money; it was also potentially destructive. Florence argued that advertising was both dangerous and undemocratic because it diverted money and energy away from national concerns.[3] In voicing this opinion, Florence was likely drawing on the negative attitude toward advertising that had existed throughout North America during the Depression. By encouraging unnecessary purchases and interfering with the individual's ability to make "rational" economic decisions, advertising became a scapegoat for the economic malaise of the 1930s.[4]

Hone and Florence represented opposite ends of a continuum of opinion that focused upon the tension between support for the war effort and the pursuit of profit. In many public pronouncements, the Second World War was portrayed as a fight for democracy and freedom. Personal responsibility, "economic stabilization," and "common cause" were buzzwords in federal government literature explaining the war effort to Canadians. Moreover, coupon rationing and other regulations, including wage and price ceilings, were trumpeted in government publications as "democratic" and "fair."[5] As a result, businesses, like individuals, were closely monitored by both government agencies and voluntary consumer groups to ensure that they were doing their part for the war effort.[6] Creating consumer demand was, therefore, a highly contentious pursuit in the midst of a world war. So it would seem unlikely that tourism should be much of a concern in British Columbia during the early 1940s. But it was. It was a concern for both Hone and Florence. It was a concern for the province's tourism promoters. And it was certainly a concern for the 1.7 million Americans and countless Canadians who visited British Columbia during the war (see Table 4.1).

Tourism during the Second World War has not, however, garnered much interest among Canadian historians. In many ways, this is not surprising

Table 4.1

US tourists arriving at border crossings en route to Vancouver, 1939-45 (January-October)

Year	Tourists
1939	307,417
1940	298,076
1941	272,758
1942	205,322
1943	183,599
1944	259,226
1945	369,250

Source: Vancouver Tourist Association Annual Reports, 1939-45.

since tourism promoters' experiences during the war were very different from those of their brethren in manufacturing. Tourism promoters' expertise did not result in invitations to join C.D. Howe in Ottawa alongside the "dollar-a-year" men whose feats in coordinating armament manufacturing and distribution have earned them pride of place in historians' accounts of Canada's domestic war effort. The prominent place of Howe's inner circle in our understanding of business practices on the home front during the war derives in part from the fact that Canadian historians have done little to explore the activities of businesspeople outside the resource extraction and manufacturing industries during the war – particularly those businesspeople involved in the tertiary sector of the economy. This "service" sector would grow rapidly in size and importance during the postwar era.[7] Canadian historians have generally concluded that a lack of travel and leisure opportunities during the war created the "pent-up" urge to spend and travel that ushered in the postwar boom. Tourism, they suggest, all but disappeared during the war.[8]

Much of the historical literature on the war emphasizes the role that the conflict played in retooling and expanding Canada's industrial capacity. British Columbia's experience during the war reflected these developments. Ship and aircraft construction boomed in British Columbia, and unemployment was minimal. In Victoria the war dramatically increased demand for lumber, cement, shipbuilding, and housing.[9] Yet, when the war ended, so did the cities' industrial booms. After the war, Vancouver's shipbuilding industry declined significantly, and aircraft manufacturing all but disappeared as the city returned to its traditional role as a service centre for the hinterlands of the province and pioneered a less traditional path for itself in a greatly expanded tourism industry.[10]

Moreover, tourism was also championed as an important element in postwar reconstruction. According to British Columbia's deputy minister of trade and industry, E.G. Rowebottom, tourism initiatives would likely "contribute substantially towards the solution of our Post-war Rehabilitation problems." "Experience has shown," he announced in November 1942, "that the building of roads, trails, cabins, and shelters in surroundings such as are provided by our Provincial Parks appeals immensely to precisely such men as are likely to be involved in those problems." A series of road improvement projects making the province's parks more accessible, Rowebottom explained, would provide "our demobilized men with work well calculated to readjust them easily and agreeably, while at the same time employing them profitably on improvements of a necessary and permanent nature."[11]

More surprising than the tendency of historians of the Second World War to overlook the story of tourism is the tendency among tourism scholars to give short shrift to important developments that occurred during the war.[12] The present consensus among tourism scholars locates the rapid expansion of tourism in the immediate postwar era and suggests that a long period of austerity from 1930 through 1945 created a "pent-up" urge for tourist travel that (like the demand for consumer items and procreation) burst forth after the war and resulted in something akin to an orgy of travel.[13] Even in the growing international literature focusing on tourism and leisure activities, the war often occupies only a one-dimensional and tightly scripted role as the foil to the great postwar boom in consumption and tourist travel that emerged in the 1950s and 1960s.[14] Higher incomes, increased leisure time, and improved transportation all contributed to the postwar boom in tourism. And indeed, the figures in Table 4.1 suggest that the war disrupted British Columbia's tourism industry quite significantly. Yet, while there is little doubt that the postwar era witnessed remarkable growth in tourism both in Canada and throughout the world, our present understanding of the postwar boom lends itself too much to this "spasmodic" interpretation.

In embracing this explanation, tourism scholars have followed earlier studies of the war that suggested that insufficient disposable incomes combined with government regulations to make leisure and consumption peripheral to the lives of many on the home front.[15] Adding weight to this interpretation is a body of literature that offers us a reassuring image of wartime business practices. Focusing upon the close relationship between the manufacturing sector and the federal government, much of the historical literature on the Second World War trumpets the coinciding aims of business and government.[16] Overlooked, however, are the experiences of businesses not directly involved in armament production.[17]

Detailed case studies of the wartime experience of tourist destinations such as Hawaii, Florida, Newfoundland, and seaside resorts in England confirm the war's disruptive influence on tourist travel, but they also suggest that the scale of this disruption varied substantially. Hawaii, for example, became part of the theatre of war. Florida, conversely, was isolated from the direct impacts of the war, and as a result its tourist trade was not as adversely affected.[18] Such detailed examinations of tourism during the Second World War, however, are few in number and have been overshadowed by the majority of studies, which counterpose a dearth of tourist travel during the war to the dramatic expansion of travel in the postwar era.

An investigation of tourism promotion in British Columbia during the war can provide a more complex understanding of the relationship between leisure, consumption, and the Second World War in two ways. First, focusing on the tourist industry as well as the tourists highlights the important role that tourism promoters played in promoting opportunities for tourist travel both during and after the war. Tourism promoters in British Columbia responded to the war with more reserved (but creative) advertising campaigns that responded to the changing situation on the home front. Second, documenting private enterprise and government initiatives underscores the importance of the war period for the development of an organizational and material infrastructure that contributed to a rapid expansion of tourist travel in the 1950s and 1960s.

Taken together these factors underline the need to modify our current understanding of both the experience on the Canadian home front during the war and the nature of the postwar tourist boom that followed. In British Columbia, the Second World War served as an opportunity for tourism promoters to consolidate their industry. In doing so, they were preparing to take a leading role in the province's postwar economy. Their task was an awkward one, however, as the war not only disrupted established patterns of consumption and transportation but also called the ethics of tourism promotion and advertising into question. As the first half of this chapter demonstrates, the advertising activities of British Columbia's tourism promoters during the war are best understood as comprising two different phases. In the first phase, which lasted through 1941, the province's tourism promoters endeavoured to sustain earlier levels of tourist travel to the province. A second phase, triggered by the entry of the United States into the war, was marked by a concerted attempt to inculcate in American soldiers and civilians a desire to visit British Columbia once the war was over. The second half of this chapter examines the central role that the British Columbia Government Travel Bureau (BCGTB) played during the immediate postwar years as tourism promoters scrambled to prepare for what they predicted would be a dramatic increase in tourist travel.

"Business as Usual": British Columbia Tourism Promotion, 1939-41

Housed in the provincial Department of Trade and Industry, the recently formed BCGTB responded to the war as part of a provincial government campaign to stabilize and expand British Columbia's share of Canadian and international industry. For British Columbia's two largest cities, Vancouver and Victoria, as well as several small communities throughout the province, tourism had long been instrumental in attracting first investment and population and then tourist expenditures. But these efforts had often been uncoordinated as local tourism promoters frequently worked at cross-purposes in their attempts to lure tourists to the province. During the Second World War, tourism promoters would continue to play an important role in the province's development – but in a more coordinated manner.

The chief force behind this new coordinated approach to tourism was the BCGTB. The trials and tribulations of the war would test the mettle of the bureau's staff and tourism promoters throughout the province; they would also, however, provide a series of opportunities to consolidate the BCGTB's position and to ensure that the tourist industry would gain a lasting position alongside forestry, fishing, and mining among the province's largest industries. "Despite the chaotic state of affairs in Europe," Deputy Minister of Trade and Industry E.G. Rowebottom matter-of-factly reported in 1940, "British Columbia was still able to show satisfactory progress in the fields of Trade and Industry." His confidence was bolstered by his observation that "industrial and financial interests" in eastern Canada as well as Great Britain and the United States were, to a previously unparalleled extent, viewing British Columbia "as the logical field for expansion and investment."[19]

This expansion was not serendipitous. The provincial government played an important role in securing this prosperity. When hostilities broke out, for example, British Columbia was the first province to send a representative from its Bureau of Industrial and Trade Extension to Ottawa to advance the province's economic interests and ensure its fair share of industrial opportunities.[20] Existing tensions between British Columbia and federal politicians meant that, even in a national emergency, the provincial government acted quickly to guard against the inequalities of Canadian federalism and to further the province's economic concerns.[21] Aware of the power of tourism to lure investment as well as tourist expenditures to British Columbia, the government looked upon the newly created BCGTB as one more tool with which to protect and expand the provincial economy.

Tourist travel, according to the BCGTB, was a commodity, and one of the bureau's chief tasks involved providing the documentation necessary to classify and catalogue the existing information about the province's attractions so that they could be more readily consumed by visitors.[22] Among its many duties during the war, the BCGTB focused on bringing US tourists' dollars into the province – currency crucial to the purchase of war materials from the United States.[23] The importance of US currency to the Canadian war effort and the crucial role that the tourist industry was expected to play in securing these funds were evident early in 1940, when Leo Dolan, head of the Canadian Travel Bureau, contacted the Victoria Chamber of Commerce. Dolan sought the chamber's assistance in convincing firms throughout the country to "adopt the uniform practice of allowing visitors a set rate of premium on United States currency." His suggestion was warmly received by the chamber – an organization abundantly aware of the importance of tourist dollars (and return visitors).[24] Shortly after the outbreak of the war, in fact, chamber manager and VIPB commissioner George Warren informed the Gyro Club that tourism promotion could play an important role in furthering the war effort and in supporting the British Empire. According to Warren, diverting US tourist traffic from Europe to Canada would serve the interests of Canada and the empire.[25]

In April 1940, Dolan arrived in person as part of his cross-country tour to coordinate the nation's tourism plans for the year. He attended the Victoria chamber's annual meeting in April and delivered a speech in which he confidently asserted that 1940 would prove to be "the biggest tourist year ever experienced in the history of Canada." This possibility, he claimed, was due in part to the war itself. Travel dollars that had been earmarked for Europe, the West Indies, and South America, he explained, were sure to be directed toward Canada. Moreover, these travel dollars were crucial to the war effort itself since they provided Canada with much-needed American currency. Dolan concluded his speech by reminding his audience of the importance of good public relations in the tourist industry, and he urged caution to those who might drive away American tourist dollars by criticizing American neutrality.[26]

Dolan was not alone in his belief that the war itself offered a unique opportunity for tourism promoters in British Columbia. In 1940 the Vancouver Junior Board of Trade put forward a detailed beautification plan for the city designed to take advantage of the increase in tourism that, the organization understood, would likely come at the expense of travel to Europe.[27] And, in March 1940, Sidney Smith, chairman of the Kamloops Tourist Bureau, predicted that "British Columbia is going to enjoy a tremendous increase in tourists" in the coming year. This situation arose, he suggested, as a result of "well-known conditions brought about by the war, such as the exchange situation and the fact that American tourists will not be going to many parts of the world that have enjoyed this business up until a few months ago."[28] A BCGTB advertising campaign aimed at Prairie and Ontario residents was based on a similar optimism. It aimed to sell British Columbia as "The Riviera of Canada" in an attempt to attract tourists no longer able to travel to the West Indies, South America, and other destinations along the Atlantic because of the war.[29]

Capitalizing upon this opportunity would not be easy, however. In December 1939, J. Gordon Smith announced that the BCGTB was taking steps designed to combat adverse publicity surrounding tourist experiences in Canada that was apparently being circulated by "foreign agents" determined to limit US tourist traffic in Canada. To alleviate fears that American tourists in Canada could have their vehicles impounded and that American men would be conscripted into the Canadian Armed Forces, Smith announced that the BCGTB was designing a pamphlet assuring Americans that border restrictions were minimal and reminding them that they would benefit from a favourable currency exchange rate.[30] In January 1940, Smith himself took action by attending a convention of the American Roadbuilders Association in Chicago in an attempt to use picture displays and his own powers of persuasion "to offset reported German propaganda designed to discourage travel in Canada."[31]

Another threat to effective tourism promotion was located closer to home. The BCGTB's 1940 campaign included a cooperative advertising effort with the Washington State Progress Commission and the Oregon Highway Commission that featured full-page advertisements in leading US magazines such as *Life* and *National Geographic*. These ads also stressed the minimal border restrictions and the favourable exchange rate. This campaign ran into one unanticipated snag – the greed of local merchants. The Greater Vancouver Tourist Association (GVTA), the latest incarnation of the Greater Vancouver Publicity Bureau, received complaints from American tourists who were refused the 10 percent premium on their US currency by Vancouver merchants. Convinced that the 10 percent premium was an effective drawing card, the GVTA pleaded with local merchants to "play the game and cooperate."[32]

Moreover, during the summer of 1940, a flurry of travel restrictions arose, complicating travel between Canada and the United States. Canadians were now required to obtain visas and passports before entering the United States, and, although Americans did not require such documentation to enter Canada, they were required to produce their passports when returning to the United States.[33] Fearful of facing difficulty in returning to the United States, many American tourists opted to avoid the complications involved in travelling to Canada. While the BCGTB carried out an energetic publicity campaign to allay what it considered to be misconceptions on the part of American tourists – misconceptions fostered to a certain extent, it concluded, by enemy propaganda – it could also take heart from the fact that the record-breaking number of visitors from other Canadian provinces joined with British Columbians vacationing within their own province, to "more than offset the decline in travel from the United States."[34]

Tourism promoters in Vancouver also moved quickly to combat the adverse publicity surrounding the war, and their chief weapon in this battle was advertising. "With the declaration of war," the GVTA reported in 1940, "rumors spread throughout the United States that military conscription was being enforced in Canada ... [and] that this Dominion was a virtual 'armed camp.'" Fortunately, "through the medium of press releases and advertisements in national publications by this Association and other tourist promotion bodies throughout the Dominion, this false impression was gradually overcome." Indeed, a "constant barrage of promotional material" was utilized to sell Americans on the advantages of visiting Canada. Such advertisements emphasized both the ease with which Americans could travel to Canada and the 10 percent premium on American money.[35]

Aware of the need to ease the concerns of potential American visitors, the GVTA stressed a "business as usual" theme in its advertising during the first year of the war. In 1941, however, it opted for a very different approach. Now convinced that Americans were more curious than nervous about Canada's war effort, the GVTA hoped to build upon potential American pro-Canada sympathies. The war was now "mentioned prominently in all advertising and in many cases the fact stressed that Americans should come and see for themselves how Canada was participating shoulder to shoulder with the rest of the Empire." Tourist groups across the country, the GVTA reported, "were aggressive in arranging military parades and displays" for the dual purpose of attracting both visitors to Canada and their sympathy and support for the war effort.[36] Indicative of this approach, and of the newfound recognition of the tourist trade within government bureaucracies, was the appearance of Prime Minister Mackenzie King in a 1941 appeal to US tourists (see Figure 4.1).[37] While E.G. Rowebottom lamented the general "marketing problems" caused by the war, his Department of Trade and Industry report for 1941 began on a more upbeat note. "British Columbia's remarkable advantages for tourist travel are being recognized to [an] increasing extent each year," he triumphantly announced. Rowebottom also proclaimed that, despite wartime conditions, the tourist industry could boast "healthy progress" for the year.[38] The key to this success was advertising.

For the first two years of the war, recreational travel remained, on the whole, relatively undisturbed. "Mild regulatory measures were in force," the BCGTB reported, "but fuel and tires were still freely purchasable." The bureau's publicity campaign had helped to maintain a high level of visits from the United States despite the restrictive border regulations. In the early years of the war, then, British Columbia's tourism promoters continued to pursue promotional possibilities. Late in 1939, for example, when representatives from the interior of the province sought immediate action to increase the number of tourists visiting their region, the BCGTB advocated a radio and newspaper campaign urging British Columbians to visit the interior. Such campaigns, it was hoped, would supplement the already very favourable tourism conditions brought on by the war.[39] In 1940 Sidney Smith, chairman of the Kamloops Tourist Bureau, went so far as to urge members of his bureau to campaign even harder for financial support from the business community now that the country was at war. Anxious to raise funds for promotional campaigns, Smith was worried by the intense competition that the Tourist Bureau would face from both the Red Cross and the Salvation Army.[40] The drive to maintain a high level of tourist visits to British Columbia remained the central aim of tourism promotion efforts during the first two years of the war. A different set of

Figure 4.1 "Canada speaks." Mackenzie King and his dog Pat did their part for Canada's tourism industry during the war by appealing to Americans' sense of duty and assuring them that they would face no restrictions on their freedom of movement. According to King, their tourist expenditures would "be used for the defence of the ideals of freedom and justice."

Source: Canadian Government Travel Bureau, *Canada Calls You* (Ottawa, c. 1941). Reproduced with the permission of the Canadian Tourism Commission.

initiatives during the 1942-45 period would lay the groundwork for the industry's dramatic rise in the postwar era.

"Salesmanship in Reverse": British Columbia Tourism Promotion, 1942-45

In 1942 the situation on the home front changed abruptly. When rubber and fuel rationing caused day trips to replace extended vacations, American tourists all but disappeared from inland resorts. In the spring of 1942, Canadian Travel Bureau chief Leo Dolan spelled out the meaning of rubber rationing for visiting American tourists. Regulations governing the sale of automobile tires and tubes, he explained in a 28 May 1942 press release, were essentially the same as those in the United States. "The only tires and tubes which an American motorist can purchase in Canada," he explained, "are used tires or tubes and then only when he has been in Canada for more than 1 week ... and only if a tire or tube is essential to the continued operation of the vehicle."[41] Victoria and Vancouver still benefited from their proximity to Washington, but wartime restrictions in both the United States and Canada now meant a severe drop in tourist travel.[42] By May 1942, wartime conditions had produced a noticeable slump in tourism in the southeastern portion of the province. The Associated Boards of Trade of Eastern British Columbia ascribed this slump, in part, to the combination of gas and rubber restrictions.[43] Such restrictions led to a rethinking of the BCGTB's advertising strategy.

Its advertising and publicity campaign was, from 1942 on, scaled back considerably. Demands for industrial products such as gasoline and rubber, as well as for "all forms of transportation," meant that "positively no direct appeal was made for tourist travel."[44] Instead, the bureau sought only to keep "the name of British Columbia constantly before the public." The result was a "token" advertising campaign in which the message was "Not now, but later. Buy War Bonds now, and save for that grand Post-war Vacation." This reserved appeal for tourist travel mirrored advertisements for consumer goods in both Britain and the United States.[45] According to one contemporary observer, Canadian tourism promoters' more reserved approach to advertising was not matched by their counterparts in Latin American countries, who had apparently gone "all out in their efforts to win friends and influence people to visit south of the Rio."[46]

Yet the motivations behind this more conservative policy are themselves revealing. By November 1942, some prominent tourism promoters viewed continued advertising not as a drain on the war effort but as a potential public relations disaster. Aware that many Americans were solidly in support of their government's attempts to restrict unnecessary travel in aid of the US war effort, British Columbia's assistant deputy minister of finance, J.V. Fisher, proclaimed such advertising to be out of step with public opinion. Fisher advocated a restriction on travel promotion in the United States, not as a form of patriotism, but as a business strategy. "We must retain the good-will of all Americans," he suggested, and "throw out the suggestion of good travel in the days to come." The BCGTB agreed, and the province's direct mail campaign was suspended until the end of the war. Henceforth, British Columbia's tourism promoters would focus on keeping the idea of a visit to the province in the minds of Americans, without pressuring them to travel immediately (see Figure 4.2).[47] In Ottawa, the Canadian Travel Bureau followed a similar approach. During

Figure 4.2   "Comrades in war." Indicative of BC tourism promoters' new approach to advertising in light of the US entry into the war, this ad appeared in the October 1943 issue of *Sunset* magazine. The Greater Vancouver Tourist Association followed the BCGTB's lead with its own "Salesmanship in Reverse" campaign.
Source: Sunset 91, 4 (1943): 2.

the early years of the war, the CTB embarked upon an information campaign aimed at assuaging potential American visitors' concerns about crossing the Canadian border. By 1942 the CTB faced funding cutbacks and similarly reoriented its now scaled-back advertising campaigns to emphasize postwar travel possibilities.[48] While the BCGTB and CTB adopted similar promotional strategies during the war, the former seems to have enjoyed a greater degree of latitude for its tourism work than did the latter. In 1941, as a bureau deeply ensconced within Mackenzie King's wartime government, the CTB found itself transferred, along with the Canadian Broadcasting Corporation, the National Film Board, and the Board of Public Information, to the Department of National War Services – a telling reflection of the official view that tourism promotion was far from a pressing concern.[49] The BCGTB, by contrast, remained comfortably in place in the BC Department of Trade and Industry. It is likely that, since the provincial government was not saddled with direct responsibility for coordinating the national war effort, the BCGTB was less constrained in mounting its token advertising campaigns.

Similarly, civic bureaus were also in a better position to continue their promotional activities. By 1943 the combination of wartime restrictions and the GVTA's enthusiasm for advertising had produced a policy that the association termed "Salesmanship in Reverse." Obliged to restrict spending to essential commodities and to reserve transportation space for military personnel, potential visitors were asked to buy war bonds now and "to prepare themselves for a travel spree when the war is over and the last battle is won."[50] While federal tourist traffic reports for 1942 suggested that American visits to Vancouver had decreased by 24 percent from 1941, the GVTA remained pleased with the overall tourist traffic for the year. While travel restrictions reduced the number of tourists travelling to the city from California, tourists from Washington and Oregon were still able to travel comfortably to Vancouver. The increased wartime payrolls in those two states helped to offset the decreased tourist expenditures from California.[51] Along with the increased payrolls, Washington and Oregon boasted large military camps where American infantrymen trained before serving overseas. The GVTA made sure its promotional literature reached these men so that they might spend their furloughs visiting Vancouver.[52]

In 1944 tourist travel from the United States to Vancouver rebounded considerably and increased by 44 percent over the previous year. The majority of these tourists were members of the armed forces. Although they spent less money in Vancouver than did nonmilitary visitors before the war, these visitors – the GVTA consoled itself – travelled far and wide passing on word of the city's attractions.[53] Buoyed by this development, the GVTA undertook "no direct newspaper, magazine or outdoor advertising" during the year.[54]

Some tourism promoters were unwilling to follow suit. In June 1944, for example, the Victoria Chamber of Commerce was alarmed to learn that some of Vancouver's less tourist-conscious politicians had appealed to the BCGTB to instruct potential visitors not to visit British Columbia during the war. Vancouver City Council was reacting to the city's lack of available accommodations for these visitors.[55] Aware that a similar accommodation shortage did not exist on Vancouver Island and that proprietors up-island required a continuous influx of tourists to stay afloat, the Victoria Chamber of Commerce opposed the Vancouver City Council proposal and, in fact, created a special committee to reiterate to E.C. Carson, the provincial minister of trade and industry, the dangers of such a policy.[56] Clearly some tourism promoters were anxious to return to a policy of direct promotion.

Further evidence of the returning acceptability of advertising could be found both on Vancouver Island and throughout the Pacific Northwest. In September 1944, J.V. Johnson and George Warren reported to the Victoria Chamber of Commerce on the recent meeting of the Pacific Northwest Tourist Association – a promotional organization representing tourism promoters in British Columbia, Washington, and Oregon.[57] The meeting had been focused primarily on raising a $1.6 million advertising fund to promote the Pacific Northwest. Much discussion had also been devoted to the Alaska Highway, including the resolution sent to Prime Minister King and President Roosevelt "asking for the removal of many restrictions by both the Canadian and American Governments in connection with interchange of travel, trade etc., between the two countries."[58]

By 1945 the Department of Trade and Industry could confidently announce that "the tide of industrial expansion is definitely flowing towards the West" and that, as a result, "business is moving to British Columbia." While tourism officially retained its "relatively inconspicuous place in the economic scheme," the BCGTB remained pleased with tourism development overall.[59] Even reports from the hard-to-reach interior of the province were upbeat. Interior resort owners reported that visitors were "being turned away from many resorts."[60] Moreover, in 1945 the GVTA was still practising "Salesmanship in Reverse" by discouraging nonessential travel, but it could rejoice in the knowledge that "the 'Essential Travel' was tremendous." After all, it reported, "thousands of people, largely those in uniform, took advantage of our travel service."[61] After reaching a "low point in 1943," Vancouver's tourist traffic increased steadily until, in 1945, the only "limiting factors" were accommodation and transportation.[62]

When the war did finally end, the expected influx of tourists arrived as well. Tourists were arriving in greater and greater numbers and, for 1946 at least, were relatively free-spending.[63] Soon the "token" efforts of the later war years were replaced by newspaper and magazine advertising campaigns more expensive than anything seen before. These campaigns, coupled with the industry's more coordinated approach to regulation and promotion, paved the way for the tourist invasion that followed. Indeed, in 1946, to take advantage of the immediate postwar travel boom, the GVTA resumed direct advertising for the first time since 1942.[64] Yet this "boom" was far less dramatic and sustained than many scholars have suggested. In fact, by 1947 the GVTA reported that "much of the backlog of travel which existed after the war due to the curtailment during war years has now been used up." Convinced that "travel in the ensuing years will not be so much a pent-up desire of several years to go to a certain place, but will be a matter of planning each year's vacation as it comes up," the GVTA embarked upon a large-scale promotional campaign.[65] Direct advertising's place in Vancouver's tourist industry had been restored, and, despite the restrictions placed upon promotional activities, the GVTA was pleased with the way in which tourism had remained an important contributor to the city's development during the war.

During the war, private entrepreneurs, civic tourism promoters, and government officials had consolidated tourism's position as a "senior partner" among British Columbia's major industries. This consolidation was a complicated story. It involved the dilemmas of commercial promotion during a time of official austerity – a dilemma that could be resolved partly by using advertising to bring American tourists and dollars into the country to further the war effort. The behaviour of tourism promoters in British Columbia closely resembled that of American businesspeople who, according to Roland Marchand, between 1939 and 1941, "found themselves torn between pressures to convert rapidly to all-out defense production and their eagerness to exploit improving markets for domestic goods."[66] As the rest of this chapter suggests, this consolidation also involved both a great deal of regulatory intervention on the part of the provincial government and the recognition that a significant shift in the tourist market had occurred.

A Visible Hand: Expert Advice and the Governing Authority of the BCGTB

The Second World War had brought an industrial and economic boom to Victoria, Vancouver, and US cities along the Pacific Coast, and the decades that followed the war have been acknowledged as an era of unrivalled economic prosperity throughout North America.[67] The growth in automobile ownership is particularly revealing. As late as 1941, just one in eight Canadians owned an automobile. By 1965, however, automobile registrations had quadrupled, and many families owned more than one vehicle.[68] Most important for the tourist industry in British Columbia was the fact that this prosperity was particularly evident on the Pacific Coast of the United States. By the end of 1962, California had surpassed New

York as the most populous state. Moreover, buoyed by the dramatic expansion of the aerospace industry, Californians saw their total personal income double from approximately $30 billion in 1955 to $60 billion in 1965 (for a per capita income of over $3,000). Californians were also more likely than other Americans to own a car and thus to travel.[69] Indeed, a 1954 study estimated that the populations of Washington, Oregon, and California combined to spend over $1.4 billion on recreational travel that year.[70]

Conclusions about tourism's postwar "boom" tend to focus primarily on these increased opportunities for travel. Carlos Schwantes, for instance, describes the tourism "boom" in the Pacific Northwest in terms in line with other "spasmodic" models: "When gasoline rationing ended, tourists withdrew money from their bulging savings accounts, cashed in their war bonds and stamps, and took to the road in record numbers."[71] Hal Rothman, focusing on the American west, similarly explains that, "after the war, more widespread distribution of wealth in American society gave greater numbers of people the means to travel, and previously inaccessible places were more easily reached because of new and better roads."[72] Neglected, for the most part, in scholarly examinations of tourism's postwar boom is the role of the state in managing and expanding the tourist industry.

What now seems clear is that the postwar era is most accurately divided into two periods: a short, dramatic rise in consumption through 1946, and then a longer, more stable period of growth shaped and managed by government intervention through the 1950s and 1960s. Doug Owram, for instance, has noted a brief unleashing of "pent-up" demand for consumer goods through 1946 that caused a degree of "economic instability," but he also suggests that, "by 1947 or so, the postwar rush to buy, the resultant inflation, and then the slump in demand, seemed to have been accommodated without any great difficulty."[73] Tourist travel in British Columbia certainly followed this pattern.

As the BCGTB had predicted, the end of the war brought a boom to British Columbia's tourist industry. Tourist travel in the province during 1946, for example, set a record for tourist expenditures and "imposed a heavy strain" on accommodations, particularly in Vancouver.[74] Yet this travel boom was neither unending nor uncomplicated. While an increasing number of travellers arrived in the province in 1947, the BCGTB reported that "individual expenditures were being scaled down." Moreover, the competition for US tourists and US dollars was heating up and becoming, in the words of a BCGTB annual report, "intense" and even "ruthless."[75] And there were other, less predictable problems with which to contend. Rationing remained a concern – though one that was reportedly understood and tolerated by the tourists themselves. More complicated was the securing of hard-to-obtain unrationed goods. On this matter, the BCGTB could offer individual tourist resort and camp operators only its encouragement and the suggestion that they make use of local food supplies.[76] In 1948, along with stringent new provincial government regulations concerning auto insurance for out-of-province tourists, tourism promoters in British Columbia had to contend with a major flood and a railway strike.[77]

The BCGTB's answer to the overall situation was effective advertising and sound regulation of tourist accommodation, while generally encouraging proprietors to maintain a strong work ethic. Just like the middle-class managerial intelligentsia in the federal bureaucracy that embraced the promise of rationality and lauded the power of the expert to determine government policy, British Columbia's travel bureau officials stepped forward to provide guidance and advice to tourist resort operators and local publicity bureaus in an effort to maximize the efficiency of tourism promotion campaigns.[78]

Regulation

Throughout the war, the BCGTB remained confident that, once the war was over, tourism would rebound quickly to "occupy a place of much greater significance than before." The fact that tourism had not been wiped out entirely in 1943 was, it surmised, a sign that it had, like mining or forestry, matured as "an industry as definitely and as strongly founded as any of those on which our economic structure is reared."[79] In fact, the BCGTB drew upon the increasingly prevalent rhetoric of Keynesianism to suggest that tourism "may easily be the shock-absorber to ease us over the difficult transition period from war-time to peace-time production."[80] To ensure these results, decisive action had been required on the part of the province's tourism promoters during the war itself.

If heightened border regulations and gasoline and rubber shortages meant that American tourists could not be lured over the border as in previous years, the BCGTB found another way of building the tourism industry – one that was, in its view, long overdue. During the war, the BCGTB undertook a number of organizational initiatives designed to produce a more coordinated approach to provincial tourism promotion.[81] These initiatives helped British Columbia's tourism promoters to negotiate the economic upheaval of the war itself. But more importantly they also laid the groundwork for the industry's dramatic expansion in the postwar era.

As the first element in this plan, the BCGTB had created the British Columbia Tourist Council in 1938 as an advisory body. The council consisted of both government mandarins and representatives from local tourism promotion organizations. The Tourist Council immediately pursued policies that would increase tourist travel into the interior of the province, endorsed a more systematic approach for marking historical sites, and worked toward increasing communication between local tourist bureaus.[82] Throughout the war, the Tourist Council was involved in many of the important BCGTB decisions concerning publicity and played an active part in helping to coordinate the industry as a whole.

Another key initiative arose in response to the sharp increase in the number of auto courts operating in British Columbia. In August 1938, 300 auto camps were operating in the province. By 1946 this number had more than doubled.[83] In November 1943, in response to this rapid increase, the bureau moved to create the Auto Courts and Resorts Association of British Columbia (ACRA), a representative body made up of resort owners that would provide the industry with a more united and influential voice in the province's economic affairs. According to E.G. Rowebottom, before this organization had been created, "it frequently happened that operators working in the same area and whose interests were more-or-less identical were barely on speaking terms." This new association divided the province into administrative districts for the purpose of coordinating promotional efforts and improving communication between tourist resort operators.[84] Together with the Tourist Council, the ACRA ensured improved communication between the BCGTB and private tourism promoters.

In 1945, concerned with what was bound to be intense competition for the tourist dollar after the war, the BCGTB continued its plan to further consolidate the province's tourist industry – this time by regulating tourist resorts directly through a Tourist Camp Act. The act's regulations focused upon "cleanliness, sanitation and fire hazards," and during the next three years inspectors scurried throughout the province evaluating newly opened resorts and ensuring that the quality of existing establishments had not deteriorated. By 1948 almost two-thirds of the province's 1,070 resorts had been inspected and graded.[85] CTB chief Leo Dolan praised British Columbia for its leadership in the field of tourist accommodation regulation, and by 1954 most other provinces had adopted a similar grading system.[86]

To further coordinate the activities of the province's tourism entrepreneurs, the BCGTB introduced a seasonal newsletter in December 1945 to provide a "medium for exchange of ideas" between resort operators and the government.[87] Here the BCGTB was following the lead of its federal counterpart, the CTB, which had introduced its own newsletter in 1940.[88] The BCGTB newsletter quickly became an important forum through which the bureau passed along the latest advice from tourism experts to tourism promoters and resort operators throughout the province.[89] Potential and current auto-court operators, for example, were encouraged to adopt modern conveniences such as flush toilets and to coordinate the colours of their establishments with the natural surroundings. The *Newsletter* also offered advice on how to paint guest rooms so that they would be more pleasing and "cozy."[90]

The BCGTB's push toward integrating and coordinating tourism promotion in British Columbia was an attempt to get the many different local promotional bureaus working in unison. The frequent meetings of the Tourist Council, which began in November 1939, were supplemented by the arrival of the ACRA in 1943 and the Tourist Camp Act in 1945. Together with the token publicity campaigns, these organizational and infrastructure initiatives were designed to keep the province's tourism engine idling high enough so that the province would not be left behind at the starting line when the war ended and the race for tourists began. With the war over, British Columbia's tourism promoters drew upon these wartime initiatives to develop the tourist industry through the twin strategies of regulation and advertising.

The BCGTB was clearly the leading organizational force behind the growth of the tourist industry in British Columbia. For the bureau, the "essence" of this industry remained "good roads and comfortable accommodations reasonably priced." While it could not directly control the former, it could certainly influence the latter through its regulatory powers.[91] The provincial government designed the Tourist Camp Act, for example, as an attempt to protect individual operators and to promote and protect the welfare of "the tourist industry throughout British Columbia as a whole." As such, the Tourist Camp Act was expected to deliver a great deal. The regulations were, in fact, designed "to stabilize a great factor in [the] provincial economy, preserve natural resources to the greatest common use, protect the legitimate operator, foster the industry through the establishment of basic minimum standards and protect the tourist whose comfort and satisfaction is of paramount importance to all of us." These regulations were apparently "well received by the industry as an initial step in the right direction."[92] Maintaining basic standards, it was thought, would maximize the tourist industry's positive effects upon the provincial economy.

Tourism entrepreneurs offered a similar view of their industry's ameliorative effects. P.M. Cowan and F.R. Brason, the proprietors of the 2400 Court in Vancouver, understood tourism's contributions to the provincial economy this way: "The tourist Industry buys largely the finished or processed product, which means the employment of a far greater number of persons, than is the case where the raw materials are sold and shipped out of the country. It helps the small business, allows scope for personal development with a small amount of capital, and affords employment to a large number of unskilled workmen and those partially disabled." Cowan and Brason reiterated the usual list of necessary elements – including quality roads, modern accommodation, and unique "Canadian" merchandise –

to enable this industry to continue to provide such benefits for the province. But along with advocating cooperation between communities, they supported a central role for the government in the continued growth of the tourist industry. Plans for new auto courts and vacation resorts, they argued, should be submitted for approval to the government in advance, and the grading and classifying of these establishments should be done by "men knowledgeable" of the "entire province." As part of this central role for government, they suggested that the best way for British Columbia to lead the way in the growth of the tourist industry was for the premier himself to create a new administrative position in the provincial bureaucracy: a deputy minister for the tourist industry who would focus entirely on the tourist industry itself.[93] Government regulation of the tourist trade, like the promise of more interventionist macroeconomic policies, offered the assurance of expert advice during a time when many Canadians feared a return to Depression-era conditions.

Support for increased government regulation of the tourist business was also voiced by the newly formed Interior British Columbia Resort Owners' Association. In a submission to the British Columbia Commission on Forest Resources, the association, whose members included owners of auto camps as well as fishing and hunting lodges in the province's southern central interior, advocated a number of regulations with the aim of elevating "the standard of service and accommodation of the various resorts with a view to encouraging post-war tourist business." Included among the suggestions were calls to ensure that all tourist resorts were subject to inspection and classification, the centralization of advertising signs along primary roads to "improve the scenic beauty of the country," and a call to ensure that "the extensive exploitation of resort sites by any corporation or company be viewed with concern."[94]

In the eyes of the BCGTB, regulations for tourist accommodation were not onerous; instead, they provided "healthy inducement" to improve these establishments. With the cooperation of the Department of Health, regular inspections were generally carried out within the friendly and courteous atmosphere that existed between government inspectors and tourist camp operators.[95] Sometimes, however, the interests of the inspectors and the camp operators diverged. As John Keane explains with reference to Claus Offe's wide-ranging examination of the western welfare state, government administrative initiatives aimed at regulating individual activity are faced with a daunting and contradictory task, for "they are forced to reorganize and restrict the mechanisms of capitalist accumulation in order to allow those mechanisms to spontaneously take care of themselves."[96] By regulating tourist camp operators, the BCGTB found itself facing just such a dilemma. Indeed, members of its Licensing Authority were, at times, uncomfortable enforcing the act. Staunch supporters of private enterprise, they struggled with the role that they played in limiting entrepreneurial opportunities. Their concerns were particularly heartfelt when they considered the plight of returning veterans, who, they suggested, "should be given every opportunity to establish themselves in the tourist industry." Unfortunately, however, some applications had to be declined. Members of the Licensing Authority saw their responsibilities as extending beyond individual applications and situations. Theirs was a broader responsibility defined by their understanding that British Columbia's "recreational economy rests largely upon their decisions." Sometimes, the BCGTB *Newsletter* explained, individual applications had to be turned down if it meant preserving a lake for fishing or protecting local game.[97]

Moreover, some resort operators expressed their displeasure with the licensing of resorts – not because licences were difficult to acquire but because they were too liberally awarded. In May 1949, for instance, the BCGTB reported that "several local associations have written the Bureau calling attention to what they consider the adequacy of tourist facilities in their area and requesting that further license applications be refused." To such requests, the BCGTB replied that it could not refuse these applications unless these new camps would endanger conservation and natural resources. In defending the Licensing Authority, the BCGTB pointed out the inconsistent position of the local associations: "Most of the operators who have been represented by the letters received are firm believers in the principle of free enterprise and would be among the first to protest restrictions in other fields."[98] In contrast to these local associations, the Licensing Authority remained more consistent in its views, taking the position that "free enterprise is one of the bulwarks of democracy and one of the most cherished of Canadian heritages." "To block off 50 miles of highway, say, and prohibit anyone from building an auto court on his own property," it argued, "would be a violation of private and personal rights." While the authorities "agreed in some instances to discourage further applications by pointing out existing conditions and by demonstrating the fallacy of investing without investigating public need," they were unwilling to sacrifice the greater good of the community for the immediate concerns of individual tourist resort operators.[99] Following the principles of the new liberalism, the BCGTB had emerged as a visible hand actively guiding the development of the tourist industry.

Advertising
While regulation formed one important strand of BCGTB activities, advertising was the other. By 1947 the BCGTB's newspaper and magazine campaign "was conducted on a better than pre-war basis," and its appropriation had risen to $62,000 from $40,000 the previous year. These advertising campaigns were aimed at the western states and eastern Canada in

an attempt to lengthen the tourist season.[100] By 1948, with the restrictions on freedom of movement lifted, the BCGTB felt comfortable reverting to its practice of direct mail advertising by introducing a "small specially prepared folder in full colour, extending a cordial invitation to 'Visit British Columbia.'"[101]

Advertising, however, was a tricky business in which there was much potential for wasting money. For this reason, the BCGTB recommended to tourist accommodation operators the hiring of a qualified advertising agent. Expert advice would direct one's message "to a definite type of class or prospect."[102] Advertising also had a reputation for dishonesty, and the BCGTB joined with others, including R.H. Baker, manager of the GVTA from 1945 to 1949, in stressing the importance of honest and accurate advertising.[103] Advertising, after all, was "an investment" – an effort to reap long-standing rewards.[104] Short-term gains at the price of discouraging the tourist from a return visit were harmful not just to the individual resort owner but also to the industry as a whole.

Sound advertising increased one's ability to tap into the rapidly expanding tourist market – a market that was becoming increasingly diversified, particularly in terms of class and gender. The BCGTB closely monitored American publications and US government reports in its attempt to keep on top of the latest developments in the tourist industry. This information was reprinted and passed on to the tourist operators of the province through the BCGTB *Newsletter*, inaugurated in 1945. One lesson that the bureau learned, and worked diligently to pass on to accommodation operators, was that new classes of tourists were emerging. An article in *Traveltime* magazine suggested that tourism was now the second largest industry in the United States (steel was number one) and that the war had "greatly increased the interest in travel." "Former G.I.'s, their families and friends – millions of average-income Americans – who never traveled much before," the article stated, "are now planning trips ranging from long weekends to extended vacation trips." In addition, "new union contracts calling for higher incomes and longer vacations," along with "higher incomes for wage earners everywhere," had contributed to the opening up of "a whole new segment of the travel market." Readers of the BCGTB *Newsletter* were being introduced here to a new type of tourist: the "class B travellers who must always *watch the budget.*"[105]

Because "class B" travellers had different desires and expectations than did white-collar workers, the BCGTB encouraged resort owners to pay more attention to the specific type of tourist whom they were best equipped to attract. Too many resort owners, the bureau warned, had been appealing to the wrong crowd. As the editors of the BCGTB *Newsletter* observed in January 1948, "there seemed to be an assumption that the only people who travel and take vacations are white-collar workers and the business executive type." In reality, they argued, "the aristocracy of labor has time on its hands!" The unionized labourer was now ready to be wooed by tourist advertising: "Through the year he has not lived in such expensive housing as his non-organized fellowman – on the average – he has not been called upon for the same clothing and other expenses – his children, again on the average, are off his hands at an earlier age and he therefore has more ready cash for vacation expenses than the white collar worker!" Resort owners were admonished to direct their appeals to the Boeing workers in Seattle and concentrate their advertising efforts on a particular audience – "and a little psychology" applied to travel literature might help as well.[106]

A "little psychology" could also be applied to tourist brochures to take advantage of another growing segment of the tourist market: women. When statistics appeared suggesting that women were emerging as an important factor in the tourist industry, the BCGTB gave a prominent position in its July 1948 *Newsletter* to an article from the *Travel Agent* by Albert K. Dawson. Dawson cited a survey appearing in the *Ladies Home Journal* that confirmed suspicions about who really wore the "travel-pants" in American families. The survey suggested that women made travel decisions by a two-to-one ratio over men. In fact, it claimed, 73 percent of the destinations were chosen by women, while 64 percent of the time women decided upon the mode of transportation. "Now that the postwar travel honeymoon seems to be about over," Dawson suggested, tourism promoters were anxious to discover what "the average woman wants."[107] The "average woman" here was defined as "an unmarried employed woman with a vacation of from two to four weeks and with from $100 to $400 to spend" who was "aged someplace between 25 and 45."

Acknowledging that these women travelled to have a good time, Dawson speculated as to what sort of "good time" these "average women" would seek on vacation: "Boiling it all down and cutting out the frills, a good time in her opinion means a place where there are *lots of men* – 'eligible men' – men in her own age group." Unmarried women, he concluded, only travelled to find mates. This was not a characteristic shared by men: "It's a funny thing about women, you know. They can't have a good time by themselves. With men it's different. Thousands of men go off on hunting trips, fishing trips, canoeing trips, have a perfectly wonderful time and never even see a woman – except perhaps a passing squaw – for weeks at a time. But did you ever hear of a woman going off on a vacation to a place where she knew in advance there would be no men? Well I never did either." Resorts with "tennis courts, hiking trails, a dance floor, a lake and canoes" were not enough, he continued. "Who is your customer going to play tennis with, or go hiking with – just another girl? And who will she go canoeing with in the moonlight?" To bolster his position, Dawson drew the reader's attention to a recent article in *Mayfair* magazine entitled "How to Trap a Man on Your Vacation."[108]

Armed with this information, what were tourism promoters in British Columbia and elsewhere to do? "With all this in mind," Dawson suggested, "it might be well to begin revamping your literature and your promotion plans with an eye to the feminine trade. Cut out some of those bathing beauties and put a few men on your front cover for a change." Women were, apparently, not well disposed toward tourist brochures that suggested that beautiful models would offer competition in their attempts to "trap a man." In truth, "the finest resort picture" that Dawson had ever seen was an advertisement for Bermuda that "showed one girl, just an ordinary girl, surrounded by three attractive men!" He also alluded favourably to a prewar endeavour in which "cruising steamers used to take along a bunch of extra men as 'assistant cruise directors' whose sole duty was to dance with the wallflowers."[109]

The BCGTB evidently found Dawson's pronouncements on the tourist industry so valuable that the following issue of its newsletter, in September 1948, again provided ample space for his views – this time accompanied by a response to his original article from a woman in Seattle. Miss Terry Britten agreed with much of what Dawson had suggested. Speaking for the "average woman," Britten admitted that, "if we get just rest, a change of scenery, and not even a suggestion of a romantic interest, we're disappointed." She went on to say that "this applies just as much to married women as to single. A married woman also gets a big thrill if one of the opposite sex shows a little interest." While Britten was not entirely convinced by the travel expert's claim "that women can't have a good time by themselves," she did concede that women preferred "to have a few men around to see them having a good time." She encouraged tourist associations to redesign their promotional materials to show men, "or a woman surrounded by men, on their covers."

The problem, as Britten saw it, lay in getting both men and women to visit the same resorts: "Must we then, advertise the abundance of men to the women and the abundance of women to the men?" Undaunted, the *Travel Agent* writer acknowledged the problem that this approach entailed: different messages to different clienteles and a concomitant increase in advertising costs. Dawson then suggested that, since "women are willing, as a rule, to pay more for their vacations than men," one possible solution "would be to give the gents an economic edge. In other words, charge the boys $50 for a week's board and room and charge the girls $100." In addition, since men, "as a rule, are willing to put up with less privacy than women, so one might house the men in bunk houses at a lower rate than the ladies who require single and double rooms with bath."[110] It is not clear that many tourism promoters in British Columbia adopted Dawson's suggestions wholeheartedly. What is certain is that in the immediate postwar era advertising campaigns began to offer very different views of women.

Historians investigating the impact of the Second World War on the status of women have noted the conflicting nature of public pronouncements on women's position in society. The more active and public roles that women enjoyed during the war were often acknowledged by employers, the government, and the press. Frequently, however, such acknowledgments were undermined and even trivialized by a conflicting discourse in which women were patronized and objectified sexually. The overall effect of women's wartime activity on female emancipation was thus muted, and a new, more restrictive attitude toward women's activities emerged during the 1950s in which women were very much confined to household duties and rendered subordinate to their husbands.[111]

What remains underexamined are representations of women in advertisements for consumer goods and leisure activities not associated with the household. Leisure was an increasingly important component of postwar life in North America, and, as Albert Dawson and others were now emphasizing, women played a central role in making decisions about vacations. How did British Columbia's tourism promoters address potential female consumers?

BCGTB advertisements during and after the war reflected – and even accentuated – the contradiction outlined by previous scholars studying the rhetoric surrounding women and work. Between the early 1940s and the early 1950s, a number of BCGTB ads appeared featuring women in nontraditional roles. Included were women exploring the province alone by car, hunting, and fishing (see Figures 4.3 to 4.6).[112] Some BCGTB advertisements were more ambiguous. One ad appearing in the June 1947 edition of *Sunset* magazine (see Figure 4.7) featured three young women gazing across the water at a passing boat. Entitled "Land of the Pleasure Cruises," the ad promised "sun-flecked sheltered waters," "colorful Indian villages," and the "exhilarating beauty" of the province's "rugged mountains, glaciers and evergreen forests." The role of the women, however, remains unclear. Are they simply three friends enjoying British Columbia's scenery? Perhaps they are examples of the "wallflowers" that Dawson hoped would be entertained by "assistant cruise directors." Perhaps, alternatively, they were employed here by the BCGTB to lure American men north to spend their US currency. Whatever their purpose, they were part of the growing presence of women in BCGTB ads – a presence that likely reflected both the growing awareness of women's spending power and the increasing resonance of heterosexuality in tourism promotion campaigns.

By the late 1940s and early 1950s, however, while women continued to

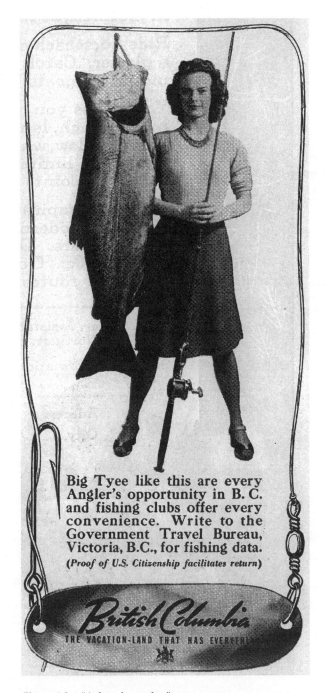

Figure 4.3 "A female angler."

Source: Sunset 86, 6 (1941): 10. Courtesy of University of Washington Libraries, Special Collections Division, UW 23583z.

Figure 4.4 "Happy moments."

Source: *Sunset* 106, 5 (1951): 21. Courtesy
of University of Washington Libraries,
Special Collections Division, UW 23588z.

Figure 4.5 "Let's go to ... British Columbia."

Source: *Sunset* 99, 6 (1947): 4. Courtesy of University of Washington Libraries, Special Collections Division, UW 23585z.

Figure 4.6 "A female hunter."

Source: *Sunset* 105, 4 (1950): 24. Courtesy of University of Washington Libraries, Special Collections Division, UW 23587z.

BRITISH COLUMBIA
Land of Pleasure Cruises

Sail the sun-flecked sheltered waters of British Columbia, past colorful Indian villages. Enjoy for yourself the exhilarating beauty of its rugged mountains, glaciers and evergreen forests. British Columbia offers relaxation in an atmosphere of Canadian hospitality, with an infinite variety of vacation opportunities. This is the vacation land of real values, where your travel dollar goes further. No passport is needed.

For information, write today
BRITISH COLUMBIA GOVERNMENT TRAVEL BUREAU
Victoria, B.C., Canada

M-8

Figure 4.7 "British Columbia: Land of pleasure cruises."
Source: *Sunset* 98, 6 (1947): 11. Courtesy of University of Washington Libraries, Special Collections Division, UW 23584z.

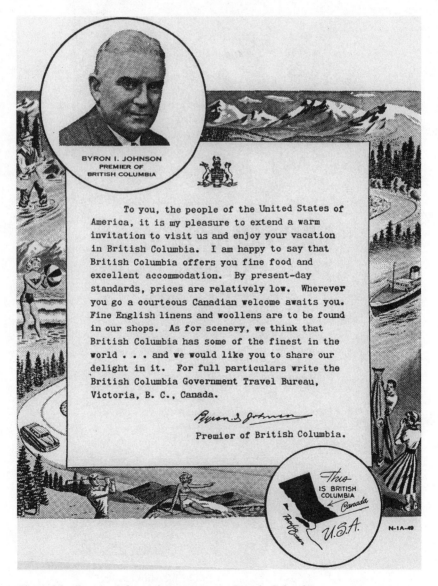

Figure 4.8 Premier Johnson's invitation to British Columbia.
Source: British Columbia Archives, Premiers' papers, Box 84, File 10.

appear as fishers in BCGTB ads, they all but disappeared as hunters and drivers as the typical advertisement emphasized more and more the familiar portraits of both the companionate wife and the family at play. After 1952 women could be seen fishing and occasionally golfing, but they were increasingly shown taking tea while the men pursued outdoor activities. Illustrative of this retrenchment is the BCGTB advertisement featuring BC premier Byron Johnson that was used to open both the 1949 and the 1950 advertising campaigns (see Figure 4.8). Placed in forty-seven newspapers covering eleven different states in the western and southwestern United States, the ad resulted in more enquiries than any other ad during the campaigns. The ad included a personal message from the premier to the people of the United States encouraging them to take advantage of the province's "fine food and excellent accommodation." Along with the standard promise of a "courteous Canadian welcome" and some of the finest scenery in the world, Johnson promised potential visitors the opportunity to purchase "fine English linens and woolens ... in our shops." Increasingly in the postwar era, the British flavour of the province was not an essence subtly present in the visitor's imagination but a set of commodities that the visitor could purchase and cart home as a souvenir.

The border surrounding Johnson's message is also revealing – literally in the case of the scantily clad female figure who inhabits it. Active amid the mountains, forests, and rivers is a man enjoying two of the province's chief recreational opportunities: golf and fishing. Always nearby, and not nearly as active, is his female companion. In one scene, she amuses herself with a beachball while he fishes. When he lands the fish, she will commemorate his accomplishment by photographing him with his catch. When he golfs, she lies mermaid-like on a rock apparently marking the trajectory of his shot.[113] If this advertisement reflected a turn away from the more emancipatory images of women employed during the 1940s, the bikini-clad woman was suggestive of a more lasting change in tourism promotion campaigns: an increasing emphasis on the possibilities of heterosexual gratification.[114]

BCGTB films also acknowledged the increasing resonance of heterosexuality in advertising.[115] *The Okanagan Valley: British Columbia's Orchard Playground*, a film released by the bureau in the late 1940s, explicitly acknowledged the emerging heterosexual "norm." Audience members were told that surfboarding behind a power boat was a popular pastime in the region, and the men in the audience were urged to "Try this with your best girl." Other episodes in the film were marked by less than tasteful double entendres. To publicize the region's orchards, the film featured a woman looking at a peach while the narrator slyly exclaimed "What a peach!" A few moments later a woman holds a watermelon in front of her chest as the narrator continues in the same vein: "More juicy watermelon."[116]

The acknowledgment of heterosexuality could also be more implicitly incorporated into promotional campaigns. In August 1950, Elsie Parker and her husband visited Vancouver as a result of her election as "Queen for a day."[117] The GVTA's role in this publicity stunt was characteristic of an increasingly favoured method of obtaining exposure. Utilizing the popularity of the Mutual radio show *Queen for a Day*, which reached ten million listeners, the GVTA arranged to host one of the winners. On the show, a winner was "elected in Hollywood and is the winner of numerous prizes among which is a trip by plane to some far off place where she is regally entertained." After her trip, the winner would regale the listening audience with details of her experiences – a public relations coup for the city visited.[118] After Parker had reported on her experiences, GVTA members were informed that the publicity stunt had been well worth the expense. Included in the Parkers' vacation experience was "a day's salmon fishing in Howe Sound where she and her escort landed seven nice salmon. These were well photographed, and the two largest fish were packed in ice and taken back to Hollywood with them by plane." The GVTA was also pleased to report that "the fish did not diminish in size when she described her Vancouver experiences" on the air.[119]

Several other local Vancouver tourism initiatives had heterosexual dimensions. A campaign led by the Vancouver Junior Chamber of Commerce in the mid-1950s featured a "Couple of the Week" who were selected and entertained by campaign organizers.[120] In the early 1960s, the GVTA began to fancy Vancouver as a honeymoon destination and sought to incorporate this theme into its promotional material – which was becoming increasingly focused on film. In August 1960, the GVTA embarked upon an attempt to create two films (a thirteen-minute trailer to be shown in cinemas before feature films, and a twenty-eight-minute "documentary type" version). The thirteen-minute version was aimed, in part, at teenagers and would focus on the experiences of a young honeymooning couple visiting Vancouver. The strategy was to highlight "the tourist attractions, perhaps some hotel accommodation, very light on narration and high on music." The twenty-eight-minute version would include this shorter film but would supplement it with "suitable industrial and civic enterprise."[121] The film was clearly designed to appeal as well to the emerging baby boom generation. D. Bennett of Parry Films, for example, stressed that "emphasis should be placed on the youth of the city."[122]

The timing of this new emphasis on heterosexuality and the female consumer deserves comment. First, there is a striking difference here between these tourism promotion initiatives and more general advertising campaigns. As Roland Marchand has documented, advertisers in the 1920s and 1930s were already convinced that women made 80 percent of consumer purchases and thus were already targeting women as an important audience.[123] British Columbia's tourism promoters, and the experts whose advice they were following, were just coming to recognize that women were wearing the "travel-pants" in the 1940s. In terms of recognizing the role of women as consumers, tourism promoters were behind the times. Second, while tourism promoters in British Columbia were behind the advertising industry when it came to recognizing the importance of the female market, they appear to have anticipated advertisers' embrace of the sexual sell. As Valerie J. Korinek demonstrates, advertisements for household products in *Chatelaine* magazine adopted the sexual sell in the early 1960s.[124] Tourism promoters in British Columbia were already being encouraged to adopt this approach in the late 1940s.

What, then, explains the timing of these two developments? Two points seem to be particularly worthy of note. First, the early embrace of the sexual sell was likely motivated by the intense increase in competition between tourist destinations following the Second World War. Increasingly popular destinations such as Hawaii had fully embraced the sexual sell in the 1930s, and British Columbia now found itself in direct competition with these campaigns.[125] Second, the delayed recognition of women as an important tourist market was likely dictated in part by the changing rationale of tourism promotion. Until the 1930s, tourism promotion in British Columbia was simply regarded as the most direct and efficient form of boosterism. It targeted agricultural and industrial investment. And, because of this, it primarily targeted men. When tourism promotion was reinvented as a method of soliciting increased aggregate consumer demand, women came to be considered a useful target market. Moreover, women's increasing visibility as consumers and consumer advocates on the home front in the 1940s likely convinced tourism experts such as Albert K. Dawson, as with the BCGTB, to sit up and take notice.[126] Finally, this new emphasis on heterosexuality likely reflected the fact that tourism promoters were paying greater attention than ever before to determine – through market research – who was most likely to be lured to British Columbia for a vacation. As the instability of the immediate postwar years was superseded by a sustained period of economic expansion, the province's tourism promoters would continue to gather information zealously profiling potential tourists – a segment of society, they were now convinced, that was larger than ever.

Conclusion

By 1949 BCGTB publications and pronouncements exuded confidence in British Columbia's tourist industry based on what was considered to be a lengthy and diversified list of factors contributing to the industry's success: the cumulative effect of continual advertising, regional and national promotion on behalf of the federal government, improvements in accommodation, the provincial highway development program, the BCGTB's own inspections carried out under the auspices of the Tourist Camp Act, the province's abundance of fish and game, and the development of local attractions by local tourism promoters.[127] In fact, in 1950 the BCGTB announced in its annual report that "the tourist movement to British Columbia has assumed such dimensions as to make it one of the first-ranking industries in the Province."[128] It was no coincidence that advertising and government regulation topped the BCGTB's list of important elements in the province's tourism success. They had been the keys to the industry's consolidation during the Second World War, and they would become the twin pillars of tourism "management" in the postwar era.

Hedley S. Hipwell, GVTA president from 1947 until 1950, summarized tourism's future potential in his 1950 annual report. Hipwell saw British Columbians as "stockholders" who, while "fully aware of the inexpendable stock which we have on hand," were nonetheless too conservative in their approach to convince others to travel to visit the province. "Profits are made on a confident approach to a market," he explained in 1950, "and with full knowledge of, and pride in, the 'product' which is being sold."[129] By ignoring the central role that the provincial government had played in coordinating the province's tourism industry, Hipwell's "stockholder" metaphor misrepresented the nature of tourism's growth in the immediate postwar era. The guiding hand of the state had played a leading role not only in advertising campaigns but in regulating the behaviour of tourist industry entrepreneurs as well.

As the following chapters demonstrate, tourism did indeed experience a postwar "boom," but the nature of this boom can be better understood by reconceptualizing how tourism was experienced and promoted during, and in the immediate aftermath of, the war. While the war effort occupied much of everyday life for Canadians, leisure pursuits did not disappear. In fact, leisure activities were often deemed essential to a strong war effort. A small but varied literature is emerging that suggests that, in the face of increasingly stringent government regulations and ever-expanding wartime demands for labour and supplies, Canadians retained a healthy interest in leisure activities. In their study of leisure activities in Alberta, for example, Donald G. Wetherell and Irene Kmet have discovered that, despite expressed concerns about the appropriateness of leisure activities during the war, festivals and agricultural fairs continued to attract large crowds. So too did professional hockey as Canadian civilians and soldiers joined with team owners to defeat campaigns to curtail or cancel professional hockey during the war. Moreover, as Jeff Keshen has recently demonstrated, professional sports magnates were not the only civilians anxious to protect their economic interests. Even in the face of strict government price and wage controls, many Canadians also retained a healthy interest in making a profit by circumventing government regulations through black market activities.[130]

Tourism offered both an opportunity for rigorous outdoor activity and a chance to escape from the strains and concerns of the war effort. While the number of tourists visiting British Columbia during the war did not approach the record years of the late 1920s, the story of tourism during the war is far more complicated than the existing "spasmodic" explanation suggests. The postwar travel boom did not mark the return of a once vanished industry. Nor did it indicate the arrival of mass tourism where no similar industry had existed before. The 1940s instead saw the consolidation of tourism as an industry in British Columbia – an industry that would, by the mid-1960s, rival forestry and mining in its importance to the provincial economy. By working to create consumer demand, British Columbia's private sector and government tourism promoters used the war as an opportunity to increase their province's share of the Confederation pie. They worked hard to maintain acceptable levels of US tourists, but they also benefited greatly from the increasing numbers of Canadians visiting their province.

By June 1944, Premier Hart looked forward with confidence to the coming years in which British Columbia would be comfortably positioned to help its residents, and especially the returning veterans, to "make their homes and rebuild their lives in the peace and security which they have won for themselves and for us all."[131] But as this chapter has demonstrated, the province's tourism promoters had not been content to leave civilians and returning veterans to "rebuild their lives" alone – they worked diligently to ensure that tourism became an increasingly central component of civilian life. It would be wrong to discount the notion that some sort of pent-up urge played a role in fostering the immediate postwar tourism boom. Before discounting that thesis entirely, one would wish to investigate more completely the motivations and decisions of the tourists themselves. However, by not factoring in the promotional activities of the province's tourism promoters, we risk overlooking an important aspect of the postwar boom: the role that promoters played in creating demand for leisure activities *before the "boom" occurred*. In doing so, we also risk ascribing an unrealistic amount of agency to consumers. Tourists, as Karen Dubinsky reminds us, "are made, not born."[132] The decision to travel during the postwar era was made within a particular context – one in which tourism promoters had spent much of the war coordinating their promotional efforts and refining their advertising campaigns. If the activities of British Columbia's tourism promoters are any indication, then the Second World War should be recorded not as a bleak period in which tourist travel vanished entirely because customers and promoters were deeply immersed in the war effort but as a time in which the shape of the tourism industry was transformed and consolidated.

Anticipating the postwar boom in April 1947, representatives from tourism promotion bodies throughout the Pacific Northwest gathered in Seattle for a Pacific Northwest Tourist Conference hosted by the University of Washington under the heading "Building a Billion-Dollar Business." Participants included BC premier John Hart and E.G. Rowebottom, the province's deputy minister of trade and industry, who was then serving as the president of the Canadian Association of Tourist and Publicity Bureaus. The two-day conference focused on tourism's potential in the region, with presentations addressing issues such as state involvement; publishing; the role of restaurants, parks, and highways in attracting tourists; accommodation management; advertising; and the relationship between tourism and public education.[133] This was a conference about *managing* the tourist industry in the Pacific Northwest in the face of increasingly intense *competition*. These two themes are the subjects of the remaining chapters.

5
Differentiation, Cultural Selection, and the Postwar Travel "Boom"

If more people spent more time in places like this we'd have a heck of a lot fewer inmates in institutions.

— An anonymous psychiatrist commenting
on Victoria's Olde England Inn, c. 1960[1]

But there isn't an Empire any more ... it's a Commonwealth. And we just stole the word evergreen from Oregon. But Totem, now that's original with us, and it's a good gimmick.

— Former GVTA vice president Harry Duker on why
Vancouver's new sports stadium should be named
Totem Stadium, 1954[2]

In the late 1940s, while the number of visitors to Canada was certainly increasing (see Table 5.1), tourist expenditures were not increasing as rapidly as before. Moreover, retail prices in the United States had peaked in August 1948 and had since dropped, while Canadian prices, conversely, continued to rise. The result was the elimination or narrowing of the "price differential" that Canadian merchants had been enjoying. Consumer items with a foreign feel to them continued to sell briskly, however. "Fine English china still leads the field in retail sales to tourists," the Canadian Government Travel Bureau[3] report on Canadian tourism for 1949 announced, "followed by English and Canadian silverware, woolens, leather goods, blankets and luggage."[4] Before the war, the tourist trade in British Columbia was measured both by expenditure and its contribution to the upbuilding of industrial development; tourism in the postwar era was increasingly identified with, and rationalized by, its own cash value. Consumer purchases were now considered the primary measure of tourist activities. Consequently, maximizing tourism's economic potential required a promotional strategy that encouraged tourists to spend money while on vacation.

Tourism's potential contribution to the province's economic growth was nicely summarized by Earle C. Westwood, British Columbia's minister of recreation and conservation, in a September 1957 speech to the GVTA entitled "B.C. as the Playground of North America in Our Future." Having surveyed the natural wonders of the province, Westwood informed his audience that "we have but scratched the surface in the utilization of these recreational resources." His emphasis then turned quickly to the economics of leisure. Westwood quoted a writer in *Business Week* who, in 1955, had emphasized the potential of "leisure-time spending" this way: "Spending money on leisure is no longer considered an economic waste. In fact, the future economy of America will be built upon leisure-time spending. There is just so much food, and clothing, and shelter, and other things needed for bare existence. There is no foreseeable limit to what we need and can use as our leisure time increases." And there could be no doubt, Westwood informed his audience, that leisure time was indeed increasing along with the population and the opportunities for mobility.[5]

The key problems facing the tourist industry, according to Westwood, were familiar ones for the province: its lack of proximity to the continent's major population centres and the intense competition that British Columbia faced from other tourist markets. Westwood's solution was to minimize the province's disadvantages and maximize its advantages: "The merchandising of the tourist industry is no different from the merchandising of any product. The sales talk must be convincing, the product must be attractively packaged, and it must live up to its advertisements."[6] Tourism promoters in British Columbia thus remained convinced that they needed to play an active role in building up a tourist industry if they were to harvest the fruits of their interwar and wartime endeavours.

Surveying Canada as a whole, CGTB chief Leo Dolan offered a similar synopsis. Canada's "rapid industrialization," he explained to a meeting of the National Retail Hardware Association in Toronto, had "contributed to a marked increase in real income and thus to higher living standards" for its population. The average Canadian now earned "more than double the income of his forbearers at the turn of the century," Dolan announced. "And he has been able to achieve all this and at the same time enjoy greater leisure. In 1900 the average manufacturing employee worked 57 hours a week. Today he works 41 hours a week, a decline of more than one quarter in working hours."[7] More leisure time meant, at

Table 5.1

US tourists arriving at border crossings en route to Vancouver, 1946-49 (January-October)

Year	Tourists
1946	518,995
1947	535,281
1948	537,348
1949	587,998

Source: Greater Vancouver Tourist Association Annual Reports.

least potentially, more tourism. More tourists visiting Canada, in turn, meant increased aggregate demand for Canadian consumer goods and services. In the postwar era, opportunities for "souvenir shopping" appeared frequently in CGTB promotional campaigns. As Alisa Apostle confirms, "shopping was held to account for anywhere between 5 to 30 percent of tourist expenditures, not including food."[8] Securing this additional consumer demand, however, was no easy task. Throughout the late 1940s and 1950s, federal tourism promoters emphasized the increasingly keen competition that Canada faced from other countries that also coveted the spending power of American consumers.[9] Competition from the United States itself proved to be an even more pressing concern for postwar tourism promotion in Canada. The spectre of US competition reached its height in 1951 when it was announced that for the first time ever more money had been spent in the United States by Canadian tourists than had been pumped into the Canadian economy by American visitors.[10] The ensuing concern about this deficit in the nation's tourism balance of payments not only spoke to the extent to which tourism expenditures were now recognized by governments as an important factor in the Canadian economy but also served to emphasize the need for a successful promotional strategy – one that would differentiate Canada from the United States and its other tourism competitors.

There were, as Dolan explained to the GVTA in 1959, sixty-one domestic campaigns in the United States that were "either state financed or have more than $100,000 annually to spend to keep United States citizens visiting their own land." There was a time, he continued, when Canada could rely upon its proximity to the US as a "tremendous asset." Now, however, "magazines and newspapers are filled with advertisements sponsored by the multi-million[-dollar] travel budgets of transportation interests encouraging people to leave California or New York in the morning and be in London or Copenhagen for dinner the same night." "In short," he lamented, "potential Customers Canada once had almost for the asking, are now going to Europe, to the Orient, to the Middle East, to Russia and far-off corners of the world with an expenditure of not much more money necessary to visit Canada."[11]

The pursuit of differentiation did not take place solely on a national level. BC tourism promoters were well aware of the intense international competition that they faced in the postwar era. Yet, as Karen Dubinsky has demonstrated, Canadian tourism promoters envisioned their task in nationalist terms – an approach that seems to have muted the BCGTB's concern with competition from other provinces.[12] British Columbia's tourism promoters remained focused primarily upon competition from outside Canada. Before the Second World War, the BCGTB reported in 1958, "there was comparatively little competition. Now seventy-two countries and forty-nine States and two Territories actively compete for our market."[13] The importance of differentiating British Columbia from other destinations was reflected in a letter written to *Holiday* magazine in December 1948 by one disgruntled visitor to Victoria. Mrs. Henry A. Berger of Chicago offered a very critical indictment of the city based on recent experiences she had shared with her daughter. Mrs. Berger reported that their trip had begun inauspiciously when they were forced to endure an overcrowded boat ride into the city. Their mood did not improve when their hotel staff visibly protested having to serve them tea after the official sitting time. The overpriced and underprepared meal left them further disgruntled. What really seemed to have floored Berger, however, was the Americanization of the city. She found Victoria inundated with "neon signs, many hamburger and milk bars, slot machines, etc." instead of the "quaint old streets" that she had expected.[14] The province's tourism promoters were alert to such disappointed visitors. Increasingly convinced that the tourism effort was an industry itself, they were also more and more conscious of the need to produce a tourism product that would not disappoint people such as Mrs. Berger. This chapter illustrates the ways in which they commodified history in their attempt to differentiate British Columbia from competing tourist destinations. This was a process, to borrow Sylvia Rodriguez's useful synopsis, in which ethnicity was "objectified, sanitized, and sold."[15]

An Industry in Itself

The shift in thinking about tourism was most noticeable in postwar Victoria. As early as 1934, David Leeming had suggested that tourism had reached an unparallelled level of importance for the city. Now others were beginning to add their support to the late mayor's vision. While George Warren retained his dominant presence in Victoria publicity circles during the postwar era and, indeed, retained his position as commissioner of the VIPB until 1960, other key tourism promoters in the city during the 1950s and 1960s appear to have been drawn primarily from businesses directly related to the tourist industry. In March 1963, for example, when the VIPB was reorganized to become the Victoria Tourist, Convention and Publicity Bureau, its new directors included Howard McKay of the Hudson's Bay Company; Conway Parrott, the general manager of Vancouver Island Coach Lines; local hotel proprietor Sam Lane; and Leslie Parkinson, the manager of the Empress Hotel.[16]

Tourism's heightened position in Victoria would not go unchallenged, however. Some members of the business community remained uncomfortable with the idea of basing the city's economic future primarily on tourism. Major H.C. Holmes, a local real estate agent, was one Chamber of Commerce member who expressed concern about the rising prominence of tourism. In 1949 he was alarmed by a suggestion from the chamber's

Tourist Trade Group that a lack of natural resources and an unfavourable location meant that large-scale industrial development was not practicable in Victoria. Holmes preferred instead to see Vancouver Island pursue an economic development strategy more along the lines of Switzerland, a country that had "practically no raw material, but yet was a large Industrial center of Europe, and imported over 90 per cent of [the] raw material used in its manufacturing plants."[17] Tourism and other industries, he suggested, could exist comfortably side by side.

The tourist industry, transformed in the Depression and consolidated in the war, was thus, by the 1950s, becoming a source of tension within Victoria's local business community. By 1954, for example, Conway Parrott, head of the chamber's Tourist Trade Group and a leading proponent of developing Victoria as a "Convention City," expressed his concerns to the chamber's board of directors about the forthcoming establishment of a pulp mill in the Victoria area. While Parrott "recognized the need for local industry," he was deeply worried about the possibility of the mill polluting the city and jeopardizing the city's tourist allure.[18] In March 1954, having been recently elected president of the Victoria and Island Publicity Bureau, Parrott continued his steadfast opposition to industrial pursuits that might endanger the tourist business, this time opposing the planned establishment of a Royal Canadian Navy torpedo range in Saanich Inlet. The range, Parrott feared, "might prove a severe deterrent to local residents and visitors alike who might frequent Saanich Inlet waters and Butchart's Gardens."[19] Not everyone agreed with Parrott. Stuart Keate, publisher of the Victoria *Daily Times*, strongly supported the establishment of the pulp mill and argued that "nothing should be done to discourage additional payrolls from settling here." The torpedo range probably came with "a great deal of nuisance attached," Keate admitted, but as a matter of "national security" it was something that the business community should not challenge too vehemently.[20] What is striking here, of course, is the dissimilarity between Parrott's pronouncements and those of earlier promoters, such as Herbert Cuthbert in the 1910s and 1920s. No longer employed primarily as a strategy to lure industrial development to Victoria, tourism had now become an industry in itself – an industry with its own strategies, characteristics, and, most importantly, interests, which were, in the eyes of many of its proponents, increasingly incompatible with other industries, such as forestry and manufacturing.

A 1957 *Canadian Business* profile of Vancouver and Victoria confirmed the Victoria business community's acceptance of tourism as the city's economic foundation. In a comparison of the two cities' achievements and motivations, R.H. Francis found that the debate surrounding tourism's role had largely subsided, and he cited Arnold Webb, managing secretary of the Victoria Chamber of Commerce, to illustrate the new consensus.

"We recognize we play second fiddle to Vancouver industrially," Webb explained, "but Victoria is Victoria and we are not willing to make sacrifices merely to be big." The city certainly sought economic growth, but it did not "seek smokestacks." A plethora of larger industries would threaten the city's "assets," Webb explained, in a veiled reference to tourism. To capitalize most fruitfully upon these assets, Francis reported, the city's tourism promoters concentrated their efforts on what made Victoria "different and attractive to the U.S. visitor" – namely its British character. The American tourist, Francis explained, "savors the atmosphere of a more leisurely age. He sees the tweedy garb of the older inhabitants, he enjoys eating crumpets and watching cricket." And the tourism promoters were happy to oblige, comfortable in their understanding that their actions reflected "not just a clinging to the past which happens to appeal to tourists" but in fact stemmed from the city's "character inherited from early British residents of the city."[21] By the early 1960s, it was clear to many that Victoria's future lay squarely in the realm of tourism promotion. A January 1961 article in the Victoria *Daily Times* nicely summarized the city's plight. A recent survey of Victoria's economy emphasized the importance of both tourism and government to the city's future development and suggested that there was "little likelihood that the primary industries in the capital region would increase much in the future."[22] As Peter A. Baskerville explains, many residents of postwar Victoria "did not view lack of industry as a major problem." Instead, they could take comfort in a 1951 study that suggested that "retail sales per capita were 2.3 times greater than the national average and about double the provincial average." This heightened consumer demand, Baskerville confirms, was attributed to the city's tourists rather than "to a high local income."[23]

Conversely, a more economically diversified Vancouver could see tourism potentially as one of many industries. Tourism in Vancouver, however, was seen by its chief proponents as a key ingredient in the city's overall economy. The GVTA's 1954 Declaration of Policy endorsed this point. The association was to serve as "a non-profit community organization, which will enable business firms and individuals to work together collectively" in an attempt to develop the tourist industry. In publicizing the greater Vancouver area "as a tourist mecca and playground and as a convention area," it hoped to "foster, develop, create and promote good will to all visitors in the interests of our civic and provincial economy."[24] Like the VIPB, the hospitality industry was well represented among the GVTA's senior officers. Fred Evans, the president and managing director of the Devonshire Hotel, for example, served on the board of directors from 1953 to 1956, while Colin McCartney, GVTA vice president in 1963, was the manager of the Hotel Vancouver. Frank Baker, a city alderman and the owner of the Colonial House Restaurant, served as GVTA vice president from

1958 to 1961 and president in 1962 and 1963. The GVTA also boasted significant representation from the public relations and advertising fields. Peard Sutherland, vice president in 1949 and 1950, was the assistant public relations manager for the BC Telephone Company. Harry Duker, who chaired the GVTA's Finance Committee in 1948 and 1949 and served as the association's vice president in 1951, was the former manager of Duker & Shaw Ltd., an outdoor-advertising firm. Harold Merilees, a longtime public relations manager with BC Electric who had served terms as president of both the Advertising Association of the West and the BC Public Relations Society, served in a variety of capacities with the GVTA throughout the 1950s, including vice president from 1956 to 1959. He served as president in 1960 and 1961 before taking over the day-to-day operations of the association as its managing director in 1962.

A March 1965 GVTA news release nicely summarized what, for Vancouver's tourism promoters, tourism promotion was all about. According to GVTA president Jack Bain, "more than 7,200 men and women ... are directly on the payrolls of companies whose prime function is to service visitors." Bain also cited UBC economists in arguing that "this volume of foreign dollars spent in Greater Vancouver helps to keep taxes down." Burnaby reeve and GVTA director Alan Emmott explained the relationship between tourism, the service sector, and the public in terms of a "'chain reaction' of profits which results from the tourist industry, and pointed out that many people living in Burnaby, a residential area, made their money out of some aspect of tourism, and spent it in their own neighbourhood."[25] L.W. Lane, Jr., the publisher of *Sunset* magazine, employed a more colourful metaphor to make the same point: "A tourist dollar puts a billiard ball to shame in its ricochet effect within an economy."[26] Such pronouncements reflected early optimistic estimations regarding the extent to which tourist expenditures had a multiplying effect upon local economies.[27]

Throughout the 1930s and 1940s, tourism promoters such as E.H. Adams had joined with prominent civic leaders such as Gerry McGeer to emphasize the importance of tourist expenditures. In the postwar era, however, the chief concern for the province's tourism promoters was no longer depression or war; it was competition. "Did you know," GVTA publicity commissioner M.J. McCormick asked the association's members in 1951, "that Mr. and Mrs. U.S. Citizen spent almost $700 million dollars in travel OUTSIDE the U.S.A. last year, but that only 44% of this amount was spent in Canada[?]" Increased competition from Mexico, the Caribbean, and Europe, among other destinations, he explained, was clearly cutting into Canada's share of the lucrative US market.[28] To meet the challenges of postwar competition, BC tourism promoters embarked upon a concerted effort to differentiate the province's attractions from those of competing destinations. In doing so, they drew selectively from the province's complex past.

"Selling the Sizzle Instead of the Steak": The Lessons of Differentiation

> We travel to see something unlike what we are familiar with at home, and we usually plan to take away with us something that is not available at home, or which will in the future represent to us that which we enjoyed in our travels. Let us emphasize our differences within this region and between this and other regions, and see that symbols of these differences are available. We may have to develop or discover these unique features, but they should be as standard and distinctive as the tartans of Scotland.
>
> — UBC commerce professor E.D. McPhee, 1955[29]

As Conway Parrott's 1953 campaign against the building of a pulp mill suggested, Victoria's tourism promoters knew what sold the city and did their best to maintain their chosen image. CGTB chief Leo Dolan advocated the continued expansion of the Canadian tourist industry along similar lines. "In all conscience," he explained, "I hope never to see Canada's tourist areas a replica of some sections of California, or of Florida, or of Europe. Let us keep our attractions as something that is distinctively Canadian." Here he focused on history, arts, and humanities and encouraged GVTA members to follow the examples of the Stratford Theatre, British Columbia's own 1958 centennial celebrations, and Fredericton's Beaverbrook Gallery. "Our visitors," he explained, "don't want only to visit night clubs and the sort of thing they can get bigger and better at home in the United States."[30] A July 1951 GVTA tourist opinion survey supported Dolan's suggestions. A compiled list of "Complaints" and "Compliments" revealed that visitors to the city were apparently unimpressed with the poor directional signs and generally found it difficult to find their way to the city's chief attractions. They were further dismayed by the dearth of Mounties and Indians – typically Canadian attractions that they had been anticipating.[31]

Faced with intense competition in the postwar era, the province's tourism promoters came increasingly to adopt a position held by R.E. Jefferson of McKim Advertising Ltd. in Vancouver. During the early 1950s, McKim was one of more than half a dozen advertising firms employed by the BCGTB. According to Jefferson, tourism promoters needed to focus on "selling the sizzle instead of the steak." Gimmicks were necessary to succeed in the international battle for tourists. Jefferson offered three international examples. One was "the Indian Maharajah who greeted American tourists in his pink palace, put them up in his guest house and gave them rides on elephants." Jefferson also praised "the imaginative innkeeper in France's Dijon who installed faucets in every room which dispensed red and white wines" and the date grower in California who attracted customers to his roadside stand with the promise of "a continuous movie showing the sex life of the date."[32]

Some promoters seem to have taken Jefferson's food metaphor literally, for the scramble to differentiate British Columbia from other tourist destinations included a concerted attempt to Canadianize and commodify food. Leo Dolan, for example, played an active part in encouraging the growth of a distinct Canadian cuisine for the travel industry. In March 1950, he called for more information to be distributed "on how to cook and serve Canadian food." Such typically Canadian foods included "Ontario's own special blueberry pie; Prince Edward Island Clam Chowder; ... Winnipeg Goldeneye; ... [and] Quebec Soup au Pois." British Columbia was represented in Dolan's smorgasbord of Canadian cuisine by "Lion's Gate Pancakes."[33]

GVTA vice president J.V. Hughes echoed Dolan's suggestions. "We have not in the catering business drawn sufficiently on those foods native to our Province," he lamented, "and when we do, we use little if any imagination in featuring them on our menus." In short, he explained, "we do not capitalize on our native assets."[34] These calls to market distinctively Canadian foods demonstrate the extent to which tourism promoters had embraced the necessity of employing "gimmicks" to lure tourists to British Columbia. Their most lucrative "native asset," however, was history. Buffeted by the pressures of the modern world, many scholars now argue, North Americans by the mid-twentieth century sought solace and escape in a variety of historical half-truths and fictions. In his study of the representation of Seminole Indians in Florida, for example, Jay Mechling explains that the popularity of Seminole tourist sites increased as Americans sought to escape from modern anxieties as varied as fear of nuclear annihilation and a dread of the deadening conformity of North American consumer culture.[35] In fact, the antimodernist desire for stability has proven to be a powerful stimulus to the creation of a number of reassuring ethnic stereotypes. The popularity of the Nova Scotia "fisher folk," indigenous architecture in Santa Fe, New Mexico, and the romantic imagery of Cannery Row in Monterey, California, for example, all speak to this desire to look to the past for relief from the onrush of modernity.[36] Travellers visiting British Columbia similarly embraced simplified representations of two of the province's ethnic groups.

The importance of selling British Columbia's history was emphasized by many individuals, including the provincial librarian and archivist. In

1954 Willard Ireland addressed the annual general meeting of the GVTA on the subject of "British Columbia – A Panorama of Development." As part of his recipe for development, Ireland informed his audience "that the early history of our Province could and should be capitalized for the benefit of our Tourist Industry."[37] The call for increased use of the province's British character and Indian lore in the 1930s had been heeded by the end of the war. In her 1945 examination of the expanding tourist industry for *Canadian Business*, Lyn Harrington praised British Columbians for making use "of the Indian theme in such places as Thunderbird Park in Victoria" and for ensuring that "English traditional ways and motifs" offered American tourists something "different."[38]

Three years later, in his September 1948 profile of Victoria in *Holiday* magazine, Ronald John Williams commented favourably upon the city's British atmosphere. Williams drew his readers' attention to the Tudor-style architecture of the local shops and the city's hanging flower baskets. Until recently, he explained, all of the city's police officers "wore the uniform of the English bobby"; now, he reported approvingly, these uniforms had been "retained in the downtown area as a concession to the tourist-trade boosters." Williams praised the city's "British" cultural activities, which included cricket, lawn bowling, and afternoon tea, and commented favourably upon the city's exclusive gentlemen's clubs. He was particularly delighted with the exclusivity of the Union Club, where one could "observe a concentration of rugged British tweeds, ruddy cheeks and close-clipped army mustaches."

Williams dwelled at length on the Empress Hotel and praised its "terraced lawns and magnificent gardens." Entering the hotel, he explained, was like "going into Durham Cathedral." Even the hotel's occupants, he reported, offered a respite from the modern world. Of the several elderly women who lived in the Empress, Williams had this to report: "To watch a group of these stately dowagers at this social ritual is, in the word of one enchanted Seattle girl, 'something straight from the world of Queen Victoria.'" Williams also highlighted the "Britishness" of consumer goods. "The shops are more English than Canadian," he reported, "and feature such merchandise as imported British woolens, tweeds, and homespuns, and English chinaware bearing the respected marks of Wedgwood, Spode, Crown Derby and Royal Doulton, all of which are priced lower than in the United States." He also directed visitors to the city's antique shops.[39]

Williams's enthusiasm for the city's "British" character was shared by Sam Lane, vice chairman of the Victoria Chamber of Commerce's Tourist Trade Group and a fervent supporter of preserving Victoria's historical landmarks. In 1957, for example, Lane succeeded in gaining chamber support for the preservation of Fort Rodd Hill, Fisguard Light House, and several forts for use as a historical park.[40] Lane was also responsible for the

Tourist Trade Group's decision to adopt the crumpet as a publicity symbol. During a mid-1950s promotional tour of Washington state, Lane had borrowed from the rhetoric surrounding the Cold War to coin the slogan "Come behind the crumpet curtain and see Victoria" and had taken to distributing crumpets to those whom he came in contact with along the way. Lane also carried with him an eighteenth-century English horn that he sounded whenever the party entered a new city.[41]

Lane was not simply an ambassador for Victoria's tourist industry but also part of the industry himself. He and his wife owned the city's Olde England Inn, which by 1960 had taken the commodification of Englishness to new heights. The Lanes' inn boasted canopy beds and 500-year-old suits of armour apparently "dented by musket fire," while guests were served by waitresses sporting the "attire of the Middle Ages." The Lanes, along with their three children, lived in a three-storey residence that was "an exact replica of the house in which Shakespeare was born" and managed to obtain permission from the director of Shakespeare's Birthplace Trust to erect a replica of Anne Hathaway's cottage. Lane attributed the success of the inn and its restaurant to an increased desire on the part of visitors to escape "paper cup service and menus that read differently but taste alike." He believed that "the bulk of his guests visit[ed] his establishment to escape chromium fittings, juke boxes and other devices of modern insanity." "Modern gimmicks," he explained, "would put me out of business overnight."[42]

The commodification of Englishness was not Victoria's prerogative alone. In the mid-1950s, several Vancouver hotels sought to capitalize on this historical theme. In January 1955, the *Canadian Hotel Review* reported that three Vancouver hotels now offered visitors theme lounges concentrating on English history. The Hotel Vancouver's Mayfair Room focused on the days of George III and included a twenty-foot-tall mural of London as well as ornamental grille screens covered in dark green vine. The Sylvia Hotel's Tilting Room boasted murals as well, but they offered a medieval theme and included a scene of a noble family setting out for a tournament. Twin canopies, like those that would have covered the entrance to the royal tent, were supplemented with medieval-themed coasters and napkins as well as a ceiling designed to look like stone. Armour, shields, and banners decorated the walls. The Cavalier Grill at the Hotel Georgia focused on the England of James I, and its entrances featured "hand hammered copper sheeting which [had] been treated with acid to darken its color." Cedar strips and pennants lined its walls.[43]

The commodification of the past and the emphasis on encouraging tourist expenditures are best illustrated, however, by the enhanced interest that tourism promoters showed in Aboriginal culture. Turn-of-the-century tourism promoters made scant reference to Aboriginals. Aboriginal culture was first appropriated by the province's tourism promoters on a regular basis during the Depression. In 1945 the Royal Bank added its voice to the chorus calling upon tourism promoters across the nation to utilize the country's "Indian lore" to a greater extent in luring tourists to Canada.[44] Aboriginal culture shared at least two characteristics with its British counterpart that made it ideal for the purposes of tourism promotion: it was both increasingly uncommon and appeared to be suitably "foreign" to visitors from the United States. The province's British-born population had peaked as a percentage of the total provincial population in 1921 at 31.6 percent, declining only slightly during the 1920s before plummeting in the postwar era to 12.4 percent in 1961. The province's Aboriginal population was, of course, considerably smaller, declining from 10.9 percent in 1901 to 2.2 percent in 1951 before rising slightly throughout the 1950s and 1960s to 3.5 percent in 1971.[45] Both groups were thus diminutive in size in comparison with the rest of the provincial population. More importantly, though, these cultures shared a history of roughly 200 years of contact, conflict, and colonization.[46] In capitalizing upon the new cachet of Native culture, however, British Columbia's tourism promoters offered the more comforting vision of the province's Natives as quaint and mysterious people who maintained a safe enough distance from the modern world to retain their uniqueness but still managed to reap the benefits of modern architecture and education.

The growing acceptance and commodification of Native culture can be seen through three BCGTB films produced between 1942 and 1964. In the 1942 version of *Vancouver Island: British Columbia's Island Playground*, the audience was directed to take note of Victoria's Thunderbird Park, located, the film boasted, close to where potlatches had once been held. Here was a place where "weird totems, armorial bearings of an ancient and mysterious people, gaze with unseeing eyes toward the modern city that has grown from a trading post stockade." A mysterious aura was emphasized – although it was not so mysterious that potential tourists would be frightened away from purchasing authentic Indian articles such as sweaters, socks, and tuques. What this interpretation omitted was the conflicting and painful memories of federal bureaucrats who, throughout the first half of the twentieth century, had tried to end these potlatches on the ground that they inhibited the spread of European values regarding property.[47]

In describing Forbidden Plateau, a recreation area near Courtenay, the narrator informed the audience that an Indian legend proclaimed the area taboo and warned that those who journeyed there would not return. While the narrator reassured the audience that this was "just an old Native superstition," he also refashioned this legend for the purposes of tourism promotion: the area was a "land of bewitching loveliness" – so bewitching, in fact, that visitors might not want to leave. "In the stillness of the scene, one can imagine the mystic beat of tomtoms and the weird chant of the council fire," he continued. With drums beating in the background, the narrator concluded his pitch: "Yesterday Indian land of taboo, today a matchless paleface playground."[48]

Another film, *Highway 16*, released six years later, offered a similar description of an Indian village named Kispiox near the Skeena River. This village also possessed "weird totems." "Behind the village is a limitless region taboo to those hidden children of the wilderness," explained the narrator. Yet the mystic and mysterious Indians apparently lived harmoniously with modern society. In the village of Kitwangaha, he continued, the "Natives live comfortably in large homes," while "education facilities are provided, and healthy recreation [is] enjoyed by the youngsters." While changes to the Indian Act in 1951 encouraged the integration of Native children into the province's public school system and ended the prohibition of the potlatch, the everyday reality of the province's Aboriginal population bore little resemblance to the BCGTB's saccharine representation of Native life.[49] Totem poles were prominent in this film as well, appearing as "silent monuments" to a "brave" and "noble" people and their "mystic beliefs." Here too the film emphasized shopping and encouraged the audience to enjoy leisurely stopovers to purchase Indian handicrafts. Lest potential visitors concern themselves that these educated and well-housed Indians were too modern, the narrator turned to a "wolf totem" that stood "as a silent sentinel ... unshaken by the gleaming planes that wing us to the airways of the world."[50]

An updated version of *Vancouver Island* was released in the mid-1950s but retained the same description of Native imagery.[51] A third version completed in the early 1960s, however, offered a different view. This time, it was explained, the totem poles in Thunderbird Park recorded "the legends of our Native Indians." These were not "weird" totems; they were now "our" totems. The description of Forbidden Plateau now emphasized the fresh mountain air, the meadows, and the different types of flowers. An Indian legend did indeed pronounce the area "forbidden," but the narrator now confidently assured the audience that "you will find nothing forbidding here." Native history here had been almost fully domesticated and cleansed of its complexity. The totem poles at Alert Bay had watched as steam power had rendered sailing ships redundant and planes had allowed people to fly in "great birds." They stood now as "silent guardians of the past" and helped to demonstrate that "the past, present, and future are as one."[52] The uneasiness surrounding the use of Native culture prevalent in the early decades of the century had disappeared completely by the 1960s. Native culture was now eagerly employed to boost souvenir sales.

The most forceful demands for the increased use of Native lore came from Vancouver. By 1949, even the uniforms of the GVTA's female counter staff were being redesigned to capitalize on the increasing popularity of Aboriginal culture. The uniforms now sported a "Travel Advisor" insignia containing a "thunder bird motif."[53] In 1950 the GVTA had a hand in creating an organization designed to concentrate solely on increasing the use of Aboriginal themes in promoting British Columbia. In August of that year, the GVTA agreed to donate $500 to an organization termed the "Totem-Land" Society, confident that the work this group hoped to accomplish would produce great results for the tourist industry.[54] Vancouver Mayor Charles E. Thompson served as president, while Harry Duker, GVTA director and director of special events for the Vancouver Board of Park Commissioners, served as secretary-treasurer. Duker was the real force behind the organization. He had arrived in Vancouver in 1907 from St. Louis, Missouri, hoping to land a position on a local professional baseball team. Duker failed to make the team and became the team's club secretary instead. He would go on to become known as "Vancouver's Club Man" and was associated with over twenty different local organizations over the next sixty years.[55]

At a 1950 board of directors meeting, GVTA comptroller A.L. Woods praised the new society, noting that "we have in this Province a great deal of interesting Indian lore that could be 'sold' to the rest of the world. California has been 'selling' her Missions for years and is still doing so. Our British Columbia Indians' Totem Poles lend themselves to much colorful advertising, and the whole idea should be grist for our mill."[56] At the same meeting, Duker addressed the GVTA board of directors and outlined the future possibilities of the organization. He was confident that the "Totem-Land" theme would lend itself well to advertising campaigns featuring Vancouver and British Columbia and insisted that the organization "would prove of great value in luring more tourists and interesting them in something distinctively British Columbian." The "other uses" that Duker foresaw for the slogan and "totem pole publicity" included letterheads, envelopes, invoices, shipping labels, and even the cancellation stamps used for mailing machines.[57]

According to the official letterhead, the "Totem-Land" Society was incorporated under the provincial Societies Act ostensibly "to Foster and Protect Indian arts and Promote Goodwill Among All Canadians." Given the number of "tourist conscious" men sitting on its executive, however, a cynical observer might easily conclude that the society's aims were primarily economic. In 1962, for example, Charles E. Thompson served as immediate past president, while the presidential duties were performed by R. Rowe Holland. Halford D. Wilson served as first vice president, and Duker himself held the position of honorary secretary-treasurer.[58] All four men were affiliated with the GVTA.

One of Duker's chief aims was to champion the use of Native imagery in place of what he saw as unnecessarily vague alternatives. Informed that the provincial government was contemplating introducing promotional licence plates in 1964 with the slogan "'Beautiful' British Columbia," Duker was adamant that the slogan itself was insufficient. According to him, the "Totem-Land" Society saw "undoubted merit in including some descriptive data on the license plates, as is being done in some of our Provinces and in many of the neighbouring States." But the society was concerned that "the word 'beautiful' is too general and not exclusively symbolic of British Columbia." According to Duker, the society's opinion was shared by the Vancouver *Daily Province,* which had suggested that the term "beautiful" was "too platitudinous and advocated a more meaningful and original word." Not surprisingly, Duker's alternative suggestion was "Totem-Land." His rationale placed little emphasis on the possibilities of protecting and fostering Indian arts or promoting goodwill among Canadians and focused to a great extent on the more measurable advantages that such a slogan offered. "The totem poles of British Columbia are historic monuments and are recognized as such by the Government, hence the restoration work that is being done to preserve them for posterity." Moreover, "Totem-Land" was "a short word and would easily incorporate with other license plate data." And finally Duker's preferred slogan would "provoke the curiosity of strangers and may influence some of them to come to British Columbia to explore something of our Indian history and totem lore."[59]

The Fort Langley and District Board of Trade enthusiastically endorsed Duker's proposal and cited the slogan's uniqueness as its chief selling point. "No other place on this continent," the board's secretary, Mrs. M.S.W. Mackenzie, suggested, "can lay claim to these historic monuments but British Columbia ... So let us honour our native indians [sic] and be proud of our Totem pole Emblems by having them on our license plates."[60] In differentiating British Columbia from competing tourist destinations, tourism promoters had increasingly emphasized the province's British and Native heritages; they provided, however, no suggestion that these two cultures had ever been in conflict. Even the construction of the province's first tourist information centre at the Douglas border crossing south of Vancouver in the mid-1950s was influenced by the desire to convince American tourists that they were visiting a foreign land that boasted two "foreign" cultures. "The lofty presence of the Red Ensign beside the building," the BCGTB reported, "adds to the feeling that the traveller is entering a different land."[61] The erection of "an authentic 40-foot totem-pole immediately south of the building" similarly convinced "a great number of visitors to stop at the Centre."[62]

Indeed, the complexities of colonization (not to mention the sobering impact of decolonization) were nowhere to be seen in promotional literature, in historically themed hotel dining rooms, or on vehicle licence plates. A GVTA news release publicizing Aboriginal culture in the early 1960s nicely illustrates this point. "British Columbia's Coast Indians were prolific totem pole carvers," the news release explained. "Very few Indians now, however, have the techniques or prowess necessary to carry out this art. While much of the earlier handiwork unhappily has been lost through neglect, some splendid examples have been preserved." Here the GVTA deftly avoided explaining why Aboriginal totem poles were few and far between. There was, of course, no indication here of European involvement in this "neglect." The number of Aboriginal artists capable of producing these objects had simply diminished.[63] Such selective explanations are illustrative of what Renato Rosaldo has termed "Imperialist Nostalgia" – a common endeavour in which we absolve our complicity in imperialism by mourning the passing of a society that we helped to transform or subdue.[64] By reducing Native culture to the useful and marketable symbol of the totem pole, British Columbia's tourism promoters encouraged visitors to the province to embrace its history in a simplistic but comforting way – one that encouraged consumption rather than contemplation (see Figures 5.1 to 5.6).

Harry Duker remained Vancouver's foremost proponent of the use of Aboriginal imagery throughout the 1950s and 1960s. In 1954 he waged a public campaign urging the provincial government to purchase a collection of "Indian paintings" by the Vancouver artist Mildred Valley Thornton. In purchasing these paintings depicting "native Indian chiefs," most of whom were now dead, Duker reasoned, the provincial government could ensure that the paintings were kept in their "rightful place" – "where they can be seen by our citizens and visitors." Such an undertaking would both provide "enjoyment for all who see the pictures" and preserve "a valuable record for future generations."[65] That year he waged an unsuccessful battle to have Vancouver's new sports stadium termed "Totem Stadium." His rationale was familiar: the mere mention "of the word 'totem' to any listener anywhere," he claimed, "immediately suggests British Columbia."[66]

Duker was also adamant that Aboriginal culture be prominently displayed at Vancouver's airport. In an August 1965 letter to the *Province,* he championed the use of recognizable cultural artifacts at the airport as opposed to the "loosely termed 'modern art'" that all too frequently appeared in air terminals around the globe. To this end, Duker suggested that a large totem pole be erected outside the airport. Such an artifact, he claimed, would act both as "a tribute to our native brethren, and as a unique symbol of our province." He also suggested that display cases inside the airport exhibit "handicrafts from the backgrounds of our ethnic peoples."[67]

Yet Duker's activities and suggestions should not simply be seen as a

Figure 5.1 A "coronation vacation." Aware of visitors' interest in the province's British heritage, the BCGTB embraced the occasion of Queen Elizabeth II's coronation to make sure that Mounties, Royal Guards, and Red Ensigns were featured prominently in postwar advertising campaigns.

Sources: (left) *Sunset* 110, 4 (1953): 26; (right) *Sunset* 111, 1 (1953): 8. Courtesy of University of Washington Libraries, Special Collections Division, UW 23590 and UW 23591.

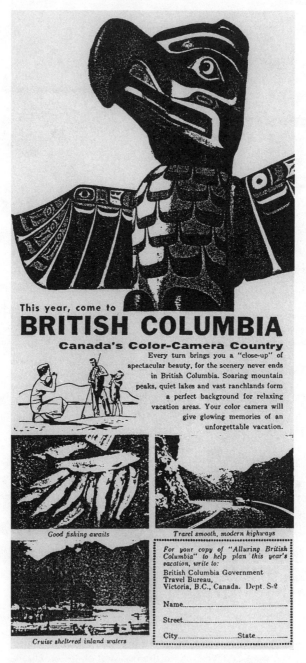

Figure 5.2 "Canada's color-camera country." Native imagery even dominated BCGTB ads ostensibly focusing on the province's natural beauties.

Source: Sunset 116, 5 (1956): 38.

Figure 5.3 "Chief Chinook." British and
Aboriginal cultures are united in this 1950 Puget
Sound Navigation Company ad. The conflicts and
repercussions of colonization are submerged
beneath a happy facade in which the gram-
matically challenged Chief Chinook takes on the
role of tourism promoter by encouraging readers
to return a coupon in exchange for schedules
and maps.

Source: Sunset 104, 5 (1950): 29. Reproduced with the
permission of Washington State Ferries.

Figure 5.4 "Everything's different in British Columbia." The quest for differentiation reached new extremes in the early 1960s when this two-page BCGTB ad began to appear regularly in *Sunset* magazine. Potential US visitors to British Columbia were encouraged to enjoy, along with the ubiquitous Mountie, the province's foreign "stamps, flags, uniforms [and] coloured money." They could also enjoy the unique experience of filling up their vehicles with "a bigger, 'Imperial gallon.'" "Unusual" Aboriginal place names such as Nanaimo and Tsawwassen were also emphasized, as were the province's "Handsome Sikhs" – "the only colony in North America." By the 1960s, the marketable "differences" began to include Vancouver's Chinatown.

Source: Sunset 130, 3 (1963): 56-57.

A dozen things you can't do anywhere else but VANCOUVER, Canada

1 Ride a twin-seat chairlift over 4,000 feet up for an unforgettable view of city and shoreline.

2 Walk across sidewalk-width suspension bridges in the canyons of the Capilano and Lynn Rivers.

3 Spend days in world-famous 1,000 acre Stanley Park.

4 Beachcomb and swim on one of the beaches that outline Vancouver.

5 Fish for a fighting Tyee salmon, perhaps with your hotel in sight.

6 See a stage presentation at new *Queen Elizabeth Theatre* and *Playhouse*, a musical at *Theatre Under The Stars*, or the fun-filled *Pacific National Exhibition*.

7 See colorful Chinatown, second largest outside Asia.

8 Highlight your dining with fresh Boundary Bay crab and tiny Pacific Coast shrimp.

9 See B.C. Lions in a professional Canadian Football game at new Empire Stadium.

10 See one of the world's most beautiful university campuses – a magnificently landscaped peninsula.

11 Enjoy historic pleasures: a sunset over the Gulf Islands, an outbound ship, a band playing in a beachside park.

12 Take home souvenirs of native Indian crafts, British china and woolens, and Commonwealth imports.

See the Fraser Valley

East of Vancouver lies the Fraser Valley. Colorful farmlands roll from either side of the river to snow-capped mountains behind. In 2 hours' drive you reach the world-famous Fraser Canyon, a route of B.C.'s gold seekers in 1860.

Fish the Sunshine Coast

Fast ferries take you north-west from Vancouver to the Sunshine Coast. This is B.C.'s Pacific outdoors at its best – fine beaches, campsites, fishing spots, and inviting communities. Tiny harbours and fiords are favorite haunts of yachtsmen.

MAIL THIS COUPON TODAY

GREATER VANCOUVER VISITORS AND CONVENTION BUREAU
596 W. Georgia Street,
Vancouver 2, British Columbia

Please rush me your full-color Visitor's Kit.

Name...........................

Address.........................

City.................State...........

Figure 5.5 "A dozen things you can't do anywhere else but Vancouver, Canada." In 1963 tourism promoters in Vancouver embarked upon a new method in their campaign to differentiate the city from other tourist destinations: a lengthy list of experiences unique to Vancouver and its surrounding area.

Source: Sunset 30, 3 (1963): 5. Reproduced with the permission of Tourism Vancouver.

You'll have fun exploring VANCOUVER ISLAND BRITISH COLUMBIA, CANADA

Forests that are centuries old. Canada's highest waterfall. So many trout and salmon you'd wonder where they came from. High mountains and deep lakes. And at many a turn in the road, warm, sandy beaches. You'll wish you could wrap it all up and pack it home as a souvenir.

MAIL COUPON FOR FREE BROCHURE

Vancouver Island Publicity Bureau,   S3
786 Government Street,
Victoria, B.C., Canada

Please send me your colorful brochure on "Canada's Treasure Island".

NAME.................................

ADDRESS..............................

....

Figure 5.6 "You'll have fun exploring Vancouver Island." By 1963 tourism and shopping were so entwined that tourism promoters on Vancouver Island could equate the visitor's entire travel experience with the desire to purchase souvenirs.

Source: *Sunset* 130, 5 (1963): 44. Reproduced with the permission of Tourism Victoria.

brazen attempt to capitalize upon Aboriginal culture. It is clear that Duker sympathized with the plight of the province's Aboriginal population and likely saw his effort to commodify their culture as one that would benefit them as well. In 1966, for instance, he publicly reprimanded H.A. Tasker, a magistrate in Tahsis, for his demeaning statements about Nootka Indians at Friendly Cove. Duker offered this condemnation on behalf of the Vancouver Civic Unity Association, which he chaired.[68] A year later, moved by a visit to the Indian pavilion at Expo '67 in Montreal, he again publicly sympathized with Canada's Aboriginal peoples. The Indian pavilion, Duker explained, had been "an agonized 'cry out' of protest," and "responsible Canadians, whatever their racial origin, deplore what can only be regarded as discrimination against our native Indians." Indeed, Duker yearned for "a feeling of mutual responsibility" to emerge "between our native Indians and all other Canadians." To this end, he encouraged Aboriginal people to scrutinize Canada's Bill of Rights in an attempt to extract themselves from the discriminatory regulations of the Indian Act. Duker's ideal solution to the plight of Aboriginal people was itself contradictory. The Bill of Rights, he hoped, would accelerate "their speedy assimilation as a sustaining unit in the new pattern for Canada which is presently emerging."[69] Whatever his altruistic goals, however, his efforts remained part of an expanding effort in the postwar era to differentiate British Columbia from other popular tourist destinations.

In recent years, historians have begun to explore the relationship between tourism and colonialism in North America. While maintaining that "the unsettled issues of conquest did not disappear, even if tourists could not see them," Patricia Nelson Limerick offers this brief synopsis of tourism's symbolic power in the American west of the early twentieth century: "The war was over; white people had won; the West was subdued; the West was an occupied terrain, and the tourists were the army of occupation."[70] Tourism, then, helped to confirm conquest. Hal Rothman has gone so far as to suggest that tourism's tendency to reward outsiders at the expense of local populations makes "tourism the most colonial of economies ... as a result of its psychic and social impact on people and their places." "Tourism, and the social structure it provides," he argues, "makes unknowing locals into people who look like themselves but who act and behave differently as they learn to market their place and its, and their, identity. They change every bit as much as did African workers in the copper mines of the Congo or the diamond mines of South Africa."[71] In the Canadian context, Patricia Jasen has convincingly demonstrated the extent to which nineteenth-century travel writing helped to "bolster public enthusiasm" for bringing northern Ontario "fully under white control" while confirming "established stereotypes of the Native population."[72]

In the case of British Columbia, we can see tourism and colonialism

connected even more explicitly. Tourism promotion in British Columbia
aided in the process of "resettlement" in two ways.[73] In its first incarnation between 1900 and 1930, tourism promotion served as an efficient and
effective form of boosterism. It was, as Herbert Cuthbert revealingly explained, "the modern colonizer." In luring well-to-do entrepreneurs and
settlers to take up new lives in the province, tourism promotion functioned as a principal method of securing Anglo-Saxon hegemony over the
land and the provincial economy. Tourism's second incarnation, I have
argued, took shape during the 1930s – a period in which civic leaders and
politicians were anxious for solutions to the economic and cultural malaise that they saw around them. For three decades, tourism promotion
offered the cities of Vancouver and Victoria the opportunity to increase
both their populations and their industrial production. As a crisis of "overproduction," of course, the Great Depression rendered increased production unnecessary and increased immigration unwelcome.[74] As tourism
promotion was refashioned as a method of soliciting increased aggregate
demand, it came to aid the process of resettlement in a different manner. In selling British Columbia's history and commodifying British and
Aboriginal cultures, tourism promoters encouraged visitors and the host
population to embrace a selective reimagining of the province's past –
one that substituted "imperialist nostalgia" for the complicated and often
ugly realities of colonialism. British Columbians, Cole Harris reminds us,
"associate colonialism with other places and other lives – a racially seg-
regated South Africa, Joseph Conrad's fear-ridden Congo – where they
can easily condemn its brutalities" yet remain "largely oblivious" to colonialism's impact on their home province: "They turn the Fraser Canyon
into a gold rush trail, a place where rugged land and sturdy miners met;
a gondola gives them scenery and a touch of 'gold pan Pete.' The equation is simple and powerful, but leaves out thousands of human years
and lives."[75] It also leaves out roughly 200 years of conflict between the
two ethnic groups most forcefully represented in the province's promotional travel literature. Having contributed directly to the colonial process in its first phase, tourism promotion then contributed to a process
of selective amnesia in its second phase – a process that normalized European control of the land and encouraged both visitors and hosts to reimag-
ine the "resettlement" of British Columbia as benign, comforting, and
consumable fare.

Conclusion

In 1964 L.J. Crampton, head of recreation economics research at Stanford
University, addressed a meeting of the Canadian Tourist Association in
Saskatoon. Crampton was one of a growing number of tourism "experts"
on the Pacific Coast who were bringing the tools of social science to the

study of tourist behaviour. His lesson for those in attendance was that climate and scenery were no longer sufficient for tourism success. Times had changed, he explained: "In reality, what the tourists want, what they will buy, what we must sell them is, instead, what all successful areas are selling – an enjoyable experience." Tourism promoters, Crampton argued, "must think of themselves as 'peddlers of fun' rather than as promoters of an outstanding bit of mountain scenery or a lake that will consistently produce trophy fish." "Scenery and climate and other natural attractions," he reminded his audience, "are only the building blocks upon which this opportunity for enjoyment can be built, not the sole reason for visitation."

Crampton divided the promoter's task into two complementary procedures. The first was "product development." Tourism promoters must develop features and facilities to lure tourists to their particular area. Attractive scenery and comfortable climates were everywhere; guaranteeing potential visitors the maximum amount of fun and excitement was the only way to woo them away from similarly endowed destinations. One key product in need of constant development, according to Crampton, was "service." Hospitality and service, he argued, were crucial to tourism success and complemented the other key to product development: differentiation. In detailing the tourism success enjoyed by the Cherokee Indian community in North Carolina, Crampton was blunt: "The secret of their success has been in the differentiation of their product to provide a specific reason to visit this community to obtain fun and enjoyment." Only after this first phase of "product development" had been accomplished did the second phase, promotion and advertising, make sense. Here Crampton advocated targeting specific audiences in concentrated areas so as to maximize the impact of advertising expenditures.[76] By the early 1960s, British Columbia's tourism promoters had embraced the lessons of differentiation and would have agreed with much of what Crampton had to say. The story of how these lessons were implemented, however, is the story not only of the commodification of British and Aboriginal cultures but also of an increased commitment by the provincial government to recognize tourism as an important element in its postwar province-building schemes. It became part and parcel of the "new" British Columbia that its citizens must be "tourist conscious." These developments are the subject of the following chapter.

6
Tourism as a Public Good: The Provincial Government Manages the Postwar "Boom," 1950-70

It must be made clear to our citizens and merchants alike, that
every single citizen benefits from this golden tide.

— GVTA president George Bradley, 1956[1]

The British Columbia Government Travel Bureau's changing status throughout the postwar era reflected the provincial government's growing recognition of tourism. From its inception in 1937-38 through to 1956, the
bureau remained under the control of the Department of Trade and Industry – a reflection of tourism's earlier role as a means of attracting industrial
and agricultural investment. In 1957 the BCGTB became one of five units
comprising the newly created Department of Recreation and Conservation – a new department reflecting the growing importance of recreation
and leisure activities in the lives of British Columbians.[2] This arrangement lasted until 1967, when the growing importance of tourism (now
recognized by the government as the province's third largest industry)
necessitated the creation of a government department focusing solely on
the tourist trade: the Department of Travel Industry.[3]

BCGTB expenditures over this period tell a similar story. BCGTB budgets,
along with those of its federal counterpart, the Canadian Government
Travel Bureau (as the CTB was known after 1945), expanded dramatically
during the postwar era.[4] The BCGTB's expenditures on promotional activities during the early 1950s ranged between $60,000 in 1953-54 and
$98,000 in 1951-52 and 1956-57. With the transfer of the bureau to the
new Department of Recreation and Conservation in 1957, however, came
a dramatic increase in promotional expenditures. In 1957-58, for instance,
expenditures on tourism promotion climbed to over $193,000, and by
1966-67 they had reached over $860,000. The creation of the Department
of Travel Industry brought a further increase in expenditures to just under
$1.7 million in 1969-70.[5] A comparison between BCGTB promotional ex-
penditures and those of the Greater Vancouver Tourist Association (GVTA)
makes clear the leading role that the state bureau played in advertising
British Columbia as a tourist destination (see Table 6.1). In 1963, for instance, the GVTA spent less than $37,000 on promotional endeavours,
while the BCGTB expenditures topped $400,000.

Table 6.1

Greater Vancouver Tourist Association and British Columbia Government Travel Bureau expenditures, 1950-70 (1960 $)

	GVTA		BCGTB	
	Advertising	Total	Advertising	Total
1950	NA	NA	$102,875	$238,842
1955	NA	$61,246	$67,062	$161,667
1960	NA	$98,912	$210,303	$279,399
1965	$48,163	$215,349	$548,400	$797,964
1970	$49,314	$259,478	$1,294,253	$1,766,855

Notes: The revised figures have been rounded to the nearest dollar. GVTA figures are for the calendar year listed. BCGTB figures are for the fiscal year completed during that year.
Sources: Greater Vancouver Tourist Association Annual Reports, 1950-71; Government of British Columbia Public Accounts, 1950-70.

Several studies now illustrate the degree to which the postwar economic boom was "managed" through government intervention. Dominique Marshall, for instance, has revealed the important role that the federal government envisioned for family allowances in promoting postwar consumption in its efforts to avoid a return to economic depression after the Second World War. Throughout the 1950s and 1960s, Robert M. Campbell explains, the federal government abandoned its ostensible commitment to Keynesian fiscal policy in favour of a less discretionary and invasive monetary approach to regulating the economy. This approach was supplemented, however, by a number of ad hoc initiatives, including a campaign to encourage public works construction during the winter to offset seasonal unemployment, a determined effort to alleviate regional disparities through subsidies and tax credits, as well as a number of policies designed to protect domestic industries from foreign competition. All of these various initiatives, together with welfare state provisions such as medicare and unemployment insurance, were employed in an effort to manage and maintain the postwar economic boom. Indeed, by the late 1950s, according to Joy Parr, the welfare state combined with private medical insurance plans to provide Canadians with a sense of security that, in turn, increased their willingness to purchase goods.[6]

In their attempts to "manage" the postwar tourist "boom," British Columbia's tourism promoters similarly adopted a managerial approach and acknowledged a sizable role for governments in developing the tourist industry. In many ways, the activities and approach of the provincial government's travel bureau closely resembled the ambitious "state-initiated social engineering" initiatives examined by James C. Scott. The BCGTB shared with other state organizations of the postwar era a determination to bring about an "administrative ordering of nature and society" through a systematic process of measuring and quantifying human behaviour in order to produce efficient but simplistic models that would serve to guide government policy. The bureau's initiatives also adhered to what Scott has termed a "high-modernist ideology" – an enhanced, even exaggerated, confidence in the virtues of science, technology, and rational planning.[7]

With government recognition of tourism's importance fully secured, the stage was set for tourism promotion to benefit from two key developments of the postwar era: the expansion of state intervention, and the proliferation of a type of propaganda that historian Paul Rutherford terms "civic advocacy."[8] The first half of this chapter focuses on the state. It explores the ways in which tourism promoters' efforts to maintain a high level of consumer demand for British Columbia's attractions throughout the postwar era relied upon direct actions by the state. Tourism's postwar "boom" began in the 1940s – a time, Shirley Tillotson explains, when "the whole notion of state-sponsored, expert-managed social and economic planning was just taking hold in Canada."[9] The growing confidence in expert planning and state intervention forcefully shaped the scale and scope of postwar tourism promotion, most obviously through a growing reliance on market research surveys. The second half of the chapter examines civil society. Here I focus on the manner in which the BCGTB and local tourism organizations sold the importance of the tourist industry to British Columbians. As Paul Rutherford explains, the postwar era witnessed a dramatic expansion of civic advocacy propaganda in which governments, corporations, and voluntary associations variously urged citizens to stop drinking and driving, combat drug abuse, support tax cuts, or save the whales.[10] By examining a variety of educational initiatives ranging from more traditional didactic endeavours, including publicity campaigns as well as university and public school initiatives, to more unconventional and innovative enterprises, including an attempt to provide hospitality without any human hosts at all, this chapter documents the extent to which tourism was sold as a public good – that is, as an industry that benefited everyone and, therefore, deserved everyone's support.

Travel Surveys and BCGTB Advertising Campaigns
For UBC School of Commerce professor E.D. McPhee, a frequent speaker on issues concerning tourism in the Pacific Northwest, the government's central role in fostering the tourist industry was essential. In fact, he endorsed arguments that considered tourism a component of national life whose "benefits are so widespread, so difficult to tie down to any particular providers of goods and services, only a representative institution can properly and equitably finance such an effort." Governments, McPhee argued, through business taxation, needed to play a major role

in financing the tourist industry.[11] Moreover, he explained, governments should also play a leading role in financing adequate surveys of tourists' "wants and wishes."[12]

The importance of tourist expenditures was similarly championed before the Pacific Northwest Trade Association by Dr. Weldon B. Gibson, director of economic research at the Stanford Research Institute.[13] Increased tourist travel would come, he explained, not only from higher incomes and advances in transportation but also from changes in the makeup of a growing US population that was migrating west and growing older. As a result, he predicted, the next two decades would bring an increase in the number of potential visitors with more leisure time. To facilitate the industry's expansion, Gibson, like many others, advocated greater attention to advertising. But he also underscored the importance of another component of tourism promotion: research. "Tourist research," Gibson explained, was being undertaken not just by federal government departments in Canada and the United States but also by "states, counties and communities, territories, provinces, private groups, bureaus of business research and applied research organizations." Moreover, he reported, "bureaus of business research" at colleges and universities in the Pacific Northwest were becoming "very active in analyzing the tourist industry." Most of these studies employed surveys to determine the number of tourists visiting a particular destination in the Pacific Northwest. However, there was as yet no overall appraisal of tourism's importance to the region. Such an overall analysis, Gibson suggested, would provide crucial information regarding tourists' motivations and the effectiveness of promotional efforts.[14]

The absence of reasonably complete travel statistics had long been a frustrating limitation for tourism promoters. "With the other basic industries," E.G. Rowebottom lamented during the Second World War, "the matter is realitively [sic] simple – so many board feet, so many tons, so many cases – but with Tourism the statistics are all so very personal – how many were in the party, how long did they stay, where did they go, how much did they spend – that there can be no compulsion." Visitors could only be "invited" to cooperate and divulge such information.[15] With the increasing recognition by governments of social science and market research techniques, it is not surprising that Canadian tourism promoters embraced these tools. In 1947, for example, the Canadian Government Travel Bureau (CGTB) established a separate statistics division in order to chart and measure the impact of its advertising initiatives. That year the CGTB hired the Cockfield, Brown and Co. advertising firm to conduct market research surveys of American tourists.[16] Tourism promoters in British Columbia similarly embraced the promise of market research. BCGTB campaigns in the early 1950s reflected survey results indicating that US tourists visiting Canada were primarily interested in "touring and sightseeing" rather than attractions such as fishing and hunting. In 1951 the BCGTB placed greater emphasis on what it termed "the totem theme" in an attempt to "emphasize the different or foreign features which are of importance to tourist and sightseeing visitors." The use of totem poles also allowed the BCGTB to establish "a symbol," or trademark, that would serve as a lasting reminder of British Columbia.[17] While such surveys provided tourism promoters with some detailed information on tourist behaviour, the most significant surveys were undertaken in the early 1960s. By 1960, in fact, the BCGTB was carrying out continuous travel surveys through its reception centres. The bureau remained convinced, however, that much more information was required in order to allow it to conduct its promotional campaigns on a more scientific basis.[18]

Determined to obtain such information, the bureau embarked upon a detailed survey of travellers between the United States and British Columbia during the summer of 1962 and published the results in a booklet entitled *Tourist '62*.[19] Like its federal counterpart, the BCGTB contracted out the survey duties to a private firm. The *Tourist '62* survey, commissioned by the BCGTB and conducted by Regional Marketing Surveys Limited of Vancouver, confirmed many earlier hypotheses while rejecting others. The company conducted 626 personal interviews with US visitors en route to, or returning from, Vancouver Island by ferry and a further 1,003 interviews with US visitors travelling by car through the Douglas border crossing. The survey indicated that over 70 percent of US tourists visiting the province came from California, Oregon, and Washington and logically recommended that promotional efforts be concentrated along the US Pacific Coast. The visitors were also older than average and possessed above-average incomes. Few visitors made less than $5,000 a year, and most made between $7,500 and $12,000 annually. Almost half of the province's visitors came from the "upper-middle and upper classes even though these classes represent a segment of 15% of the population." They were "typically in the professions, law, medicine, teaching and senior management." "Middle class" tourists or "white collar workers" represented roughly one-third of these visitors, while "skilled labourer[s]" accounted for a further 15 percent. Overall, the survey concluded, "our visitors are sophisticated, moderately wealthy, and middle aged." The survey reported with some surprise, however, that "the 'typical' tourist group – the happy family with a couple of children along," was not quite so typical. In fact, it was more common for couples to travel without children.[20] The survey also offered valuable detailed information about tourists' activities while on vacation and highlighted the importance of convincing visitors to extend their stay, noting that only 6 percent of visitors stayed in the province for longer than a week and that even convincing visitors to stay just one day longer would result in increasing the province's tourist revenue by 40 percent.

The survey also revealed that tourists in British Columbia overwhelmingly expressed an interest in visiting the province's two largest cities and, of course, taking in the province's scenery. In fact, 85 percent of those surveyed visited only the Victoria and Greater Vancouver areas, a pattern that the provincial government and many interior communities hoped to change. The survey confirmed suspicions that visitors were more interested in obtaining a sense of being in a "foreign" country through shopping and visiting historical attractions than they were in "fishing, camping and the outdoor life." Finally, the survey indicated that nearly half of the province's visitors planned their summer vacations between January and June, while 20 percent planned their trips even earlier than that. Such information, the report explained, reinforced the importance of reaching potential visitors during the winter and spring.[21] A similar examination of tourist behaviour resulted in a sustained campaign to both lengthen British Columbia's tourist season and decrease the significant fluctuations in tourist travel throughout the year.

Lengthening the Season

In the postwar era, the BCGTB was not content simply to lure tourists to the province; it worked with other promotional organizations to influence *when* these visitors travelled as well. British Columbia's tourism promoters had long been interested in extending the tourist season. In the 1920s, for instance, they had embarked upon a "Prairie Winter" campaign to lure residents of Alberta, Saskatchewan, and Manitoba west to enjoy British Columbia's more temperate climate. By September 1947, the goal of lengthening the tourist season was described in the increasingly popular Keynesian language of the day. In a report to the GVTA board of directors, GVTA secretary-manager R.H. Baker underscored his concern with the increasing number of working-class vacationers who were joining the growing number of people receiving paid vacations for the first time. "If all these new vacations are to be in July and August," he lamented, "the feast and famine aspect of tourist business will only be aggravated." To combat this situation, Baker advocated a concerted effort on the part of tourist groups to try to spread vacations throughout the year. California, he reported, "has taken the lead in this campaign in the hope that others will follow." "During the next few years you will probably hear a lot about the advantages as an employer, or employee, of having vacations spread out so factories are not literally closed down for weeks during the summer, with idle machines adding up losses for all." Vancouver, he suggested, had a great deal to gain from such a campaign, and he advocated a complementary campaign that would encourage British Columbians themselves to spread their vacations throughout the year. This approach "would have the twofold advantage of making more accommodation available in the summer months at our own resorts, and provide the margin of business to enable our transportation and accommodation people to broaden their season and provide facilities for visitors."[22]

Throughout the postwar era, the BCGTB played a prominent role in this endeavour. In 1949, for example, it modified both the text and the timing of advertising copy in an attempt to "lengthen" the tourist season. The resulting slight increases in tourist traffic from the United States in both the spring and autumn were viewed as encouraging. Discussions with large employers were also pursued with "a view to encouraging those without children of school age to take vacations in the off-season."[23] Similarly, the GVTA's choice of magazines for advertising copy in 1949 reflected its determination both to reach potential travellers with "better than average" incomes and to extend the tourist season as much as possible. Hence, advertisements were placed in *Kiwanis* magazine and *Rotarian* magazine "on the theory that service club members had better than average incomes" and "were unquestionably more travel-conscious than other groups." In an effort to reach business executives in eastern North America, the GVTA took out an advertisement in *Forbes* magazine. In the immediate postwar years, the GVTA embarked upon a sustained attempt to increase visitors from eastern Canada during the fall and winter. To this end, the association took out colour advertisements in *Time* and *Saturday Night* magazines in October and November. This sustained campaign to extend the tourist season beyond the summer months was already paying dividends by 1949 in increased tourist visits in fall and winter.[24] Throughout the postwar era, tourism promoters worked vigorously, primarily through advertising campaigns, to expand the travel season (see Figures 6.1 to 6.3). Their efforts appear to have been successful. By 1964 the BCGTB was reporting that the tourist season had been successfully extended into September and October to a greater extent than ever before.[25]

Conventions
In a 1959 visit to Vancouver, CGTB chief Leo Dolan encouraged the GVTA to focus its efforts on the now central aims of tourism. He was disturbed by the growing focus on conventions, which he considered a "specialized job" that was the responsibility of individual communities. Overall he emphasized the GVTA's role in bringing tourists to the city and spoke out against what might prove to be alluring ties between other industries and the tourist trade. "In other words," he explained, "this organization should not be promoting industry, that is the job for the Vancouver Chamber of Commerce."[26] Dolan's admonishments were misplaced. In the postwar era, even conventions were understood by BC tourism promoters not as

SEPTEMBER IS
'Spring Time' in B.C.

Yes, right now the Spring or Tyee Salmon are running in the famous coastal waters of British Columbia. Here is sport-fishing at its finest, fishing which attracts anglers from all over the world. You'll catch Spring Salmon from 6 lbs. to 60 lbs. in size, and excellent Coho, too, the fightingest fish that every took your lure. Take two weeks and come now. Excellent accommodation at all fishing centres. For further details, write:

BRITISH COLUMBIA
GOVERNMENT TRAVEL
BUREAU
Victoria, B.C.   M-48-49

Figure 6.1 "September is 'spring time' in B.C." Some BCGTB ads attempted to equate autumn with spring.

Source: Sunset 103, 4 (1949): 4. Courtesy of University of Washington Libraries, Special Collections Division, UW 23586z.

Figure 6.2 A year-round "green world" of "happy valleys." Other ads simply urged tourists to visit the province outside the usual summer months.

Sources: (left) *Sunset* 107, 4 (1951): 20; (right) *Sunset* 114, 4 (1955): 38. Courtesy of University of Washington Libraries, Special Collections Division, UW 23592z and UW 23589z.

Figure 6.3 Vancouver as a year-round destination. Greater Vancouver Tourist Association ads throughout the 1950s emphasized this point as well. A 1951 ad informed readers that "vacation fun" was available "12 months of the year."

Sources: Sunset 107, 1 (1951): 15. Reproduced with the permission of Tourism Vancouver.

a method for attracting investment but as an important source of tourist expenditure.

In the 1950s and 1960s, British Columbia's tourism promoters became increasingly interested in encouraging groups and organizations to hold conventions in the province. According to one mid-1960s BC Chamber of Commerce delegate, the province's seasonal tourist industry could avoid its "feast and famine" cycles by boosting the number of conventions. "The convention delegate long ago earned the reputation of being a 'big spender,'" he reasoned. "This is certainly true today when most delegates have either corporate expense accounts or a larger than average supply of discretionary spending dollars." Moreover, "increasingly, the convention delegate is taking his wife, and sometimes family, along with him – accommodation enjoys double occupancy and the retailer welcomes mom while pop attends sessions." Convention delegates patronized most visitor services, including accommodation, nightclubs, restaurants, and transportation. Attendance at conventions was often combined with holidays; "better still, the delegate likes what he sees and returns for a vacation visit."[27]

Interest in promoting conventions was motivated by the recognition that convention visitors tended to spend three times as much as their nonconvention counterparts and thus made a significant contribution to the province's tourism income.[28] By the early 1950s, the BCGTB deemed conventions to be important enough components in its campaign to smooth out the seasonal fluctuations in tourist traffic that additional messages encouraging "convention traffic" were included in the bureau's general and regional tourism folders.[29] In 1960 the BCGTB reported, the province hosted over 200 conventions with almost 50,000 delegates.[30] Two years later the bureau created its own Conventions Section, with a mandate to "co-ordinate the convention sales story for the Province" and encourage the development of the convention business throughout British Columbia.[31] By 1963 the bureau had created a new brochure entitled *British Columbia, the Memorable Land for Conventions* and was embarking upon both a direct mailing campaign and a national advertising program aimed at bringing the province to the attention of convention executives.[32]

Field personnel from the BCGTB's Convention Section travelled the province visiting and classifying accommodation and endeavouring "to assist new operators with the problems of management and promotion of their establishments." The Convention Section also worked diligently to promote "pre- and post-convention tours" in an attempt to lengthen delegates' visits in the province, and the BCGTB even made staff available to assist in "planning and operating" the conventions themselves.[33] By 1965 the bureau estimated that convention delegates alone were responsible for spending over $5.5 million in British Columbia.[34]

In coordinating the province's convention business, the BCGTB's efforts mirrored the work of the province's civic tourist associations. By 1953 the GVTA was increasingly aware of the fact that many other cities boasted convention departments involved in actively recruiting conventions in an effort to keep a city's accommodation consistently filled. These departments pursued this aim both by regulating the number of delegates attending such conventions and by scheduling conventions so as to avoid conflicts. The time had come, GVTA president Ivor Neil implied, for Vancouver to adopt such a department. GVTA commissioner J.V. Hughes recalled the suggestion by the manager of a convention bureau in the United States that such "long range planning" made it possible to "obtain a continuous flow of conventions ... which keeps accommodation filled practically to capacity the whole of the year."[35]

By 1954 the GVTA was seriously considering the creation of a Convention Bureau, and the following year the GVTA gained membership in the International Association of Convention Bureaus – an association that worked as a "clearing house for confidential information regarding conventions held in member cities all over the continent."[36] By 1957 the GVTA's own Convention Bureau was up and running and, by year's end, had secured four conventions totalling over 3,000 visitors – the successful outcome of a close collaboration with the local hotels. It had also "serviced" a total of forty-five conventions totalling over 14,500 visitors, each gathering valued at roughly "$100 per head in new money to our business community."[37] So important were conventions to the association that in 1962 it changed its name from the Greater Vancouver Tourist Association to the Greater Vancouver Visitors and Convention Bureau (GVVCB).

Victoria's tourism promoters similarly embraced the possibility of convention business. In July 1951, the Victoria Chamber of Commerce's Tourist Trade Group succeeded in obtaining permission to set up its own Convention Committee to encourage the holding of conventions in the city.[38] The group's endeavours included a concerted attempt to develop visible local ceremonies to entertain convention delegates. In January 1953, for example, Conway Parrott explained that "his group was trying strenuously to develop Victoria as a Convention City and urged that some form of military ceremony be held as often as possible in the summer evenings at the Parliament Buildings to *develop a traditional ceremony* that would help to keep tourists interested in stopping over in the City."[39] So important were conventions deemed to the local economy that by the late 1960s L.C. Parkinson, chairman of the chamber's Tourist and Convention Advisory Committee, was instructing his fellow chamber members to include "'Victoria THE Convention City' in their advertising and correspondence."[40]

The BCGTB's role throughout the era remained a coordinating one. The bureau's duties, as the 1956 report aptly explained, were "essentially those of a sales organization" and its "functions ... very similar to those of sales management in industry." BCGTB members were thus expected to "keep in close touch with those responsible for the 'commodity, packaging, and distribution'" aspects of tourism promotion. Moreover, the bureau's public relations and promotional activities required close contact not only with the game and parks branches of the government but also with the various Chambers of Commerce and tourist bureaus "which function as retail outlets in the merchandising set-up of tourism."[41] In pursuing these objectives, the BCGTB took a leading role in developing strategies for the province's tourism promotion campaigns. Along with recognizing the advantages of market research studies and sustained campaigns to lengthen the tourist season and lure conventions to the province, the bureau undertook a determined effort to encourage tourists to visit areas of the province beyond Vancouver and Victoria.

Regional Coordination and the Campaign Against Uneven Tourism Development

> We, with all due modesty, cannot help but claim that we are
> entering British Columbia's half-century – and cannot help but
> observe that 'B.C.' also stands for BOOM COUNTRY.
>
> — Phil Gaglardi, highways minister, 1955[42]

As minister of highways from 1952 to 1968, Phil Gaglardi presided over an era of unprecedented road construction in British Columbia. In addition to making significant upgrades to the Cariboo Road through the Fraser Canyon, for example, the provincial government played a leading role in completing the long-awaited new Trans-Canada route through Rogers Pass, thus alleviating the need for drivers to endure "white knuckle drives" between Golden and Revelstoke.[43] Between 1952 and 1958, in fact, W.A.C. Bennett's new Social Credit government spent more money on highway development than had been spent on the province's highways by every previous provincial administration.[44]

Highways, as the primary means of communication, according to the BC Chamber of Commerce, were "major factors in the development of a civilized society." In advocating the continuation of the province's road-building campaign, the chamber not only underscored the importance of highways in servicing industries but also recognized "the great importance of tourism" to the national economy.[45] By 1962 tourism was sharing top billing with subjects such as education and free enterprise as part of the BC chamber's annual General Policy Statements. Its first "tourism" statement recognized that the tourist industry annually created "millions of dollars of new wealth that penetrates into every segment of the provincial economy benefiting directly and indirectly every man, woman and child."[46] The chamber's General Policy Statement on "Tourism & Recreation" in 1964 focused more intently on tangible goals such as the construction of highways and vacation resorts together with accommodation and recreation facilities, the development of community attractions, and the solicitation of conventions. There was, the chamber claimed, "a need to attract group business throughout British Columbia, including conventions, sales meetings, seminars and special events such as fishing derbies, winter carnivals, etc. which will attract groups of people to visit this Province throughout the year." "In order to achieve this objective," it maintained, "it will be necessary to increase substantially the expenditure for external advertising by the Provincial Government."[47]

The provincial government, not the private sector, was thus expected to take the lead in funding promotional campaigns. Smaller communities throughout the province were particularly insistent that the provincial government take a leading role in developing the tourist industry in the more remote regions of the province. Indeed, the BC Chamber of Commerce functioned as a sort of clearing house through which such demands were passed along to the government.

The limited impact of tourism on many of the province's smaller communities was implicitly alluded to in 1951 by GVTA comptroller A.L. Woods when he saluted one of the GVTA's "best investments" over the past year: a press tour around "the British Columbia circle." The tour included stops in Hope, Princeton, Vernon, Salmon Arm, Kamloops, and Vancouver.[48] That this circle tour, which covered but a small portion of the province, could be considered a circle tour of British Columbia would have infuriated the fledgling tourism organizations elsewhere in the province, but it was also indicative of the limitations that the underdeveloped road system and a limited advertising budget had placed on the ability of communities in the northern parts of the province to reap tourism's rewards.

The newly created Alaska Highway offered some promise but was by no means an instant boon for the tourist industry. In April 1949, for example, *Sunset* magazine profiled the road and reported that the trip "takes time and money" and "should not be attempted in less than a month." Its overall report was even less complimentary. "In short, the trip as sightseeing trip for *tourists* is not recommended." Only for "ardent fishermen, adventurers, experienced campers, and those who balance hardships ... against the thrills of exploring new frontiers and areas of historical significance" was the Alaska Highway a suitable journey.[49]

Even more accessible areas outside Vancouver and Victoria that were gaining recognition in the mid-1950s struggled to compete with the province's two major centres. *Sunset* magazine followed a complimentary 1956 article profiling British Columbia's Okanagan with an article the following year on the province's "Big Bend"-Kootenay region. For the family, the region offered a promising area to drive through with ample opportunities for camping, fishing, swimming, and boating. The more "rugged outdoorsman" was encouraged to try his hand at "big game hunting, backpacking or mountain climbing." The magazine compared the region to England's Lake District – "though on a grander scale and with more than a touch of the frontier added." *Sunset* did warn potential travellers, however, that the Big Bend road itself was "good (if not fast)" and that they should not expect "the big motor hotels that line some of the major highways south of the border," for the short tourist season ruled out "most of the frills."[50]

In the mid-1950s, the BC Chamber of Commerce became a forum through which the province's smaller and more remote communities made their pitch to benefit more fully from the tourist industry. Since its reinception in 1951, the BC Chamber of Commerce met annually to consider resolutions from its member organizations and to develop General Policy Statements. Chief among submissions from its constituent organizations throughout the province in the postwar era was a concern that areas outside the Lower Mainland and Victoria benefit from the tourist boom. These requests for provincial government involvement were not restricted solely to road-building projects – although improvements were indeed important.[51] Small communities throughout the province, in fact, sought government action and expenditure on a number of different fronts in their attempts to obtain a piece of the tourist pie. Demands for increased parkland and camping facilities were accompanied by demands for financial support for publicity endeavours as well as regulations governing recreation sites and local fish stocks.[52]

While these communities were anxious to obtain a share of visitor expenditures, they also saw tourism, as Victoria and Vancouver had seen it earlier in the century, as a means to induce industrial and agricultural development. The desire to increase recreational opportunities for local inhabitants also influenced these communities' pursuits. During the postwar era, these communities found the provincial government receptive to their demands. The most powerful political figure of the era was W.A.C. Bennett, Social Credit leader and premier of the province from 1952 to 1972. Bennett's governments focused on building infrastructure, luring US investment, and harnessing the province's hydroelectric power potential. His governments were also dedicated to "ameliorating regional disparities" as part of the premier's "Northern Vision."[53]

In a 1956 address to the Pacific Northwest Trade Association, Bennett outlined what he considered to be the proper role of government in industrial development. Because the government represented "the interests of all the citizens of British Columbia," he explained, it had a responsibility to "assist in the development of our economy wherever and whenever possible." "While the main impetus to industrial expansion in British Columbia will be given by the initiative of private enterprise in the search for profitable opportunities," he continued, "the government will play a major role in the development of the province." The aims of the Bennett government, then, "while allowing the freest play of private initiative, must be to ensure that the needs and welfare of the community are adequately taken care of."[54] Historian Jean Barman attributes Bennett's political success to his tendency to put "forward policies held together more by their innovative character than by their ideological consistency." "A strong verbal commitment to free enterprise," she explains, "cheerfully coexisted with a willingness to use the power of the state to set capitalism's direction."[55] A similar tendency on the part of the province's smaller communities and the BC Chamber of Commerce created a consensus in which tourism was employed as a strategy to alleviate regional economic disparities.[56]

As a government bureau, the BCGTB was responsible for the welfare of the tourist industry throughout the province, and, by the time W.A.C. Bennett came to power in 1952, the bureau was already focused on promoting the province's less developed regions. To this end, in 1950, the BCGTB distributed regional tourist folders for the first time featuring the Lower Fraser Valley and the Kamloops-Cariboo region.[57] The following year a folder featuring the "Okanagan-Fraser Canyon Loop" was created, and in 1952 regional attractions were featured in thirty-two radio spots.[58] By 1954 increased interest in travel through British Columbia to Alaska necessitated the production of a folder entitled "The Great North Road through British Columbia."[59]

These regional brochures were abandoned in 1959 as the bureau adopted a province-wide approach to promotion. In 1961, however, the BCGTB embarked upon a new method of encouraging regional tourism promotion by inaugurating a matching grant plan in which it provided dollar-for-dollar matching assistance in each of the eight designated regions of the province. This initiative marked the decentralization of the provincial government's tourism promotion administration. The grants, totalling $50,000 the first year, were to be "applied against the cost of selected promotions, such as advertising, literature production, displays and exhibits, national and international tourist association memberships, regional signs, and administration of community tourist promotion offices." By the end of 1961, five such regions had taken advantage of their full grant quota.[60]

GVTA president Frank Baker recognized the significant impact that the matching grant program had on his financially challenged association. In 1962, he explained, the GVTA as a member of "Region B," comprising greater Vancouver, the Sunshine Coast, and the Fraser Valley, now had $32,000 available for promotional endeavours. A year earlier, without the matching grant program, the association had been able to direct just $17,000 toward promotional advertising. The tripling of the funds made available by the provincial government the following year meant that "Region B" could anticipate spending $96,000 on promotion in the coming year. According to GVTA managing director Harold Merilees, the matching grants program was "the most constructive and forward looking plan of its kind in Canada."[61] From 1962 through 1964, the BCGTB increased the grant to $150,000 and raised it to $175,000 in 1965.[62] In 1966 the program was reorganized, with the government funding 60 percent of these promotional initiatives.[63] These matching grants reflected an increasingly modern and bureaucratic approach to tourism promotion in which the province was divided into promotional zones in an effort to address local needs more directly and manage information more efficiently.

The needs of British Columbia's more remote communities were similarly served by the establishment of *Beautiful British Columbia* magazine in 1959. Under the direction of the BCGTB, this attractive colour magazine quickly gained a popular following in Canada and abroad. By 1967 the magazine boasted over 83,000 subscribers, nearly two-thirds of whom lived outside Canada.[64] The magazine published four issues a year and did much to showcase the province's northern and interior communities. The spring 1960 issue, for example, highlighted the attractions of Nelson, Osoyoos, Kitimat, and Kispiox, while the summer 1961 issue contained articles such as "Williams Lake – Heart of the Cariboo," "Pleasure Puts the O.K. in Okanagan," and "Hunting Moose with a Camera."[65]

By the mid-1960s, increased advertising expenditures and the techniques of market research had been combined in order to mount a systematic campaign aimed at overcoming the legacy of tourism's earlier uneven development. This push to spread tourist expenditures more evenly throughout the province was part of the provincial government's broader commitment to the tourist industry in the postwar era. The expanded activities and budget of the BCGTB, including its eventual reorganization into its own government department in 1967, signalled the acceptance of systematic and coordinated tourism promotion as a tool in managing the postwar economy.

Teaching "Tourist Consciousness": Selling Tourism as a Public Good

> Each year thousands of tourists are attracted to the Fraser Valley
> by its scenic beauty. Its countryside has often been compared with
> that of beautiful Switzerland. Visitors are impressed by the many

mountain ranges which surround the area and they also find the
greenness of the valley, due to our abundant rainfall, unusual and
pleasant.[66]

The above quotation is not an excerpt from a tourist pamphlet; it is, in
fact, the introductory paragraph from a prize-winning essay written by
Joyce Williams in 1963 when she was a grade ten student at Abbotsford
Junior Secondary School. Exploring how she came to write this essay –
and indeed how tourism promotion infiltrated the curriculum of British
Columbia's school system – provides us with an opportunity to examine
the extent to which the province's tourism promoters responded to the
intense competition of the postwar era by attempting to make the average British Columbian "tourist conscious."

Increasingly tourism promoters concluded that they must retain and expand public support for their industry if they were to triumph in the competitive battle for tourists. Complementing their efforts to differentiate
the province's attractions from those of competing tourist destinations were
concerted attempts to improve British Columbians' hospitality. While other
countries had embraced the possibilities of the tourist industry, GVTA president Hedley S. Hipwell lamented in 1950, Canadians were not yet fully
appreciative of all that it offered. Advertising, he argued, was not the only
solution. More attention must also be directed toward the province's
attractions, its highways, its accommodations, and the overall quality of
its tourist reception – namely hospitality. In short, Hipwell explained, the
"travel industry must be treated as *big business!*"[67]

Gaining government support for tourism promotion at the provincial
level had been an important achievement, but this alone could not guarantee a healthy tourist industry. Equally important, in light of increasing
competition, was the necessity of securing popular recognition and support for tourism. In the remainder of this chapter, I trace the increasing
emphasis that tourism's proponents placed on educating their fellow citizens. These educational initiatives were pursued in two ways: the gathering and publicizing of statistical data that documented the industry's
contributions to local economies, and the socialization of service sector
employees and schoolchildren.

Drawing on Dominion Bureau of Statistics findings in 1951, GVTA publicity commissioner M.J. McCormick argued that one way for Vancouver
to maximize its tourist revenue in increasingly difficult times was to make
a determined effort to lengthen the stay of US visitors through *"Service,
Courtesy,* and *Hospitality."*[68] To this end, McCormick recommended the
modernizing and streamlining of the GVTA's headquarters to improve service to its visitors. He also emphasized the necessity of improving visitors' ability to locate points of interest and popular attractions through

an expanded number of directional signs and maps. A "new official civic guide book" and a "new shopping reference guide," he reasoned, would also increase tourist expenditures.[69]

In a July 1958 submission on advertising policy, the GVTA's advertising firm, Cockfield, Brown and Co., identified two key concerns: selling Vancouver to the world and selling the GVTA to Vancouver. Selling Vancouver's attractions to the world had long been part of the GVTA mandate. But just as central to the company's recommendations was the desire to increase public support for the association. To this end, it advocated the expansion of the GVTA's educational program "to cover a large number of groups who come into daily contact with tourists." Store clerks, in particular, could "be told how best tourists can be served: how to handle difficult situations such as the discount on the American dollar; the sort of questions tourists ask and where information can be obtained." Its specific recommendations also included the suggestion that "Vancouver schoolchildren could work on projects with the title of 'Why Vancouver is a good tourist centre,' or, 'Vancouver and the Tourist Industry.'" The GVTA, the advertising company suggested, should not only sponsor such assignments but also ensure that "winning essays were rewarded fittingly."[70]

Shortly after the Second World War, CGTB chief Leo Dolan suggested that, because the tourist industry was "Canada's most important means of securing U.S. dollars, it must be the concern of every Canadian from the bootblack to the banker."[71] British Columbia's tourism promoters shared this view. Convincing the larger business community of this fact, however, was no easy matter. Indeed, a great deal of effort was required to illustrate the industry's importance.[72] In the 1930s, tourism promoters successfully campaigned to have the provincial government recognize tourism as an important economic activity in its own right. Now they were broadening their campaign to influence civil society as well. This time the fruit of their earlier efforts, the BCGTB, played a key role in the pursuit of this aim. The campaign to sell the merits of the tourist industry to British Columbians included a BCGTB advertisement that appeared in sixty small weekly newspapers across the province in May 1949. Titled "It's Your BC," the ad encouraged British Columbians to visit different parts of the province but focused primarily on illustrating the important role that tourism played in the province's economic development. "British Columbia," the ad explained suggestively, "is noted for its courtesy, for its friendly attitude towards 'the stranger within its gates.'"[73]

Civic organizations similarly emphasized the industry's contributions. In 1959 the Victoria Chamber of Commerce inaugurated a Tourist Appreciation Week aimed at impressing upon the public the importance of the industry.[74] A second such week held the following year was helped markedly by local radio, newspaper, and television media and resulted in the distribution of 7,988 Tourist Appreciation Week buttons – a feat that the chamber's Tourist Trade Group considered demonstrative of the public's "mounting interest" in their endeavours.[75] By 1961 the new chairman of the Tourist Trade Group was encouraging chamber members to continue employing Tourist Appreciation Week as a "weapon of some force" to counter the "apathy displayed by many citizens and some merchants towards tourism."[76]

In January 1960, GVTA assistant manager C.R. Porter presented to the organization's Executive Committee a plan from the Membership Committee to produce a "Shopping, Services and Sightseeing Guide." Such a guide, the committee suggested, provided a number of advantages, including the ability to offset the cost of publication by accepting member advertising and the opportunity to "tap a revenue source now lost to commercial guides."[77] When the guide came off the press in May 1961, however, GVTA members thought that it would play another useful role: increasing membership.[78] By offering an explicit demonstration of tourism's role in increasing revenue for local businesses, GVTA members hoped that the brochure would increase recognition and support for their work.

A similar rationale informed a later attempt by the GVTA to publicize the degree to which tourist expenditures permeated the provincial economy. While the CGTB employed a series of National Film Board films to convince Canadians of the importance of the tourist dollar, tourism promoters in British Columbia embarked upon more local and interactive campaigns.[79] In 1968, for example, the GVTA's second annual Convention Week included a "dollar bill hunt" designed to "highlight the importance of the convention industry to Greater Vancouver." Thirty thousand one-dollar bills were employed as the 2000 delegates to the Canadian Institute of Mining and Metallurgy Convention were asked to "exchange their own currency for one dollar bills in a special series." When the bureau released the serial numbers of the bills, those people receiving the special bills became eligible for prizes, which included, not surprisingly, two totem poles valued at ten to fifteen dollars each. By May 1968, almost 400 dollar bills had been traced, with one bill travelling as far as Campbell River.[80] British Columbia's tourism promoters thus did not lack creativity when it came to educating their fellow British Columbians about the importance of the tourist industry.

Business, Tourism, and Education
Examinations of the relationship between business and education in the postwar era have, for the most part, focused on the extent to which businesses attempted to inculcate "free enterprise" values either through advertising campaigns or through a determined effort to infiltrate the university or public education system. Peter McInnis, for instance, has documented

the extent to which Canadian business leaders publicly championed the values of "free enterprise" in their attempts to ward off excessive state intervention in the form of an expansive welfare state.[81] In the American context, Elizabeth Fones-Wolf has demonstrated that US corporate leaders were keen to offer financial support to institutions and pursue closer personal ties with educators at universities as well as primary and secondary schools in an attempt to "create an educational climate more favorable to business and the capitalist system."[82] Tourism promoters in British Columbia followed similar strategies but focused on championing the importance of the tourist industry itself rather than the free-enterprise system as a whole. In doing so, they portrayed tourism as a "public good" – as a practice and economic pursuit that benefited all members of society and thus deserved widespread public support.[83]

One of the province's more outspoken tourism promoters on the topic of education was Ralph D. Baker, who sat on the GVTA's board of directors throughout the 1950s and served as a vice president of the association from 1953 until 1955. Baker had been sent to Canada in 1936 by Standard Oil to be the sales manager of its British Columbia Division.[84] He was also a member of the Pacific Northwest Trade Association – an international body composed of boards of trade and chambers of commerce throughout the Pacific Northwest.[85] For Baker, business and education were interdependent yet complementary pursuits. Both attempted "to meet the needs and wants of the community and to promote the general welfare." But they also tended to pursue these aims separately and along what appeared to be "divergent courses." Business, he explained, tended to focus primarily on more immediate needs, while education took the more "leisurely" route of exploring the past to find solutions to future problems. As a result, he claimed in 1952, education frequently became too preoccupied with the past and failed to focus enough on present-day concerns. Baker and many other tourism promoters looked forward to a greater degree of collaboration between business and education.[86]

Delegates involved in a roundtable discussion on tourism at the 1955 Pacific Northwest Trade Association conference in Vancouver, for example, focused on the need for what they termed "internal promotion" – the educating of host communities to prioritize tourism.[87] Lee Jacobi of Cole and Weber Advertising in Seattle similarly stressed the importance of education in the tourism industry. Jacobi advocated educating tourist workers through film and literature as well as classroom instruction. He also championed better education for the tourists themselves through an expansion in the number of information centres and directional aids, including signs and road markings indicating desirable routes through cities.[88] For tourism promoters, then, education could serve two purposes: it could increase recognition and support for the industry throughout the business community, and it could provide important information to both tourism industry workers and tourists themselves.

In his address to the 1955 Pacific Northwest Trade Association conference, Professor McPhee, director of the University of British Columbia's School of Commerce, took a decidedly academic approach to his subject, "The Business of Tourism." He began by defining his terms. "Tourism," he explained, "is the business of selling goods and services to persons who are away from home for a period and who spend money in the place they visit which is earned elsewhere."[89] McPhee acknowledged that he was conflating the supposedly distinct categories of "travel" and "tourism"; however, while conceding that "the number of travelers is not an exact measure of the number of tourists," McPhee encouraged his audience not to miss the key point: people travelling across provincial, state, and national boundaries were "spending money in our cities and countryside which would not be spent there if 'tourism' were not accepted as a natural part of our mores and customs."[90] For McPhee and other "tourist conscious" citizens, the distinction between "high" travel and "low" tourism was moot. The fact that travellers spent money in places other than where it was earned made them de facto tourists.

To reveal the inner workings of the industry to his audience, McPhee relied upon a small but increasing number of research studies. Surveys in Victoria, Vancouver, and Washington between 1952 and 1954 all suggested that 50 percent of tourist expenditures went directly to hotels, motels, auto courts, and restaurants. The Washington survey suggested that 13 percent of tourist expenditures were directed to transportation costs (including gasoline and automobile repairs), 11 percent to entertainment, and 26 percent to retail sales. Many people, McPhee argued, were benefiting from tourism without contributing their fair share. This situation arose, he explained, both from a desire on the part of many businesspeople to let others carry the costs of promotional efforts and from the fact that tourism was viewed by many as a "fad or a hobby" unworthy of serious economic consideration. The only way to correct such behaviour, McPhee explained, was to offer concrete evidence of tourism's importance. This could be done most effectively by increasing research efforts.[91]

British Columbia's tourism promoters undertook their educational initiatives at a time when Vancouver's business leaders were increasingly recognizing the opportunities afforded by a closer relationship between business, the provincial school system, and the University of British Columbia. By 1952 the Vancouver Board of Trade had recognized these possibilities and was involved in educational programs on a number of fronts. In the mid-1940s, for example, the Board of Trade entered into an arrangement with the financially struggling School of Commerce at UBC whereby the board provided an annual grant of $1,000 toward a university course on "merchandising." Within a few years, courses on advertising and "sales management" were also available. The board also attempted to "stimulate the interest of high school students in vocational matters" by providing prizes for "job studies" analyzing the province's industries. And, at the local level, the board sponsored "B-E Day" – "Business-Education Day" – an opportunity twice a year for the board to introduce Vancouver's teachers and principals "to the complexities and problems of business and the way in which management is attempting to maintain progress."[92] Tourism promoters in the postwar era similarly focused their efforts on gaining recognition and support for their activities through a number of educational initiatives. Anxious to obtain the empirical facts necessary to demonstrate their industry's importance, British Columbia's tourism promoters turned to an institution capable of providing the necessary information: the province's university.

Travel Surveys and the University of British Columbia

The 1950s and 1960s witnessed a noticeable increase in emphasis on specialized education in the business world. More and more companies sought employees with university business training to fill their management positions. New executives were expected to be experts in "organizational theory, rate of return accounting, and planning techniques." This new emphasis could be seen on Canadian university campuses as well. Between 1960 and 1970, for instance, the number of full-time university students in Canada pursuing business degrees tripled from roughly 5,500 to 16,000. Over the same time period, the number of MBA candidates in the country increased tenfold from 200 to over 2,000.[93]

Tourism promoters similarly saw a role for the university in their pursuits. In April 1946, for example, GVTA president Leo Sweeney voiced his concern that UBC was not giving the tourism industry due recognition. Sweeney was particularly frustrated by his experience at a recent meeting that he attended with university officials in which many other industries were discussed but not tourism. To help rectify this situation, he suggested the establishment of a prize or trophy to be presented to the winner of an oratory or essay contest that addressed the "tourist field," with the hope that such a competition might stimulate greater recognition on the part of students of the importance of the tourist industry.[94] It is unclear what became of his suggestion, but within a decade the university and the GVTA would enjoy a close working relationship.

Vancouver's first serious foray into the gathering of tourism statistics came as a result of GVTA commissioner J.V. Hughes's participation in a Pacific Northwest Trade Association meeting in the early 1950s. During one of the association's sessions on tourism, Hughes heard a description of a tourist survey carried out by university students. On his return to

Vancouver, he approached E.D. McPhee about the possibility of the university undertaking a continuous survey of visitors' "habits and trends." For Hughes, such a survey would serve two functions. It would provide "authentic information" for the local business community on the value of tourist expenditures, and it would "disclose many facts which would be of assistance to everyone interested in tourist promotion." McPhee acceded to the request, and Professor Stanley Oberg assumed responsibility for the survey. It was quickly incorporated into a university course on marketing. Questionnaires were created and distributed through the GVTA's headquarters from May through September seeking basic information concerning visitors' place of origin, length of stay, and details surrounding their expenditures, while also soliciting general "suggestions and comments" on their experiences in Vancouver.[95]

The preliminary results of the initial survey were announced at the GVTA's annual meeting, while a more detailed analysis was provided in the form of a graduating thesis prepared by a School of Commerce student – an achievement that Hughes deemed worthy of a $100 service award.[96] These surveys were conducted on an annual basis so as to establish patterns of tourist behaviour.[97] In April 1955, for example, Gordon Richardson completed his graduating thesis focusing on tourist behaviour in Vancouver. Because Richardson had had to pay for the drawing of graphs, and for making copies of the thesis, the GVTA contributed a service award of $100 and passed a resolution supporting the awarding of this payment on an annual basis.[98] In effect, this award cemented the relationship between the GVTA and the School of Commerce at UBC and guaranteed that one student a year would work for the tourist industry.

These studies provided the GVTA with important details about tourist behaviour. In 1956, for instance, a thesis by Ralph Kitos indicated that the number of visitors and the length of their stays in Vancouver had declined from 1955.[99] The UBC surveys also offered another possibility. GVTA president Ivor Neil hoped that the association's recent arrangement with UBC would "disclose to the whole business community a set of authentic facts, resulting in our members becoming more increasingly aware of the value to them of allocating funds for the work in which our Association is engaged."[100]

By the mid-1960s, these university initiatives were paying off not simply in additional information about tourist behaviour but also in more tangible ways. In April 1966, it was announced that the GVTA had hired William D.S. Earle, a recent UBC commerce graduate, to help run its expanding convention business as its assistant manager of the Convention Department. GVTA general manager Harold Merilees – an enthusiastic proponent of university graduates in tourism – hoped that this was a portent of things to come and pushed for an agreement with universities in which selected commerce students would be hired during the summer by hotels, motels, transportation companies, and tourist information centres. Such experience would also help the GVTA recognize the best prospective tourism promoters of the future. "The best prospects," Merilees explained, "should, after graduation, be sent abroad to study procedures in other selected areas for the period of three to six months and then brought back to put into practice in B.C. what they have learned." The end result would be a highly trained workforce: "Instead of just having people stumble into the industry," he explained, they would now be "specially trained for it."[101] The training of service sector personnel was another important component of tourism's educational initiatives.

Anxious to shore up support for the tourist industry, tourism promoters had effectively colonized the curriculum of the province's university and could now depend upon undergraduate research assignments in their efforts to convey the importance of the tourist industry to members of the general public. To increase public awareness of what was considered appropriate behaviour toward tourists visiting the province, tourism promoters organized educational initiatives aimed at inculcating in service sector workers an appropriate hospitality ethic.

Teaching Hospitality

> Travel competition is getting keener each year. The need for courtesy, friendliness, service to our visitors from all our people must be kept constantly to the fore.

> — GVTA comptroller A.L. Woods, 1950[102]

The importance of establishing Vancouver's reputation as a "friendly city" was emphasized by GVTA president George C. Bradley in 1957 when he urged store clerks and service station attendants to "extend the warmest of welcome[s] to our guests." He also called upon merchants and citizens to "play their part in making Vancouver a colorful city" by employing "unusual window displays of unique merchandise" and raising Canadian ensigns on flagpoles. Such endeavours, he suggested, served as the "lowest cost advertising medium" in the form of "word of mouth publicity from tourists who have visited this area and have found a friendly and enjoyable atmosphere."[103]

At least one observer, addressing the GVTA in December 1950, sounded the alarm concerning what he saw as an unacceptable decline in the level of hospitality offered to visitors. According to A.E. Dal Grauer, then head of BC Electric, the standard of hospitality in "Western Cities" had declined markedly since the war. Perhaps the problem was postwar abundance.

Grauer found that "people seem to have been thrown off stride morally and spiritually." He argued for a "restoration of courtesy" and suggested that the GVTA embark upon a campaign in the coming year designed to highlight the importance of courtesy.[104]

Public pronouncements were not enough, however, and organized educational initiatives were also a favoured solution. The move to expand educational opportunities for those interested in embarking upon a career in the tourist industry in Canada began almost immediately after the Second World War had ended. In October 1945, the Ontario Agricultural College planned to offer a short training course lasting seven months that would provide students, initially restricted to returning servicepeople, with both "classroom instruction" and "laboratory work." The course would focus on cooking and accounting as well as "the actual construction and maintenance of a resort hotel."[105] In 1945-46 a tourist industry training course for returning veterans was created at the University of Toronto's Department of Institutional Management and flourished briefly before being transferred to the neighbouring Ryerson Institute of Technology in 1949.[106]

In its attempt to improve hospitality standards, the GVTA enlisted the help of oil companies and requested that service stations be advised "to pay special attention to tourists in the matter of giving that little extra service on windshield, tires, etc., that creates good-will." The GVTA also asked the Retail Merchants' Association to emphasize among retail merchants the "value of courtesy to tourists."[107] Not content to leave training initiatives to individual companies, the GVTA joined with similar associations across the country in the late 1940s to hold Tourist Service Education weeks sponsored nationally by the Canadian Association of Tourist and Publicity Bureaus. In British Columbia, where such weeks were known as Tourist Courtesy weeks, the BCGTB and GVTA organized the week-long campaigns. These campaigns, aided by the Junior Chamber of Commerce, included the distribution of posters, bumper cards, and leaflets. In newspapers and in radio advertisements, as well as through "stunts," organizers sought to "arouse public interest in the value of courtesy to visitors."[108]

By 1957, in his annual report for the Victoria Chamber of Commerce's Tourist Trade Group, Sam Lane underscored the necessity of developing "an education curriculum in the catering and hosting arts." A preliminary effort had been made that year, he reported, in conjunction with the BCGTB, and a Hospitality Academy had been created. Unfortunately, the city's population had not shown a great degree of interest in the project, although tourism workers themselves had responded warmly to an educational bus tour.[109] Both the provincial government and the BC Chamber of Commerce supported and actively participated in similar initiatives throughout the postwar era. By 1957 the BCGTB had initiated a series of

Tourist-Clinic Workshops in cooperation with the provincial wing of the Canadian Restaurant Association and the British Columbia Hotels' Association. The detailed organization of the clinics, held in Chilliwack, Penticton, Kelowna, Kamloops, Nanaimo, and Victoria, was left to local boards of trade and the regional branches of organizations such as restaurant and hotel associations.[110] As with postwar initiatives regarding advertising and regulation, the BCGTB continued to coordinate and direct the province's tourism promotion efforts.

In January 1963, the BC Chamber of Commerce's newsletter profiled and endorsed two more innovations in tourism promotion. Hostesses representing the Kamloops Chamber of Commerce had taken to visiting local restaurants in the mornings to distribute information kits highlighting local attractions. The chamber also praised the Princeton Chamber of Commerce's proposed Tourist Clinic, which would aim to provide "people working in the service industries with better information about the attractions in the community and area." The chamber hoped that "all personnel who deal with the public will thus increase their effectiveness as good-will ambassadors when dealing with tourists."[111]

A more wide-ranging BCGTB educational initiative occurred in 1959 when the bureau noted a need for a counselling service to aid new accommodation operators and entered into an arrangement with the provincial Department of Education to appoint an "Institute Counsellor" responsible for coordinating "the various educational facilities in the restaurant-motel-hotel field ... [and arranging] clinics and instructional classes."[112] By 1968 the provincial Department of Education, in cooperation with the Department of Travel Industry, was offering a one-week "travel counsellors course," which focused on training tourist information centre operators (among others) in the following fields: public relations, geography, transportation, history, industrial and natural resources, recreation, accommodation, sources of information, border regulations, highway systems, special attractions, and provincial parks. This was a five-day course offered at Vancouver City College, with the only charge being five dollars for a manual.[113]

While such training courses were aimed primarily at adults, the province's tourism promoters did not ignore younger British Columbians. Always on the lookout for free publicity and an opportunity to increase tourism's profile, BC tourism promoters went so far as to enlist the help of the province's schoolchildren. As early as September 1948, the GVTA was supplying material to Vancouver high schools for use in classroom lessons about the "industry, history, development and future of Vancouver," and as early as 1951 tourism promoters were beginning to consider how the province's many schoolchildren might be utilized to further the interests of the tourist industry. In February of that year, one GVTA member suggested that the support of schoolchildren might even prove useful for the association's financial drive.[114]

In the early 1960s, the recently formed Fraser Valley Tourist Association (FVTA) embarked upon a new attempt to increase tourism's stature throughout the community. Essay and poster contests for high school students were held in schools throughout the district. The best essays were then to be publicized through purchased advertising space in newspapers and on radio.[115] In March 1963, the FVTA distributed promotional material to over thirty schools throughout the Fraser Valley in the hope of interesting "a great number of our students to become better acquainted with the proud history which is our heritage."[116] The importance of heritage, however, was closely tied to publicity and tourism. In his message to local school principals, FVTA president René Pelletier was more forthcoming. "This Association hopes to use the achievements and the name of Simon Fraser in its advertising campaign and tourist promotion," he explained, and was "attempting to have this part of the country known as 'The Land of Simon Fraser.'" In seeking principals' cooperation in organizing essay and poster contests among local high school students, Pelletier emphasized that a poster should not simply be of any format but "be such that it can be adapted for use on Billboards, crests, stationery letterheads or lapel buttons." Both the essays and the posters were to take as their theme "The Land of Simon Fraser."[117] Cash prizes for both competitions were furnished by the Bank of Montreal and by Pelletier himself.[118]

The FVTA's initiative combined a desire to educate with a recognition of the potential public relations benefits of associating schoolchildren with its endeavours. Some tourism promoters took a different stance and viewed the province's schoolchildren as potential tourist industry employees whose opinions of the industry needed to be shaped from an early age. In response to a 1969 questionnaire from Canadian Pacific Airlines concerning what needed to be done to improve training facilities for tourist workers, one GVTA member offered the following blunt appraisal: "I feel that more emphasis must be put on the service industries to the student in the primary and secondary grades."[119] In their determined attempts to promote an ethic of hospitality throughout civil society, tourism promoters thus adopted a variety of educational strategies ranging from community tourism clinics to public school essay contests. When it came to focusing directly on how hospitality affected the experience of tourists visiting British Columbia, however, the province's tourism promoters demonstrated a willingness to embrace a number of unconventional approaches.

Hospitality without Hosts

In his 1955 address to the Pacific Northwest Trade Association, McPhee objected to what he saw as the overly generic quality of much of the region's promotional material. Too many promotional efforts, he maintained, were hindered by general assertions that tourist destinations or attractions were "unsurpassed, glorious, magnificent," and "tremendous." More specific and detailed descriptions, he explained, were necessary. McPhee encouraged promoters to acknowledge the increasing differentiation of their clientele. "Who wants what you have – young people with families or middle aged people?" he asked. Moreover, he explained, promoters in the Pacific Northwest had relied for too long on the region's scenery as its primary selling point. Beautiful scenery, he reminded his audience, was also available in Colorado and California. In British Columbia, he argued, more needed to be made of the province's many parks as well as its recreational opportunities. Such efforts would complement the overall thrust of tourism promotion: to emphasize the possibility of experiences that the tourist could not obtain at home.[120] As we saw in Chapter 5, promotional activities after the war suggested that the province's tourism promoters were indeed aware of this necessity.

Yet for McPhee promotional material was only part of the solution. Once these tourists arrived, he argued, more needed to be done to direct their experience. "The tourism business in Britain is made more attractive and easy," he maintained, "by planned routes which tell you mile by mile the things to see, the things you could see, points of historic interest in the land you are passing through." Similarly, he argued, tourism literature in British Columbia and elsewhere in the Pacific Northwest should "help a tourist to know where to go and how long he should allow to buy the goods and services you want sold." Directional signs were therefore another useful component in directing the tourist experience.[121] Such endeavours were increasingly important as the international competition for tourists increased.

Formal attempts to inculcate an ethic of hospitality through classroom initiatives were supplemented by other less traditional forms of socialization. For example, organizations such as the GVTA also encouraged hospitality by creating hospitality clubs. The task of soliciting and maintaining subscriptions for the association remained the domain of the GVTA's overwhelmingly male membership under the auspices of what they termed the Captain Vancouver Club. Performing more "traditional" hospitality tasks, however, was reserved for women. Indeed, an important stage in the development of hospitality services in Vancouver was the establishment of the Lady Vancouver Club in 1963. Its initial fifty volunteers quickly went to work supplying maps and brochures while conducting questionnaires at the Blaine border crossing on 3-4 July 1963.[122]

Lady Vancouver Club activities focused on promoting GVTA aims and objectives and emphasized "the role of women as hostesses in their home town." Their activities included volunteering for office work during rush periods, operating information booths at conventions, greeting arriving groups from ships and trains, arranging tours of homes and gardens, formulating ideas for crests and souvenirs, and even forming a "Bare Flagpole Committee to encourage the flying of Canada's flags in good condition and at appropriate times."[123] According to the GVTA, the club was the first of its kind in North America.[124] It benefited from a $500 grant from the GVTA, and, according to club secretary Emily Ostapchuk, the members' motivations were based on civic and provincial pride.[125] In 1965 the club embarked upon a goodwill tour of the southwest United States with one of the members dressed as Captain Vancouver and the others sporting straw sailor hats with blue ribbons.[126]

At one level, the image of these women impersonating Captain Vancouver and male sailors may have been subversive – a subtle challenge to the gendered compartmentalization of GVTA activities. However, even this "naval" tour of the southern United States was no match for the admittedly kitschy but clearly hypermasculine role-playing that the male members of the GVTA embraced when they embarked upon "Operation Daffodil" – a promotional campaign aimed at luring Prairie residents to Vancouver to take advantage of the Lower Mainland's "early" spring. In 1970 a typical "Operation Daffodil" drive witnessed GVTA members embrace the martial language of an invading army as they travelled to Alberta in what was termed the "Invade Alberta" campaign. In an announcement aimed at the ears of chilly Albertans, the operation's "Supreme Commander," Vancouver Mayor Tom Campbell, joined with his "Field Marshall," GVTA president Alan Emmott, to offer the following joint statement: "The people of Alberta must be liberated – for too long they have suffered the lack of an early Spring. All who agree to come over to our side peacefully will be given the privileges of British Columbians, namely the right to golf, fish, sail and ski in February and March."[127] Clearly these two military strategists were conflating British Columbia's southwestern tip with the entire province. They were also clearly enjoying their tourism promotion responsibilities. But the martial imagery here also suggests that, regardless of the importance of Lady Vancouver Club endeavours, tourism promotion remained, culturally at least, primarily a male preserve.

Much has been written about the way in which tourist experiences are shaped and determined by the tourist gaze – the manner in which tourist sites are contrived and constructed.[128] In the postwar era, tourism promoters in British Columbia were now in a better position than ever before to control the tourist gaze effectively. They did so by employing a number of modern techniques in an effort both to encourage proper deportment among workers in the tourist industry and to direct tourists efficiently from one attraction to the next.

One initiative involved employing modern surveillance techniques in an effort to have service sector employees engage in self-discipline. To this end, the GVTA utilized contests to provide incentives for hospitable behaviour on the part of local workers. In 1965 the GVTA sponsored an anonymous committee to select ten "typically courteous public-spirited employees" from throughout the business community as winners of the GVTA's "Spring Hospitality Contest."[129] Winners were chosen from "categories," including retail clerks, hotel and motel staff, taxi drivers, and car hops – in short, "any male or female whose duties bring them into direct touch with tourists and/or convention delegates." Nominees were inspected secretly by committee members. GVTA managing director Harold Merilees underlined the importance of hospitality, and thus of such a competition, by reminding GVTA members that the tourist travel and convention business was now the province's second largest industry and was worth over $185 million annually. Greater Vancouver's share of this "large economic melon" was over $100 million, and the "most important factors in maintaining the phenomenal growth of this lucrative business" were "COURTESY AND ACCURATE INFORMATION." It was on these bases that nominees would be judged.[130]

The winners' prize, part of Air Canada's attempt to publicize its new "high-speed jet service" between Vancouver and New York, was a five-day, round-trip, all-expenses-paid tour of New York's World Fair in May. The winners, honoured with a lunch at the Pacific National Exhibition's Dogwood Dining Room, were drawn primarily from the service sector and consisted of a ship's pilot, a waitress, a head waiter, a bus driver, a district supervisor for the provincial Fish and Game Branch, a Vancouver police traffic officer, a hotel doorman, a gasoline service station manager, a maid-housekeeper, and a retail saleswoman.[131]

Noticeably absent from this list of winners were Vancouver cabbies – a group that had been recently lambasted in local newspapers as being among "the world's scruffiest taxi-drivers." Cabbies for Black Top Cabs were made aware of the GVTA competition, but the company offered a more tangible suggestion as to why hospitality might be improved: "At all times we should be most courteous and ever helpful to our passengers, a good percentage of whom are tourists," a company bulletin explained. "We should conduct ourselves in this manner if for no other reason than to promote the receiving of larger tips."[132]

By the 1950s, the province's tourism promoters had also begun to embrace the possibility of controlling the tourist gaze and ensuring visitor satisfaction even without the intervention of hospitality workers. In the mid-1950s, for example, the Victoria Chamber of Commerce took a more active role in steering tourists toward the city's attractions. Besides endorsing a plan that would see the creation of more sightseeing signs marking important historical and geographical attractions, the chamber approved

Sam Lane's suggestion of creating directional signs throughout the city "to focus tourist attention on points of interest." Drawing on a theme long associated with the city, Lane's signs would include a bird emblem.[133] By 1957 a yellow line guiding visitors with cars throughout the city had become a reality through the work of the VIPB together with support from the civic politicians of Victoria, Saanich, Esquimalt, and Oak Bay.[134] And by June of that year, the chamber was declaring the city's system of roadside markers and painted yellow lines on the roadways such a success that it sought the means of extending the system throughout the island.[135]

The increasing desire to control the tourist gaze and to guide visitors to appropriate attractions efficiently was reflected in one GVTA member's lament that Vancouver was "the worst marked city on the Continent" and paled in comparison to the US federal highway system of frequent numbered markers for roads through cities.[136] The attempt to guide visitors along an appropriate tourist route was thus not a strictly Victoria phenomenon. A "49 Mile Drive" in San Francisco served a similar purpose, and in 1957 the GVTA attempted to revive and enlarge an earlier plan to create a scenic drive for Vancouver.[137] By March 1958, the GVTA considered itself as having moved closer to realizing this aim of establishing a fifty-nine-mile scenic drive of Vancouver.[138] According to J.V. Hughes, the benefits of a scenic drive were threefold: it provided visitors with "an opportunity to properly see the beauty spots to best advantage," it inevitably meant cash-generating stops along the way, and it meant visitors would return home "as better ambassadors."[139]

Establishing scenic drives and otherwise ensuring that tourists had an enjoyable experience in Vancouver meant removing some less enjoyable scenes. When the president of the South Burnaby Board of Trade brought to the GVTA's attention the existence of some unsightly squatters' shacks along Burrard Inlet, the GVTA enthusiastically took up the board's case by drafting letters to anyone who might have influence – including the CPR, the Municipality of Burnaby, the National Harbours Board, and the Department of Indian Affairs – to urge a cleanup.[140] Hospitality and differentiation were thus two sides of the same coin. To ensure maximum tourist enjoyment required not only an efficient and welcoming host population but also a determined effort to direct tourists' attention toward some aspects of the province's social realities and away from others.

The drive to sell tourism to British Columbians as a public good thus embraced a wide variety of initiatives. Having secured state support for their endeavours, the province's tourism promoters set their sights on civil society with the hope of creating a "tourist conscious" province. Their initiatives included forays into university and public school curricula, concerted efforts to train and monitor service sector employees, and a campaign to improve directional signage in order to limit the occurrence of unpleasant travel experiences, all in an effort to manage and maximize the postwar tourist "boom."

Conclusion

As Reg Whitaker and Gary Marcuse remind us in their study of Canada's Cold War, "the capitalism that produced the goods after the war was not quite the old unregulated *laissez-faire* capitalism of the 'Dirty Thirties.' It was a capitalism managed and assisted by the state."[141] As tourism promoters' activities in the postwar era suggest, however, governments played an important role in *selling the goods* as well. The BCGTB employed market research surveys and expanded advertising campaigns in order to sell consumer goods to visitors while participating in a vigorous campaign to sell tourism as a public good to British Columbians.

The provincial government, through its funding initiatives and its direct involvement in promotional campaigns, played a central role in developing the province's tourist industry. As a mature industry, an increasing number of tourism promoters argued, tourism required the tools and approaches that had gained currency elsewhere. Thus, when Dan Wallace, acting director of the Canadian Government Travel Bureau, addressed the annual meeting of the Victoria Chamber of Commerce in 1965, he suggested that it was now "right to speak with respect of 'the travel *industry*.'" And, because tourism was an "industry," it required more "extensive market research" as well as an increasing effort to relate "travel promotion expenditure to the returns to be expected on this investment."[142]

Tourism promoters in British Columbia had, in fact, been pursuing such goals since the end of the Second World War, and they had been leaning heavily on the provincial government in the process. Their activities testify to the fact that British Columbia's postwar tourism boom was not simply a reflexive reaction to pent-up tourist demand but rather a process managed (but by no means fully controlled) by the province's tourism promoters. The final decision about how much to travel and where to visit certainly rested with consumers, but, as this chapter demonstrates, promoters harnessed the spending power and bureaucratic management style of the provincial government as they worked diligently to influence both consumer behaviour and the conduct of those British Columbians whom tourists were likely to meet.

Conclusion:
From Tourist Trade to
Tourist Industry

"What is a tourist?" asked Roland Wild in a 1955 article for *Saturday Night* magazine. "What does he want and where does he spend his money?"[1] Wild's questions appear seamlessly linked, for today we generally assume that a tourist is someone who visits a place other than his or her home community and whose impact upon society is measured primarily in terms of the dollars spent there. Indeed, a chief concern in many host communities today is that tourists will choose to settle permanently.[2] As the early chapters of this book demonstrate, however, there was a time when Wild's second question would not have followed so naturally from his first. During the first three decades of the twentieth century in British Columbia, tourism promoters concentrated on luring investment to the province. After 1930, however, tourism became increasingly equated with consumption, and the industry's success was measured primarily in terms of tourist expenditures. Between 1920 and 1970, tourism was effectively incorporated into North America's growing culture of consumption. Two brief anecdotes, both focusing on tourism promoters' attitudes toward Aboriginal imagery, capture the essence of this incorporation.

A 1903 exchange between Herbert Cuthbert, then a leading member of the Tourist Association of Victoria (TAV), and J.S. Bloomfield, an artist hired to design the cover for *An Outpost of Empire* for the TAV, recalls an era in which the investment imperative dictated tourism promoters' activities.[3] When Cuthbert asked the artist to provide a sketch for the booklet, Bloomfield produced one of an Indian. Cuthbert's reply was polite but direct. The Tourist Association, he explained, had "endeavored to avoid using the Indians in our illustrations as much as possible because while it is true they are probably very picturesque when found in the interior, ... those found on the coast are otherwise." He directed Bloomfield to produce instead a cover illustration of Esquimalt Harbour.[4]

Cuthbert's objection was not based, however, solely on his personal opinion of Native people. "I showed the sketch to some of our principal subscribers and some of our newspaper men and I must admit that they all took ... a decided objection to the Indian," Cuthbert explained. "There is such a local prejudice against anything with Indians or references to Indians," he maintained, that Bloomfield's design could never gain acceptance. Cuthbert requested instead a sketch "that will represent some feature in the history of this City or Island as an Outpost of Empire without using the glorified Indian." A "sailor, a soldier, a miner or lumberman" would prove acceptable as representing an incident or feature typical of the city.[5] Fittingly Cuthbert's alternative suggestions reflected contemporary Anglo-Saxon martial and industrial ideals. The choice of the harbour itself also reinforced the desired effect of the tourist literature: to help potential visitors see Victoria as a lively and productive commercial centre.

By the mid-1960s, as a second anecdote suggests, the rationale behind tourism promotion in British Columbia was quite different. In January 1966, the Greater Vancouver Visitors and Convention Bureau (GVVCB), then the latest incarnation of the Greater Vancouver Tourist Association, hit upon what its members considered to be a stroke of promotional genius. With Canada's 1967 centennial celebrations on the horizon, the GVVCB planned to commission a 100-foot-tall totem pole to be presented to "honour our capital city at Ottawa" and erected on Parliament Hill. According to the bureau's manager, Harold Merilees, such an endeavour had several benefits. First, it "would be a newsworthy reversal of the usual pattern. Instead of requesting a Centennial grant from Ottawa," he explained, "we would be making a tangible contribution to our capital city commemorating Canada's Centennial." Second, and most obviously, the totem pole would "remain as a permanent advertisement for British Columbia for all who would see it and photograph it on Parliament Hill." Third, its journey from Vancouver to Ottawa would also generate publicity since it would be shipped by truck across the western half of the country, be "exhibited in the principal cities en route," and make an appearance at the World's Fair in Montreal. Fourth, there was an additional possibility for publicity – one in keeping with an emerging trend in tourism initiatives that championed behind-the-scenes or "back region" experiences.[6] Merilees insisted that the "actual work of carving by our native Indian craftsmen would provide a big attraction" for both residents and visitors during 1966 – British Columbia's centennial – either in Stanley Park in Vancouver or in Thunderbird Park in Victoria.[7]

Grant Deachman, the federal Member of Parliament for the riding of Vancouver-Quadra, responded to Merilees's proposal with cautious optimism. Deachman was keen on the proposal but expressed "grave doubts that the government will permit the erection of a totem pole or any other exhibit of regional culture on the sacred grounds of Parliament Hill." "The granting of permission to a city or province to erect something on

Parliament Hill," he cautioned, "would blow up a competition to end all competitions." One is tempted here to imagine the unfolding of a provincial rivalry in which the 100-foot-tall BC totem pole would be quickly joined by, among other provincial symbols, a 100-foot-tall Nova Scotia lobster and a 100-foot-tall PEI potato – all cluttering the grounds of Parliament Hill.

Deachman voiced an alternative idea. The National Museum was scheduled to move into a new building to be completed in 1969 that would surely "be one of the most important buildings in Ottawa and a national tourist attraction." This building, Deachman suggested, "should be the permanent home for a Vancouver totem." "In fact," he explained optimistically, "it could become the signature piece of that building." For the present time, he offered, the centennial totem pole "should be given a very prominent place in Ottawa" (his suggestion was that the pole be temporarily located at the corner of Elgin and Sparks Streets, which represented "the hub of city foot and vehicular traffic," and then moved into the National Museum). "When the time comes to install it at the Museum," Deachman enthusiastically explained, "it should be moved to the new site with great ceremony." "An Anglican Bishop should bless it," he continued. "A Catholic Bishop should throw holy water on it and a Rabbi should cut a piece off it."[8]

Deachman's pronouncements here reveal a great deal about the exalted place of Aboriginal culture in British Columbia's tourism promotion efforts by the 1960s. But the playful way in which Deachman suggested the totem pole be welcomed into the museum belied another aspect of tourism promotion: the manner in which promoters now tipped their collective caps to the playfulness and pastiche of postmodernity. In his proposal, religion and Native culture were reduced to a decidedly decontextualized spectacle. The historical precedence for such a ceremony – most obviously missionary activity in the Canadian west by various religious denominations (and the conflict and complexity that these activities entailed) – was neatly expunged from this proposed ceremony. Native culture here served a solely commercial purpose: to sell visitors to Ottawa on the prospect of visiting Vancouver and leaving behind a sizable portion of their disposable income in the process.[9] By the 1960s, tourism promotion was understood primarily as a method of encouraging visitors to spend as much money as possible in a given geographical location, and from the middle part of the century tourism promoters had embraced the colour and allure of Aboriginal culture to help sell visitors on the prospect of visiting the city – and leaving behind their money. The aims of Deachman and Merilees are of a piece with the motives of tourism promoters today. Tourist behaviour today is measured by the amount of money that tourists spend at a given destination. Other revealing aspects of this exchange highlight key developments examined in this book: the equation of totem poles with advertisements, the recognition by politicians of tourism's importance, and, of course, the allusion to the intense competition between tourist destinations for travellers during the postwar era.

This book has examined not only the developments that took place between these two episodes but also tourism promoters' changing conceptions of just what a tourist was. Indeed, the changing makeup of the tourism promoters themselves throughout the twentieth century is itself indicative of the changing nature of tourism promotion. At the turn of the century, local boosters such as Herbert Cuthbert dominated the public discussions surrounding tourism and its potential contributions to prosperity in British Columbia. They saw tourism primarily as a promotional strategy that would capitalize upon the utilitarian outlook of tourists who were both repulsed and excited by the impact of industrial capitalism. By the 1930s, a new group of tourism promoters held sway. Men such as David Leeming and Charles Webster presided over local tourist organizations whose membership increasingly reflected the growing centrality of the service sector in the provincial economy. It was at this time that the rationale behind tourism promotion was transformed to embrace a consumerist orientation that identified tourist visits with tourist expenditures. This orientation was confirmed in the postwar era as veteran advertising men such as Harold Merilees and Harry Duker stepped forward to lead more aggressive and innovative campaigns for tourists in the 1950s and 1960s.

In tracing the changing conceptions of tourism among tourism promoters in British Columbia, this book has also examined the formation of a tourist industry. It would be misleading to refer to tourism promotion efforts in British Columbia before the Second World War as comprising a tourist "industry" – although the term was employed by many tourism promoters themselves. Tourist "trade" is a far more fitting term. Before the economic dislocation of the Great Depression, tourism promotion was viewed by many people, and the provincial government in particular, as an unimportant activity. Moreover, before the government belatedly recognized tourism's possibilities in the late 1930s, tourism promotion was generally pursued in an uncoordinated manner in a very limited portion of the province. The advent of state intervention was the crucial development that transformed the tourist trade into a tourist industry. Not surprisingly, it also marked the decline of a Pacific Northwest-regional approach to tourism promotion that targeted eastern industrialists and signalled the ascendence of a provincial government travel promotion bureaucracy that enjoyed a reasonably comfortable working relationship with its federal counterpart and focused its energies on targeting consumers in the western United States. During the Second World War, the provincial government's travel bureau embarked upon a campaign to coordinate the province's tourism promotion activities. It also commenced a drive to cat-alogue both the province's attractions and the characteristics of potential visitors to the province. The period from 1930 to 1945, then, was a crucial one for the tourist industry and thus for the history of consumerism more generally. Throughout the postwar era, the elements of the modern tourist industry were put in place: expanded advertising campaigns, intensified consumer marketing research, and the creation of a receptive and hospi-table host population. Such state intervention set the stage for an inva-sion of civil society during the postwar era. In 1955, for example, when *Saturday Night* journalist Roland Wild posed the questions "What is a tourist?" and "What does he want and where does he spend his money?" he could be confident that answers were now being provided – by under-graduate students at the University of British Columbia whose assigned task for their graduating essays was to supply market research informa-tion for tourism promoters in Vancouver.

Wild also expressed confidence in something else. "The tourist," he concluded, "has been recognized as a commodity."[10] This book has exam-ined and detailed the process by which tourists came to be defined entirely by the amount of food and accommodation and the number of souvenirs that they purchased on their visits to British Columbia. It has also demon-strated the extent to which British Columbia's history was commodified in an attempt both to lure these visitors to the province and to convince them to spend as much money as possible once they had arrived there. The commodification of the tourist is best illustrated by the comments of Earl McCallum of the Seattle *Times,* who in 1961 offered his views on how British Columbia's tourism promoters could best capitalize upon the Seattle World's Fair. In doing so, he echoed the regular campaigns carried out and coordinated by the BCGTB and emphasized the province's scenery and "foreign" attractions. Yet McCallum's advice also echoed another emerging characteristic of the BC promoters' approach to tourism – a ten-dency to measure tourist activities as one would the reservoir held back by a dam. "For 1962," McCallum insisted, "collective effort should result in a volume of visitors that is 'head and shoulders' above 1961."[11] Yet tour-ism promoters faced an awkward dilemma. For the purposes of managing the postwar tourist "boom," visitors to British Columbia were recorded, questioned, and catalogued. For McCallum and others, they were increas-ingly viewed impersonally as components of economic development. As this book has demonstrated, however, one of the key concerns of tourism promotion was hospitality. Tourists might comprise a "volume" that flowed into the province, but they were not, GVVCB president Alan Emmott re-minded Vancouverites, "chickens to be plucked" – a revealing term that acknowledged the plight of the individual consumer who was confronted with the assembled apparatus that the tourist industry now boasted.[12] The story of tourism in twentieth-century British Columbia is not simply the story of a seemingly insatiable consumer demand spasmodically slaking its thirst whenever the opportunity arose. It is, more accurately, the story of how this formidable apparatus of consumer culture was put in place and set to work.

Appendix:
Key tourism promotion organizations in British Columbia, 1901-72

Vancouver
Vancouver Tourist Association, 1902-9
Vancouver Information and Tourist Association, 1909-22
Greater Vancouver Publicity Bureau, 1922-35
Greater Vancouver Tourist Association, 1936-51
Vancouver Tourist Association, 1952-56
Greater Vancouver Tourist Association, 1957-61
Greater Vancouver Visitors and Convention Bureau, 1962-72

Victoria
Tourist Association of Victoria, 1902-6
Victoria Development and Tourist Association, 1906-8
Vancouver Island Development Association, 1908-18
Victoria and Island Development Association, 1918-22
Victoria and Island Publicity Bureau, 1922-63
Victoria Tourist, Convention and Publicity Bureau, 1963-
Tourist Trade Development Association of Victoria, 1935-[39?]

Government of British Columbia
Provincial Bureau of Information (and Publicity), 1901-37
Bureau of Industrial and Tourist Development, 1937-38
British Columbia Government Travel Bureau, 1938-

International Organizations
Pacific Northwest Tourist Association, 1916-22
Puget Sounders and British Columbians Associated, 1923-35
Evergreen Playground Association, 1935-[?]

Notes

Introduction: Tourism and Consumer Culture

1 On these anticipatory concerns during the mid-1980s, see J.L. Granatstein, *Yankee Go Home? Canadians and Anti-Americanism* (Toronto: HarperCollins, 1996), 251-54.

2 For classic critiques of consumers from both a Marxist and a liberal perspective, see Max Horkheimer and Theodor Adorno, "The Culture Industry: Enlightenment as Mass Deception," in *Dialectic of Enlightenment*, trans. John Cumming (New York: Continuum, 1993 [1969]), 120-67, and John Kenneth Galbraith, "The Dependence Effect," in *The Affluent Society* (New York: New American Library, 1958), 124-30. For a more recent and self-deprecating critique, see Steven Waldman, "The Tyranny of Choice," in *Consumer Society in American History: A Reader*, ed. Lawrence B. Glickman (Ithaca: Cornell University Press, 1999), 359-66.

3 Patricia Jasen, *Wild Things: Nature, Culture, and Tourism in Ontario 1790-1914* (Toronto: University of Toronto Press, 1995), 5. Jasen was directing this observation toward the distinction made between tourists and travellers by Paul Fussell and Daniel Boorstin.

4 "About WTO," <http://www.world-tourism.org/aboutwto/eng/menu.html>, (accessed 7 July 2004).

5 World Tourism Organization, *Tourism Highlights 2002* (Madrid: World Trade Organization, c. 2002), 2.

6 Statistics Canada, *National Tourism Indicators Quarterly Estimates: First Quarter 2003* (Ottawa: Ministry of Industry, 2003), viii, 18-19.

7 Ibid., xii.

8 Alisa Apostle, "Canada, Vacations Unlimited: The Canadian Government Tourism Industry, 1934-1959" (PhD diss., Queen's University, 2003), 88-89.

9 Ibid., 206-08.

10 Tourism British Columbia, *The Value of Tourism* (Victoria, 1999), 3.

11 Vancouver *News Herald*, 8 August 1938, 9.

12 Vancouver *Sun*, 10 June 1954, 8.

13 Ross Nelson and Geoffrey Wall, "Transportation and Accommodation: Changing Inter-relationships on Vancouver Island," *Annals of Tourism Research* 13 (1986): 254.

14 British Columbia Ministry of Tourism, *The Economic Impact of Tourism Industries in British Columbia* (Victoria, 1992), 28-32.

15 Gary Cross, *Time and Money: The Making of Consumer Culture* (London: Routledge, 1993), 95-96; Karen Dubinsky, *The Second Greatest Disappointment: Honeymooning and Tourism at Niagara Falls* (Toronto: Between the Lines, 1999), 118-19. On Canadian debates regarding the issue of paid vacations, see Shirley Tillotson, "Time, Swimming Pools, and Citizenship: The Emergence of Leisure Rights in Mid-Twentieth-Century Canada," in *Contesting Canadian Citizenship: Historical Readings*, ed. Robert Adamoski et al. (Peterborough: Broadview, 2002), 207-09.

16 Stanley Lebergott, *Pursuing Happiness: American Consumers in the Twentieth Century* (Princeton: Princeton University Press, 1993), 136.

17   City of Vancouver Archives (CVA), Add. Mss. 426, Harold Merilees fonds, Vol. 3, File 1, Don Finlayson, "The Impressions of a Caravanner," *Forward: Official Publication of the Vancouver Junior Board of Trade* (1937): 3.

18   On the underdeveloped nature of the province's road system at this time, see Cole Harris, "Moving amid the Mountains, 1870-1930," *BC Studies* 58 (1983): 27-30, and "The Struggle with Distance," in *The Resettlement of British Columbia: Essays on Colonialism and Geographical Change*, ed. Cole Harris (Vancouver: UBC Press, 1997), 172-74.

19   On this phenomenon, see Donald F. Davis, "Dependent Motorization: Canada and the Automobile to the 1930s," *Journal of Canadian Studies* 21, 3 (1986): 125.

20   See, for instance, John A. Jakle, *The Tourist: Travel in Twentieth-Century North America* (Lincoln: University of Nebraska Press, 1985); Warren James Belasco, *Americans on the Road: From Autocamp to Motel, 1910-1945* (Baltimore: Johns Hopkins University Press, 1997 [1979]); Clark Davis, "From Oasis to Metropolis: Southern California and the Changing Context of American Leisure," *Pacific Historical Review* 61, 3 (1992): 357-86.

21   On the important role that tourism played in fostering a shared sense of American identity in the late nineteenth and early twentieth centuries, see Marguerite S. Shaffer, *See America First: Tourism and National Identity 1880-1940* (Washington, DC: Smithsonian Institution Press, 2001). On the close relationship between consumer culture and the project of Canadian nation building during the middle of the twentieth century, see Apostle, "Canada, Vacations Unlimited." For two recent edited collections exploring the links between tourism, consumption, and identity, see *Seeing and Being Seen: Tourism in the American West*, ed. David M. Wrobel and Patrick T. Long (Lawrence: University Press of Kansas, 2001), and *Being Elsewhere: Tourism, Consumer Culture, and Identity in Modern Europe and North America*, ed. Shelley Baranowski and Ellen Furlough (Ann Arbor: University of Michigan Press, 2001).

22   Richard Wightman Fox and T.J. Jackson Lears, "Introduction," in *The Culture of Consumption: Critical Essays in American History 1880-1980*, ed. Richard Wightman Fox and T.J. Jackson Lears (New York: Pantheon, 1983), x.

23   Don Slater, *Consumer Culture and Modernity* (Cambridge, MA: Polity Press, 1997), 24-31.

24   Celia Lury, *Consumer Culture* (New Brunswick, NJ: Rutgers University Press, 1996), 29-36. For a witty exposition on the immense scope of our consumer culture and the extent to which a consumer ethos pervades even the most minute decision-making processes – including the decision to swat a black fly, see Bill McKibben, "Consuming Nature," *Consuming Desire: Consumption, Culture, and the Pursuit of Happiness*, ed. Roger Rosenblatt (Washington, DC: Island Press, 1999), 87-95.

25   For a brief summary of celebrations and critiques of consumerism, see Michael Schudson, "Delectable Materialism: Second Thoughts on Consumer Culture," in *Consumer Society in American History: A Reader*, ed. Lawrence B. Glickman (Ithaca: Cornell University Press, 1999), 342-58.

26   Keith Walden, *Becoming Modern in Toronto: The Industrial Exhibition and the Shaping of a Late Victorian Culture* (Toronto: University of Toronto Press, 1997), 195-99. The "moral panic" surrounding single women is discussed in Carolyn Strange, "From Modern Babylon to a City upon a Hill: The Toronto Social Survey Commission of 1915 and the Search for Sexual Order in the City," in *Patterns of the Past: Interpreting Ontario's History*, ed. Roger Hall, William Westfall, and Laurel Sefton MacDowell (Toronto: Dundurn Press, 1988), 255-77. The liberating opportunities of Eaton's department store are examined in Cynthia Wright, "Feminine Trifles of Vast Importance: Writing Gender into the History of Consumption," in *Gender Conflicts: New Essays in Women's History*, ed. Franca Iacovetta and Mariana Valverde (Toronto: University of Toronto Press, 1992), 229-60.

27   On the former, see Bryan Palmer, "The Theatre of Mass Culture: The First Act," in *Working Class Experience: Rethinking the History of Canadian Labour, 1800-1991*, ed. B.D. Palmer, 2nd ed. (Toronto: McClelland and Stewart, 1992), 229-36. The latter is explored briefly in Suzanne Morton, *Ideal Surroundings: Domestic Life in a Working-Class Suburb in the 1920s* (Toronto: University of Toronto Press, 1995), 44-49.

28   Doug Owram, *Born at the Right Time: A History of the Baby Boom Generation* (Toronto: University of Toronto Press, 1996).

29 Joy Parr, *Domestic Goods: The Material, the Moral, and the Economic in the Postwar Years* (Toronto: University of Toronto Press, 1999).

30 Palmer, "The Theatre of Mass Culture."

31 Lizabeth Cohen, "The New Deal State and the Making of Citizen Consumers," in *Getting and Spending: European and American Consumer Societies in the Twentieth Century*, ed. Susan Strasser, Charles McGovern, and Matthias Judt (Cambridge, UK: Cambridge University Press, 1998), 111.

32 Gary Cross, *An All-Consuming Century: Why Commercialism Won in Modern America* (New York: Columbia University Press, 2000), 69, 75, 79, 86.

33 Cross, *Time and Money*, 128-53; quotations at 128.

34 Ibid., 164, 176.

35 Dean MacCannell, *The Tourist: A New Theory of the Leisure Class* (New York: Schocken Books, 1976), 13.

36 John Urry, *The Tourist Gaze: Leisure and Travel in Contemporary Societies* (London: Sage, 1990). More satisfying is Urry's more recent study, which acknowledges the role of tourist sites as "centres for consumption" in which "goods and services are compared, evaluated, purchased and used." John Urry, *Consuming Places* (London: Routledge, 1995), 1. For a more recent examination that recognizes tourists' complex motivations for travelling, see Julia Harrison, *Being a Tourist: Finding Meaning in Pleasure Travel* (Vancouver: UBC Press, 2002).

37 Colin Campbell, "Consuming Goods and the Good of Consuming," in *Consumer Society in American History*, 29. Similarly limiting is Hal Rothman's claim that through tourism "people acquire intangibles – experience, cachet, [and] proximity to celebrity." As contemporary tourism promoters remind us at length, there is a great deal of tangible consumption taking place as well. See Hal Rothman, "Shedding Skin and Shifting Shape: Tourism in the Modern West," in *Seeing and Being Seen*, 111.

38 Ellen Janet Nightingale Berry, "The Tourist's Image of a City: Vancouver, B.C." (MA thesis, University of British Columbia, 1979), 243.

39 Raymond Williams, "Advertising: The Magic System," in *The Cultural Studies Reader*, ed. Simon During (London: Routledge, 1993), 320-36.

40 On the interaction between tourism and the environment, see Alexander Wilson, *The Culture of Nature: North American Landscape from Disney to the Exxon Valdez* (Toronto: Between the Lines, 1991). The role of tourism entrepreneurs and, increasingly, corporations in the tourist industry is explored in Belasco, *Americans on the Road*, and in Hal Rothman, *Devil's Bargains: Tourism in the Twentieth-Century American West* (Lawrence: University Press of Kansas, 1998). The experience of tourist industry workers is an important theme in Dubinsky, *The Second Greatest Disappointment*, and Urry, *The Tourist Gaze*. For an insightful examination of the interaction between host indigenous peoples and European tourists in nineteenth-century Canada, see Jasen, *Wild Things*.

41 Fox and Lears, "Introduction," x-xi.

42 E.A. Heaman, *The Inglorious Arts of Peace: Exhibitions in Canadian Society during the Nineteenth Century* (Toronto: University of Toronto Press, 1999), 106.

43 Valerie J. Korinek, *Roughing It in the Suburbs: Reading Chatelaine Magazine in the Fifties and Sixties* (Toronto: University of Toronto Press, 2000).

44 Keith Walden, "Speaking Modern: Language, Culture, and Hegemony in Grocery Store Window Displays," *Canadian Historical Review* 70, 3 (1989): 285-310.

45 Fox and Lears, "Introduction," x.

46 On such resistance in Canada, see Julie Guard, "Women Worth Watching: Radical Housewives in Cold War Canada," in *Whose National Security? Canadian State Surveillance and the Creation of Enemies*, ed. Gary Kinsmen et al. (Toronto: Between the Lines, 2000), 73-88. For a fascinating account of consumer activism in the postwar United States, see Lizabeth Cohen, *A Consumers' Republic: The Politics of Mass Consumption in Postwar America* (New York: Knopf, 2003).

47 Heaman, *The Inglorious Arts of Peace*, 106. In his recent survey of money and power in the modern era, Niall Ferguson jarringly reminds us that "experimental research shows that most people are remarkably bad at assessing their own economic best interest, even

when they are given clear information and time to learn." Niall Ferguson, *The Cash Nexus: Money and Power in the Modern World, 1700-2000* (New York: Basic Books, 2001), 11.

48 One recent exception to this trend is Russell Johnston, *Selling Themselves: The Emergence of Canadian Advertising* (Toronto: University of Toronto Press, 2001).

49 For Frank, the enthusiasm that scholars have shown concerning reception and resistance "has led us to overlook and even minimize the equally-fascinating doings of the creators of mass culture, a group as playful and even as subversive in their own way as the heroic consumers who are the focus of so much of cultural studies today." Thomas Frank, *The Conquest of Cool: Business Culture, Counterculture, and the Rise of Hip Consumerism* (Chicago: University of Chicago Press, 1997), x.

Chapter 1: Boosterism and Early Tourism Promotion in British Columbia, 1890-1930

1 Todd, better known to many people by her married name, Irene Baird, would go on to write several novels, including *Waste Heritage* (Toronto: Macmillan, 1939).

2 Irene Todd, "A Cruise down the North Pacific Coast," *Saturday Night* 6 August 1921: 17.

3 Ibid.

4 On the "experience" of modernity, see Marshall Berman, *All that Is Solid Melts into Air: The Experience of Modernity* (New York: Viking Penguin, 1988 [1982]), and David Harvey, *The Condition of Postmodernity: An Enquiry into the Origins of Cultural Change* (Oxford: Blackwell, 1990), Chapter 2. The dramatic transformation of daily life and the arrival of modernity in late-nineteenth-century Toronto are detailed in Keith Walden, *Becoming Modern in Toronto: The Industrial Exhibition and the Shaping of a Late Victorian Culture* (Toronto: University of Toronto Press, 1997).

5 Leo Marx, *The Machine in the Garden: Technology and the Pastoral Ideal in America* (New York: Oxford University Press, 2002 [1964]), 195.

6 David Louter, "Glaciers and Gasoline: The Making of a Windshield Wilderness, 1900-1915," in *Seeing and Being Seen: Tourism in the American West*, ed. David M. Wrobel and Patrick T. Long (Lawrence: University Press of Kansas, 2001), quotation at 257.

7 Both *Saturday Night* and *Maclean's* were popular Canadian magazines aimed at a general audience. They were established in Toronto in 1887 and 1905 respectively. *Sunset* magazine was founded in 1898 by the Southern Pacific Railway to boost investment and settlement along the Pacific Coast. By the 1920s, *Sunset* had emerged as the preeminent leisure and recreation magazine in the western United States.

8 In her study of tourism in nineteenth-century Ontario, for example, Patricia Jasen underscores the extent to which a romantic fascination with wilderness lured travellers to destinations such as Niagara Falls and the Thousand Islands. See Patricia Jasen, *Wild Things: Nature, Culture, and Tourism in Ontario, 1790-1914* (Toronto: University of Toronto Press, 1995).

9 Bill Parenteau, "Angling, Hunting, and the Development of Tourism in Late Nineteenth Century Canada: A Glimpse at the Documentary Record," *Archivist* 117 (1998): 10-19; Darrin M. McGrath, "Salted Caribou and Sportsmen-Tourists: Conflicts over Wildlife Resources in Newfoundland at the Turn of the Twentieth Century," *Newfoundland Studies* 10, 2 (1994): 208-25; Gerald L. Pocius, "Tourists, Health Seekers, and Sportsmen: Luring Americans to Newfoundland in the Early Twentieth Century," in *Twentieth-Century Newfoundland: Explorations*, ed. James Hiller and Peter Neary (St. John's: Breakwater, 1994), 47-77.

10 See George Colpitts, "Wildlife Promotions, Western Canadian Boosterism, and the Conservation Movement, 1890-1914," *American Review of Canadian Studies* 28, 1-2 (1998): 103-30.

11 See James B. Wolf, "A Grand Tour: South Africa and American Tourists between the Wars," *Journal of Popular Culture* 25, 2 (1991): 99-116.

12 Howard Johnson, "The 'Jamaica 300' Celebrations of 1955: Commemoration in a Colonial Polity," *Journal of Imperial and Commonwealth History* 26, 2 (1998): 120-37.

13 Robert A.J. McDonald, "Politics before Parties: Modernity and Province-Building, 1871-1903," paper presented at the BC Studies Conference, Kamloops, May 2001.

14 See Jean Barman, *The West beyond the West: A History of British Columbia*, rev. ed. (Toronto: University of Toronto Press, 1996), Chapter 9.

15 See, for example, Jackson Lears, *No Place of Grace: Antimodernism and the Transformation of American Culture, 1880-1920* (Chicago: University of Chicago Press, 1994 [1981]); George Cotkin, *Reluctant Modernism: American Thought and Culture, 1880-1900* (New York: Twayne, 1992). The determination of some Torontonians to produce and maintain an orderly community is documented in Carolyn Strange, "From Modern Babylon to City upon a Hill: The Toronto Social Survey Commission of 1915 and the Search for Sexual Order in the City," in *Patterns of the Past: Interpreting Ontario's History*, ed. Roger Hall, William Westfall, and Laurel Sefton MacDowell (Toronto: Dundurn Press, 1988), 255-77.

16 "The Beauties of Halcyon, B.C.," *Saturday Night* 18 April 1908: 4.

17 Ernest McGaffey, "The Island of Discovery," *Sunset* 30, 5 (1913): 405.

18 Mrs. Arthur Spragge, "The Last Great Valley," *Maclean's* June 1915: 22.

19 Indeed, Canada boasted many different tourist destinations noted for their health-giving properties. See, for example, Andrew Sackett, "Inhaling the Salubrious Air: Health and Development in St. Andrews, N.B., 1880-1910," *Acadiensis* 25, 1 (1995): 54-81. On the popularity of health-cure vacations in Ontario, see Jasen, *Wild Things*, 107-12. On the emergence of such "health-giving" vacations in the United States, see Cindy Aron, *Working at Play: A History of Vacations in the United States* (New York: Oxford University Press, 1999), Chapter 1. Similar concerns motivated travellers to the American far west. See Anne Farrar Hyde, *An American Vision: Far Western Landscape and National Culture, 1820-1920* (New York: NYU Press, 1990), 149-50.

20 E.A. Vandeventer, "The West Makes the Open Road Alluring," *Sunset* 54, 5 (1925): 5.

21 J.E. March, "Ski-Riders of Revelstoke," *Maclean's* 1 February 1928: 42.

22 "Travel," *Saturday Night* 7 July 1928: 10-11.

23 Similar concerns about maintaining the appropriate balance between physical and intellectual pursuits motivated social reformers to champion baseball as an antidote to the enervating effects of modern life. See Colin D. Howell, *Northern Sandlots: A Social History of Maritime Baseball* (Toronto: University of Toronto Press, 1995), 15-16, 20, 26.

24 George G. Eldredge, "On Vacation Values," *Sunset* 13, 3 (1904): 254-55.

25 Gladys Denny Shultz, "Mental Health Problems in the Business World," *Sunset* 62, 4 (1929): 38, 44. On US employers' increasing emphasis on the important role that vacations played in increasing productivity during the 1920s, see Aron, *Working at Play*, 197-205.

26 On travellers' quests for sublime experiences in Ontario, see Jasen, *Wild Things*. Visitors to the Yosemite Valley in California were also enchanted by its awe-inspiring natural wonders. See Peter J. Blodgett, "Visiting 'The Realm of Wonder': Yosemite and the Business of Tourism, 1855-1916," *California History* 69, 2 (1990): 120, 127, and Anne F. Hyde, "From Stagecoach to Packard Twin Six: Yosemite and the Changing Face of Tourism, 1880-1930," *California History* 69, 2 (1990): 156. The landscape of the American far west and the American reliance on European rhetorical conventions and conceptions of beauty, Hyde argues, combined to make the sublime a staple of travellers' recollections and railway guidebooks. See Hyde, *An American Vision*, 17-20, 109. The European fascination with (and aversion to) dangerous mountains are evocatively detailed by Simon Schama, *Landscape and Memory* (Toronto: Vintage Canada, 1996 [1995]), 447-513.

27 Mary Adelaide Snider, "Walking the Flume," *Saturday Night* 16 August 1913: 29, 35.

28 Kitty Hardcastle, "Drinking from Mountain Streams," *Saturday Night* 27 September 1913: 29.

29 McGaffey, "The Island of Discovery."

30 E. Alexander Powell, "Autobirds of Passage: The Island Highway," *Sunset* 33, 3 (1914): 529.

31 Norman Lambert, "The New British Columbia," *Maclean's* October 1915: 20.

32 Guy E. Rhoades, "Bella Coola: The Norway of Canada," *Saturday Night* 23 May 1925: 25.

33 Charles Lugrin Shaw, "The Valley of the Past," *Maclean's* 15 March 1922: 27.

34 Donald A. Wright, "W.D. Lighthall and David Ross McCord: Antimodernism and English-Canadian Imperialism, 1880s-1918," *Journal of Canadian Studies* 32, 2 (1997): 134-53; Ross D. Cameron, "Tom Thomson, Antimodern Nationalism, and the Ideal of Manhood," *Journal of the Canadian Historical Association*, New Series 10 (1999): 185-208.

35 Hyde, *An American Vision*, 216.

36   Edward W. Sandys, "A Gleam from a Glacier," *Saturday Night* 8 February 1890: 7.
37   W.E. Raney, "On the Old Cariboo Road," *Saturday Night* 25 February 1899: 4. This theme of the traveller as "hero" is explored in Susan L. Blake, "A Woman's Trek: What Difference Does Gender Make?" *Women's Studies International Forum* 13, 4 (1990): 347-55.
38   Hardcastle, "Drinking from Mountain Streams." On the tendency of female explorers to celebrate their successful triumphs over dangers and the sense of empowerment that resulted from such achievements, see Dea Birkett, *Spinsters Abroad: Victorian Lady Explorers* (Oxford: Blackwell, 1989).
39   Percy Gomery, "Looking for a Road across British Columbia," *Journal of the Canadian Bankers' Association* July 1922: 441.
40   Powell, "Autobirds of Passage: The Island Highway," 530.
41   The emerging role of science and its centrality in travellers' quests to "systematize" nature during the latter half of the eighteenth century is detailed in Mary Louise Pratt, *Imperial Eyes: Travel Writing and Transculturation* (London: Routledge, 1992), 29-34.
42   Hamilton M. Laing, "Gardens of the Desert," *Canadian Magazine* May 1920: 21-32.
43   "Sport on the Cariboo Road," *Saturday Night* 11 March 1899: 7.
44   Snider, "Walking the Flume."
45   E. Alexander Powell, "Autobirds of Passage: The Cariboo Trail," *Sunset* 33, 4 (1914): 742.
46   Spragge, "The Last Great Valley."
47   Lambert, "The New British Columbia."
48   "The Beauties of Halcyon, B.C."
49   Ian Ousby, *The Englishman's England: Taste, Travel, and the Rise of Tourism* (Cambridge, UK: Cambridge University Press, 1990). On the scientific and collecting activities undertaken by female travellers, see Birkett, *Spinsters Abroad*.
50   Anne Farrar Hyde has noted a similar tendency to combine utilitarian observations with romantic conventions among travellers to the American far west. See Hyde, *An American Vision*, 65-67.
51   Robert A.J. McDonald, "Victoria, Vancouver, and the Economic Development of British Columbia, 1886-1914," in *Town and City: Aspects of Western Canadian Urban Development*, ed. Alan F.J. Artibise (Regina: Canadian Plains Research Center, University of Regina, 1981), 31-36; quotation at 31.
52   Carlos A. Schwantes, "Tourists in Wonderland: Early Railroad Tourism in the Pacific Northwest," *Columbia* 7, 4 (1993-94): 22-23.
53   E.J. Hart, *The Selling of Canada: The CPR and the Beginnings of Canadian Tourism* (Banff: Altitude Publishing, 1983), 7, 8, 16.
54   Hyde, *An American Vision*, 108, 149, 161, 165, 175, 240, 266.
55   Hart, *The Selling of Canada*, 14-19.
56   Charles N. Forward, "The Evolution of Victoria's Functional Character," in *Town and City*, 359.
57   Paul-Andre Linteau, *The Promoters' City: Building the Industrial Town of Maisonneuve, 1883-1918*, trans. Robert Chodos (Toronto: James Lorimer, 1985), 64-73.
58   Paul Rutherford, "Tomorrow's Metropolis: The Urban Reform Movement in Canada, 1880-1920," *Canadian Historical Association, Historical Papers* (1971): 203-24; quotation at 211.
59   Janet Northam Russell and Jack W. Berryman, "Parks, Boulevards, and Outdoor Recreation: The Promotion of Seattle as an Ideal Residential City and Summer Resort," *Journal of the West* 26, 1 (1987): 15.
60   On the "booster" mentality of the period, see Alan F.J. Artibise, "Boosterism and the Development of Prairie Cities, 1871-1913," in *Town and City*, 211-16.
61   David Neufeld, "Security, Approval, and Mastery – Symbols of Saskatoon: The Cultural Baggage of Some Settlers in Western Canada," *Prairie Forum* 13, 2 (1998): 159-72.
62   City of Victoria, *Victoria Illustrated* (Victoria: Ellis-*Colonist*, 1891).
63   University of Washington Archives (UWA), Daniel Hunt Gilman papers, Box 4, File 24, Seattle Chamber of Commerce, *Facts Seattle* (January 1893).
64   Russell and Berryman, "Parks, Boulevards, and Outdoor Recreation."
65   Tom Zimmerman, "Paradise Promoted: Boosterism and the Los Angeles Chamber of Commerce," *California History* 64, 1 (1985): 22-33; quotation at 22.

66 Forward, "The Evolution of Victoria's Functional Character," 356-57.

67 McDonald, "Victoria, Vancouver, and the Economic Development of British Columbia, 1886-1914," 36-39.

68 Victoria City Archives (VCA), Victoria Chamber of Commerce (VCC) fonds, 32 B 1, Minute Book, Volume 1, Regular Quarterly Meeting, 6 October 1890. The Victoria Chamber of Commerce was founded in 1863. In 1878, its name was changed to the British Columbia Board of Trade. In 1921, the organization reverted back to its original name, the Victoria Chamber of Commerce.

69 VCA, VCC fonds, 32 B 1, Minute Book, Volume 1, 8th Meeting of Council, 2 December 1890; 12th Meeting of Council, 7 April 1891.

70 VCA, VCC fonds, 32 B 1, Minute Book, Volume 2, Quarterly General Meeting, 15 October 1897; 11th Meeting of Council, 20 December 1898.

71 VCA, VCC fonds, 32 B 1, Minute Book, Volume 2, Quarterly General Meeting, 13 October 1899.

72 VCA, VCC fonds, 32 B 1, Minute Book, Volume 2, 4th Meeting of Council, 1 September 1900; 5th Meeting of Council, 2 October 1900.

73 VCA, VCC fonds, 32 B 5, Clipping Album, Victoria *Daily Colonist*, 7 September 1901, "Meeting of B. of T. Council."

74 British Columbia Board of Trade, *Victoria, British Columbia: Past and Present* (Victoria: Colonist Presses, c. 1900).

75 VCA, VCC fonds, 32 B 1, Minute Book, Volume 2, 6th Meeting of Council, 3 December 1901.

76 Kenneth Lines, "A Bit of Old England: The Selling of Tourist Victoria" (MA thesis, University of Victoria, 1972), 26.

77 Victoria *Daily Colonist* 27 May 1917: 15.

78 See, for example, Linteau, *The Promoters' City*, 145-62.

79 On local initiatives to develop British seaside resorts, see Richard Roberts, "The Corporation as Impresario: The Municipal Provision of Entertainment in Victorian and Edwardian Bournemouth," and John K. Walton, "Municipal Government and the Holiday Industry in Blackpool, 1876-1914," in *Leisure in Britain, 1780-1939*, ed. John K. Walton and James Walvin (Manchester: Manchester University Press, 1983), 137-57, 159-85.

80 *Daily Colonist* 7 July 1900: 7.

81 *Daily Colonist* 3 March 1901: 5.

82 *Daily Colonist* 23 November 1901: 5.

83 By 19 February 1902, the committee had obtained subscriptions totalling over $3,700, and the Provisional Committee was confident (a confidence that was understandable given the mayor's position as president of the association) that the city would make available an annual grant from funds that had been directed in previous years to private advertising schemes. *Daily Colonist* 20 February 1902: 6. On civic boosters' claims that they were acting in the interests of the entire community, see Artibise, "Boosterism and the Development of Prairie Cities, 1871-1913," 214-15.

84 *Daily Colonist* 20 February 1902: 6.

85 Cameron and Jones, for example, were both Liberals. In 1903 Cameron secured the Victoria City seat in the provincial legislature as a member of British Columbia's newly formed Liberal Party, while Jones was an original member, and later the president, of the city's Sir Wilfrid Laurier Club. D.R. Ker, like Herbert Cuthbert, was a Conservative. In fact, Cuthbert was a supporter of Conservative premier Richard McBride and vociferously endorsed the premier's campaign to obtain "better terms" from the federal government. *Daily Colonist* 30 October 1930: 5; *Daily Colonist* 3 October 1933: 1-2; *Daily Colonist* 14 July 1923: 1, 8; *Daily Colonist* 26 November 1909: 3; *Daily Colonist* 21 October 1908: 3. The members of the Provisional Committee were drawn from at least two different mainstream Protestant denominations. Cameron and Fraser were both Presbyterian, while Ker and Lugrin were Anglican. *Daily Colonist* 30 October 1930: 5; *Daily Colonist* 31 January 1911: 3; *Daily Colonist* 14 July 1923: 1, 8; *Daily Colonist* 15 June 1917: 1, 4.

86 Fraser and Mayor Hayward, for example, served as manager and president, respectively, of the BC Protestant Orphans' Home. *Daily Colonist* 31 January 1911: 3; *Daily Colonist* 9

July 1919: 1. On the philanthropic efforts of contemporary businesspeople, see Linteau, *The Promoters' City*, 36, and Diana Pederson, "'Building Today for the Womanhood of Tomorrow': Businessmen, Boosters, and the YWCA, 1890-1930," *Urban History Review* 15, 3 (1987): 225-42. Their concern for the overall economic welfare of the city is indicated by the fact that virtually all of the Provisional Committee members were associated with the city's Board of Trade.

87 Evidence certainly exists to suggest that many cities were, indeed, determined to focus their efforts on attracting free-spending visitors. As Catherine Cocks has shown in her study of American city festivals, city beautiful endeavours could be closely related to what I refer to as the "expenditure imperative" – the determination to maximize visitor expenditures. See Catherine Cocks, "The Chamber of Commerce's Carnival: City Festivals and Urban Tourism in the United States, 1890-1915," in *Being Elsewhere*, 89-107. And there are, indeed, other documented references to early-twentieth-century tourism promoters in the United States explaining their motivations in terms of tourist expenditures. See, for example, David Louter, "Glaciers and Gasoline: The Making of a Windshield Wilderness, 1900-1915," and Peter Blodgett, "Selling the Scenery: Advertising and the National Parks, 1916-1933," in *Seeing and Being Seen*, 265, 280. Nevertheless, in the case of British Columbia, a strong connection between traditional boosterism and tourism promotion lasted well into the 1920s.

88 *Daily Colonist* 6 March 1907: 3.

89 E.A. Heaman, *The Inglorious Arts of Peace: Exhibitions in Canadian Society during the Nineteenth Century* (Toronto: University of Toronto Press, 1999), 155.

90 Lugrin arrived in Victoria in 1897 after a successful career in law and journalism in his home province of New Brunswick. During the 1880s, he authored several works documenting the natural resources and vacation opportunities of New Brunswick. *Daily Colonist* 15 June 1917: 1, 4.

91 *Daily Colonist* 20 February 1902: 6.

92 Ibid.

93 Ibid.

94 VCA, VCC fonds, 32 B 5, Clippings Album, *Daily Colonist* 19 July 1902: 5-6.

95 VCA, "Tourism" Clipping File, *Daily Colonist* 4 February 1903: 5.

96 Victoria *Daily Times* 27 April 1906: 1.

97 VCA, CRS 97, Tourist Association of Victoria (TAV) papers, 3 A 4, Secretary's Letterbooks, Cuthbert to E.J. Coyle, Asst. General Passenger Agent, CPR, Vancouver, 8 August 1903; Cuthbert to [no addressee], 9 December 1903; Cuthbert to Mayor, Victoria, 10 December 1903.

98 VCA, TAV papers, Secretary's Letterbooks, Cuthbert to Coyle, 14 August 1903.

99 VCA, VCC fonds, 32 B 1, Minute Book, Volume 2, 8th Meeting of Council, 14 November 1902.

100 VCA, VCC fonds, 32 B 1, Minute Book, Volume 2, 20th Meeting of Council, 22 May 1903.

101 *Daily Colonist* 15 June 1917: 10.

102 *Daily Colonist* 29 April 1903: 5.

103 VCA, TAV papers, Secretary's Letterbooks, Cuthbert to Mayor, 2 September 1903; Cuthbert to Premier Richard McBride, 2 September 1903.

104 *Daily Colonist* 6 July 1904: 3.

105 *Daily Colonist* 7 May 1904: 3.

106 Tourist Association of Victoria, *An Outpost of Empire* (Victoria: Colonist Printing and Publishing, 1905), 1.

107 *The Hotel Dallas* (Victoria: Province Print, c. 1895).

108 Tourist Association of Victoria, *Victoria, British Columbia, Canada: Tourist Resort of the Pacific Northwest* (Victoria: Colonist Presses, c. 1902). According to a 1903 TAV pamphlet, "Victoria's pleasant summer days, of sunshine, and bracing breezes offer health to the body and repose to the mind." TAV, *Picturesque Victoria, British Columbia, Canada: The Tourist Resort of the Pacific Northwest* (Victoria: Colonist Printing, 1903). The 1905 TAV publication, *An Outpost of Empire*, expanded upon this characteristic, explaining that "the

city has earned for itself a very enviable reputation" as a health resort. For people feeling "run down through over work, or suffering from nervous prostration on account of mental worry, or because of living in high altitudes, there is no city in which such speedy and effectual relief will be found as in Victoria" (Victoria: Colonist Printing and Publishing, 1905). A later edition of *An Outpost of Empire* explained that Victoria's "combination of magnificent scenery and almost perfect climate is going to be instrumental in making Victoria one of the largest and richest residential cities on the continent." TAV, *An Outpost of Empire: Victoria, British Columbia, Canada: "The Evergreen City of Canada"* (Victoria: Colonist Presses, 1907).

109 TAV, *Picturesque Victoria* (1903).
110 TAV, *An Outpost of Empire* (1907).
111 Vancouver Island Development Association, *Victoria, British Columbia: A Most Attractive City on the Pacific Coast* (Victoria, 1915).
112 See, for example, British Columbia Board of Trade, *Victoria, British Columbia: Past and Present* (c. 1900); TAV, *An Outpost of Empire* (1905); and TAV, *Picturesque Victoria* (1903).
113 TAV, *An Outpost of Empire* (1905).
114 TAV, *Picturesque Victoria* (1903). The British character of Kelowna was similarly publicized and celebrated in promotional material regarding orchards. Jason Patrick Bennett, "Apple of the Empire: Landscape and Imperial Identity in Turn-of-the-Century British Columbia," *Journal of the Canadian Historical Association* New Series 9 (1998): 63-92.
115 *Victoria ... the Capital City of the West* (Victoria: BC Print and Engraving Company, c. 1900).
116 TAV, *Impressions of Victoria, British Columbia, Canada: The "Empress" City of the Golden West* (Victoria: Colonist Presses, 1907).
117 *Daily Colonist* 3 April 1906: 6.
118 *Daily Colonist* 7 March 1906: 7.
119 *Times* 9 February 1906: 4.
120 *Daily Colonist* 13 July 1904: 5; *Daily Colonist* 9 February 1906: 2; *Daily Colonist* 10 January 1907: 3.
121 VCA, TAV papers, Secretary's Letterbooks, Cuthbert to H.H. Jones, Permanent Home Building Society, Victoria, 17 August 1903.
122 VCA, TAV papers, Secretary's Letterbooks, Cuthbert to Mrs. Joan Dunsmuir, Victoria, 22 September 1903.
123 VCA, TAV papers, Secretary's Letterbooks, Cuthbert to James Thompson, HBC, Victoria, 18 February 1904.
124 VCA, TAV papers, Secretary's Letterbooks, Cuthbert to Mayor and Board of Aldermen, Victoria, 6 November 1903.
125 VCA, "Tourism" Clipping File, *Daily Colonist* 28 January 1903: 4.
126 Vancouver *Daily Province* 24 June 1902: 3.
127 *Province* 26 June 1902: 2.
128 *Province* 11 July 1902: 1.
129 *Province* 5 July 1902: 1.
130 "Headquarters Established," *Province* 12 July 1902: 1; *Province* 21 July 1902: 1.
131 Robert A.J. McDonald, *Making Vancouver: Class, Status, and Social Boundaries, 1863-1913* (Vancouver: UBC Press, 1996), 169.
132 *Province* 5 July 1902: 1.
133 Ibid.
134 *Province* 28 June 1902: 1.
135 *Province* 14 July 1902: 1.
136 "Exhibits for Tourists," *Province* 21 July 1902: 2.
137 *Province* 7 July 1902: 1.
138 *Province* 9 July 1902: 2. The visitors' ethnicity is not stated.
139 *Province* 21 February 1908: 2.
140 Robert A.J. McDonald, "Business Leaders in Early Vancouver, 1886-1914" (PhD diss., University of British Columbia, 1977), 320-21; McDonald, *Making Vancouver*, 123-24.
141 On these antimodern activities, see Ian McKay, *The Quest of the Folk: Antimodernism and Cultural Selection in Twentieth-Century Nova Scotia* (Montreal: McGill-Queen's University

Press, 1994); Cameron, "Tom Thomson, Antimodern Nationalism, and the Ideal of Manhood"; Michael Dawson, "'That Nice Red Coat Goes to My Head like Champagne': Gender, Antimodernism, and the Mountie Image: 1880-1960," *Journal of Canadian Studies* 32, 3 (1997): 119-39; and Michael Dawson, *The Mountie from Dime Novel to Disney* (Toronto: Between the Lines, 1998), Chapter 2.

142   Marguerite S. Shaffer, "Seeing America First: The Search for Identity in the Tourist Landscape," in *Seeing and Being Seen*, 171-72.

Chapter 2: From the Investment to the Expenditure Imperative

1   Warren James Belasco, *Americans on the Road: From Autocamp to Motel, 1910-1945* (Baltimore: Johns Hopkins University Press, 1997 [1979]), 7.

2   Norman Hayner, "Auto Camps in the Evergreen Playground," *Social Forces* 9 (1930): 256-57.

3   Along with Belasco, *Americans on the Road*, see, for example, James H. Morrison, "American Tourism in Nova Scotia, 1871-1940," *Nova Scotia Historical Review* 2, 2 (1982): 41; Carlos A. Schwantes, "Tourists in Wonderland: Early Railroad Tourism in the Pacific Northwest," *Columbia* 7, 4 (1993-94): 30; Gerald D. Nash, "Stages of California's Economic Growth, 1870-1970," *California Historical Quarterly* 51, 4 (1972): 323; and Anne Farrar Hyde, "From Stagecoach to Packard Twin Six: Yosemite and the Changing Face of Tourism, 1880-1930," *California History* 69, 2 (1990): 154-69.

4   Victoria *Daily Colonist* 24 April 1906: 6.

5   Victoria *Daily Times* 8 December 1908: 4; *Times* 30 January 1909: 5.

6   Vancouver *Daily Province* 20 January 1909: 13; *Province* 21 January 1909: 10.

7   *Times* 13 October 1916: 1; *Times* 27 October 1916: 13; *Times* 27 November 1916: 15; Victoria City Archives (VCA), Victoria Chamber of Commerce (VCC) fonds, 31 F 7, Minute Book, 15th Meeting of Council, 6 October 1916; 17th Meeting of Council, 27 October 1916.

8   VCA, VCC fonds, 31 F 7, Minute Book, 25th Meeting of Council, 2 March 1917.

9   In November 1921, for example, Premier John Oliver made it known that rural districts in the province had expressed their frustration concerning the government's funding of the PNTA because it was perceived to be advertising only Vancouver and Victoria. VCA, VCC fonds, 32 A 3, Minute Book, Report of Joshua Kingham to President and Council, 27 October 1916; *Times* 27 October 1916: 13; *Times* 25 November 1921: 1.

10   VCA, VCC fonds, 31 F 7, Minute Book, 25th Meeting of Council, 2 March 1917.

11   *Daily Colonist* 13 July 1904: 5.

12   *Daily Colonist* 31 January 1906: 8; *Daily Colonist* 25 February 1906: 5. On the history of the See America First movement and its connection to the broader theme of American nation building, see Marguerite S. Shaffer, *See America First: Tourism and National Identity, 1880-1940* (Washington, DC: Smithsonian Institution Press, 2001).

13   *Daily Colonist* 3 February 1906: 6.

14   *Daily Colonist* 6 April 1906: 12.

15   VCA, VCC fonds, 32 A 3, Minute Book, Report of Joshua Kingham to President and Council, 27 October 1916.

16   Kenneth Lines, "A Bit of Old England: The Selling of Tourist Victoria" (MA thesis, University of Victoria, 1972), 47-49.

17   VCA, VCC fonds, 32 B 7, Scrapbook, "Declares Victoria Has Basis for Largest Industry," *Times* 13 May 1921: 7.

18   University of Oregon Archives (UOA), Ax 27, Lee D. Drake papers, Box 3, File 2, Herbert Cuthbert, "Tourist Travel: How It Is Aiding in Rural Upbuilding," address before the Washington State Chamber of Commerce, 6 December 1922.

19   UOA, Drake papers, Box 3, File 2, Herbert Cuthbert, Secretary's Report to the Sixth Annual Meeting of the PNTA, 24 November 1922. Unlike many publicity organizations, the PNTA's advertising copy was not contracted out to an advertising agency but devised by the PNTA itself under the watchful eye of Cuthbert. This mode of operation was favoured not only as a cost-saving device but also because the organization considered tourist advertising "different from the ordinary run of business that went to advertising agencies." UOA, Drake papers, Box 3, File 2, Minutes of 6th Annual Meeting of the PNTA, 24 November 1922.

20   Pacific Northwest Tourist Association, *The Pacific Northwest: The World's Greatest Out of Doors* (Seattle: PNTA, c. 1917).
21   UOA, Drake papers, Box 3, File 2, PNTA Minutes of Directors' Meeting, 7 March 1923; John Hart to Cuthbert, 24 April 1923.
22   *Daily Colonist* 20 August 1920: 14.
23   UOA, Drake papers, Box 3, File 2, PNTA Minutes of Directors' Meeting, 7 March 1923.
24   *Times* 26 December 1916: 16.
25   *Times* 5 October 1920: 5.
26   *Daily Colonist* 28 August 1921: 13.
27   Lines, "A Bit of Old England," 47.
28   Roland Marchand, *Advertising the American Dream: Making Way for Modernity, 1920-1940* (Berkeley: University of California Press, 1985), 6-7.
29   Pamela Walker Laird, *Advertising Progress: American Business and the Rise of Consumer Marketing* (Baltimore: Johns Hopkins University Press, 1998), 246.
30   Russell Johnston, *Selling Themselves: The Emergence of Canadian Advertising* (Toronto: University of Toronto Press, 2001).
31   *Daily Colonist* 23 September 1951: 4 (magazine section); *Daily Colonist* 8 July 1964: 1-2.
32   Lines, "A Bit of Old England," 57-58; *Daily Colonist* 16 January 1954: 13; *Daily Colonist* 31 December 1921: 1; *Daily Colonist* 8 July 1964: 1-2.
33   *Daily Colonist* 8 July 1964: 1-2.
34   *Daily Colonist* 11 March 1960: 14.
35   Lines, "A Bit of Old England," 55-59.
36   Vancouver *Sun* 1 March 1939: 26.
37   The association's board of directors sought a membership of 2,500 members and fully expected to reach that number in the coming years. After all, the board explained, "this Association is the only one in the city whose membership is open to any citizen. The class of business or profession has no effect on the qualification for membership." Nor was there a membership fee. City of Vancouver Archives (CVA), Add. Mss. 633, Greater Vancouver Visitors and Convention Bureau (GVVCB) papers, Series B, Volume 4, File 20, Greater Vancouver Publicity Bureau, *Report of the Board of Directors for the Year 1926*, 20.
38   Ibid.
39   CVA, GVVCB papers, Series B, Volume 4, File 20, GVPB, *Report of the Board of Directors for the Year 1928*, 19; *Times* 13 February 1924: 8, 13.
40   GVPB, *Report of the Board of Directors for the Year 1926*, 9.
41   Ibid., 10; *Times* 25 February 1927: 11.
42   *Times* 25 February 1927: 11; GVPB, *Report of the Board of Directors for the Year 1926*, 9-10; *Daily Colonist* 21 February 1929: 22.
43   *Times* 25 February 1927: 11.
44   *Times* 13 February 1924: 8, 13.
45   GVPB, *Report of the Board of Directors for the Year 1926*, 12-13.
46   *Daily Colonist* 5 October 1927: 4.
47   Victoria and Island Publicity Bureau (VIPB), *"Follow the Birds" to Victoria, B.C.* (Victoria, 1922); VIPB, *"Follow the Birds" to Victoria, B.C.* (Victoria, 1928).
48   *Daily Colonist* 5 October 1927: 4.
49   Laird, *Advertising Progress*, 185-86.
50   Marchand, *Advertising the American Dream*, 153-54.
51   GVPB, *Report of the Board of Directors for the Year 1928*, 10.
52   Marchand, *Advertising the American Dream*, 92. According to Mary Vipond, 30 percent of Canadians owned radios by 1931. Mary Vipond, *The Mass Media in Canada*, rev. ed. (Toronto: James Lorimer, 1992), 39.
53   Jackson Lears, *Fables of Abundance: A Cultural History of Advertising in America* (New York: Basic Books, 1994), 334-35.
54   Marchand, *Advertising the American Dream*, 93.
55   By the early 1930s, for example, the US Park Service was using the radio to deliver a series of lectures on the Park Service in an attempt to reach the one million potential visitors listening in. Peter Blodgett, "Selling the Scenery: Advertising and the National Parks,

1916-1933," in *Seeing and Being Seen: Tourism in the American West,* ed. David M. Wrobel and Patrick T. Long (Lawrence: University Press of Kansas, 2001), 284.

56 *Times* 13 February 1924: 11.
57 GVPB, *Report of the Board of Directors for the Year 1928,* 11.
58 Ibid., 1.
59 Ibid., 1.
60 Ibid., 2.
61 Laird, *Advertising Progress,* 239.
62 These calculations are based on the GVPB's raw data. See GVPB, *Report of the Board of Directors for the Year 1926,* 14.
63 *Times* 25 February 1927: 11.
64 GVPB, *Report of the Board of Directors for the Year 1926,* 14.
65 Ibid.
66 *Daily Colonist* 21 February 1929: 15.
67 GVPB, *Report of the Board of Directors for the Year 1928,* 6. On the widespread use of the "invisible export" concept, see Alisa Apostle, "Canada, Vacations Unlimited: The Canadian Government Tourism Industry, 1934-1959" (PhD diss., Queen's University, 2003), 54.
68 *Times* 25 February 1927: 11.
69 *Daily Colonist* 21 February 1929: 15.
70 GVPB, *Report of the Board of Directors for the Year 1928,* 6-7.
71 CVA, GVVCB papers, Series B, Volume 4, File 20, GVPB, *Report of the Board of Directors for the Year 1929,* 1.
72 GVPB, *Report of the Board of Directors for the Year 1928,* 12.
73 Lears, *Fables of Abundance,* 237.
74 CVA, GVVCB papers, Series B, Volume 4, File 20, *Publicity Bureau of Greater Vancouver Annual Report 1931,* "President's Message," 1-2.
75 GVPB, *Publicity Bureau of Greater Vancouver Annual Report 1931,* 1.
76 Laird, *Advertising Progress,* 184; Lears, *Fables of Abundance,* 161, 197; Marchand, *Advertising the American Dream,* 2, 7.
77 GVPB, *Publicity Bureau of Greater Vancouver Annual Report 1931,* 1.
78 Ibid.
79 GVPB, *Publicity Bureau of Greater Vancouver Annual Report 1931,* "Ways and Means," 1.
80 British Columbia Archives and Records Service (BCARS), GR 709, Department of Highways, Highways Records 1926-71, Box 2, File 3, C15, GVPB tourism promotion booklet, *100 for 1,* c. 1931.
81 GVPB, *Publicity Bureau of Greater Vancouver Annual Report 1931,* 3-4.
82 CVA, GVVCB papers, Series B, Volume 4, File 20, GVPB, *Publicity Bureau of Greater Vancouver Annual Report 1932,* "Advertising."
83 CVA, GVVCB papers, Series B, Volume 4, File 21, GVPB, *Publicity Bureau of Greater Vancouver Annual Report 1933,* "President's Address."
84 Ibid., "Commissioner's Report."
85 GVPB, *Publicity Bureau of Greater Vancouver Annual Report 1931,* "Membership," 1.
86 CVA, GVVCB, Series B, Volume 4, File 21, GVPB, *Publicity Bureau of Greater Vancouver Annual Report 1934,* "President's Message."
87 GVPB, *Publicity Bureau of Greater Vancouver Annual Report 1933,* "Commissioner's Report."
88 *Daily Colonist* 10 February 1931: 5; *Times* 18 November 1931: 4.
89 *Times* 12 February 1932: 1, 5.
90 University of British Columbia Archives (UBCA), S.F. Tolmie papers, Box 19, File 19-4, *Daily Colonist,* 10 February 1933, "The Tourist Industry."
91 *Times* 8 February 1933: 1, 18.
92 CVA, GVVCB papers, Series B, Volume 4, File 21, GVPB, *Publicity Bureau of Greater Vancouver Annual Report 1935,* "President's Report."
93 Ibid.
94 GVPB, *Publicity Bureau of Greater Vancouver Annual Report 1935,* "Commissioner's Report."
95 Ibid.

96   GVPB, *Publicity Bureau of Greater Vancouver Annual Report 1935*, "Advertising Committee Report."

97   GVPB, *Publicity Bureau of Greater Vancouver Annual Report 1935*, "Convention and Entertainment Committee Report."

98   CVA, GVVCB papers, Series B, Volume 4, File 21, GVPB, *Publicity Bureau of Greater Vancouver Annual Report 1936*, "Commissioner's Report."

99   On the development of market research in Canada, see Johnston, *Selling Themselves*, Chapter 6.

100 *Times* 14 February 1938: 14.

101 UBCA, Tolmie papers, Box 3, File 3-29, H.B. Thomson to Tolmie, 26 September 1930.

102 UBCA, Tolmie papers, Box 3, File 3-29, Henry B. Thomson, Chairman, Liquor Control Board, to Tolmie, 26 April 1932. On the English use of the garden to mark the conquest of new territory, see Patricia Seed, *Ceremonies of Possession in Europe's Conquest of the New World, 1492-1640* (Cambridge, UK: Cambridge University Press, 1995), 16-40.

103 UBCA, Tolmie papers, Box 22, File 22-9, Victoria *Daily Times*, 12 January 1933, "Victoria and the Tourist Business"; Ottawa *Evening Journal*, 22 December 1932, "Don't Americanize."

104 BCARS, Add. Mss. 9, G.G. McGeer papers, Box 14, File 6, E.H. Adams, "Tourist Trade," Address to the Canadian Chamber of Commerce, Vancouver, 9 September 1937.

105 See, for example, Tourist Association of Victoria (TAV), *Victoria, British Columbia, Canada: Tourist Resort of the Pacific Northwest* (c. 1902); TAV, *Picturesque Victoria, British Columbia, Canada: The Tourist Resort of the Pacific Northwest* (1903); and TAV, *An Outpost of Empire* (1905). A noteworthy exception is the Vancouver Tourist Association publication *The Sunset Doorway of the Dominion: Vancouver, B.C.* (Vancouver, c. 1905), which encouraged visitors to visit an Indian village near North Vancouver. Its description of the Aboriginal population, however, revealed the extent to which the authors felt it necessary to overcome the reader's conceptions of Native people. "These people are industrious, frugal, devout," the pamphlet explained, "and entitled to the sympathy felt the world over for the noble red men of the forest."

106 Robert F. Burkhofer, Jr., *The White Man's Indian: Images of the American Indian from Columbus to the Present* (New York: Vintage, 1979 [1978]), 61; Daniel Francis, *The Imaginary Indian: The Image of the Indian in Canadian Culture* (Vancouver: Arsenal Pulp Press, 1992), 52. The desire to retain a "progressive" reputation in the hope of obtaining statehood meant that city boosters in Santa Fe, New Mexico, played down indigenous cultures before 1912. Chris Wilson, *The Myth of Santa Fe: Creating a Modern Regional Tradition* (Albuquerque: University of New Mexico Press, 1997). A similar desire to sell Canada as a "progressive society" to prospective settlers and investors meant that the federal government's Department of Indian Affairs attempted to tightly constrain and script Aboriginal performances. Paige Raibmon, "Theatres of Contact: The Kwakwaka'wakw Meet Colonialism in British Columbia and at the Chicago World's Fair," *Canadian Historical Review* 81, 2 (2000): 179-80, 184. Not all boosterism campaigns in British Columbia avoided employing Aboriginal imagery. In 1910 the Grand Trunk Pacific began to select "Indian names" for several of its townsites. Frank Leonard, "Grand Trunk Pacific and the Establishment of the City of Prince George, 1911-1915," *BC Studies* 63 (1984): 34. More revealing, perhaps, was the decision by boosters in Kelowna to employ references to the Okanagan peoples' early recognition of the land's fecundity in an attempt to lure settlers. As Jason Bennett explains, such references were tightly circumscribed, and Kelowna's boosters made sure to emphasize that the Okanagan were not fellow residents but "a 'feature' of the natural landscape amongst the foliage and fauna." Jason Patrick Bennett, "Apple of the Empire: Landscape and Imperial Identity in Turn-of-the-Century British Columbia," *Journal of the Canadian Historical Association* New Series 9 (1998): 73.

107 E.A. Heaman, *The Inglorious Arts of Peace: Exhibitions in Canadian Society during the Nineteenth Century* (Toronto: University of Toronto Press, 1999), 182, 188, 193, 199, 300.

108 Paul Schullery, "Privations and Inconveniences: Early Tourism in Yellowstone National Park," in *Seeing and Being Seen*, 241.

109 Patricia Nelson Limerick, "Seeing and Being Seen: Tourism in the American West," in *Seeing and Being Seen*, 45.

110   Lears, *Fables of Abundance*, 163.
111   Jeffrey Steele, "Reduced to Images: American Indians in Nineteenth-Century Advertising," in *Dressing in Feathers: The Construction of the Indian in American Popular Culture*, ed. S. Elizabeth Bird (Boulder: Westview Press, 1996), 45-47.
112   Quoted in Francis, *The Imaginary Indian*, 181-82.
113   It is clear, however, that Native peoples in the Pacific Northwest interacted with tourists at some level during the late nineteenth century. As Paige Raibmon notes, "tourists and anthropologists encouraged Aboriginal people to present and commodify their authentic selves at the same time as government officials and missionaries discouraged such displays." Paige S. Raibmon, "Authentic Indians: Episodes of Encounter from the Late Nineteenth-Century Northwest Coast" (PhD diss., Duke University, 2000), 30.
114   BCARS, Add. Mss. 522, C.C. Pemberton papers, Volume 1, "Tourist Trade Development Association" File, Submission by W.T. Straith, Chairman, Beautification Committee, TTDA. Contained in T.H. Eslick to Pemberton, c. November 1935.
115   BCARS, GR 1222, Premiers' papers, Box 137, File 10, George I. Warren to Premier, 11 May 1936.
116   Jackson Lears, "Packaging the Folk: Tradition and Amnesia in American Advertising, 1880-1940," in *Folk Roots, New Roots: Folklore in American Life*, ed. Jane S. Becker and Barbara Franco (Lexington, MA: Museum of Our National Heritage, 1988), 122-25, 131-32; see also Lears, *Fables of Abundance*, 383-84. On the antimodernist interest in Nova Scotia folk imagery, see Ian McKay, *The Quest of the Folk: Antimodernism and Cultural Selection in Twentieth-Century Nova Scotia* (Montreal: McGill-Queen's University Press, 1994).
117   Burkhofer, *The White Man's Indian*, 61, 176.
118   According to John Jakle, for instance, "pent-up buying power and increased leisure time after World War II served to flood North American highways with vacationers." John A. Jakle, *The Tourist: Travel in Twentieth-Century North America* (Lincoln: University of Nebraska Press, 1985), 185. On the pent-up demand for tourism in British Columbia, see John Douglas Belshaw and David J. Mitchell, "The Economy since the Great War," in *The Pacific Province: A History of British Columbia*, ed. Hugh Johnston (Vancouver: Douglas and McIntyre, 1996), 330.
119   Cindy Aron, *Working at Play: A History of Vacations in the United States* (New York: Oxford University Press, 1999), 238.
120   Peter Blodgett, "Selling the Scenery: Advertising and the National Parks, 1916-1933," in *Seeing and Being Seen*, 289. In an insightful article, Michael Berkowitz has recently argued that the 1930s were a turning point in the development of tourism in the United States, and he points to two key factors: an increase in the number of people securing paid vacations, and the activities of tourism promoters as playing a key role in this development. Michael Berkowitz, "A 'New Deal' for Leisure: Making Mass Tourism during the Great Depression," in *Being Elsewhere: Tourism, Consumer Culture, and Identity in Modern Europe and North America*, ed. Shelley Baranowski and Ellen Furlough (Ann Arbor: University of Michigan Press, 2001), 185-212.
121   Karen Dubinsky, *The Second Greatest Disappointment: Honeymooning and Tourism at Niagara Falls* (Toronto: Between the Lines, 1999), 140; Alan A. MacEachern, "No Island Is an Island: A History of Tourism on Prince Edward Island, 1870-1939" (MA thesis, Queen's University, 1991), 119-20.
122   In the United States, for example, the percentage of disposable personal income spent on recreation pursuits between 1930 and 1939 averaged 4.88 percent, while between 1921 and 1929 it averaged 4.06 percent. Those with money, it seems, increasingly chose to spend it on recreation activities. Marion Clawson and Jack L. Knetsch, *Economics of Outdoor Recreation* (Baltimore: Johns Hopkins University Press, 1966), 318-19.
123   CVA, GVVCB papers, Series B, Volume 4, File 21, GVPB, *Publicity Bureau of Greater Vancouver Annual Report 1938*, "Publications and Editorial Committee."

Chapter 3: Entitlement, Idealism, and the Establishment of the BCGTB, 1935-39

  1   R. Ross Nelson, "The Presentation of Landscape: Rhetorical Conventions and the Promotion of Tourism in British Columbia, 1900-1990" (PhD diss., University of British Columbia, 1994), 202-11.

2   Ibid., 211-13, 218.
3   Alvin Finkel, *Business and Social Reform in the Thirties* (Toronto: James Lorimer, 1979).
4   Bliss suggests that the roots of the Depression can be found both in the dislocation caused by the First World War and by the protectionist policies pursued by various governments. Michael Bliss, *Northern Enterprise: Five Centuries of Canadian Business* (Toronto: McClelland and Stewart, 1987), 412.
5   Ibid., 425.
6   Finkel, *Business and Social Reform*, 31-35.
7   Lara Campbell, "'A Barren Cupboard at Home': Ontario Families Confront the Premiers during the Great Depression," in *Ontario since Confederation: A Reader*, ed. E.-A. Montigny and L. Chambers (Toronto: University of Toronto Press, 2000), 284-306; Lara Campbell, "'We Who Have Wallowed in the Mud of Flanders': First World War Veterans, Unemployment, and the Great Depression in Ontario, 1929-1939," *Journal of the Canadian Historical Association* New Series 11 (2000): 125-49.
8   Lizabeth Cohen, "The New Deal State and the Making of Citizen Consumers," *Getting and Spending: European and American Consumer Societies in the Twentieth Century*, ed. Susan Strasser, Charles McGovern, and Matthias Judt (Cambridge: Cambridge University Press, 1998), 115, 123.
9   Robert M. Campbell, *Grand Illusions: The Politics of the Keynesian Experience in Canada, 1945-1975* (Peterborough: Broadview Press, 1987), 36.
10   For example, on 27 January 1928, the chamber went on record opposing recently imposed custom regulations that called upon tourists to furnish a bond on items such as sporting and camera equipment. The same day a motion was passed requesting that Victoria City Council reconsider its decision not to renew the licence of the Victoria Auto Camp. Victoria City Archives (VCA), Victoria Chamber of Commerce (VCC) fonds, 32 A 1, Regular Meeting of the Board of Directors, 27 January 1928.
11   VCA, VCC fonds, 32 A 1, Quarterly Luncheon Meeting, 9 November 1931.
12   VCA, VCC fonds, 32 A 1, Board of Directors Meeting, 7 March 1932.
13   VCA, VCC fonds, 32 A 1, Regular Meeting of the Board of Directors, 18 September 1933; Joint Meeting of the Victoria Chamber of Commerce and the VIPB, 15 June 1932.
14   Victoria *Daily Times* 11 December 1931: 1-2; *Times* 3 January 1939: 1; *Times* 3 January 1939: 4; Victoria *Daily Colonist* 4 January 1939: 2.
15   *Daily Colonist* 27 August 1929: 3.
16   VCA, VCC fonds, 32 A 1, Board of Directors Meeting, 6 November 1934.
17   *Times* 22 November 1934: 13.
18   *Times* 22 November 1934: 13; *Daily Colonist* 23 November 1934: 3.
19   *Times* 23 November 1934: 15; *Daily Colonist* 24 November 1934: 2.
20   *Times* 22 November 1934: 13; *Daily Colonist* 19 January 1935: 1-2.
21   *Daily Colonist* 19 January 1935: 1-2.
22   Ibid.
23   *Daily Colonist* 16 March 1935: 1, 3.
24   *Times* 16 March 1935: 1.
25   *Daily Colonist* 16 March 1935: 1, 3.
26   British Columbia Archives and Records Service (BCARS), Add. MSS. 522, C.C. Pemberton papers, Volume 1, "Tourist Trade Development Association" File, Mayor Leeming to Pemberton, 26 November 1934.
27   BCARS Pemberton papers, Volume 1, "Tourist Trade Development Association" File, "The TTDA of Victoria and Vancouver Island: A Brief Description of Its Form, Purposes, and Possibilities," n.d.
28   Ibid.
29   Ibid.
30   BCARS, Pemberton papers, Volume 1, "Tourist Trade Development Association" File, B.A. McKelvie, "Observations as a Result of Island Tour by Delegation from the Tourist Trade Development Association of Victoria and Vancouver Island," n.d.
31   Ibid.
32   BCARS, Pemberton papers, Volume 1, "Tourist Trade Development Association" File, Leeming to Pemberton, 13 April 1935.

33   BCARS, Pemberton papers, Volume 1, "TTDA Historic Objects and Natural Features Preservation Committee" File, Minutes of the TTDA Historic Landmarks and Natural Features Preservation Committee, 31 January 1935.
34   BCARS, Pemberton papers, Volume 1, "Tourist Trade Development Association" File, Excerpts from articles appearing in the Victoria *Daily Colonist* written by B.A. McKelvie on "Vancouver Island's Urgent Need for a New Deal." Endorsed and distributed by the Island Council of the Tourist Trade Development Association of Victoria and Vancouver Island, n.d.
35   McKelvie, "Observations."
36   Alisa Apostle, "Canada, Vacations Unlimited: The Canadian Government Tourism Industry, 1934-1959" (PhD diss., Queen's University, 2003), 32, 47-48; quotation at 32.
37   BCARS, GR 709, Highways Records, Box 2, File 3, C15, GVPB booklet, *100 for 1*, c. 1931.
38   University of British Columbia Archives (UBCA), Add. MSS. S.F. Tolmie papers, Box 3, File 3-28, Tolmie to A.J.T. Taylor, Ottawa, 13 November 1931.
39   "Canada's Tourist Trade – $250,000,000.00 a Year," Canadian Bank of Commerce *Monthly Commercial Letter*, April 1932, in UBCA, Tolmie papers, Box 3, File 3-29, Henry B. Thomson, Chairman, Liquor Control Board, to Tolmie, 26 April 1932.
40   UBCA, Tolmie papers, Box 22, File 22-9, Point Grey *News*, 19 May 1932, "The Tourist Trade."
41   UBCA, Tolmie papers, Box 19, File 19-4, *Times*, 23 September 1933, "The Tourist Business."
42   UBCA, Tolmie papers, Box 19, File 19-4, Ashcroft *Journal*, 30 April 1932, "Canada's Tourist Trade."
43   UBCA, Tolmie papers, Box 22, File 22-9, Prince Rupert *News*, 21 May 1932, "Who Gets Tourist Dollar?" The only present alternative, the *News* suggested, was securing a reasonable rate from a railway company that would allow tourists to transport their vehicles by rail into the city.
44   A similar enthusiasm in the United States and France led to the creation of the US Travel Bureau in 1937 and the French Tourism Commissariat in 1935. Michael Berkowitz, "A 'New Deal' for Leisure," and Bertram Gordon, "French Cultural Tourism and the Vichy Problem," in *Being Elsewhere: Tourism, Consumer Culture, and Identity in Modern Europe and North America*, ed. Shelley Baranowski and Ellen Furlough (Ann Arbor: University of Michigan Press, 2001), 203, 242.
45   See Senate of Canada, *Report and Proceedings of the Special Committee on Tourist Traffic* (Ottawa: King's Printer, 1934). For a detailed examination of the special committee as well as a discussion of the prominent role that tourism came to play in the Maritimes in the 1920s and 1930s, see Shelley Kyte, "'V-8 or Make and Break' – An Investigation of the Development of Tourism in Canada: A Case Study of Nova Scotia" (MA thesis, Queen's University, 1997). For a detailed overview of both the Senate committee and the creation of the CTB that places these developments in the broader international context of tourism promotion initiatives, see Apostle, "Canada, Vacations Unlimited," Chapter 1.
46   Apostle, "Canada, Vacations Unlimited," 31-32. On the promotion of tourism in Canada's national parks, see Alan MacEachern, *Natural Selections: National Parks in Atlantic Canada, 1935-1970* (Montreal: McGill-Queen's University Press, 2001).
47   Senate of Canada, *Report and Proceedings of the Special Committee on Tourist Traffic*, viii-ix.
48   National Archives of Canada (NAC), D. Leo Dolan papers, MG 30, E 259, Volume 1, "Minister 1" File, Memorandum, Dolan to Minister, 8 January 1935.
49   NAC, Dolan papers, Volume 1, "Minister 2" File, Memorandum, Dolan to W.J. Bennett, Private Secretary, Department of Transport, 8 April 1937.
50   Apostle, "Canada, Vacations Unlimited," 58.
51   NAC, Dolan papers, Volume 1, "Minister 1" File, Memorandum, Dolan to Minister, 8 November 1934.
52   Ibid.
53   *Daily Colonist* 12 May 1936: 1, 5; Robin Fisher, *Duff Pattullo of British Columbia* (Toronto: University of Toronto Press, 1991), 208.
54   NAC, Dolan papers, Volume 1, "Minister 2" File, telegram, Cromie to Dolan, 5 December 1935.
55   NAC, Dolan papers, Volume 1, "Minister 2" File, telegram, Dolan to Cromie, 6 December

1935; Memorandum, Dolan to Minister C.D. Howe, 7 December 1935. Howe and the Liberals, led by Mackenzie King, defeated the Conservatives in the October 1935 federal election.

56 On Pattullo's campaign promises and his ongoing battle with the federal government, see Fisher, *Duff Pattullo*, Chapters 7 and 8.

57 BCARS, Add. MSS. 3, T.D. Pattullo papers, Microfilm A-1807, Volume 62, File 3a, R.J. Cromie, Publisher, Vancouver *Sun*, to Pattullo, 21 February 1935.

58 BCARS, Pattullo papers, Microfilm A-1807, Volume 62, File 3a, Pattullo to Cromie, 22 February 1935.

59 BCARS, Pattullo papers, Microfilm A-1807, Volume 62, File 3a, Cromie to Pattullo, 23 February 1935.

60 BCARS, Pattullo papers, Microfilm A-1807, Volume 62, File 3a, Pattullo to Cromie, 25 February 1935. Pattullo's reluctance to embrace the possibilities of the tourist industry, for example, differs markedly from the enthusiasm shown toward the tourist trade by Nova Scotia's premier Angus L. Macdonald. On Macdonald, see Ian McKay, "Tartanism Triumphant: The Construction of Scottishness in Nova Scotia, 1933-1954," *Acadiensis* 21, 2 (1992): 5-47.

61 *Province* 6 March 1935: 1; Vancouver *Sun* 6 March 1935: 1; *Sun* 7 March 1935: 1, 10; *Sun* 8 March 1935: 1, 4.

62 *Sun* 6 March 1935: 1. The five Liberal MLAs were S.S. McKeen, Robert Wilkinson, Gordon Wismer, Helen Smith, and Vancouver mayor G.G. McGeer.

63 *Sun* 11 March 1935: 1.

64 *Sun* 6 March 1935: 1; *Times* 6 March 1935: 1; *Sun* 8 March 1935: 1, 4; *Times* 8 March 1935: 1.

65 *News Herald* 7 March 1935: 4.

66 *Sun* 8 March 1935: 1.

67 *Sun* 12 March 1935: 8. The twelve included nine Liberals (N.W. Whittaker, Saanich; L.A. Hanna, Comox; R. Wilkinson, Vancouver-Point Grey; George M. Murray, Lillooet; Dr. J. Allen Harris, South Okanagan; S.S. McKeen, Vancouver-Point Grey; George S. Pearson, Alberni-Nanaimo; Byron Johnson, Victoria; and J.D. Gillis, Yale), one Labour MLA (Tom Uphill, Fernie), and two former Conservatives (R.W. Bruhn, Salmon Arm, of the Non Partisan Independent Group, and R.H. Pooley, Esquimalt, of the Unionist Party of BC).

68 *Sun* 13 March 1935: 1.

69 *Sun* 15 March 1935: 1.

70 *Sun* 27 August 1935: 4.

71 On the creation of the Economic Council, see Fisher, *Duff Pattullo*, 260.

72 *Sun* 15 March 1935: 20.

73 *Daily Colonist* 24 July 1935: 6.

74 BCARS, GR 1222, Premiers' papers, Box 129, File 11, G.E. Curtis, Secretary, Board of Trade of the City of New Westminster, to Hon. John Hart, Minister of Finance, 18 March 1936.

75 BCARS, Premiers' papers, Box 129, File 11, M.C. Ironside, Secretary, Nanaimo Board of Trade, to Pattullo, 15 January 1936.

76 *Times* 25 March 1936: 11; Vancouver *News Herald*, 25 March 1936: 8.

77 *Times* 4 November 1937: 1-2; Government of British Columbia, *Report of the Department of Trade and Industry 1939*, FF13; Meg Stanley, "Creating Beautiful British Columbia: Pattullo's Promotion of Tourism," paper presented to the BC Studies Conference, Kelowna, October 1994, 13-14.

78 *Times* 15 February 1938: 5.

79 *Sun* 25 November 1938: 2; *Times* 25 November 1938: 15; *Province* 25 November 1938: 16.

80 *Daily Colonist* 11 January 1939: 2.

81 For example, the Liberal Party publicly recognized the importance of the tourist industry at its 1932 convention, and in June 1934 Pattullo himself speculated about the possibility of creating a provincial Ministry of Tourist Traffic. Stanley, "Creating Beautiful British Columbia," 11; Fisher, *Duff Pattullo*, 215-16.

82 BCARS, Premiers' papers, Box 35, File 2, J. Gordon Smith, "Summary of Suggestions for Improved Promotion of the Tourist Industry," 17 July 1936.

83 *Daily Colonist Magazine* 11 June 1950: 3; *Daily Colonist* 29 September 1951: 16.
84 *Daily Colonist* 28 June 1942: 5; Government of British Columbia, *Public Accounts* (1930-31), N 98.
85 University of Victoria Archives (UVA), 86-30, Caravan across British Columbia 1930 fonds, Scrapbook, Vancouver *Province,* 6 May 1931, "Auto Caravan Justified by Results."
86 *Daily Colonist* 28 May 1938: 2.
87 Smith, "Summary of Suggestions."
88 Government of British Columbia, *Public Accounts* (1938-39).
89 *Province* 11 May 1936: 20.
90 *Times* 17 September 1937: 13.
91 Smith, "Summary of Suggestions."
92 Ibid., Appendix A.
93 Ibid.
94 NAC, RG 20, Department of Industry, Trade and Commerce papers, A9, Volume 1578, File 3610-B-1, J. Gordon Smith to Dolan, 8 December 1938; Dolan to Smith, 23 December 1938; Smith to Dolan, 16 December 1938; Dolan to Smith, 22 December 1938; Dolan to Smith, 23 December 1938; Dolan to W. Lloyd Craig, 14 November 1938.
95 NAC, Dolan papers, Volume 1, "Minister 1" File, Memorandum, Dolan to Minister, 8 January 1935. An additional 3 percent was targeted at the American southeast.
96 Senate of Canada, *Report and Proceedings of the Special Committee on Tourist Traffic,* 260.
97 NAC, Dolan papers, Volume 1, "Minister 2" File, Paul B. Thompson, Advertising Representative, *Sunset* magazine, to CTB, 20 November 1936.
98 BCARS, Premiers' papers, Box 148, File 6, Warren to Dolan, 31 March 1938.
99 NAC, Department of Industry, Trade and Commerce papers, A9, Volume 1578, File 3610-B-1, W. Lloyd Craig, Bureau of Industrial and Tourist Development, to Dolan, 4 April 1938.
100 NAC, Department of Industry, Trade and Commerce papers, A9, Volume 1578, File 3610-B-1, Dolan to Craig, 9 April 1938.
101 NAC, Department of Industry, Trade and Commerce papers, A9, Volume 1578, File 3610-B-1, Smith, Commissioner, Bureau of Tourist Development, Department of Trade and Industry, to Dolan, 23 November 1938.
102 Smith, "Summary of Suggestions." In 1935, following established advertising practices, the CTB divided the country into five regions for the purpose of advertising Canada in the United States. In 1949, this model would be abandoned in favour of promotional material that highlighted the country's nine provinces. See Apostle, "Canada, Vacations Unlimited," 111, 285. Smith, of course, was anxious for the CTB to go beyond simply incorporating these marketing zones into existing (and for him far too vague) publicity campaigns and instead allow promoters from each region to conduct regional campaigns with federal funds. There is no evidence, however, to suggest that he got his way.
103 On McGeer's proposals for monetary reform, see David Ricardo Williams, *Mayor Gerry: The Remarkable Gerald Grattan McGeer* (Vancouver: Douglas and McIntyre, 1986), especially Chapter 7. McGeer's own lengthy tome on the subject was published in 1935. See G.G. McGeer, *The Conquest of Poverty: Or, Money, Humanity, and Christianity* (Hawthorne, CA: Omni, 1967 [1935]).
104 BCARS, McGeer papers, Box 14, File 6, "Memorandum Re Development of Tourist Trade," McGeer to Mayor George Miller, 8 January 1937.
105 BCARS, McGeer papers, Box 14, File 5, CBO radio broadcast, Ottawa, c. 1937.
106 Ibid.
107 BCARS, McGeer papers, Box 14, File 5, *Liberty,* 28 May 1938, editorial by Associate Publisher Wilber M. Philpott.
108 BCARS, McGeer papers, Box 14, File 6, Leo Dolan, Chief, CTB, address to British Hotelmen, Waldorf Astoria Hotel, New York City, 10 May 1938.
109 City of Vancouver Archives (CVA), Add. MSS. 633, Greater Vancouver Visitors and Convention Bureau (GVVCB) papers, Series B, Volume 4, File 21, GVPB, *Publicity Bureau of Greater Vancouver Annual Report 1937,* "Secretary-Manager's Report."
110 Ibid.
111 GVPB, *Publicity Bureau of Greater Vancouver Annual Report 1938,* "President's Report."

112 Ibid.
113 Ibid.
114 The unemployed were protesting reduced government relief grants and a municipal ban on "collecting" on city streets. For a firsthand account of the strikes and the "Bloody Sunday" clash with authorities, see Steve Brodie, *Bloody Sunday Vancouver – 1938: Recollections of the Post-Office Sit-Down of Single Unemployed* (Vancouver: Young Communist League, 1974).
115 BCARS, Premiers' papers, Box 148, File 6, 24 June 1938, George Warren to Pattullo (22 June 1938, Wm. J. Clark, Manager, Dominion Hotel, Victoria, to Warren, VIPB).
116 BCARS, Premiers' papers, Box 148, File 6, 24 June 1938, George Warren to Pattullo (22 June 1938, A. Playfair, Sunset Inn, Qualicum Beach, to Warren).
117 BCARS, Premiers' papers, Box 148, File 6, 24 June 1938, George Warren to Pattullo (22 June 1938, Wm. J. Clark, Manager, Dominion Hotel, Victoria, to Warren, VIPB).
118 BCARS, Premiers' papers, Box 148, File 6, 24 June 1938, George Warren to Pattullo (17 June 1938, E.W. Hudson, Manager, Hotel Georgia, Vancouver, to Warren).
119 UBCA, Alexander Maitland Stephen papers, Box 2, *British Columbia Job-Seekers Journal* 1, 1; emphasis added. Many thanks to Todd McCallum for sharing his research notes on the Stephen papers with me.
120 Ibid.
121 Brodie, *Bloody Sunday*, 7 (illustration).
122 UBCA, Stephen papers, Box 2, "Tourist Guide!" sheet, issued by Single Unemployed Committee.
123 Cited in Niall Ferguson, *The Cash Nexus: Money and Power in the Modern World, 1700-2000* (New York: Basic Books, 2001), 396. The relationship between tourism and peace remains a hotly debated topic. For a spirited celebration of tourism's potential contribution to world peace, see L.J. D'Amore, "Tourism: A Vital Force for Peace," *Futurist* 22 (1988): 23-28, and "Tourism: The World's Peace Industry," *Recreation Canada* 48, 1 (1990): 24-33. For a more guarded appraisal of tourism's possibilities, see Turgut Var, John Ap, and Carlton Van Doren, "Tourism and World Peace," in *Global Tourism: The Next Decade*, ed. William F. Theobald (Oxford: Butterworth Heinemann, 1994), 27-39.
124 Berkowitz, "A 'New Deal' for Leisure," in *Being Elsewhere*, 204.
125 See Shelley Baranowski, "Strength through Joy: Tourism and National Integration in the Third Reich," in *Being Elsewhere*, 213-36.
126 GVPB, *Publicity Bureau of Greater Vancouver Annual Report 1938*, "Secretary-Manager's Report."
127 University of Victoria Archives (UVA), Caravan across British Columbia 1930 fonds, Scrapbook, *Province*, n.d. [Burns Lake, 21 June 1930], "Northern Poet Is Inspired by Alaska Caravan."
128 CVA, Add. MSS. 426, Harold Merilees fonds, Volume 3, File 5, *British Columbia Presents the Big Bend Highway* (Victoria: Queen's Printer, 1940), 3.

Chapter 4: The Second World War and the Consolidation of the BC Tourist Industry, 1939-50

1 British Columbia Archives and Records Service (BCARS), GR 1222, Premiers' papers, Box 35, File 3, Jules Hone, Hone Tours, Montreal, to Premier Pattullo, 18 August 1941.
2 In devising his program, Hone astutely tailored his message differently for Canada's two major linguistic groups (and in doing so undoubtedly undermined his potential contribution to national unity). French Canadians would be encouraged to "visit those parts of Western Canada first discovered by our ancestors under the French Regime" and to witness with their own eyes "their present-day splendor, wonderful material advance, and glorious future." English Canadian travellers, conversely, were encouraged to visit the western achievements of "British daring, resourcefulness and faith." BCARS, Premiers' papers, Box 45, File 7, Hone to Premier John Hart, 13 January 1942.
3 BCARS, Premiers' papers, Box 45, File 7, Vancouver *News Herald*, G. Florence to Editor, 20 August 1943.
4 The attack on advertising by both government and consumers during the 1930s is documented in James P. Wood, *The Story of Advertising* (New York: Ronald Press Company, 1958),

417-31; Jackson Lears, *Fables of Abundance: A Cultural History of Advertising in America* (New York: Basic Books, 1994), 235-47; and Frank Fox, *Madison Avenue Goes to War: The Strange Military Career of American Advertising, 1941-1945* (Provo: Brigham Young University, 1975), 17-24. As Fox has suggested, advertising's potential to interfere with the efficient distribution of materials for the war effort meant that the advertising industry in the United States found itself with little public support during the early 1940s. See Fox, *Madison Avenue Goes to War*, 25-44. Market research and opinion polling would gain a permanent foothold in Canada during the 1930s and 1940s, and its success in this regard was due in part to the pollsters' claims that their work bolstered "democracy." See Daniel J. Robinson, *The Measure of Democracy: Polling, Market Research, and Public Life, 1930-1945* (Toronto: University of Toronto Press, 1999).

5   Government of Canada, *Wartime Economic Stabilization to Keep down the Cost of Living in Canada: What It Is, How It Works, Why It Must Be Supported* (Ottawa: King's Printer, 1944). Government of Canada, *Canada's Wartime Measures for Economic Stability to Keep down the Cost of Living* (reference handbook) (Ottawa: King's Printer, 1944). Terry Copp has illustrated the important role that concepts such as "liberty" and "democracy" played in mobilizing support for the war effort in Ontario. Terry Copp, "Ontario 1939: The Decision for War," *Ontario History* 86, 3 (1994): 269-78. Popular support for these measures – especially in the early months after their implementation – was confirmed by polling results during the war. Robinson, *The Measure of Democracy*, 71-72. These polls, carried out by the Canadian Institute of Public Opinion, Robinson warns us, were, like many polls of the era, not entirely representative of the Canadian public. On Canadians' decreasing support for rationing, see Jeff Keshen, "One for All or All for One: Government Controls, Black Marketing, and the Limits of Patriotism, 1939-1947," *Journal of Canadian Studies* 29, 4 (1994-95): 111-43. Doug Owram has recently argued that the concept of "home" was far more central to Canadians' understanding of the war effort than abstract concepts such as "democracy" and "freedom." It seems likely, however, that such concepts often overlapped and that contributing to the war effort could be experienced and understood as a defence of both home and democratic ideals. See Doug Owram, "Canadian Domesticity in the Postwar Era," in *The Veterans Charter and Post-World War II Canada*, ed. Peter Neary and J.L. Granatstein (Montreal: McGill-Queen's University Press, 1998), 207.

6   On the cooperation between female consumers and the federal Wartime Prices and Trade Board, see Joy Parr and Gunilla Ekberg, "Mrs Consumer and Mr Keynes in Postwar Canada and Sweden," *Gender and History* 8, 2 (1996): 214-15. The enforcement efforts of the Wartime Prices and Trade Board are detailed in Keshen, "One for All or All for One."

7   On the increasing centrality of the service sector to the Canadian economy during the postwar era, see Kenneth Norrie and Douglas Owram, *A History of the Canadian Economy*, 2nd ed. (Toronto: Harcourt Brace, 1996), 510. On the service sector's increasing percentage of GNP at the expense of primary industries in Canada, see William L. Marr and Donald G. Paterson, *Canada: An Economic History* (Toronto: Gage, 1980), 21-22. For an international survey of the rise of the service sector, see Scott Lash and John Urry, *The End of Organized Capitalism* (Cambridge, UK: Polity Press, 1987), especially Chapter 6.

8   See, for example, Alexander Wilson, *The Culture of Nature: North American Landscape from Disney to the Exxon Valdez* (Toronto: Between the Lines, 1991), 27. The frustrations involved in securing necessary parts for automobiles during the war and the concomitant reduction in even short automobile excursions are explored in Robert Bothwell, *Years of Victory: 1939-1948* (Toronto: Grolier Limited, 1987), 32-34. Some scholars point to government restrictions on foreign exchange and on travel to the United States as evidence of the curtailment of tourist travel across the country. See, for example, Norrie and Owram, *A History of the Canadian Economy*, 521, and Robert Bothwell, Ian Drummond, and John English, *Canada since 1945: Power, Politics, and Provincialism*, rev. ed. (Toronto: University of Toronto Press, 1989), 55. In fact, government restrictions did decrease tourist travel by Canadians to the United States, but these restrictions are a poor measure of the scope of American tourism in Canada and of Canadian domestic tourism. Indeed, such conclusions rest uncomfortably with contemporary accounts. See, for example, Lyn Harrington's observation that during the war "Canadians turned for recreation to the resources

of their own country," with the result that, "in some of our provinces, holidays-with-pay legislation has crowded camps, cabins and hotels to capacity." Lyn Harrington, "The Yankee Dollah!" *Canadian Business* October 1945: 58-59, 128-32.

9 Harry Gregson, *A History of Victoria, 1842-1970* (Victoria: Victoria Observer Publishing, 1970), 220. On the war's impact on industry in Vancouver, see Norbert MacDonald, *Distant Neighbors: A Comparative History of Seattle and Vancouver* (Lincoln: University of Nebraska Press, 1987), 141, as well as Alan Morley, *Vancouver: From Milltown to Metropolis*, 2nd ed. (Vancouver: Mitchell Press, 1969), 190-91. On industrial expansion in British Columbia during the war, see Jean Barman, *The West beyond the West: A History of British Columbia*, rev. ed. (Toronto: University of Toronto Press, 1996), 262, as well as John Douglas Belshaw and David J. Mitchell, "The Economy since the Great War," in *The Pacific Province: A History of British Columbia*, ed. Hugh Johnston (Vancouver: Douglas and McIntyre, 1996), 320-22, and Margaret A. Ormsby, *British Columbia: A History* (Vancouver: Macmillan, 1958), 481-82.

10 On the decline of Vancouver's wartime industry, see MacDonald, *Distant Neighbors*, 141.

11 BCARS, GR 520, British Columbia Commission on Forest Resources papers, Box 9, File 8, Number 32, E.G. Rowebottom, Deputy Minister of Trade and Industry, "Memorandum on Travel Industry and Its Bearing on Post-War Rehabilitation," November 1942.

12 Two recent exceptions are Bertram M. Gordon, "Warfare and Tourism: Paris in World War II," *Annals of Tourism Research* 25, 3 (1998): 616-38, and Valene L. Smith, "War and Tourism: An American Ethnography," *Annals of Tourism Research* 25, 1 (1998): 202-27.

13 On the pent-up demand for tourism in British Columbia, see Belshaw and Mitchell, "The Economy since the Great War," 330. A similar position is held by Hal Rothman concerning the American west; Hal K. Rothman, "Selling the Meaning of Place: Entrepreneurship, Tourism, and Community Transformation in the Twentieth-Century American West," *Pacific Historical Review* 65, 4 (1996): 544. On the more general "pent-up" demand for consumer goods (and babies) in Canada, see Doug Owram, *Born at the Right Time: A History of the Baby Boom Generation* (Toronto: University of Toronto Press, 1996). James Overton's study of tourism in Newfoundland reminds us that the postwar tourist boom did not occur everywhere in North America at the same time. A lack of infrastructure in Newfoundland, for example, hindered tourism development into the 1960s. See James Overton, *Making a World of Difference: Essays on Tourism, Culture, and Development in Newfoundland* (St. John's: ISER, 1996), 30.

14 In his study of tourism in North America, for example, John Jakle maintains that "travel for recreation fell off sharply" during the war. John A. Jakle, *The Tourist: Travel in Twentieth-Century North America* (Lincoln: University of Nebraska Press, 1985), 185. A similar decrease for Australia is recorded in Richard White, "The Retreat from Adventure: Popular Travel Writing in the 1950s," *Australian Historical Studies* 109 (1997): 101. John Urry has even suggested that the tourist boom that arrived after a long period of austerity resulted in the holiday camp becoming a "symbol of post-war society" in Britain. See John Urry, *The Tourist Gaze: Leisure and Travel in Contemporary Societies* (London: Sage, 1990), 32-33, 36. A more nuanced understanding of tourism in the United States during the war is offered by Warren James Belasco. He suggests that travel expenditures increased in the later years of the Depression and resulted in a tourism boom during 1940-41 when the "war-related boom put more Americans than ever on the road, both for business and for pleasure, and with more to spend" – a boom that was curtailed by gasoline rationing in 1942. See Warren James Belasco, *Americans on the Road: From Autocamp to Motel, 1910-1945* (Cambridge, MA: MIT Press, 1979), 155, 169-70.

15 Many scholars maintain that, while the civilian experience in Canada during the war was not as bleak as it had been during the First World War, rationing was still a fundamental part of daily life and that even the rapid expansion of industrial employment that accompanied war production failed to provide civilians with an existence, or a disposable income, very different from the suffering of the 1930s. Michael Bliss, *Northern Enterprise: Five Centuries of Canadian Business* (Toronto: McClelland and Stewart, 1987), 448. On the "collective" experience of rationing and austerity during the war, see Robert Bothwell, "'Who's Paying for Anything These Days?': War Production in Canada 1939-1945,"in *Mobilization*

for Total War: The Canadian, American, and British Experience 1914-1918, 1939-1945, ed. N.F. Driesziger (Waterloo: Wilfrid Laurier University Press, 1981), 63; Bothwell, *Years of Victory,* 52; Ted Barris and Alex Barris, *Days of Victory, Canadians Remember: 1939-1945* (Toronto: Macmillan, 1995), 74-75; and J.L. Granatstein, *Canada's War: The Politics of the Mackenzie King Government, 1939-1945* (Toronto: Oxford University Press, 1975), 186.

16   Indeed, several historians have commented upon the manner in which business leaders allied themselves with the government (and Canada's soldiers) by taking a leading role in the war effort. The cozy relationship between the manufacturing sector and the government is detailed in Bliss, *Northern Enterprise,* 450-53; Granatstein, *Canada's War,* 159-200; and Bothwell, "'Who's Paying for Anything These Days?'"

17   An important exception is Jeff Keshen's analysis of consumers' frustrations with clothing manufacturers who continued to charge the ceiling rate for clothing that had been simplified and trimmed of its frills. See Keshen, "One for All or All for One," 123.

18   The scope and timing of these disruptions varied substantially. In Hawaii regular tourists were evacuated in 1942, but military authorities and civic leaders continued to employ metaphors of tourism to combat homesickness among the visiting US troops and to mediate the ethnic tensions that resulted when the islands' population, one-third of which was of Japanese ancestry, welcomed over a million American soldiers and war workers. David Farber and Beth Bailey, "The Fighting Man as Tourist: The Politics of Tourist Culture in Hawaii during World War II," *Pacific Historical Review* 65, 4 (1996): 641-60. At least one early study of Florida, however, emphasizes the continuity of tourism in that state throughout the war. See Ben F. Rogers, "Florida in World War II: Tourists and Citrus," *Florida Historical Quarterly* 39, 1 (1960): 34-41. In his study of tourism in twentieth-century Newfoundland, James Overton confirms that the war caused tourism development there to suffer "a setback," but he also directs our attention to the "large numbers of service personnel associated with American and Canadian military bases" in Newfoundland who became "captive visitors who spent their leisure time hunting, fishing, sightseeing and generally relaxing." Overton, *Making a World of Difference,* 24. Seaside resorts in England were all affected by the war, but even there the fate of the towns could vary considerably. Blackpool welcomed 37,500 evacuees and, located on the west coast, "retained its vitality throughout the war." The more vulnerable resorts on the east coast, however, "became very run down." The Isle of Man, a popular tourist destination before the war, "was turned into a large-scale prison-camp." James Walvin, *Beside the Seaside: A Social History of the Popular Seaside Holiday* (London: Allen Lane, 1978), 126-28.

19   Government of British Columbia, *Report of the Department of Trade and Industry, 1940,* 19.

20   Lloyd Craig, director of the department's Bureau of Industrial and Trade Extension, arrived in Ottawa on 22 October 1939 "to ensure British Columbia's proper participation in the business resulting from Canada's war effort." Ibid. The long-term effects of the federal government's favouritism toward central Canadian industries during the war are detailed in Ernest R. Forbes, "Consolidating Disparity: The Maritimes and the Industrialization of Canada during the Second World War," *Acadiensis* 15, 2 (1986): 3-27.

21   On British Columbia's battle with its partners in Confederation during the 1930s and early 1940s, see Robin Fisher, *Duff Pattullo of British Columbia* (Toronto: University of Toronto Press, 1991), 242-51.

22   *Report of the Department of Trade and Industry, 1940,* 21.

23   Canadians not directly associated with the tourist industry also championed tourism's possible contributions to the war effort. In a letter to Premier Pattullo, W.S. Beaton, the mayor of Sudbury, Ontario, endorsed the prospect of Canadians writing to friends and relatives to encourage them to visit Canada by emphasizing the fact that because of the exchange rate their money would go further. While this increase in travel from the United States would undoubtedly make relations between the two countries more cordial, Beaton underscored the most important possible result from such a campaign: "the fact of their spending money in Canada will greatly assist the 'War Effort.'" BCARS, Premiers' papers, Box 158, File 5, W.S. Beaton, Mayor, Sudbury, to Pattullo, 12 February 1941.

24   Victoria City Archives (VCA), Victoria Chamber of Commerce (VCC) fonds, 32 A 1, Board of Directors Minutes, 11 January 1940.

25 Victoria *Daily Colonist* 3 October 1939: 4.

26 VCA, VCC fonds, Annual Meeting Minutes, 15 April 1940.

27 BCARS, Add. MSS. 9, Gerry McGeer papers, Box 14, File 5, "Prepare for Tourist" Campaign Bulletin by Vancouver Junior Board of Trade, in H.J. Merilees, National Tourist Traffic Committee, Junior Chamber of Commerce, Montreal, to McGeer, House of Commons, 25 January 1940.

28 BCARS, Add. MSS. 497, Sidney J. Smith papers, Volume 3, File 4, Smith, Chairman, Kamloops Tourist Bureau, to Mayor and City Council, 7 March 1940.

29 Vancouver *Sun* 7 October 1939: 1.

30 Victoria *Daily Times* 22 December 1939: 1.

31 Vancouver *News Herald* 27 January 1940: 16.

32 *News Herald* 11 January 1940: 9; ibid.

33 These restrictions were eased later in the year, but their immediate impact was to greatly increase travellers' concerns about cross-border travel. Government of British Columbia, *Report of the Department of Trade and Industry, 1941,* 22.

34 Ibid., 21-22.

35 City of Vancouver Archives (CVA), Add. MSS. 633, Greater Vancouver Visitors and Convention Bureau (GVVCB), Series B, Volume 4, File 20, Vancouver Tourist Association, *Annual Report,* 1940, 5. The RCMP were convinced that Communists were responsible for at least some of these rumours. See RCMP security bulletins 36, 26 August 1940, and 41, 20 March 1941, in *RCMP Security Bulletins: The War Series, 1939-1941,* ed. Gregory S. Kealey and Reg Whitaker (St. John's: Committee on Canadian Labour History, 1989), 291, 339-40.

36 CVA, GVVCB papers, Series B, Volume 4, File 22, Vancouver Tourist Association, *Annual Report,* 1941, 10-11.

37 Ibid.

38 *Report of the Department of Trade and Industry, 1941,* 19.

39 BCARS, Smith papers, Volume 3, File 1, "General Plans for 1940," BCGTB Report Presented to the BC Tourist Council, November 1939.

40 BCARS, Smith papers, Volume 3, File 1, Sidney J. Smith, Chairman, Kamloops Tourist Bureau, to Mayor and City Council, 7 March 1940.

41 National Archives of Canada (NAC), RG 20, Department of Industry, Trade and Commerce papers, A9, Volume 1572, File T-3400-9, Press Release, Leo Dolan, Chief, CGTB, "Tire and Tube Situation in Canada," 28 May 1942.

42 Government of British Columbia, *Report of the Department of Trade and Industry, 1943,* 26-27. Gasoline rationing was implemented on 1 April 1942. Restrictions on tires followed a month later. Keshen, "One for All or All for One," 120-21.

43 CVA, Add. MSS. 370, British Columbia Chamber of Commerce fonds, Volume 1, File 9, Proceedings of the 42nd Annual Convention of the Associated Boards of Trade of Eastern British Columbia, Nelson, 26-27 May 1942.

44 *Report of the Department of Trade and Industry, 1943,* 28.

45 E.S. Turner, *The Shocking Story of Advertising!* (London: Michael Joseph, 1952), 235, 241-42.

46 Harrington, "The Yankee Dollah!" 58

47 BCARS, Smith papers, Volume 3, File 1, British Columbia Tourist Council Minutes, 30 November 1942.

48 Alisa Apostle, "Canada, Vacations Unlimited: The Canadian Government Tourism Industry, 1934-1959" (PhD diss., Queen's University, 2003), 158-61, 171-72.

49 Ibid., 172-73.

50 CVA, GVVCB papers, Series B, Volume 4, File 22, Vancouver Tourist Association, *Annual Report* 1943, 3.

51 CVA, GVVCB papers, Series B, Volume 4, File 22, Vancouver Tourist Association, *Annual Report* 1942, 7-8. According to one contemporary observer, Americans living close to the Canadian border continued to visit Canada. Sometimes this necessitated pooling gas tickets, but other forms of transportation were also available. "Steamship lines on the Great Lakes," Harrington reported, "were crowded with American passengers." Harrington, "The Yankee Dollah!" 128.

52 Vancouver Tourist Association, *Annual Report* 1942, 12.

53   CVA, GVVCB papers, Series B, Volume 4, File 22, Vancouver Tourist Association, *Annual Report*, 1944, 5. On the impact of soldiers' travel experiences on the postwar tourist boom, see Smith, "War and Tourism."

54   Vancouver Tourist Association, *Annual Report*, 1944, 7.

55   The housing shortage in Vancouver is detailed in MacDonald, *Distant Neighbors*, 148-49, and in Jill Wade, *Houses for All: The Struggle for Social Housing in Vancouver, 1919-50* (Vancouver: UBC Press, 1994), Chapters 4 and 5. On the city's postwar accommodation crisis, see Patricia Roy, "Behaving as Canadians: British Columbians, 1945-1947," in *Uncertain Horizons: Canadians and Their World in 1945*, ed. Greg Donaghy (Ottawa: Canadian Committee for the History of the Second World War, 1997), 217.

56   VCA, VCC fonds, Board of Directors Minutes, 1 June 1944.

57   Documentation on this organization is sparse. Unlike the organization of the same name discussed in Chapter 2, this organization did not rely upon government funding but appears to have been yet another example of regional cooperation. The earliest evidence that I have found of its existence is an acknowledgment of the VIPB's membership in the organization. See Vancouver *Sun* 17 February 1936: 8.

58   VCA, VCC fonds, Board of Directors Minutes, 14 September 1944.

59   Government of British Columbia, *Report of the Department of Trade and Industry, 1945*, 5; *Report of the Department of Trade and Industry, 1944*, 33.

60   Additional reports suggested not only that more resorts were necessary but also that the quality of the existing resorts needed to be improved. *Report of the Department of Trade and Industry, 1945*, 30-31.

61   CVA, GVVCB papers, Series B, Volume 4, File 22, Vancouver Tourist Association, *Annual Report*, 1945, 2.

62   Ibid., 5.

63   Government of British Columbia, *Report of the Department of Trade and Industry, 1946, 1947*, 45.

64   CVA, GVVCB papers, Series B, Volume 4, File 22, Vancouver Tourist Association, *Annual Report*, 1946, 8.

65   CVA, GVVCB papers, Series B, Volume 4, File 22, Vancouver Tourist Association, *Annual Report*, 1947, 16.

66   Roland Marchand, *Creating the Corporate Soul: The Rise of Public Relations and Corporate Imagery in American Big Business* (Berkeley: University of California Press, 1998), 317.

67   For a contemporary account of the province's economic expansion in the 1940s that not only stresses the impact of the war but also ascribes the growing popularity of the province to its climate, the high wages obtained through union actions, and the province's higher level of old-age pensions and superior "social legislation" compared with other provinces, see Charles Saxon, "B.C. Rides a Boom," *Canadian Business* May 1947: 32-33, 107-10.

68   Norrie and Owram, *A History of the Canadian Economy*, 421. The proliferation of cars, and their increasing centrality to family life in the postwar era, is discussed in Owram, *Born at the Right Time*, 69-72.

69   Walton Bean, *California: An Interpretive History*, 2nd ed. (New York: McGraw-Hill, 1973), 524, 533.

70   Government of British Columbia, *Report of the Department of Recreation and Conservation, 1955*, W50.

71   Carlos Schwantes, *The Pacific Northwest: An Interpretive History* (Lincoln: University of Nebraska Press, 1989), 339.

72   Hal Rothman, *Devil's Bargains: Tourism in the Twentieth-Century American West* (Lawrence: University Press of Kansas, 1998), 202-03. John Jakle offers a similar interpretation while emphasizing that "workers enjoyed shorter work weeks and longer vacation periods." Jakle, *The Tourist*, 185.

73   Owram, *Born at the Right Time*, 17.

74   *Report of the Department of Trade and Industry, 1946, 1947*, 45.

75   Ibid.

76   BCGTB *Newsletter* 3 (1946): 1.

77   Government of British Columbia, *Report of the Department of Trade and Industry, 1948*, 52.

78   On the triumph of rational economic planning in the federal bureaucracy during the war, see Doug Owram, *The Government Generation: Canadian Intellectuals and the State, 1900-1945* (Toronto: University of Toronto Press, 1986), Chapters 10 and 11.

79   Government of British Columbia, *Report of the Department of Trade and Industry, 1943*, 27.

80   Government of British Columbia, *Report of the Department of Trade and Industry, 1944*, 31.

81   Coordination of the tourist industry had been an important rationale in the creation of the Special Senate Committee on Tourist Traffic held in 1934 as well as the annual Dominion-Provincial Tourist Conferences inaugurated in 1946.

82   Government of British Columbia, *Report of the Department of Trade and Industry, 1939*, 22.

83   Vancouver *News Herald* 8 August 1938: 9; Victoria *Daily Times* 5 July 1946: 11.

84   BCARS, Smith papers, Volume 3, File 4, Margaret Powers, Executive Secretary, Auto Courts and Resorts Association of British Columbia, to Smith, 9 February 1949; *Report of the Department of Trade and Industry, 1944*, 31; BCARS, Smith papers, Volume 3, File 1, Margaret Powers, Executive Secretary, Auto Courts and Resorts Association of British Columbia, to Smith, 9 February 1949.

85   BCGTB *Newsletter* 1 (1945): 5; *Report of the Department of Trade and Industry, 1948*, 53.

86   Apostle, "Canada, Vacations Unlimited," 234-35.

87   BCGTB *Newsletter* 1 (1945): 1.

88   Apostle, "Canada, Vacations Unlimited," 167.

89   BCGTB *Newsletter* 1 (1945): 1.

90   Ibid., 2-3; BCGTB *Newsletter* 2 (1946): 1-3.

91   *Report of the Department of Trade and Industry, 1948*, 53. According to Deputy Minister of Trade and Commerce E.G. Rowebottom, visitors to British Columbia were "strikingly unanimous" in their criticism of the province's roads. BCARS, GR 520, British Columbia Commission on Forest Resources papers, Box 9, File 8, Number 32, E.G. Rowebottom, Deputy Minister of Trade and Industry, "Memorandum on Travel Industry and Its Bearing on Post-War Rehabilitation," November 1942.

92   BCGTB *Newsletter* 1 (1945): 5. The quotation is from the BCGTB. In August 1945, G.H. Worthington of the GVTA had gone on record in singing the praises of the Tourist Camp Act. CVA, GVVCB papers, Series A, Volume 1, File 1, VTA Board of Directors Minutes, 9 August 1945.

93   BCARS, Premiers' papers, Box 75, File 4, P.M. Cowan and F.R. Brason, 2400 Court, Vancouver, to Premier Byron Johnson, 12 January 1948.

94   BCARS, British Columbia Commission on Forest Resources papers, Box 9, File 8, Number 424, Brief to the British Columbia Commission on Forest Resources from the Interior British Columbia Resort Owners' Association, c. 15 January 1945.

95   *Report of the Department of Trade and Industry, 1946, 1947*, 46.

96   John Keane, "Introduction" in Claus Offe, *Contradictions of the Welfare State* (Cambridge, MA: MIT Press, 1984), 16.

97   BCGTB *Newsletter* 2 (1946): 8.

98   BCGTB *Newsletter* 16 (1949): 14.

99   BCGTB *Newsletter* 17 (1949): 7.

100 *Report of the Department of Trade and Industry, 1946, 1947*, 46.

101 *Report of the Department of Trade and Industry, 1948*, 53.

102 BCGTB *Newsletter* 2 (1946): 13-14.

103 BCGTB *Newsletter* 3 (1946): 6.

104 BCGTB *Newsletter* 12 (1948): 1.

105 BCGTB *Newsletter* 6 (1946): 9. The tendency of war travel to increase the desire on the part of military personal after the war is discussed in Smith, "War and Tourism," 211-12.

106 BCGTB *Newsletter* 11 (1948): 2.

107 BCGTB *Newsletter* 13 (1948): 7.

108 Ibid., 8.

109 Ibid., 9.

110 BCGTB *Newsletter* 14 (1948): 6-7.

111 Helen Smith and Pamela Wakewich, "'Beauty and the Helldivers': Representing Women's Work and Identities in a Warplant Newspaper," *Labour/Le Travail* 44 (1999): 71-107;

Susannah J. Wilson, "The Changing Image of Women in Canadian Mass Circulating Magazines, 1930-1970," *Atlantis* 2 (1977): 33-44; M. Susan Bland, "Henrietta the Home-maker, and 'Rosie the Riveter': Images of Women in Advertising in *Maclean's* Magazine, 1939-50," *Atlantis* 8, 2 (1983): 61-86.

112 See, for example, *Sunset* June 1941: 10; December 1947: 4; October 1950: 24; May 1951: 21; and May 1952: 29.

113 BCARS, Premiers' papers, Box 84, File 10, L.H. Eyres, Minister of Trade and Industry, to Premier Byron I. Johnson, 10 January 1951.

114 An increasingly explicit emphasis on heterosexual fulfillment may in fact have been a continent-wide phenomenon. Karen Dubinsky's study of Niagara Falls, Ontario, for example, demonstrates that that city's tourism promoters began diligently to "sell" the honeymoon only in the postwar era. Karen Dubinsky, *The Second Greatest Disappointment: Honeymooning and Tourism at Niagara Falls* (Toronto: Between the Lines, 1999), 30, 168, 214-15, 229-37.

115 For a survey of BCGTB film production during this era, see David Mattison, "The British Columbia Government Travel Bureau and Motion Picture Production, 1937-1947," in *Flashback: People and Institutions in Canadian Film History*, ed. Gene Walz (Montreal: Media-texte Publications, 1986), 79-104.

116 BCARS, BCGTB film *The Okanagan Valley: British Columbia's Orchard Playground*, c. 1940s.

117 CVA, GVVCB papers, Series A, Volume 1, File 3, VTA Board of Directors Minutes, 21 September 1950.

118 CVA, GVVCB papers, Series A, Volume 1, File 3, GVTA Board of Directors Minutes, "Operating Report," 17 August 1950.

119 CVA, GVVCB papers, Series A, Volume 1, File 3, VTA Board of Directors Minutes, "Operating Report," 21 September 1950.

120 CVA, GVVCB papers, Series A, Volume 2, File 8, GVTA Greeting and Hospitality Committee Minutes, 8 February 1956.

121 CVA, GVVCB papers, Series A, Volume 2, File 11, GVTA Special Meeting, 30 August 1960.

122 CVA, GVVCB papers, Series A, Volume 2, File 11, Minutes of the GVTA Meeting to Inquire into Arrangements for the Production of a "Vancouver" Film, 7 November 1960.

123 Roland Marchand, *Advertising the American Dream: Making Way for Modernity, 1920-1940* (Berkeley: University of California Press, 1985), 66.

124 Valerie J. Korinek, *Roughing It in the Suburbs: Reading Chatelaine Magazine in the Fifties and Sixties* (Toronto: University of Toronto Press, 2000), 152, 155.

125 On the shift toward the heterosexual sell in Hawaii, see Jane C. Desmond, *Staging Tourism: Bodies on Display from Waikiki to Sea World* (Chicago: University of Chicago Press, 1999), 98-141.

126 On female consumer activism during the 1940s, see Julie Guard, "Women Worth Watching: Radical Housewives in Cold War Canada," in *Whose National Security? Canadian State Surveillance and the Creation of Enemies*, ed. Gary Kinsmen et al. (Toronto: Between the Lines, 2000), 73-88.

127 Government of British Columbia, *Report of the Department of Trade and Industry, 1949*, 57.

128 Government of British Columbia, *Report of the Department of Trade and Industry, 1950*, 37.

129 CVA, GVVCB papers, Series B, Volume 4, File 22, Hedley S. Hipwell, "President's Report," *Greater Vancouver Tourist Association Annual Report 1950*, 1-3.

130 Donald G. Wetherell, with Irene Kmet, *Useful Pleasures: The Shaping of Leisure in Alberta, 1896-1945* (Regina/Edmonton: Canadian Plains Research Center/Alberta Culture and Multiculturalism, 1990), 317-18; R. Bruce McIntyre, "Which Uniform to Serve the War: Hockey in Canada versus Military Service during World War Two," *Canadian Journal of History of Sport* 24, 2 (1993): 68-90; Keshen, "One for All or All for One."

131 BCARS, Premiers' papers, Box 55, File 9, Premier Hart to E.G. Rowebottom, 5 June 1944.

132 Dubinsky, "'Everybody Likes Canadians,'" in *Being Elsewhere*, 322.

133 University of Washington Archives, Business Research Bureau papers, Box 1, File 2, Pacific Northwest Tourist Conference Program, 17-18 April 1947.

Chapter 5: Differentiation, Cultural Selection, and the Postwar Travel "Boom"

1 H.P. McKeever, "You Might Say I Live in the Past," *Canadian Hotel Review* August 1960: 26-27. My thanks to Karen Dubinsky for this reference.

2 Vancouver *Daily Province* 12 August 1954: 21.
3 The Canadian Travel Bureau formally added "Government" to its name in 1945. See Alisa Apostle, "Canada, Vacations Unlimited: The Canadian Government Tourism Industry, 1934-1959" (PhD diss., Queen's University, 2003), 169.
4 National Archives of Canada (NAC), Leo D. Dolan papers, Volume 1, "Speeches" File, *An Interim Report on Canadian Tourism*, 1949.
5 City of Vancouver Archives (CVA), Greater Vancouver Visitors and Convention Bureau (GVVCB) papers, Series A, Volume 2, File 9, Speech by the Honourable Earle C. Westwood, Minister of Recreation and Conservation, to the GVTA Annual General Meeting, "B.C. as the Playground of North America in Our Future," 25 September 1957.
6 Westwood, "B.C. as the Playground of North America in Our Future."
7 NAC, Dolan papers, Volume 1, "Speeches" File, Dolan Address to the 57th Annual Congress of the National Retail Hardware Association, Toronto, 24 July 1956.
8 Apostle, "Canada, Vacations Unlimited," 294.
9 Ibid., 188, 224-25.
10 Ibid., 210-11.
11 CVA, GVVCB papers, Series A, Volume 2, File 10, Text of Speech, Leo Dolan to GVTA, 21 October 1959.
12 On the nationalist orientation of postwar tourism promotion initiatives, see Karen Dubinsky, "Everybody Likes Canadians: Canadians, Americans, and the Post-World War Two Travel Boom," in *Being Elsewhere: Tourism, Consumer Culture, and Identity in Modern Europe and North America*, ed. Shelley Baranowski and Ellen Furlough (Ann Arbor: University of Michigan Press, 2001), 320-47.
13 Government of British Columbia, *Report of the Department of Recreation and Conservation, 1958*, Q45.
14 Mrs. Henry A. Berger, "Victoria," Letter to the Editor, *Holiday* December 1948: 6-8.
15 Sylvia Rodriguez, "Tourism, Whiteness, and the Vanishing Anglo," in *Seeing and Being Seen: Tourism in the American West*, ed. David M. Wrobel and Patrick T. Long (Lawrence: University Press of Kansas, 2001), 197.
16 Victoria *Daily Colonist* 13 March 1963: 13.
17 Victoria City Archives (VCA), Victoria Chamber of Commerce (VCC) fonds, 32 A 2, Board of Directors Minutes, 25 May 1949.
18 VCA, VCC fonds, 32 A 2, Board of Directors Minutes, 19 February 1954.
19 VCA, VCC fonds, 32 A 2, Board of Directors Minutes, 19 March 1954.
20 VCA, VCC fonds, 32 A 2, Board of Directors Minutes, 19 February 1954; Board of Directors Minutes, 19 March 1954.
21 R.H. Francis, "Victoria – Vancouver: A Study in Contrasts on the West Coast," *Canadian Business* September 1957: 30-33.
22 VCA, "Tourism" Clipping File, Victoria *Daily Times* 4 January 1961, "City Faces Tough Job in Enticing Industry – Tourism Best Bet Survey Indicates."
23 Peter A. Baskerville, *Beyond the Island: An Illustrated History of Victoria* (Burlington: Windsor, 1986), 105.
24 CVA, GVVCB papers, Series A, Volume 1, File 7, GVTA Declaration of Policy, 21 October 1954.
25 CVA, GVVCB papers, Series E, Volume 10, File 96, Draft of GVVCB News Release, 4 March 1965.
26 *"Land of the Empire Builders"*: *The Pacific Northwest Dimensions and Opportunities* (Menlo Park, CA: Lane Magazine Co., 1964).
27 To estimate the impact of the tourism industry on local communities in Canada and elsewhere, tourism authorities have relied primarily upon the use of income multipliers in order to determine both the direct and the indirect impacts of tourist expenditures. This approach acknowledges the fact that money introduced into a local economy by an outside visitor changes hands several times and thus has a greater effect than would be recognized if only the initial expenditure were counted. Similarly an employment multiplier is utilized to estimate the number of related jobs that tourism produces in a given location. Charles R. Goeldner, J.R. Brent Ritchie, and Robert W. McIntosh, *Tourism: Principles, Practices, Philosophies*, 8th ed. (New York: John Wiley and Sons, 2000), 426-30. For an examination

and critique of these early pronouncements on the "multiplier effect," see Douglas Pearce, *Tourist Development*, 2nd ed. (Harlow, UK: Longman Scientific and Technical; New York: Wiley, 1989), 205-11.

28   According to the Dominion Bureau of Statistics, 85 percent of US visitors were short-term visitors who spent forty-eight hours or less in Canada. This group spent on average just $2.55 per visitor. Conversely, long-term visitors spent on average $56.89 per visitor. CVA, GVVCB papers, Series B, Volume 4, File 22, M.J. McCormick, "Publicity Commissioner's Report," *Vancouver Tourist Association Annual Report 1951*, 10.

29   E.D. McPhee, "The Business of Tourism," in *Proceedings of the 33rd General Conference of the PNTA*, Vancouver, 9-10 May 1955, 13-17.

30   CVA, GVVCB papers, Series A, Volume 2, File 10, Text of Speech, Leo Dolan to GVTA, 21 October 1959.

31   M.J. McCormick, "Publicity Commissioner's Report," *Vancouver Tourist Association Annual Report 1951*, 11-13, 16-17.

32   "Report of the Visitor and Recreation Committee," in *Proceedings of the 35th General Conference of the Pacific Northwest Trade Association*, Victoria, 14-15 May 1956, 23.

33   NAC, Dolan papers, Volume 2, "Booklets and Pamphlets" File, Script for Broadcast of *Borden's Canadian Cavalcade*, CBC Radio, 14 March 1950. Dolan also desired that more emphasis be placed on seasonal dishes such as fresh fish. NAC, Dolan papers, Volume 1, "Speeches" File, Dolan Address to Canadian Restaurant Association, 15 March 1950.

34   Roland Wild, "How Tourist Dollars Make Sense," *Saturday Night* 6 August 1955: 27.

35   Jay Mechling, "Florida Seminoles and the Marketing of the Last Frontier," in *Dressing in Feathers: The Construction of the Indian in American Popular Culture*, ed. S. Elizabeth Bird (Boulder: Westview Press, 1996), 162-63.

36   Ian McKay, *Quest of the Folk: Antimodernism and Cultural Selection in Twentieth-Century Nova Scotia* (Montreal: McGill-Queen's University Press, 1994); Chris Wilson, *The Myth of Santa Fe: Creating a Modern Regional Tradition* (Albuquerque: University of New Mexico Press, 1997); Martha K. Norkunas, *The Politics of Public Memory: Tourism, History, and Ethnicity in Monterey, California* (Albany: SUNY Press, 1993).

37   CVA, GVVCB papers, Series A, Volume 2, File 8, VTA Annual General Meeting Minutes, 24 November 1954. In a 1965 address to the Penticton Chamber of Commerce, Willard Ireland "stressed that history is like any other commodity and a Board or Chamber needs to know its product and have it well packaged if it is to be attractive to tourists." CVA, British Columbia Chamber of Commerce fonds, Volume 3, File 1, "Sell History," *BC Bulletin* 15, 2 (1965): 6.

38   Lyn Harrington, "The Yankee Dollah!" *Canadian Business* October 1945: 58-59, 128-32.

39   Ronald John Williams, "Canada's 'City of Gardens,'" *Holiday* September 1948: 91-97, 137-38. The push to discard the English-style bobby uniforms came from the police union itself, which agitated for American-style uniforms. See Jim Nesbitt and Melwyn Breen, "Victoria – Our West-Coast Garden," *Saturday Night* 8 August 1950: 3-10, 31.

40   VCA, VCC fonds, 32 A 2, Board of Directors Minutes, 22 March 1957.

41   The caravan included thirty-three members from Victoria, including Stuart Keate, president of the chamber, and George Warren, publicity commissioner of the VIPB. VCA, VCC fonds, 32 B 7, General Scrap Book, *Times*, c. May 1955, "Goodwill Party from Victoria at Spokane Festival."

42   McKeever, "You Might Say I Live in the Past."

43   "New Vancouver Lounges Exploit English History," *Canadian Hotel Review* January 1955: 18-19. My thanks to Karen Dubinsky for this reference.

44   British Columbia Archives and Records Service (BCARS), Add. MSS. 497, Sidney J. Smith papers, Volume 3, File 4, Royal Bank of Canada *Newsletter* April 1945.

45   Jean Barman, *The West beyond the West: A History of British Columbia*, rev. ed. (Toronto: University of Toronto Press, 1996), 379-80. The commodification of Native culture was preceded by a scramble to preserve Native culture that was motivated to a great extent by the belief in the nineteenth century that Aboriginal populations would soon be extinct. See Daniel Francis, *The Imaginary Indian: The Image of the Indian in Canadian Culture* (Vancouver: Arsenal Pulp Press, 1992), 16-60.

46 Early Native-white relations in British Columbia are documented most extensively in Robin Fisher, *Contact and Conflict: Indian-European Relations in British Columbia, 1774-1890,* 2nd ed. (Vancouver: UBC Press, 1992). See also the important essays on this topic in Cole Harris, *The Resettlement of British Columbia: Essays on Colonialism and Geographical Change* (Vancouver: UBC Press, 1997), as well as his "Social Power and Cultural Change in Pre-Colonial British Columbia," *BC Studies* 115-16 (1997): 45-82. More recent political conflicts involving the province's Aboriginal population are surveyed in Paul Tennant, *Aboriginal Peoples and Politics: The Indian Land Question in British Columbia, 1849-1989* (Vancouver: UBC Press, 1990).

47 On the conflict between Aboriginals and whites over the potlatch, see Tina Loo, "Dan Cranmer's Potlatch: Law as Coercion, Symbol, and Rhetoric in British Columbia, 1884-1890," *Canadian Historical Review* 73, 2 (1992): 125-65, and Douglas Cole and Ira Chaikin, *An Iron Hand upon the People: The Law against the Potlatch on the Northwest Coast* (Vancouver: Douglas and McIntyre, 1990).

48 BCARS, BCGTB film *Vancouver Island: British Columbia's Island Playground,* 1942. In its 1939 souvenir program commemorating the third annual "See B.C. First" caravan from Vancouver to the Cariboo, the Tourist Traffic Committee of the Vancouver Junior Board of Trade included a photograph of totem poles along with the caption "Weird Totems – Armorial Bearings of an Ancient Race." CVA, Add. MSS. 426, Harold Merilees fonds, Volume 3, File 1, *Official Programme, Third Annual "See B.C. First" Caravan* 1939.

49 On changing opinions toward the province's Native peoples and the uneven effects of the liberalization of the Indian Act, see Barman, *The West beyond the West,* 307-09.

50 BCARS, BCGTB film *Highway 16,* c. 1948-49.

51 BCARS, BCGTB film *Vancouver Island: British Columbia's Island Playground,* c. 1956-57.

52 BCARS, BCGTB film *Vancouver Island: British Columbia's Island Playground,* c. 1962-64. In Florida the tourist representations of the Seminole Indians underwent a similar transformation so that, by the mid-1950s, they "were now portrayed as noble children of the swamp but also as people who could pick and choose from modern conveniences without jeopardizing the virtues of their traditional ways." Mechling, "Florida Seminoles and the Marketing of the Last Frontier," 158.

53 CVA, GVVCB papers, Series A, Volume 1, File 2, VTA Board of Directors Minutes, 18 August 1949.

54 CVA, GVVCB papers, Series A, Volume 1, File 3, VTA Board of Directors Minutes, "Operating Report," 17 August 1950.

55 *Sun* 12 June 1968: 83.

56 CVA, GVVCB papers, Series A, Volume 1, File 3, VTA Board of Directors Minutes, "Comptroller's Operating Report," 12 October 1950. On the city of San Diego's campaigns to reemphasize its Spanish heritage during the 1950s in an attempt to lure tourists, see Susan G. Davis, "Landscapes of Imagination: Tourism in Southern California," *Pacific Historical Review* 68, 2 (1999): 176.

57 CVA, GVVCB papers, Series A, Volume 1, File 3, VTA Board of Directors Minutes, 12 October 1950.

58 University of British Columbia Archives (UBCA), Fraser Valley Tourist Association (FVTA) papers, File 4, Harry Duker, "Totem-Land" Society, Vancouver, to M.S.W. Mackenzie, 18 October 1962.

59 Ibid.

60 UBCA, FVTA papers, File 6, Mrs. M.S.W. Mackenzie, Secretary, Fort Langley and District Board of Trade, to Harry Duker, 11 November 1962.

61 Government of British Columbia, *Report of the Department of Trade and Industry, 1955,* W52.

62 Government of British Columbia, *Report of the Department of Recreation and Conservation, 1957,* I135.

63 CVA, GVVCB papers, Series D, Volume 6, File 33, "Totem Poles," *News from Vancouver,* c. 1960s.

64 Renato Rosaldo, "Imperialist Nostalgia," *Representations* 26 (1989): 107-22. For a similar example of this phenomenon in tourism promotion, see Leah Dilworth, "Tourists and Indians in Fred Harvey's Southwest," in *Seeing and Being Seen,* 142-64.

65 Harry Duker, "Letter to the Editor," Vancouver *Daily Province* 14 December 1954: 6.
66 Harry Duker, "Letter to the Editor," *Province* 9 July 1954: 6.
67 Harry Duker, "Letter to the Editor," *Province* 21 August 1965: 4.
68 Harry Duker, "Letter to the Editor," *Province* 20 June 1966: 4.
69 Harry Duker, "Letter to the Editor," *Province* 29 June 1967: 4.
70 Patricia Nelson Limerick, "Seeing and Being Seen: Tourism in the American West," in *Seeing and Being Seen*, 47.
71 Hal Rothman, "Shedding Skin and Shifting Shape: Tourism in the Modern West," in *Seeing and Being Seen*, 102.
72 Patricia Jasen, *Wild Things: Nature, Culture, and Tourism in Ontario, 1790-1914* (Toronto: University of Toronto Press, 1995), 81.
73 On this theme, see Harris, *The Resettlement of British Columbia*.
74 My thinking on this point has been shaped by insights offered by Michael Berkowitz. See Berkowitz, "A 'New Deal' for Leisure," in *Seeing and Being Seen*, 197.
75 Harris, *The Resettlement of British Columbia*, xi.
76 BCARS, Smith papers, Volume 3, File 4, L.J. Crampton, "Trail to the North," presented to the meeting of the Canadian Tourist Association, Saskatoon, 7 October 1964.

Chapter 6: Tourism as a Public Good

1 City of Vancouver Archives (CVA), Add. MSS. 633, Greater Vancouver and Visitors Bureau (GVVCB) papers, Series B, Volume 4, File 22, George C. Bradley, "President's Report," *Greater Vancouver Tourist Association Annual Report 1956*, 4.
2 The other four units were the Fish and Game Branch, the provincial Parks Branch, the Photographic Branch, and the Commercial Fisheries Branch.
3 *Report of the Department of Recreation and Conservation, 1957*, 7; *Report of the Department of Recreation and Conservation, 1967*, 7. On the growing recognition of recreation by governments, see Shirley Tillotson, "Time, Swimming Pools, and Citizenship: The Emergence of Leisure Rights in Mid-Twentieth-Century Canada," in *Contesting Canadian Citizenship: Historical Readings*, ed. Robert Adamoski et al. (Peterborough: Broadview, 2002), 199-221; and *The Public at Play: Gender and the Politics of Recreation in Post-War Ontario* (Toronto: University of Toronto Press, 2000).
4 On the expansion of CGTB budgets and advertising expenditures, see Alisa Apostle, "Canada, Vacations Unlimited: The Canadian Government Tourism Industry, 1934-1959" (PhD diss., Queen's University, 2003), 191, 277.
5 Government of British Columbia, *Public Accounts*, 1950-70.
6 Dominique Jean [Marshall], "Family Allowances and Family Autonomy: Quebec Families Encounter the Welfare State, 1945-1955," in *Canadian Family History: Selected Readings*, ed. Bettina Bradbury (Toronto: Copp Clark Pitman, 1992), 401-37; Robert M. Campbell, *Grand Illusions: The Politics of the Keynesian Experience in Canada, 1945-1975* (Peterborough: Broadview Press, 1987), 208-12; Joy Parr, *Domestic Goods: The Material, the Moral, and the Economic in the Postwar Years* (Toronto: University of Toronto Press, 1999), 101.
7 James C. Scott, *Seeing Like a State: How Certain Schemes to Improve the Human Condition Have Failed* (New Haven: Yale University Press, 1998), 2-4.
8 Paul Rutherford, *Endless Propaganda: The Advertising of Public Goods* (Toronto: University of Toronto Press, 2000), 8.
9 Tillotson, *The Public at Play*, 79.
10 Rutherford, *Endless Propaganda*, 8-9.
11 E.D. McPhee, "The Business of Tourism," in *Proceedings of the 33rd General Conference of the PNTA*, Vancouver, 9-10 May 1955, 13-17.
12 Ibid.
13 While Gibson dwelled at length on the important role that tourist expenditures played in the region's economy, he also acknowledged the industry's capacity to draw settlers. Dr. Weldon B. Gibson, "Pacific Northwest Tourists: A Billion Dollar Industry," in *Proceedings of the 33rd General Conference of the PNTA*, Vancouver, 9-10 May 1955, 3-8. The *Pacific Northwesterner*, the voice of the Pacific Northwest Trade Association, also continued to recognize tourism's "investment" possibilities – albeit in a secondary capacity. The

association recognized the importance of the "tourist dollar" but also appreciated the fact that tourism brought with it the possibility of increased settlement and investment. These possibilities were an additional bonus in the eyes of the association. University of Washington, Special Collections, "More Gracious Hosts," *Pacific Northwesterner* 6, 2 (1955): 1.

14   Gibson, "Pacific Northwest Tourists."

15   BCARS, GR 520, British Columbia Commission on Forest Resources papers, Box 9, File 8, Number 32, E.G. Rowebottom, Deputy Minister of Trade and Industry, "Memorandum on Travel Industry and Its Bearing on Post-War Rehabilitation," November 1942.

16   Apostle, "Canada, Vacations Unlimited," 201, 218-20.

17   The survey results were as follows: fishing 17 percent; hunting 5 percent; cruising and sailing 3 percent; resort relaxation 13 percent; city visits 11 percent; and touring and sightseeing 51 percent. Government of British Columbia, *Report of the Department of Trade and Industry, 1951*, Q58.

18   Government of British Columbia, *Report of the Department of Recreation and Conservation, 1960*, O44.

19   Government of British Columbia, *Report of the Department of Recreation and Conservation, 1962*, S51.

20   Government of British Columbia, *Tourist '62* (Victoria, 1962), 2-15.

21   Ibid., 16-35.

22   CVA, GVVCB papers, Series A, Volume 1, File 1, Board of Directors Minutes, VTA Manager's Report, 11 September 1947.

23   Government of British Columbia, *Report of the Department of Trade and Industry, 1949*, DD57.

24   CVA, GVVCB papers, Series B, Volume 4, File 22, R.H. Baker, "Manager's Report," *Greater Vancouver Tourist Association Annual Report 1949*, 10-11.

25   *Report of the Department of Recreation and Conservation, 1964*, 11. The CGTB similarly attempted to sell Canada as a year-round vacation destination. See Apostle, "Canada, Vacations Unlimited," 282.

26   CVA, GVVCB papers, Series A, Volume 2, File 10, Text of Speech, Leo Dolan to GVTA, 21 October 1959.

27   CVA, GVVCB papers, Series E, Volume 7, File 42, "Convention Business Is BIG Business," c. 1965-66.

28   CVA, GVVCB papers, Series B, Volume 4, File 23, George C. Bradley, "President's Report," *Greater Vancouver Tourist Association Annual Report 1956*, 5.

29   Government of British Columbia, *Report of the Department of Trade and Industry, 1953*, LL53.

30   Government of British Columbia, *Report of the Department of Recreation and Conservation, 1960*, O10.

31   Government of British Columbia, *Report of the Department of Recreation and Conservation, 1962*, S52.

32   Government of British Columbia, *Report of the Department of Recreation and Conservation, 1963*, U43.

33   Government of British Columbia, *Report of the Department of Recreation and Conservation, 1964*, T42.

34   Government of British Columbia, *Report of the Department of Recreation and Conservation, 1965*, Y49.

35   CVA, GVVCB papers, Series B, Volume 4, File 23, Ivor Neil, "President's Report," *Vancouver Tourist Association Annual Report 1953*, 1-2; James V. Hughes, "Commissioner's Report," *Vancouver Tourist Association Annual Report 1953*, 4.

36   CVA, GVVCB papers, Series B, Volume 4, File 23, James V. Hughes, "Commissioner's Report," *Vancouver Tourist Association Annual Report 1954*, 7.

37   CVA, GVVCB papers, Series B, Volume 4, File 23, George C. Bradley, "President's Report," *Greater Vancouver Tourist Association Annual Report 1957*, 5; James V. Hughes, "Report of the Executive Vice-President," *Greater Vancouver Tourist Association Annual Report 1957*, 9; T. Boyd Haskell, "President's Report," *Greater Vancouver Tourist Association Annual Report 1958*, 3.

38   Victoria City Archives (VCA), Victoria Chamber of Commerce (VCC) fonds, 32 A 2, Board of Directors Minutes, 18 July 1951.

39   VCA, VCC fonds, 32 A 2, Board of Directors Meeting, 16 February 1953; emphasis added.
40   VCA, VCC fonds, 32 A 5, L.C. Parkinson, Chairman, Tourist and Convention Advisory Committee, to President and Board of Directors, 26 April 1968.
41   Government of British Columbia, *Report of the Department of Trade and Industry, 1956*, Y58.
42   Phil Gaglardi, "Opportunity Unlimited," in *Proceedings of the 34th General Conference of the Pacific Northwest Trade Association*, Seattle, 31 October-1 November 1955, 23.
43   Lyndon Grove, *Focus on British Columbia* (Vancouver: Westworld, c. 1981), 17-18.
44   Jean Barman, *The West beyond the West: A History of British Columbia*, rev. ed. (Toronto: University of Toronto Press, 1996), 271, 281. While the previous coalition government had also completed several major highway projects, including the Hope-Princeton highway that provided a "circle" route between the Lower Mainland and the Okanagan, highway building came to be identified as a key component of Social Credit's province-building policy.
45   CVA, Add. MSS. 370, British Columbia Chamber of Commerce (BCCC) papers, Volume 1, File 10, *General Policy Statements and Resolutions, British Columbia Chamber of Commerce 1952-53*, 3.
46   CVA, BCCC papers, Volume 2, File 4, *Submissions Received up to 14th April, 1962 for Discussion at Eleventh Annual Meeting*.
47   CVA, BCCC papers, Volume 2, File 6, *Submissions Received up to 14th April 1964 for Discussion at Thirteenth Annual Meeting*.
48   CVA, BCCC papers, Series A, Volume 1, File 3, VTA Board of Directors Minutes, "Operating Report," 11 January 1951.
49   "Alaska Highway," *Sunset* 102, 4 (1949): 6-14.
50   "October Is a Fine Time to Visit the Okanagan," *Sunset* 117, 5 (1956): 28-30, 32, 34, 36; "Looping the Big Bend Country ... and the Watery Kootenays," *Sunset* 119, 2 (1957): 44-48.
51   Representative demands for road improvements to encourage tourist travel in the vicinities of Cranbrook, Kimberley, Vanderhoof, and Seton Portage in the mid- to late 1950s appear in the following: CVA, BCCC papers, Volume 1, File 13, *General Policy Statements*, 4th Annual Meeting of the BC Chamber of Commerce; Volume 2, File 1, *Submissions Received up to 19th March, 1959 for Discussion at Eighth Annual Meeting*; Volume 2, File 1, *Submissions Received up to 19th March, 1959 for Discussion at Eighth Annual Meeting*.
52   Examples of requests for the expansion and improvement of parks and campgrounds near both Dawson Creek and Trail are located in CVA, BCCC papers, Volume 1, File 16, *Submissions Received up to 31st March, 1958 for Discussion at Seventh Annual Meeting*, 6; Volume 2, File 2, *Submissions Received up to 1st April, 1960 for Discussion at Ninth Annual Meeting*. Suggestions for publicity endeavours came from many sources, including the Associated Boards of Trade of the Fraser Valley and Lower Mainland, the Kamloops and District Board of Trade, and the Duncan-Cowichan Chamber of Commerce. See CVA, BCCC papers, Volume 1, File 12, *Policy Statements and Resolutions Submitted to the 3rd Annual Meeting of the BC Chamber of Commerce*, 1954, 9; Volume 2, File 2, *Submissions Received up to 1st April, 1960 for Discussion at Ninth Annual Meeting*; Volume 2, File 6, *Submissions Received up to 14th April, 1964 for Discussion at Thirteenth Annual Meeting*. Requests for government regulation came from, among other organizations, the Courtney-Comox Chamber of Commerce and the Prince George Chamber of Commerce. See CVA, BCCC papers, Volume 1, File 13, *Policy Statements and Resolutions Submitted to the 4th Annual Meeting of the BC Chamber of Commerce*, 1955, 7-8; Volume 2, File 4, *Submissions Received up to 14th April, 1962 for Discussion at Eleventh Annual Meeting*.
53   Barman, *The West beyond the West*, 271, 281.
54   W.A.C. Bennett, "A New Era," in *Proceedings of the 35th General Conference of the PNTA*, Victoria, 14-15 May 1956, 26-30.
55   Barman, *The West beyond the West*, 280.
56   Tourism had long been seen as an answer to regional underdevelopment in the Maritimes. See, for example, Shelley Kyte, "'V-8 or Make and Break' – An Investigation of the Development of Tourism in Canada: A Case Study of Nova Scotia" (MA thesis, Queen's University, 1997), and Alan MacEachern, *Natural Selections: National Parks in Atlantic Canada, 1935-1970* (Montreal: McGill-Queen's University Press, 2001), Chapters 3-6.

57 Government of British Columbia, *Report of the Department of Trade and Industry, 1950*, HH62.
58 Government of British Columbia, *Report of the Department of Trade and Industry, 1951*, Q60; *1952*, FF68-69.
59 Government of British Columbia, *Report of the Department of Trade and Industry, 1953*, LL53.
60 Government of British Columbia, *Report of the Department of Recreation and Conservation, 1961*, V47.
61 CVA, GVVCB papers, Series B, Volume 4, File 23, Frank Baker, "President's Report," *Greater Vancouver Visitors and Convention Bureau Annual Report 1962*, 4; Harold Merilees, "Managing Director's Report," *Greater Vancouver Visitors and Convention Bureau Annual Report 1963*, 11.
62 Government of British Columbia, *Report of the Department of Recreation and Conservation, 1962*, S51; *1963*, U45; *1964*, T43; and *1965*, Y51.
63 Government of British Columbia, *Report of the Department of Recreation and Conservation, 1966*, T58. At a meeting of the provincial Tourist Advisory Council in March 1966, future minister of Department of Travel Industry W.K. Kiernan explained that this shift in policy was designed to allow regional boards to direct more of their own revenue toward local initiatives such as information centres and administrative expenses." CVA, GVVCB papers, Series E, Volume 7, File 50, Provincial Tourist Advisory Council Meeting, Empress Hotel, Victoria, 23 March 1966.
64 Government of British Columbia, *Report of the Department of Recreation and Conservation, 1959*, 7; *Annual Report, Department of Travel Industry, 1967*, 28.
65 *Beautiful British Columbia* spring 1960; *Beautiful British Columbia* summer 1961.
66 University of British Columbia Archives (UBCA), Fraser Valley Tourist Association (FVTA) papers, File 15, Joyce Williams, Abbotsford Junior Secondary School, grade ten, prize-winning essay, "The Land of Simon Fraser," [1963].
67 CVA, GVVCB papers, Series B, Volume 4, File 23, Hedley S. Hipwell, "President's Report," *Greater Vancouver Tourist Association Annual Report 1950*, 1-3.
68 CVA, GVVCB papers, Series B, Volume 4, File 22, M.J. McCormick, "Publicity Commissioner's Report," *Vancouver Tourist Association Annual Report 1951*, 10.
69 Ibid., 10-11.
70 CVA, GVVCB papers, Series A, Volume 2, File 10, Cockfield, Brown and Company Limited, Suggested Advertising Policy for the Greater Vancouver Tourist Association, 3 July 1958.
71 National Archives of Canada (NAC), Leo D. Dolan papers, Volume 2, "Booklets and Pamphlets" File, "24th Annual Convention and Exposition Success," *Hotel News*, Official Organ of Hotel Associations in Canada, 22, 4 (1949): 12-13.
72 On the national campaign to convince Canadians that tourism was "everybody's business," see Karen Dubinsky, "Everybody Likes Canadians: Canadians, Americans, and the Post-World War Two Travel Boom," in *Being Elsewhere: Tourism, Consumer Culture, and Identity in Modern Europe and North America*, ed. Shelley Baranowski and Ellen Furlough (Ann Arbor: University of Michigan Press, 2001), as well as Apostle, "Canada, Vacations Unlimited," 244-45, 297-313. Apostle's key arguments are also presented in "The Display of a Tourist Nation: Canada in Government Film, 1945-1959," *Journal of the Canadian Historical Association*, New Series 12 (2001): 177-97.
73 Interestingly, these advertisements retained a focus on tourism's role in promoting settlement – an emphasis that diminished markedly throughout the postwar era. BCARS, GR 1222, Premiers' papers, Box 194, File 8, Estimate and Schedule, Stewart-Lovick and Macpherson Ltd., 9 May 1949.
74 VCA, VCC fonds, 33 G 1, File 2, Victoria Chamber of Commerce, *1959 Annual Report*.
75 VCA, VCC fonds, 33 G 1, File 2, Victoria Chamber of Commerce, *1960 Annual Report*.
76 VCA, VCC fonds, 33 G 1, File 2, Victoria Chamber of Commerce, *1961 Annual Report*.
77 CVA, GVVCB papers, Series A, Volume 2, File 10, GVTA Executive Committee Minutes, 18 January 1960.
78 CVA, GVVCB papers, Series A, Volume 2, File 12, GVTA Membership Committee Minutes, 18 May 1961. By January 1962, it had been decided to change the name of the booklet to *Sightseeing, Entertainment, and Shopping*. CVA, GVVCB papers, Series A, Volume 2, File 12, GVTA Membership Committee Minutes, 31 January 1962.

79　On the CGTB's film campaign, see Apostle, "The Display of a Tourist Nation."

80　CVA, GVVCB papers, Series E, Volume 8, File 61, GVVCB News Release, [c. 1968]; Series E, Volume 8, File 62, List of Prizes for Dollar Trace Winners, n.d.; Series E, Volume 8, File 62, William D.S. Earle, Assistant Manager, Convention Bureau, to W.G. Schammann, General Manager, Discovery Inn, Campbell River, 30 May 1968.

81　Peter S. McInnis, "Planning Prosperity: Canadians Debate Postwar Reconstruction," in *Uncertain Horizons: Canadians and Their World in 1945*, ed. Greg Donaghy (Ottawa: Canadian Committee for the History of the Second World War, 1997), 231-59.

82　See Elizabeth Fones-Wolf, *Selling Free Enterprise: The Business Assault on Labor and Liberalism, 1945-1960* (Urbana: University of Illinois Press, 1994), Chapter 7; quotation at 193.

83　On the proliferating advocacy of public goods since the 1960s, see Rutherford, *Endless Propaganda*.

84　"Ralph D. Baker Chooses Canadian Citizenship," *Pacific Northwesterner* 16, 4 (1964): 6.

85　*Proceedings of the 31st General Conference of the PNTA*, Portland, 11-12 November 1954, 35.

86　Ralph D. Baker, "A Challenge and Golden Opportunity," *Pacific Northwesterner* 3, 2 (1952): 1-2.

87　Stanley M. Oberg, "Report on the Tourist Round Table," in *Proceedings of the 33rd General Conference of the PNTA*, Vancouver, 9-10 May 1955, 32-33.

88　"Report of the Visitor and Recreation Committee," *Proceedings of the 35th General Conference of the PNTA*, Victoria, 14-15 May 1956, 23.

89　E.D. McPhee, "The Business of Tourism."

90　Ibid.

91　Ibid.

92　Reg. T. Rose, "An Academic Enterprise ... Sponsored by Business," *Canadian Business* June 1952: 58-59, 78-81.

93　Michael Bliss, *Northern Enterprise: Five Centuries of Canadian Business* (Toronto: McClelland and Stewart, 1987), 500-01.

94　CVA, GVVCB papers, Series A, Volume 1, File 1, Board of Directors Minutes, VTA Manager's Report, 11 April 1946.

95　N.F. Pullen, "A Statistic Speaks Out," in *Proceedings of the 36th General Conference of the PNTA*, Yakima, WA, 1-2 October 1956, 35; CVA, GVVCB papers, Series B, Volume 4, File 23, James V. Hughes, "Commissioner's Report," *Vancouver Tourist Association Annual Report 1953*, 2; CVA, GVVCB papers, Series B, Volume 4, File 23, James V. Hughes, "Commissioner's Report," *Vancouver Tourist Association Annual Report 1954*, 5.

96　CVA, GVVCB, Series B, Volume 4, File 23, James V. Hughes, "Report of the Executive Vice-President," *Vancouver Tourist Association Annual Report 1955*, 6.

97　CVA, GVVCB papers, Series A, Volume 1, File 7, VTA Management and Finance Committee Minutes, 17 September 1953.

98　CVA, Add. MSS. 633, Series A, Volume 2, File 8, VTA Management and Finance Committee Minutes, 20 April 1955. The role of the UBC professors did not stop there, however. In May 1955, Professor McPhee approached the VTA executive vice president, James V. Hughes, with the offer of setting up a conference on tourism in Seattle to discuss ways of overcoming the lack of factual data concerning tourism. Those present at the meeting in Seattle included McPhee, Oberg, J.V. Hughes, Ernest Evans, George Warren, Charlie Johns, Dr. J. Guthrie of Washington State College, Dr. Engle of the University of Washington, Deputy Minister of Trade and Industry T.L. Sturgess, and the director of the Bureau of Economics and Statistics in Victoria, Mr. Hatcher. CVA, GVVCB papers, Series A, Volume 2, File 8, VTA Board of Directors Minutes, 19 May 1955; VTA Management and Finance Committee Minutes, 4 August 1955. And, in January 1962, Ald. Bell-Irving suggested establishing a Chair of Hotel Management at the University of British Columbia. CVA, GVVCB papers, Series A, Volume 2, File 12, GVTA Board of Directors Minutes, 15 January 1962.

99　CVA, Add. MSS. 633, Series A, Volume 2, File 9, GVTA Board of Directors Minutes, 21 February 1957. According to Roland Wild, these studies revealed that visitors to the city approved of its culinary and consumer offerings as they spent 27 percent of their money on food and 14 percent on clothing. They were, however, frustrated by the city's lack of directional signs, its Wednesday shop closings, and its antiquated liquor laws. Roland Wild, "How Tourist Dollars Make Sense," *Saturday Night* 6 August 1955: 27.

100 CVA, GVVCB papers, Series B, Volume 4, File 23, Ivor Neil, "President's Report," *Vancouver Tourist Association Annual Report 1953*, 1.
101 CVA, GVVCB papers, Series D, Volume 6, File 31, GVVCB News Release, 18 April 1966.
102 CVA, GVVCB papers, Series B, Volume 4, File 23, A.L. Woods, "Comptroller's Report," *Greater Vancouver Tourist Association Annual Report 1950*, 14.
103 George C. Bradley, "President's Report," *Greater Vancouver Tourist Association Annual Report 1956*, 5; George C. Bradley, "President's Report," *Greater Vancouver Tourist Association Annual Report 1957*, 6.
104 CVA, GVVCB papers, Series A, Volume 1, File 3, Minutes of the GVTA Annual Meeting, 2 December 1950.
105 Lyn Harrington, "The Yankee Dollah!" *Canadian Business* October 1945: 58-59, 128-32.
106 Dubinsky, "'Everybody Likes Canadians,'" in *Being Elsewhere*, 327.
107 CVA, Add. MSS. 633, Series A, Volume 1, File 3, VTA Board of Directors Minutes, "Operating Report," 11 January 1951.
108 CVA, GVVCB papers, Series B, Volume 4, File 22, R.H. Baker, "Manager's Report," *Vancouver Tourist Association Annual Report 1948*, 16-17.
109 VCA, VCC fonds, 33 G 1, File 2, Victoria Chamber of Commerce *1957 Annual Report Year Book and Business Directory*, 13-15.
110 *Report of the Department of Recreation and Conservation, 1957*, II36.
111 CVA, BCCC papers, Volume 2, File 5, *BC Bulletin* 13, 1 (1963): 6.
112 *Report of the Department of Recreation and Conservation, 1959*, Y42.
113 CVA, GVVCB papers, Series E, Volume 7, File 42, [BC Chamber of Commerce] *Intelligencer* 17, 10 (1968): 6.
114 CVA, GVVCB papers, Series A, Volume 1, File 2, VTA Board of Directors Minutes, "Manager's Report," 14 October 1948; Volume 1, File 3, Minutes of a Closed Meeting of the Joint Board of the VTA and Automobile Club, 10 February 1951.
115 UBCA, FVTA papers, File 13, Minutes of FVTA Executive Meeting, 25 June [1963].
116 UBCA, FVTA papers, File 13, René Pelletier, President FVTA, to "Editor," 23 March 1963.
117 UBCA, FVTA papers, File 13, Pelletier to Principals of Schools in the Fraser Valley, 11 March 1963.
118 UBCA, FVTA papers, File 13, Executive Committee Minutes, 26 February 1963.
119 CVA, GVVCB papers, Series E, Volume 7, File 49, CP Air Questionnaire; completed and submitted to Jack Webb, 12 December 1969.
120 McPhee, "The Business of Tourism."
121 Ibid.
122 CVA, GVVCB papers, Series A, Volume 3, File 13, GVVCB Executive Committee Minutes, 28 February 1963; Volume 3, File 13, GVVCB Board of Directors Minutes, 5 June 1963.
123 CVA, GVVCB papers, Series E, Volume 9, File 78, Mrs. C.W. Mellish, Secretary, Interim Planning Committee, Lady Vancouver Club, to GVVCB Board of Directors, 11 March 1963.
124 CVA, GVVCB papers, Series E, Volume 9, File 79, GVVCB *News from Vancouver*, 6 April 1972.
125 CVA, GVVCB papers, Series E, Volume 9, File 78, Emily Ostapchuk, Secretary, Lady Vancouver Club, to Jack Bain, President GVVCB, 8 July 1966.
126 CVA, GVVCB papers, Series D, Volume 6, File 30, VVB News Release, 25 May 1965.
127 CVA, GVVCB papers, Series E, Volume 8, File 65, "Operation Daffodil Top Secret" (card), [1970].
128 See, for example, John Urry, *The Tourist Gaze: Leisure and Travel in Contemporary Societies* (London: Sage, 1990), and Ian McKay, "History and the Tourist Gaze: The Politics of Commemoration in Nova Scotia, 1935-1964," *Acadiensis* 22, 2 (1993): 102-38.
129 CVA, GVVCB papers, Series E, Volume 7, File 38, Harold Merilees to Councillor Henry Gilbertson, Richmond, 7 May 1965.
130 CVA, GVVCB papers, Series E, Volume 7, File 38, Harold Merilees, form letter, to various recipients, 6 April 1965.

131   CVA, GVVCB papers, Series E, Volume 7, File 38, Harold Merilees to Councillor Henry Gilbertson, Richmond, 7 May 1965.
132   CVA, GVVCB papers, Series E, Volume 7, File 38, *Black Top Cab Bulletin,* April 1965.
133   VCA, VCC fonds, 32 A 2, Board of Directors Minutes, 19 November 1954; Board of Directors Minutes, 26 September 1955.
134   VCA, VCC fonds, 33 G 1, File 2, *1957 Annual Report Year Book and Business Directory,* Sam Lane, "Report of the Chairman of the Tourist Trade Group."
135   VCA, VCC fonds, 32 A 2, Board of Directors Minutes, 14 June 1957.
136   CVA, GVVCB papers, Series A, Volume 1, File 2, VTA Board of Directors Minutes, 19 August 1948.
137   CVA, GVVCB papers, Series A, Volume 2, File 9, GVTA Visitor Promotion Committee Minutes, 16 May 1957.
138   CVA, GVVCB papers, Series A, Volume 2, File 9, GVTA Board of Directors Minutes, 20 March 1958.
139   CVA, GVVCB papers, Series A, Volume 2, File 10, GVTA Meeting Regarding a Scenic Drive Minutes, 9 June 1958.
140   CVA, GVVCB papers, Series A, Volume 2, File 9, GVTA Executive Committee Minutes, 26 May 1958.
141   Reg Whitaker and Gary Marcuse, *Cold War Canada: The Making of a National Insecurity State, 1945-1957* (Toronto: University of Toronto Press, 1994), 14.
142   VCA, VCC fonds, 32 A 4, File 7, "Canada's Travel Industry," Address by Dan Wallace, Acting Director CGTB, to the Annual Meeting of the Victoria Chamber of Commerce, 15 September 1965.

Conclusion: From Tourist Trade to Tourist Industry

1   Roland Wild, "How Tourist Dollars Make Sense," *Saturday Night* 6 August 1955: 27.
2   On such concerns, see David M. Wrobel, "Introduction: Tourists, Tourism, and the Toured Upon," and Rudolfo Anaya, "Why I Love Tourists: Confessions of a Dharma Bum," in *Seeing and Being Seen: Tourism in the American West,* ed. David M. Wrobel and Patrick T. Long (Lawrence: University Press of Kansas, 2001), 4, 60-62.
3   Victoria City Archives (VCA), Tourist Association of Victoria (TAV) papers, Secretary's Letterbooks 1903-06, Cuthbert to J.S. Bloomfield, Vancouver, 12 December 1903.
4   VCA, TAV papers, Secretary's Letterbooks 1903-06, Cuthbert to S. McClure, Victoria, 20 October 1903.
5   VCA, TAV papers, Secretary's Letterbooks 1903-06, Cuthbert to J.S. Bloomfield, Vancouver, 14 November 1903. When it eventually went to press, the first edition of the pamphlet sported Flora, the Goddess of Flowers, in the foreground and British warships in the background. See Kenneth Lines, "A Bit of Old England: The Selling of Tourist Victoria" (MA thesis, University of Victoria, 1972), 35.
6   On this trend, see Dean MacCannell, *The Tourist: A New Theory of the Leisure Class* (New York: Schocken Books, 1976), 100-02.
7   City of Vancouver Archives (CVA), Greater Vancouver Visitors and Convention Bureau (GVVCB) papers, Series E, Volume 8, File 52, Memorandum from Harold Merilees to various people, including MPs and MLAs, 28 January 1966.
8   CVA, GVVCB papers, Series E, Volume 8, File 52, Grant Deachman, MP for Vancouver-Quadra, to Merilees, 7 February 1966.
9   As recent studies emphasize, it is important not to confuse Deachman's and Merilees's aims with First Nations' own reasons for participating in such cultural displays. On the variety of First Nations' motivations for participating in public ceremonial displays, see, for example, Paige S. Raibmon, "Authentic Indians: Episodes of Encounter from the Late Nineteenth-Century Northwest Coast" (PhD diss., Duke University, 2000); Susan Roy, "Performing Musqueam Culture and History at British Columbia's 1966 Centennial Celebrations," *BC Studies* 135 (2002): 55-90; Frank Goodyear, "The Narratives of Sitting Bull's Surrender: Bailey, Dix, and Mead's Photographic Western," in *Dressing in Feathers: The Construction of the Indian in American Popular Culture,* ed. S. Elizabeth Bird (Boulder: Westview Press, 1996), 29-43; and Charlotte Townsend-Gault, "If Art Is the Answer, What Is

the Question? – Some Queries Raised by First Nations' Visual Culture in Vancouver," *RACAR [Revue d'art canadienne/Canadian Art Review]* 21, 1-2 (1994): 100-10.

10 Wild, "How Tourist Dollars Make Sense," 27.

11 University of British Columbia Archives (UBCA), Fraser Valley Tourist Association (FVTA) papers, File 6, Memorandum, Earl McCallum, Director, World's Fair Edition, Seattle *Times*, to Boards of Trade and Chambers of Commerce Throughout British Columbia, 25 November 1961.

12 CVA, GVVCB papers, Series D, Volume 6, File 32, "Hospitality Stressed by Tourist Official," *News from Vancouver*, May 1969.

Bibliography

Primary Sources

Archival Collections

British Columbia Archives and Records Service (Victoria)
British Columbia Commission on Forest Resources papers
C.C. Pemberton papers
Department of Highways, Highways Records
G.G. McGeer papers
Premiers' papers
Sidney J. Smith papers
T.D. Pattullo papers

City of Vancouver Archives (Vancouver)
British Columbia Chamber of Commerce fonds
Greater Vancouver Visitors and Convention Bureau papers
Harold Merilees fonds

National Archives of Canada (Ottawa)
D. Leo Dolan papers
Department of Industry, Trade and Commerce papers

University of British Columbia Archives (Vancouver)
A.M. Stephen papers
Fraser Valley Tourist Association papers
S.F. Tolmie papers

University of Oregon Archives (Eugene)
Lee D. Drake papers

University of Victoria Archives (Victoria)
Caravan Across British Columbia 1930 fonds

University of Washington Archives (Seattle)
Business Research Bureau papers
Daniel Hunt Gilman papers

Victoria City Archives (Victoria)
"Tourism" Clipping File

Tourist Association of Victoria papers
Victoria Chamber of Commerce fonds

Newspapers and Magazines (Various Dates)
Ashcroft *Journal*
Beautiful British Columbia magazine
Ottawa *Evening Journal*
Prince Rupert *News*
Sunset magazine
Vancouver *News Herald*
Vancouver *Province*
Vancouver *Sun*
Victoria *Daily Colonist*
Victoria *Daily Times*

Magazine Articles
"Alaska Highway." *Sunset* 102, 4 (1949): 6-14.
"The Beauties of Halcyon, B.C." *Saturday Night* 18 April 1908: 4.
Berger, Mrs. Henry A. "Victoria." Letter to the Editor. *Holiday* December 1948: 6, 8.
Eldredge, George G. "On Vacation Values." *Sunset* 13, 3 (1904): 254-55.
Francis, R.H. "Victoria – Vancouver: A Study in Contrasts on the West Coast." *Canadian Business* September 1957: 30-33.
Gomery, Percy. "Looking for a Road Across British Columbia." *Journal of the Canadian Bankers' Association* July 1922: 440-44.
Hardcastle, Kitty. "Drinking from Mountain Streams." *Saturday Night* 27 September 1913: 29.
Harrington, Lyn. "The Yankee Dollah!" *Canadian Business* October 1945: 58-59, 128-32.
Laing, Hamilton M. "Gardens of the Desert." *Canadian Magazine* May 1920: 21-32.
Lambert, Norman. "The New British Columbia." *Maclean's* October 1915: 19-22.
"Looping the Big Bend Country ... and the Watery Kootenays." *Sunset* 119, 2 (1957): 44-48.
March, J.E. "Ski-Riders of Revelstoke." *Maclean's* 1 February 1928: 14, 41-42.
McGaffey, Ernest. "The Island of Discovery." *Sunset* 30, 5 (1913): 494-507.
McKeever, H.P. "You Might Say I Live in the Past." *Canadian Hotel Review* August 1960: 26-27.
Nesbitt, Jim, and Melwyn Breen. "Victoria – Our West-Coast Garden." *Saturday Night* 8 August 1950: 8-10, 31.
"New Vancouver Lounges Exploit English History." *Canadian Hotel Review* January 1955: 18-19.
"October Is a Fine Time to Visit the Okanagan." *Sunset* 117, 5 (1956): 28-36.
"Pan American Highway." *Sunset* 91, 4 (1943): 6-9.
Powell, E.A. "Autobirds of Passage: The Island Highway." *Sunset* 33, 3 (1914): 519-30.
—. "Autobirds of Passage: The Cariboo Trail." *Sunset* 33, 4 (1914): 739-48.
Raney, W.E. "On the Old Cariboo Road." *Saturday Night* 25 February 1899: 4.
Rhoades, Guy E. "Bella Coola: The Norway of Canada." *Saturday Night* 23 May 1925: 25.
Rose, Reg. T. "An Academic Enterprise ... Sponsored by Business." *Canadian Business* June 1952: 58-59, 78-81.
Sandys, Edward W. "A Gleam from a Glacier." *Saturday Night* 8 February 1890: 7.
Saxon, Charles. "B.C. Rides a Boom." *Canadian Business* May 1947: 32-33, 107-10.
Schultz, Gladys Denny. "Mental Health Problems in the Business World." *Sunset* 62, 4 (1929): 38, 44.
Shaw, Charles Lugrin. "The Valley of the Past." *Maclean's* 15 March 1922: 26-27, 54-55.
Snider, Mary Adelaide. "Walking the Flume." *Saturday Night* 16 August 1913: 29, 35.
"Sport on the Cariboo Road." *Saturday Night* 11 March 1899: 7.
Spragge, Mrs. Arthur. "The Last Great Valley." *Maclean's* June 1915: 20-22, 78.
Todd, Irene. "A Cruise down the North Pacific Coast." *Saturday Night* 6 August 1921: 17.
"Travel." *Saturday Night* 7 July 1928: 10-11.
Vandeventer, E.A. "The West Makes the Open Road Alluring." *Sunset* 54, 5 (1925): 5.

Wild, Roland. "How Tourist Dollars Make Sense." *Saturday Night* 6 August 1955: 27.
Williams, Ronald John. "Canada's 'City of Gardens.'" *Holiday* September 1948: 91-97,
137-38.

Government Publications
British Columbia Government Travel Bureau. *Newsletter.* 1945-56.
British Columbia Ministry of Tourism. *The Economic Impact of Tourism Industries in British
Columbia.* Victoria, 1992.
Canadian Government Travel Bureau. *Canada Calls You.* Ottawa, c. 1941.
Government of British Columbia. *Public Accounts.* 1930-70.
—. *Report of the Department of Trade and Industry.* 1939-56.
—. *Report of the Department of Recreation and Conservation.* 1957-67.
—. *Tourist '62.* Victoria, 1962.
—. *Tourist '63.* Victoria, 1963.
—. *Annual Report, Department of Travel Industry.* 1967-72.
Government of Canada. *Canada's Wartime Measures for Economic Stability to Keep down
the Cost of Living.* Ottawa: King's Printer, 1944.
—. *Wartime Economic Stabilization to Keep down the Cost of Living in Canada: What It Is,
How It Works, Why It Must Be Supported.* Ottawa: King's Printer, 1944.
Senate of Canada. *Report and Proceedings of the Special Committee on Tourist Traffic.* Ottawa:
King's Printer, 1934.
Statistics Canada. *National Tourism Indicators Quarterly Estimates: First Quarter 2003.* Ottawa:
Ministry of Industry, 2003.
Tourism British Columbia. *The Value of Tourism.* Victoria, 1999.

Miscellaneous Reports and Proceedings
Baker, Ralph D. "A Challenge and Golden Opportunity." *Pacific Northwesterner* 3, 2 (1952):
1-2.
Bennett, W.A.C. "A New Era." *Proceedings of the 35th General Conference of the Pacific
Northwest Trade Association.* Victoria, 14-15 May 1956: 26-30.
Gaglardi, Phil. "Opportunity Unlimited." *Proceedings of the 34th General Conference of the
Pacific Northwest Trade Association.* Seattle, 31 October-1 November 1955: 23.
Gibson, Dr. Weldon B. "Pacific Northwest Tourists: A Billion Dollar Industry." *Proceedings
of the 33rd General Conference of the Pacific Northwest Trade Association.* Vancouver, 9-
10 May 1955: 3-8.
McPhee, E.D. "The Business of Tourism" and "Pacific Northwest Tourists: A Billion Dol-
lar Industry." *Proceedings of the 33rd General Conference of the Pacific Northwest Trade
Association.* Vancouver, 9-10 May 1955: 13-17.
"More Gracious Hosts." *Pacific Northwesterner* 6, 2 (March 1955): 1.
Oberg, Stanley M. "Report on the Tourist Round Table." *Proceedings of the 33rd General
Conference of the Pacific Northwest Trade Association.* Vancouver, 9-10 May 1955: 32-33.
Proceedings of the 31st General Conference of the Pacific Northwest Trade Association. Port-
land, 11-12 November 1954.
Pullen, N.F. "A Statistic Speaks Out." *Proceedings of the 36th General Conference of the
Pacific Northwest Trade Association.* Yakima, WA, 1-2 October 1956: 35.
"Ralph D. Baker Chooses Canadian Citizenship." *Pacific Northwesterner* 16, 4 (1964): 6.
"Report of the Visitor and Recreation Committee." *Proceedings of the 35th General Con-
ference of the Pacific Northwest Trade Association.* Victoria, 14-15 May 1956: 22-24.

Tourism Promotion Pamphlets
British Columbia Board of Trade. *Victoria, British Columbia: Past and Present.* Victoria: Col-
onist Presses, c. 1900.
City of Victoria. *Victoria Illustrated.* Victoria: Ellis-*Colonist*, 1891.
The Hotel Dallas. Victoria: Province Print, c. 1895.
"Land of the Empire Builders": The Pacific Northwest: Dimensions and Opportunities. Menlo
Park, CA: Lane Magazine Co., 1964.

Pacific Northwest Tourist Association. *The Pacific Northwest: The World's Greatest Out of Doors*. Seattle: PNTA, c. 1917.

Tourist Association of Victoria. *Victoria, British Columbia, Canada: Tourist Resort of the Pacific Northwest*. Victoria: Colonist Presses, c. 1902.

—. *Picturesque Victoria, British Columbia, Canada: The Tourist Resort of the Pacific Northwest*. Victoria: Colonist Printing, 1903.

—. *An Outpost of Empire*. Victoria: Colonist Printing and Publishing, 1905.

—. *An Outpost of Empire: Victoria, British Columbia, Canada: "The Evergreen City of Canada."* Victoria: Colonist Presses, 1907.

—. *Impressions of Victoria, British Columbia, Canada: The "Empress" City of the Golden West.* Victoria: n.p., 1907.

Vancouver Island Development Association. *Victoria, British Columbia: A Most Attractive City on the Pacific Coast*. Victoria, 1915.

Vancouver Tourist Association. *The Sunset Doorway of the Dominion: Vancouver, B.C.* Vancouver, c. 1905.

Victoria ... the Capital City of the West. Victoria: BC Print and Engraving Company, c. 1900.

Victoria and Island Publicity Bureau. *"Follow the Birds" to Victoria, B.C.* Victoria, 1922.

—. *"Follow the Birds" to Victoria, B.C.* Victoria, 1928.

Films

British Columbia Government Travel Bureau. *Tourism: A British Columbia Industry*. 1940.

—. *Vancouver Island: British Columbia's Island Playground*. 1942.

—. *The Okanagan Valley: British Columbia's Orchard Playground*. c. 1943-47.

—. *Highway 16*. c. 1948-49.

—. *Vancouver Island: British Columbia's Island Playground*. c. 1956-57.

—. *Vancouver Island: British Columbia's Island Playground*. c. 1962-64.

Secondary Sources

Articles

Anaya, Rudolfo. "Why I Love Tourists: Confessions of a Dharma Bum." *Seeing and Being Seen: Tourism in the American West*, ed. David M. Wrobel and Patrick T. Long, 59-69. Lawrence: University Press of Kansas, 2001.

Apostle, Alisa. "The Display of a Tourist Nation: Canada in Government Film, 1945-1959." *Journal of the Canadian Historical Association* New Series 12 (2001): 177-97.

Artibise, Alan F.J. "Boosterism and the Development of Prairie Cities, 1871-1913." *Town and City: Aspects of Western Canadian Urban Development*, ed. Alan F.J. Artibise, 209-35. Regina: Canadian Plains Research Center, University of Regina, 1981.

Baranowski, Shelley. "Strength through Joy: Tourism and National Integration in the Third Reich." *Being Elsewhere: Tourism, Consumer Culture, and Identity in Modern Europe and North America*, ed. Shelley Baranowski and Ellen Furlough, 213-36. Ann Arbor: University of Michigan Press, 2001.

Belshaw, John Douglas, and David J. Mitchell. "The Economy since the Great War." *The Pacific Province: A History of British Columbia*, ed. Hugh Johnston, 313-42. Vancouver: Douglas and McIntyre, 1996.

Bennett, Jason Patrick. "Apple of the Empire: Landscape and Imperial Identity in Turn-of-the-Century British Columbia." *Journal of the Canadian Historical Association* New Series 9 (1998): 63-92.

Berkowitz, Michael. "A 'New Deal' for Leisure: Making Mass Tourism during the Great Depression." *Being Elsewhere: Tourism, Consumer Culture, and Identity in Modern Europe and North America*, ed. Shelley Baranowski and Ellen Furlough, 185-212. Ann Arbor: University of Michigan Press, 2001.

Blake, Susan L. "A Woman's Trek: What Difference Does Gender Make?" *Women's Studies International Forum* 13, 4 (1990): 347-55.

Bland, M. Susan. "Henrietta the Homemaker, 'Rosie the Riveter': Images of Women in Advertising in *Maclean's* Magazine, 1939-50." *Atlantis* 8, 2 (1983): 61-86.

Blodgett, Peter J. "Selling the Scenery: Advertising and the National Parks, 1916-1933." *Seeing and Being Seen: Tourism in the American West*, ed. David M. Wrobel and Patrick T. Long, 271-98. Lawrence: University Press of Kansas, 2001.

—. "Visiting 'The Realm of Wonder': Yosemite and the Business of Tourism, 1855-1916." *California History* 69, 2 (1990): 118-30.

Bothwell, Robert. "'Who's Paying for Anything These Days?': War Production in Canada 1939-1945." *Mobilization for Total War: The Canadian, American, and British Experience 1914-1918, 1939-1945*, ed. N.F. Drieziger, 57-69. Waterloo: Wilfrid Laurier University Press, 1981.

Cameron, Ross D. "Tom Thomson, Antimodern Nationalism, and the Ideal of Manhood." *Journal of the Canadian Historical Association* New Series 10 (1999): 185-208.

Campbell, Colin. "Consuming Goods and the Good of Consuming." *Consumer Society in American History: A Reader*, ed. Lawrence B. Glickman, 19-32. Ithaca: Cornell University Press, 1999.

Campbell, Lara. "'A Barren Cupboard at Home': Ontario Families Confront the Premiers during the Great Depression." *Ontario since Confederation: A Reader*, ed. E.-A. Montigny and L. Chambers, 284-306. Toronto: University of Toronto Press, 2000.

—. "'We Who Have Wallowed in the Mud of Flanders': First World War Veterans, Unemployment, and the Great Depression in Ontario, 1929-1939." *Journal of the Canadian Historical Association* New Series 11 (2000): 125-49.

Cocks, Catherine. "The Chamber of Commerce's Carnival: City Festivals and Urban Tourism in the United States, 1890-1915." *Being Elsewhere: Tourism, Consumer Culture, and Identity in Modern Europe and North America*, ed. Shelley Baranowski and Ellen Furlough, 89-107. Ann Arbor: University of Michigan Press, 2001.

Cohen, Lizabeth. "The New Deal State and the Making of Citizen Consumers." *Getting and Spending: European and American Consumer Societies in the Twentieth Century*, ed. Susan Strasser, Charles McGovern, and Matthias Judt, 111-25. Cambridge, UK: Cambridge University Press, 1998.

Colpitts, George. "Wildlife Promotions, Western Canadian Boosterism, and the Conservation Movement, 1890-1914." *American Review of Canadian Studies* 28, 1-2 (1998): 103-30.

Copp, Terry. "Ontario 1939: The Decision for War." *Ontario History* 86, 3 (1994): 269-78.

D'Amore, L.J. "Tourism: A Vital Force for Peace." *Futurist* 22 (1988): 23-28.

—. "Tourism: The World's Peace Industry." *Recreation Canada* 48, 1 (1990): 24-33.

Davis, Clark. "From Oasis to Metropolis: Southern California and the Changing Context of American Leisure." *Pacific Historical Review* 61, 3 (1992): 357-86.

Davis, Donald F. "Dependent Motorization: Canada and the Automobile to the 1930s." *Journal of Canadian Studies* 21, 3 (1986): 106-32.

Davis, Susan G. "Landscapes of Imagination: Tourism in Southern California." *Pacific Historical Review* 68, 2 (1999): 173-91.

Dawson, Michael. "'That Nice Red Coat Goes to My Head like Champagne': Gender, Antimodernism, and the Mountie Image, 1880-1960." *Journal of Canadian Studies* 32, 3 (1997): 119-39.

Dilworth, Leah. "Tourists and Indians in Fred Harvey's Southwest." *Seeing and Being Seen: Tourism in the American West*, ed. David M. Wrobel and Patrick T. Long, 142-64. Lawrence: University Press of Kansas, 2001.

Dubinsky, Karen. "Everybody Likes Canadians: Canadians, Americans, and the Post-World War Two Travel Boom." *Being Elsewhere: Tourism, Consumer Culture, and Identity in Modern Europe and North America*, ed. Shelley Baranowski and Ellen Furlough, 320-47. Ann Arbor: University of Michigan Press, 2001.

Farber, David, and Beth Bailey. "The Fighting Man as Tourist: The Politics of Tourist Culture in Hawaii during World War II." *Pacific Historical Review* 65, 4 (1996): 641-60.

Forbes, Ernest. "Consolidating Disparity: The Maritimes and the Industrialization of Canada during the Second World War." *Acadiensis* 15, 2 (1986): 3-27.

Forward, Charles N. "The Evolution of Victoria's Functional Character." *Town and City:*

Aspects of Western Canadian Urban Development, ed. Alan F.J. Artibise, 347-70. Regina: Canadian Plains Research Center, University of Regina, 1981.

Fox, Richard Wightman, and T.J. Jackson Lears. "Introduction." *The Culture of Consumption: Critical Essays in American History 1880-1980*, ed. Richard Wightman Fox and T.J. Jackson Lears, ix-xiv. New York: Pantheon, 1983.

Galbraith, John Kenneth. "The Dependence Effect." *The Affluent Society*, 124-30. New York: New American Library, 1958.

Goodyear, Frank. "The Narratives of Sitting Bull's Surrender: Bailey, Dix, and Mead's Photographic Western." *Dressing in Feathers: The Construction of the Indian in American Popular Culture*, ed. S. Elizabeth Bird, 29-43. Boulder: Westview Press, 1996.

Gordon, Bertram M. "French Cultural Tourism and the Vichy Problem." *Being Elsewhere: Tourism, Consumer Culture, and Identity in Modern Europe and North America*, ed. Shelley Baranowski and Ellen Furlough, 239-71. Ann Arbor: University of Michigan Press, 2001.

---. "Warfare and Tourism: Paris in World War II." *Annals of Tourism Research* 25, 3 (1998): 616-38.

Guard, Julie. "Women Worth Watching: Radical Housewives in Cold War Canada." *Whose National Security? Canadian State Surveillance and the Creation of Enemies*, ed. Gary Kinsmen, Dieter K. Buse, and Mercedes Steedman, 73-88. Toronto: Between the Lines, 2000.

Harris, Cole. "Introduction." *The Resettlement of British Columbia: Essays on Colonialism and Geographical Change*, xi-xxii. Vancouver: UBC Press, 1997.

---. "Moving amid the Mountains, 1870-1930." *BC Studies* 58 (1983): 3-39.

---. "Social Power and Cultural Change in Pre-Colonial British Columbia." *BC Studies* 115-16 (1997): 45-82.

---. "The Struggle with Distance." *The Resettlement of British Columbia: Essays on Colonialism and Geographical Change*, 161-93. Vancouver: UBC Press, 1997.

Hayner, Norman. "Auto Camps in the Evergreen Playground." *Social Forces* 9 (1930): 256-66.

Horkheimer, Max, and Theodor Adorno. "The Culture Industry: Enlightenment as Mass Deception." *Dialectic of Enlightenment*, trans. John Cumming, 120-67. New York: Continuum, 1993 [1969].

Hyde, Anne Farrar. "From Stagecoach to Packard Twin Six: Yosemite and the Changing Face of Tourism, 1880-1930." *California History* 69, 2 (1990): 154-69.

Jean, Dominique. "Family Allowances and Family Autonomy: Quebec Families Encounter the Welfare State, 1945-1955." *Canadian Family History: Selected Readings*, ed. Bettina Bradbury, 401-37. Toronto: Copp Clark Pitman, 1992.

Keshen, Jeff. "One for All or All for One: Government Controls, Black Marketing, and the Limits of Patriotism, 1939-1947." *Journal of Canadian Studies* 29, 4 (1994-95): 111-43.

Lears, Jackson. "Packaging the Folk: Tradition and Amnesia in American Advertising, 1880-1940." *Folk Roots, New Roots: Folklore in American Life*, ed. Jane S. Becker and Barbara Franco, 103-40. Lexington, MA: Museum of Our National Heritage, 1988.

Limerick, Patricia Nelson. "Seeing and Being Seen: Tourism in the America West." *Seeing and Being Seen: Tourism in the American West*, ed. David M. Wrobel and Patrick T. Long, 39-58. Lawrence: University Press of Kansas, 2001.

Loo, Tina. "Dan Cranmer's Potlatch: Law as Coercion, Symbol, and Rhetoric in British Columbia, 1884-1890." *Canadian Historical Review* 73, 2 (1992): 125-65.

Louter, David. "Glaciers and Gasoline: The Making of a Windshield Wilderness, 1900-1915." *Seeing and Being Seen: Tourism in the American West*, ed. David M. Wrobel and Patrick T. Long, 248-70. Lawrence: University Press of Kansas, 2001.

Mattison, David. "The British Columbia Government Travel Bureau and Motion Picture Production, 1937-1947." *Flashback: People and Institutions in Canadian Film History*, ed. Gene Walz, 79-104. Montreal: Mediatexte Publications, 1986.

McDonald, Robert A.J. "Victoria, Vancouver, and the Economic Development of British Columbia, 1886-1914." *Town and City: Aspects of Western Canadian Urban Development*, ed. Alan F.J. Artibise, 31-55. Regina: Canadian Plains Research Center, University of Regina, 1981.

McGrath, Darrin M. "Salted Caribou and Sportsmen-Tourists: Conflicts over Wildlife Resources in Newfoundland at the Turn of the Twentieth Century." *Newfoundland Studies* 10, 2 (1994): 208-25.

McInnis, Peter S. "Planning Prosperity: Canadians Debate Postwar Reconstruction." *Uncertain Horizons: Canadians and Their World in 1945*, ed. Greg Donaghy, 231-59. Ottawa: Canadian Committee for the History of the Second World War, 1997.

McIntyre, R. Bruce. "Which Uniform to Serve the War: Hockey in Canada versus Military Service during World War Two." *Canadian Journal of History of Sport* 24, 2 (1993): 68-90.

McKay, Ian. "History and the Tourist Gaze: The Politics of Commemoration in Nova Scotia, 1935-1964." *Acadiensis* 22, 2 (1993): 102-38.

—. "Tartanism Triumphant: The Construction of Scottishness in Nova Scotia, 1933-1954." *Acadiensis* 21, 2 (1992): 5-47.

McKibben, Bill. "Consuming Nature." *Consuming Desire: Consumption, Culture, and the Pursuit of Happiness*, ed. Roger Rosenblatt, 87-95. Washington: Island Press, 1999.

Mechling, Jay. "Florida Seminoles and the Marketing of the Last Frontier." *Dressing in Feathers: The Construction of the Indian in American Popular Culture*, ed. S. Elizabeth Bird, 149-66. Boulder: Westview Press, 1996.

Morrison, James H. "American Tourism in Nova Scotia, 1871-1940." *Nova Scotia Historical Review* 2, 2 (1982): 40-51.

Murphy, Peter E. "Tourism: Canada's Other Resource Industry." *Tourism in Canada: Selected Issues and Options*, ed. Peter E. Murphy, 3-23. Victoria: Department of Geography, University of Victoria, 1983.

Nelson, Ross, and Geoffrey Wall. "Transportation and Accommodation: Changing Interrelationships on Vancouver Island." *Annals of Tourism Research* 13 (1986): 239-60.

Neufeld, David. "Security, Approval, and Mastery – Symbols of Saskatoon: The Cultural Baggage of Some Settlers in Western Canada." *Prairie Forum* 13, 2 (1998): 159-72.

Owram, Doug. "Canadian Domesticity in the Postwar Era." *The Veterans Charter and Post-World War II Canada*, ed. Peter Neary and J.L. Granatstein, 205-23. Montreal: McGill-Queen's University Press, 1998.

Parenteau, Bill. "Angling, Hunting, and the Development of Tourism in Late Nineteenth Century Canada: A Glimpse at the Documentary Record." *Archivist* 117 (1998): 10-19.

Parr, Joy, and Gunilla Ekberg. "Mrs Consumer and Mr Keynes in Postwar Canada and Sweden." *Gender and History* 8, 2 (1996): 212-30.

Pederson, Diana. "'Building Today for the Womanhood of Tomorrow': Businessmen, Boosters, and the YWCA, 1890-1930." *Urban History Review* 15, 3 (1987): 225-42.

Pocius, Gerald L. "Tourists, Health Seekers, and Sportsmen: Luring Americans to Newfoundland in the Early Twentieth Century." *Twentieth-Century Newfoundland: Explorations*, ed. James Hiller and Peter Neary, 47-77. St. John's: Breakwater, 1994.

Raibmon, Paige. "Theatres of Contact: The Kwakwa̱ka'wakw Meet Colonialism in British Columbia and at the Chicago World's Fair." *Canadian Historical Review* 81, 2 (2000): 157-90.

Roberts, Richard. "The Corporation as Impresario: The Municipal Provision of Entertainment in Victorian and Edwardian Bournemouth." *Leisure in Britain, 1780-1939*, ed. John K. Walton and James Walvin, 137-57. Manchester: Manchester University Press, 1983.

Rodriguez, Sylvia. "Tourism, Whiteness, and the Vanishing Anglo." *Seeing and Being Seen: Tourism in the American West*, ed. David M. Wrobel and Patrick T. Long, 194-210. Lawrence: University Press of Kansas, 2001.

Rogers, Ben F. "Florida in World War II: Tourists and Citrus." *Florida Historical Quarterly* 39, 1 (1960): 34-41.

Rosaldo, Renato. "Imperialist Nostalgia." *Representations* 26 (1989): 107-22.

Rothman, Hal K. "Selling the Meaning of Place: Entrepreneurship, Tourism, and Community Transformation in the Twentieth-Century American West." *Pacific Historical Review* 65, 4 (1996): 525-57.

—. "Shedding Skin and Shifting Shape: Tourism in the Modern West." *Seeing and Being Seen: Tourism in the American West*, ed. David M. Wrobel and Patrick T. Long, 100-24. Lawrence: University Press of Kansas, 2001.

Roy, Patricia. "Behaving as Canadians: British Columbians, 1945-1947." *Uncertain Horizons: Canadians and Their World in 1945*, ed. Greg Donaghy, 211-29. Ottawa: Canadian Committee for the History of the Second World War, 1997.

Roy, Susan. "Performing Musqueam Culture and History at British Columbia's 1966 Centennial Celebrations." *BC Studies* 135 (2002): 55-90.

Russell, Janet Northam, and Jack W. Berryman. "Parks, Boulevards, and Outdoor Recreation: The Promotion of Seattle as an Ideal Residential City and Summer Resort." *Journal of the West* 26, 1 (1987): 5-17.

Rutherford, Paul. "Tomorrow's Metropolis: The Urban Reform Movement in Canada, 1880-1920." *Canadian Historical Association, Historical Papers* (1971): 203-24.

Sackett, Andrew. "Inhaling the Salubrious Air: Health and Development in St. Andrews, N.B., 1880-1910." *Acadiensis* 25, 1 (1995): 54-81.

Schudson, Michael. "Delectable Materialism: Second Thoughts on Consumer Culture." *Consumer Society in American History: A Reader*, ed. Lawrence B. Glickman, 341-58. Ithaca: Cornell University Press, 1999.

Schullery, Paul. "Privations and Inconveniences: Early Tourism in Yellowstone National Park." *Seeing and Being Seen: Tourism in the American West*, ed. David M. Wrobel and Patrick T. Long, 227-47. Lawrence: University Press of Kansas, 2001.

Schwantes, Carlos A. "Tourists in Wonderland: Early Railroad Tourism in the Pacific Northwest." *Columbia* 7, 4 (1993-94): 22-30.

Shaffer, Marguerite S. "Seeing America First: The Search for Identity in the Tourist Landscape." *Seeing and Being Seen: Tourism in the American West*, ed. David M. Wrobel and Patrick T. Long, 165-93. Lawrence: University Press of Kansas, 2001.

Smith, Helen, and Pamela Wakewich. "'Beauty and the Helldivers': Representing Women's Work and Identities in a Warplant Newspaper." *Labour/Le Travail* 44 (1999): 71-107.

Smith, Valene L. "War and Tourism: An American Ethnography." *Annals of Tourism Research* 25, 1 (1998): 202-27.

Steele, Jeffrey. "Reduced to Images: American Indians in Nineteenth-Century Advertising." *Dressing in Feathers: The Construction of the Indian in American Popular Culture*, ed. S. Elizabeth Bird, 45-64. Boulder: Westview Press, 1996.

Strange, Carolyn. "From Modern Babylon to City upon a Hill: The Toronto Social Survey Commission of 1915 and the Search for Sexual Order in the City." *Patterns of the Past: Interpreting Ontario's History*, ed. Roger Hall, William Westfall, and Laurel Sefton MacDowell, 255-77. Toronto: Dundurn Press, 1988.

Tillotson, Shirley. "Time, Swimming Pools, and Citizenship: The Emergence of Leisure Rights in Mid-Twentieth-Century Canada." *Contesting Canadian Citizenship: Historical Readings*, ed. Robert Adamoski et al., 199-221. Peterborough: Broadview, 2002.

Townsend-Gault, Charlotte. "If Art Is the Answer, What Is the Question? Some Queries Raised by First Nations' Visual Culture in Vancouver." *RACAR [Revue d'art canadienne/ Canadian Art Review]* 21, 1-2 (1994): 100-10.

Var, Turgut, John Ap, and Carlton Van Doren. "Tourism and World Peace." *Global Tourism: The Next Decade*, ed. William F. Theobald, 27-39. Oxford: Butterworth Heinemann, 1994.

Wade, Jill. *Houses for All: The Struggle for Social Housing in Vancouver, 1919-50*. Vancouver: UBC Press, 1994.

Walden, Keith. "Speaking Modern: Language, Culture, and Hegemony in Grocery Store Window Displays." *Canadian Historical Review* 70, 3 (1989): 285-310.

Waldman, Steven. "The Tyranny of Choice." *Consumer Society in American History: A Reader*, ed. Lawrence B. Glickman, 359-66. Ithaca: Cornell University Press, 1999.

Walton, John K. "Municipal Government and the Holiday Industry in Blackpool, 1876-1914." *Leisure in Britain, 1780-1939*, ed. John K. Walton and James Walvin, 159-85. Manchester: Manchester University Press, 1983.

White, Richard. "The Retreat from Adventure: Popular Travel Writing in the 1950s." *Australian Historical Studies* 28, 109 (1997): 90-105.

Williams, Raymond. "Advertising: The Magic System." *The Cultural Studies Reader*, ed. Simon During, 320-36. London: Routledge, 1993.

Wilson, Susannah J. "The Changing Image of Women in Canadian Mass Circulating Magazines, 1930-1970." *Atlantis* 2 (1977): 33-44.

Wright, Cynthia. "Feminine Trifles of Vast Importance: Writing Gender into the History of Consumption." *Gender Conflicts: New Essays in Women's History*, ed. Franca Iacovetta and Mariana Valverde, 229-60. Toronto: University of Toronto Press, 1992.

Wright, Donald A. "W.D. Lighthall and David Ross McCord: Antimodernism and English-Canadian Imperialism, 1880s-1918." *Journal of Canadian Studies* 32, 2 (1997): 134-53.

Wrobel, David M. "Introduction: Tourists, Tourism, and the Toured Upon." *Seeing and Being Seen: Tourism in the American West*, ed. David M. Wrobel and Patrick T. Long, 1-34. Lawrence: University Press of Kansas, 2001.

Zimmerman, Tom. "Paradise Promoted: Boosterism and the Los Angeles Chamber of Commerce." *California History* 64, 1 (1985): 22-33.

Books

Aron, Cindy. *Working at Play: A History of Vacations in the United States*. New York: Oxford University Press, 1999.

Barman, Jean. *The West beyond the West: A History of British Columbia*. Rev. ed. Toronto: University of Toronto Press, 1996.

Barris, Ted, and Alex Barris. *Days of Victory: Canadians Remember: 1939-1945*. Toronto: Macmillan, 1995.

Baskerville, Peter A. *Beyond the Island: An Illustrated History of Victoria*. Burlington: Windsor, 1986.

Bean, Walton. *California: An Interpretive History*. 2nd ed. New York: McGraw-Hill, 1973.

Belasco, Warren James. *Americans on the Road: From Autocamp to Motel, 1910-1945*. Baltimore: Johns Hopkins University Press, 1997 [1979].

Berkhofer, Robert F. *The White Man's Indian: Images of the American Indian from Columbus to the Present*. New York: Vintage, 1979 [1978].

Berman, Marshall. *All that Is Solid Melts into Air: The Experience of Modernity*. New York: Viking Penguin, 1988 [1982].

Birkett, Dea. *Spinsters Abroad: Victorian Lady Explorers*. Oxford: Blackwell, 1999.

Bliss, Michael. *Northern Enterprise: Five Centuries of Canadian Business*. Toronto: McClelland and Stewart, 1987.

Bothwell, Robert. *Years of Victory: 1939-1948*. Toronto: Grolier, 1987.

Bothwell, Robert, Ian Drummond, and John English. *Canada since 1945: Power, Politics, and Provincialism*. Rev. ed. Toronto: University of Toronto Press, 1989.

Brodie, Steve. *Bloody Sunday Vancouver – 1938: Recollections of the Post-Office Sit-Down of Single Unemployed*. Vancouver: Young Communist League, 1974.

Campbell, Robert M. *Grand Illusions: The Politics of the Keynesian Experience in Canada, 1945-1975*. Peterborough: Broadview Press, 1987.

Clawson, Marion, and Jack L. Knetsch. *Economics of Outdoor Recreation*. Baltimore: Johns Hopkins University Press, 1966.

Cohen, Lizabeth. *A Consumers' Republic: The Politics of Mass Consumption in Postwar America*. New York: Knopf, 2003.

Cole, Douglas, and Ira Chaikin. *An Iron Hand upon the People: The Law against the Potlatch on the Northwest Coast*. Vancouver: Douglas and McIntyre, 1990.

Cotkin, George. *Reluctant Modernism: American Thought and Culture, 1880-1900*. New York: Twayne, 1992.

Cross, Gary. *An All-Consuming Century: Why Commercialism Won in Modern America*. New York: Columbia University Press, 2000.

—-. *Time and Money: The Making of Consumer Culture*. London: Routledge, 1993.

Dawson, Michael. *The Mountie from Dime Novel to Disney*. Toronto: Between the Lines, 1998.

Desmond, Jane C. *Staging Tourism: Bodies on Display from Waikiki to Sea World*. Chicago: University of Chicago Press, 1999.

Dubinsky, Karen. *The Second Greatest Disappointment: Honeymooning and Tourism at Niagara Falls*. Toronto: Between the Lines, 1999.

Ferguson, Niall. *The Cash Nexus: Money and Power in the Modern World, 1700-2000*. New York: Basic Books, 2001.

Finkel, Alvin. *Business and Social Reform in the Thirties*. Toronto: James Lorimer, 1979.

Fisher, Robin. *Contact and Conflict: Indian-European Relations in British Columbia, 1774-1890*. 2nd ed. Vancouver: UBC Press, 1992.

—. *Duff Pattullo of British Columbia*. Toronto: University of Toronto Press, 1991.

Fones-Wolf, Elizabeth. *Selling Free Enterprise: The Business Assault on Labor and Liberalism, 1945-1960*. Urbana: University of Illinois Press, 1994.

Fox, Frank. *Madison Avenue Goes to War: The Strange Military Career of American Advertising, 1941-1945*. Provo: Brigham Young University, 1975.

Francis, Daniel. *The Imaginary Indian: The Image of the Indian in Canadian Culture*. Vancouver: Arsenal Pulp Press, 1992.

Frank, Thomas. *The Conquest of Cool: Business Culture, Counterculture, and the Rise of Hip Consumerism*. Chicago: University of Chicago Press, 1997.

Goeldner, Charles R., J.R. Brent Ritchie, and Robert W. McIntosh. *Tourism: Principles, Practices, Philosophies*. 8th ed. New York: John Wiley and Sons, 2000.

Granatstein, J.L. *Canada's War: The Politics of the Mackenzie King Government, 1939-1945*. Toronto: Oxford University Press, 1975.

—. *Yankee Go Home? Canadians and Anti-Americanism*. Toronto: HarperCollins, 1996.

Gregson, Harry. *A History of Victoria, 1842-1970*. Victoria: Victoria Observer Publishing, 1970.

Grove, Lyndon. *Focus on British Columbia*. Vancouver: Westworld, c. 1981.

Harris, Cole. *The Resettlement of British Columbia: Essays on Colonialism and Geographical Change*. Vancouver: UBC Press, 1997.

Harrison, Julia. *Being a Tourist: Finding Meaning in Pleasure Travel*. Vancouver: UBC Press, 2002.

Hart, E.J. *The Selling of Canada: The CPR and the Beginnings of Canadian Tourism*. Banff: Altitude Publishing, 1983.

Harvey, David. *The Condition of Postmodernity: An Enquiry into the Origins of Cultural Change*. Oxford: Blackwell, 1990.

Heaman, E.A. *The Inglorious Arts of Peace: Exhibitions in Canadian Society during the Nineteenth Century*. Toronto: University of Toronto Press, 1999.

Howell, Colin D. *Northern Sandlots: A Social History of Maritime Baseball*. Toronto: University of Toronto Press, 1995.

Hyde, Anne Farrar. *An American Vision: Far Western Landscape and National Culture, 1820-1920*. New York: New York University Press, 1990.

Jakle, John A. *The Tourist: Travel in Twentieth-Century North America*. Lincoln: University of Nebraska Press, 1985.

Jasen, Patricia. *Wild Things: Nature, Culture, and Tourism in Ontario, 1790-1914*. Toronto: University of Toronto Press, 1995.

Johnston, Russell. *Selling Themselves: The Emergence of Canadian Advertising*. Toronto: University of Toronto Press, 2001.

Kealey, Gregory S., and Reg Whitaker, eds. *RCMP Security Bulletins: The War Series, 1939-1941*. St. John's: Committee on Canadian Labour History, 1989.

King, Jane, and Andrew Hampstead. *British Columbia Handbook*. 4th ed. Chico, CA: Moon Publications, 1998.

Korinek, Valerie J. *Roughing It in the Suburbs: Reading Chatelaine Magazine in the Fifties and Sixties*. Toronto: University of Toronto Press, 2000.

Laird, Pamela Walker. *Advertising Progress: American Business and the Rise of Consumer Marketing*. Baltimore: Johns Hopkins University Press, 1998.

Lash, Scott, and John Urry. *The End of Organized Capitalism*. Cambridge, UK: Polity Press, 1987.

Lears, Jackson. *Fables of Abundance: A Cultural History of Advertising in America*. New York: Basic Books, 1994.

—. *No Place of Grace: Antimodernism and the Transformation of American Culture, 1880-1920*. Chicago: University of Chicago Press, 1994 [1981].

Lebergott, Stanley. *Pursuing Happiness: American Consumers in the Twentieth Century*. Princeton: Princeton University Press, 1993.

Linteau, Paul-André. *The Promoters' City: Building the Industrial Town of Maisonneuve, 1883-1918*. Trans. Robert Chodos. Toronto: James Lorimer, 1985.

Lury, Celia. *Consumer Culture*. New Brunswick, NJ: Rutgers University Press, 1996.

MacCannell, Dean. *The Tourist: A New Theory of the Leisure Class*. New York: Schocken Books, 1976.

MacDonald, Norbert. *Distant Neighbours: A Comparative History of Seattle and Vancouver*. Lincoln: University of Nebraska Press, 1987.

MacEachern, Alan. *Natural Selections: National Parks in Atlantic Canada, 1935-1970*. Montreal: McGill-Queen's University Press, 2001.

Marchand, Roland. *Advertising the American Dream: Making Way for Modernity, 1920-1940*. Berkeley: University of California Press, 1985.

---. *Creating the Corporate Soul: The Rise of Public Relations and Corporate Imagery in American Big Business*. Berkeley: University of California Press, 1998.

Marr, William L., and Donald G. Paterson. *Canada: An Economic History*. Toronto: Gage, 1980.

Marx, Leo. *The Machine in the Garden: Technology and the Pastoral Ideal in America*. New York: Oxford University Press, 2002 [1964].

McDonald, Robert A.J. *Making Vancouver: Class, Status, and Social Boundaries, 1863-1913*. Vancouver: UBC Press, 1996.

McGeer, G.G. *The Conquest of Poverty: Or, Money, Humanity, and Christianity*. Hawthorne, CA: Omni, 1967 [1935].

McKay, Ian. *Quest of the Folk: Antimodernism and Cultural Selection in Twentieth-Century Nova Scotia*. Montreal: McGill-Queen's University Press, 1994.

Morley, Alan. *Vancouver: From Milltown to Metropolis*. 2nd ed. Vancouver: Mitchell Press, 1969.

Morton, Suzanne. *Ideal Surroundings: Domestic Life in a Working-Class Suburb in the 1920s*. Toronto: University of Toronto Press, 1995.

Norkunas, Martha K. *The Politics of Public Memory: Tourism, History, and Ethnicity in Monterey, California*. Albany: SUNY Press, 1993.

Offe, Claus. *Contradictions of the Welfare State*. Ed. John Keane. Cambridge, MA: MIT Press, 1984.

Ousby, Ian. *The Englishman's England: Taste, Travel, and the Rise of Tourism*. Cambridge, UK: Cambridge University Press, 1990.

Overton, James. *Making a World of Difference: Essays on Tourism, Culture, and Development in Newfoundland*. St. John's: ISER, 1996.

Owram, Doug. *Born at the Right Time: A History of the Baby Boom Generation*. Toronto: University of Toronto Press, 1996.

---. *The Government Generation: Canadian Intellectuals and the State, 1900-1945*. Toronto: University of Toronto Press, 1986.

Owram, Doug, and Kenneth Norrie. *A History of the Canadian Economy*. Toronto: Harcourt Brace Jovanovich, 1991.

Palmer, Bryan. *Working Class Experience: Rethinking the History of Canadian Labour, 1800-1991*. 2nd ed. Toronto: McClelland and Stewart, 1992.

Parr, Joy. *Domestic Goods: The Material, the Moral, and the Economic in the Postwar Years*. Toronto: University of Toronto Press, 1999.

Pearce, Douglas. *Tourist Development*. 2nd ed. Harlow, UK: Longman Scientific and Technical; New York: Wiley, 1989.

Pratt, Mary Louise. *Imperial Eyes: Travel Writing and Transculturation*. London: Routledge, 1992.

Robinson, Daniel J. *The Measure of Democracy: Polling, Market Research, and Public Life, 1930-1945*. Toronto: University of Toronto Press, 1999.

Rothman, Hal. *Devil's Bargains: Tourism in the Twentieth-Century American West*. Lawrence: University Press of Kansas, 1998.

Rutherford, Paul. *Endless Propaganda: The Advertising of Public Goods*. Toronto: University of Toronto Press, 2000.

Schama, Simon. *Landscape and Memory.* Toronto: Vintage Canada, 1996 [1995].

Schwantes, Carlos. *The Pacific Northwest: An Interpretive History.* Lincoln: University of Nebraska Press, 1989.

Scott, James C. *Seeing like a State: How Certain Schemes to Improve the Human Condition Have Failed.* New Haven: Yale University Press, 1998.

Seed, Patricia. *Ceremonies of Possession in Europe's Conquest of the New World, 1492-1640.* Cambridge, UK: Cambridge University Press, 1995.

Shaffer, Marguerite S. *See America First: Tourism and National Identity, 1880-1940.* Washington, DC: Smithsonian Institution Press, 2001.

Slater, Don. *Consumer Culture and Modernity.* Cambridge, MA: Polity Press, 1997.

Tennant, Paul. *Aboriginal People and Politics: The Indian Land Question in British Columbia, 1849-1989.* Vancouver: UBC Press, 1990.

Tillotson, Shirley. *The Public at Play: Gender and the Politics of Recreation in Post-War Ontario.* Toronto: University of Toronto Press, 2000.

Turner, E.S. *The Shocking Story of Advertising!* London: Michael Joseph, 1952.

Urry, John. *Consuming Places.* London: Routledge, 1995.

---. *The Tourist Gaze: Leisure and Travel in Contemporary Societies.* London: Sage, 1990.

Vipond, Mary. *The Mass Media in Canada.* Rev. ed. Toronto: James Lorimer, 1992.

Walden, Keith. *Becoming Modern in Toronto: The Industrial Exhibition and the Shaping of a Late Victorian Culture.* Toronto: University of Toronto Press, 1997.

Walvin, James. *Beside the Seaside: A Social History of the Popular Seaside Holiday.* London: Allen Lane, 1978.

Wetherell, Donald G., with Irene Kmet. *Useful Pleasures: The Shaping of Leisure in Alberta, 1896-1945.* Regina/Edmonton: Canadian Plains Research Center/Alberta Culture and Multiculturalism, 1990.

Whitaker, Reg, and Gary Marcuse. *Cold War Canada: The Making of a National Insecurity State, 1945-1957.* Toronto: University of Toronto Press, 1994.

Williams, David Ricardo. *Mayor Gerry: The Remarkable Gerald Grattan McGeer.* Vancouver: Douglas and McIntyre, 1986.

Wilson, Alexander. *The Culture of Nature: North American Landscape from Disney to the Exxon Valdez.* Toronto: Between the Lines, 1991.

Wilson, Chris. *The Myth of Santa Fe: Creating a Modern Regional Tradition.* Albuquerque: University of New Mexico Press, 1997.

World Tourism Organization. *Tourism Highlights 2002.* Madrid: World Tourism Organization, c. 2002.

Wood, James P. *The Story of Advertising.* New York: Ronald Press Company, 1958.

Unpublished Dissertations, Theses, Papers, and Websites

"About WTO." <www.world-tourism.org/aboutwto/eng/menu.html>. (Accessed 7 July 2004).

Apostle, Alisa. "Canada, Vacations Unlimited: The Canadian Government Tourism Industry, 1934-1959." PhD diss., Queen's University, 2003.

Kyte, Shelley. "'V-8 or Make and Break': An Investigation of the Development of Tourism in Canada: A Case Study of Nova Scotia." MA thesis, Queen's University, 1997.

Lines, Kenneth. "A Bit of Old England: The Selling of Tourist Victoria." MA thesis, University of Victoria, 1972.

MacEachern, Alan A. "No Island Is an Island: A History of Tourism on Prince Edward Island, 1870-1939." MA thesis, Queen's University, 1991.

McDonald, Robert A.J. "Business Leaders in Early Vancouver, 1886-1914." PhD diss., University of British Columbia, 1977.

---. "Politics before Parties: Modernity and Province-Building 1871-1903." Paper presented to the BC Studies Conference, May 2001, Kamloops.

Nelson, R. Ross. "The Presentation of Landscape: Rhetorical Conventions and the Promotion of Tourism in British Columbia, 1900-1990." PhD diss., University of British Columbia, 1994.

Nightengale Berry, Ellen Janet. "The Tourist's Image of a City: Vancouver, B.C." MA thesis, University of British Columbia, 1979.

Raibmon, Paige S. "Authentic Indians: Episodes of Encounter from the Late Nineteenth-Century Northwest Coast." PhD diss., Duke University, 2000.

Stanley, Meg. "Creating Beautiful British Columbia: Pattullo's Promotion of Tourism." Paper presented to the BC Studies Conference, October 1994, Kelowna.

Reference Works

Encyclopedia of British Columbia. Ed. Daniel Francis. Madeira Park, BC: Harbour Publishing, 2000.

Encyclopedia of Tourism. Ed. Jafar Jafaria. New York: Routledge, 2000.

Henderson's City of Vancouver and North Vancouver Directory. 1909.

Henderson's Greater Vancouver Directory. Various dates.

Who's Who in British Columbia. Various dates.

Index

Note: Page numbers in *italics* refer to illustrations

Printed and bound in Canada by Friesens

Set in Stone by Brenda and Neil West, BN Typographics West

Copy editor: Dallas Harrison

Proofreader: Sarah Munro

Cartographer: Eric Leinberger